Endorsements for *Banking Across Boundaries*

"An innovative, well-researched and invaluable book on the importance of banks and banking to contemporary capitalism. The vital importance of their cross-boundary activity and the controversy over whether and how they really do contribute to the wealth of nations are here illuminated in novel ways."
David Harvey, Distinguished Professor, City University of New York

"A trenchant, theoretically sophisticated analysis of the reciprocal relationship between economic ideas and material developments in banking and finance. In a book sure to make economists and ordinary citizens rethink the recent financial crisis, Christophers demands that we take the long historical view and place national economies in a global context. This is a fresh, exciting, and probing call for more expansive frames of economic analysis and more critical reflection on the data that allow us to know what we think we know about productivity and finance."
Mary Poovey, Samuel Rudin University Professor in the Humanities, New York University

"In *Banking Across Boundaries* Brett Christophers walks us through a history of capitalism that considers the importance of how financial intermediation is counted in economic geographies. Crucial here is the evolution of banks' spatial anatomy and conceptions of banks' economic productiveness. Explained over three periods of capitalist development, Christophers does a splendid job in detailing how ideas and practices enable one another in how banks operate across boundaries and why they are considered to be productive in modern national accounting. This book is of great interest to all scholars of finance in the international political economy."
Leonard Seabrooke, Professor of International Political Economy and Economic Sociology, Copenhagen Business School

T0341550

Antipode Book Series

Series Editors: Vinay Gidwani, University of Minnesota, USA and Sharad Chari, London School of Economics, UK
Like its parent journal, the Antipode Book Series reflects distinctive new developments in radical geography. It publishes books in a variety of formats – from reference books to works of broad explication to titles that develop and extend the scholarly research base – but the commitment is always the same: to contribute to the praxis of a new and more just society.

Published

Forthcoming

Banking Across Boundaries

Placing Finance in Capitalism

Brett Christophers

WILEY-BLACKWELL

A John Wiley & Sons, Ltd., Publication

This edition first published 2013
© 2013 John Wiley & Sons, Ltd

Wiley-Blackwell is an imprint of John Wiley & Sons, formed by the merger of Wiley's global Scientific, Technical and Medical business with Blackwell Publishing.

Registered Office
John Wiley & Sons, Ltd, The Atrium, Southern Gate, Chichester, West Sussex, PO19 8SQ, UK

Editorial Offices
350 Main Street, Malden, MA 02148-5020, USA
9600 Garsington Road, Oxford, OX4 2DQ, UK
The Atrium, Southern Gate, Chichester, West Sussex, PO19 8SQ, UK

For details of our global editorial offices, for customer services, and for information about how to apply for permission to reuse the copyright material in this book please see our website at www.wiley.com/wiley-blackwell.

The right of Brett Christophers to be identified as the author of this work has been asserted in accordance with the UK Copyright, Designs and Patents Act 1988.

Wiley also publishes its books in a variety of electronic formats. Some content that appears in print may not be available in electronic books.

Designations used by companies to distinguish their products are often claimed as trademarks. All brand names and product names used in this book are trade names, service marks, trademarks or registered trademarks of their respective owners. The publisher is not associated with any product or vendor mentioned in this book. This publication is designed to provide accurate and authoritative information in regard to the subject matter covered. It is sold on the understanding that the publisher is not engaged in rendering professional services. If professional advice or other expert assistance is required, the services of a competent professional should be sought.

Library of Congress Cataloging-in-Publication Data
Christophers, Brett, 1971–
Banking across boundaries : placing finance in capitalism / Brett Christophers.
     p.   cm.
   Includes index.
   ISBN 978-1-4443-3829-4 (cloth) – ISBN 978-1-4443-3828-7 (pbk.)
1. Finance.   2. Banks and banking.   3. International banking.   4. International finance.
5. Capitalism.
   HG173.C574 2013
   332.1'5–dc23
                                                    2012039743
A catalogue record for this book is available from the British Library.

Cover image: William Michael Hartnett, The Banker's Table, 1877, oil on canvas. Metropolitan Museum of Art, New York. Purchase, Elihu Root Jr. Gift, 1956. Acc.n. 56.21 © 2012. Image copyright The Metropolitan Museum of Art / Art Resource / Scala, Florence.
Cover design by www.cyandesign.co.uk

Set in 10/12pt Sabon by SPi Publisher Services, Pondicherry, India

1   2013

For my mother

The bank – the monster has to have profits all the time. It can't wait. It'll die… When the monster stops growing, it dies. It can't stay one size.

John Steinbeck, *The Grapes of Wrath*

In the last paper we saw that just payment of labour consisted in a sum of money which would approximately obtain equivalent labour at a future time: we have now to examine the means of obtaining such equivalence. Which question involves the definition of Value, Wealth, Price, and Produce.

None of these terms are yet defined so as to be understood by the public. But the last, Produce, which one might have thought the clearest of all, is, in use, the most ambiguous; and the examination of the kind of ambiguity attendant on its present employment will best open the way to our work.

John Ruskin, *Unto This Last*

Contents

List of Figures

List of Abbreviations

AIG	American International Group
BBA	British Bankers' Association
BEA	Bureau of Economic Analysis (*US*)
BIS	Bank for International Settlements
CAGR	Compound annual growth rate
CSI	Coalition of Service Industries (*US*)
EC	European Community
EU	European Union
FDI	Foreign direct investment
FISIM	Financial intermediation services indirectly measured
FSUG	Financial Statistics Users' Group (*UK*)
GATS	General Agreement on Trade in Services
GATT	General Agreement on Tariffs and Trade
GDP	Gross domestic product
GNP	Gross national product
GVA	Gross value-added
IBRD	International Bank for Reconstruction and Development
IBSC	Imputed Bank Service Charge
IFSL	International Financial Services, London
IMF	International Monetary Fund
NBER	National Bureau of Economic Research (*US*)
OECD	Organization for Economic Co-operation and Development
OEEC	Organization for European Economic Co-operation
ONS	Office of National Statistics (*UK*)
SEEF	Service des Etudes économiques et financières (*France*)
SNA	System of National Accounts (*United Nations*)
UN	United Nations
UNCTAD	United Nations Conference on Trade and Development
WTO	World Trade Organization

Acknowledgments

My first and biggest thanks are reserved for my wise and wonderful wife, Agneta, and for our three equally wonderful children: Elliot, Oliver, and Emilia. Thank you, thank you, thank you. Thanks, too, to my parents and siblings.

* * *

I have been based at Uppsala University in Sweden throughout the period of researching and writing this book. The staff of the university's Library of Economic Sciences did an invaluable and incredibly efficient job in handling unrelenting volumes of inter-library loan requests. I would also like to thank all my colleagues in the Department of Social and Economic Geography and the Institute for Housing and Urban Research for creating warm and supportive working environments. A special word in this regard for Gunnar Olsson, whose particular vision and practice of scholarship – in times not necessarily conducive to either – continue to inspire.

I am extremely grateful to everyone associated with the Antipode Book Series for enabling this book to see the light of day: specifically to Rachel Pain, for responding enthusiastically to my original proposal; to Vinay Gidwani, for shepherding the manuscript through the latter stages of the process; and to Jacqueline Scott at Wiley-Blackwell for being an encouraging and accommodating editor.

The book draws upon conversations with and insights provided by many individuals. Those deserving special mention are: those I formally interviewed (and in some cases, repeatedly pestered) in carrying out the research, especially in the field of national accounting; Geoff Mann, for a close and constructive reading of the original proposal, and for ongoing dialogue around many of the book's core themes; Andrew Sayer, for helping me (probably unwittingly) to clarify some of my principal arguments; Dan Davies, for his perspectives on the world of banking; and last but definitely not least, the anonymous reviewers corralled into reading both the proposal and the final manuscript. Notwithstanding all this help, the book's arguments – especially any tenuous ones – are mine alone.

The book draws, in extensively revised form, on material previously published in two articles: "Making finance productive", *Economy and Society*, 40, 2011, pp.112–140; and "Anaemic geographies of financialisation", *New Political Economy*, 17, 2012, pp.271–291. I am grateful to the journal publishers (www. tandfonline.com) and editors for permission to reuse this material.

Finally, I am thankful for financial support in the shape of a research fellowship (2008–2011) from Jan Wallanders och Tom Hedelius Stiftelse – a foundation established and administered by, of all things, one of Sweden's largest commercial banks (Svenska Handelsbanken).

July 2012

Introduction

With regard to money, the power of ideas does more than just shape the possible. It defines the feasible.

Jonathan Kirshner (2003)[1]

This book investigates the place of finance in general, and banks in particular, vis-à-vis two of Western capitalism's emblematic boundary-forms: the geopolitical boundary separating states from one another, and the representational boundary separating activities and institutions deemed economically productive from those deemed unproductive. With a focus upon banks' crossing of boundaries of one type or the other during the course of the history of capitalism, the book is animated by a number of core questions. To what extent, at different times and in different places, have banks been cross-border as opposed to territorially-bound entities? Have banks typically been seen as economically productive or unproductive in these different places and times? And what relationship, if any, have banks' respective boundary positionings – the geographical variety and the conceptual variety – borne to each other? While a substantial existing literature provides many though not all of the answers to the first question, the second question has been only minimally considered, and the third not at all.

Offering a broad historical sweep from the era of merchant capitalism, through that of industrial capitalism, all the way up to and including today's ostensibly "financialized" capitalism, the book makes a series of claims. First, it argues that finance has been *made* productive, not in a literal sense but rather in a perceptual sense: having been considered economically unproductive for most of the long history explored here, banks were increasingly envisioned as productive during the twentieth century, particularly by means of the new calculative technology of

Banking Across Boundaries: Placing Finance in Capitalism, First Edition. Brett Christophers.
© 2013 John Wiley & Sons, Ltd. Published 2013 by John Wiley & Sons, Ltd.

national accounting. Further, the book maintains that a relationship between the two forms of boundary negotiation has gradually emerged. The question of whether banks were regarded as productive or unproductive was, for a long time, immaterial to their potential or actual geographical scope, as indeed was this geography, in turn, to the way in which they were envisioned (as productive or not). This is no longer the case. So entangled have the two types of boundary positioning become, it is claimed, that not only does the conceptual actively shape the geopolitical, but also vice versa. Simply stated, being "made" productive has helped enable (Western) banks colonize international markets, while this process of financial internationalization has itself intensified that very perception of productiveness. A virtuous – or some might say, vicious – circle has materialized.

The rest of this introduction fleshes out what the reader can expect from the book and the various rationales for it looking like it does. I firstly explain the impetus to the research and thinking which underpins the book, amongst other reasons because this impetus foregrounds why the arguments herein matter, here and now. I then outline the theoretical moorings anchoring those arguments, indicating which conceptual perspectives I have found most useful but also where, how and why my approach departs from these. This discussion also contains important signposts as to the book's empirical framing: the categories and classifications it relies upon, the questions it asks and the questions it leaves untouched. Finally, I provide a fuller rendering of the book's main line of argument, partly by way of explaining and signalling the structure of what follows, and partly to enable the reader to orient herself at any particular point in the narrative – to appreciate how the argument in one part of the book connects up to the larger story of which it is a part.

All Roads Lead to FISIM

Banking Across Boundaries is not about the financial crisis which began in 2007, but it grew directly out of a series of reflections *on* the crisis: reflections on what was actually happening to financial institutions and markets, certainly, but more explicitly on the nature of the responses the events elicited from the banking community, its champions, its critics, and politicians both inside government and outside it. I am only too aware that with a deluge of books and articles having poured forth in the past four years, the last thing the reader is likely to want is yet more commentary on the crisis; nevertheless, the question of how and why the crisis gave rise to this book is a material one and hence needs to be addressed here. In return for the reader's forbearance, however, I promise to not return to the crisis until the very end of the book, in the Afterword.

As I witnessed and tried to come to terms intellectually with the unfolding financial crisis and its myriad representations during 2007 and 2008, my thinking increasingly channelled into two distinct streams of active inquiry, and as I pursued these flows downstream both ultimately converged, to my surprise, on a concept and acronym I had never knowingly encountered before: "FISIM."

What was this FISIM? By outlining, now, the nature of these two streams of inquiry and the directions in which they led, I will not only provide a preliminary answer to this question, but more importantly demonstrate why the overall argument developed in this book is a significant one, and why FISIM and related concepts play a central role within it. The first stream of inquiry was into what I tended to think of as "conceptual" responses to the crisis, the second into "political" responses (although, as I make clear, there is assuredly no hard-and-fast distinction between them). I will take each in turn.

Productive or unproductive, is that not the question?

It was inevitable that much of the commentary about the financial crisis beginning in 2007 would focus upon the role of the banking sector in fomenting the crisis. What was perhaps less foreseeable was that a good deal of this discussion would be given over to conceptual questions rather than strictly technical or historical ones. What particularly struck me, however, *was* the crystallization of a set of arguments, very much prompted by the crisis, about the fundamental "nature" of banks as economic actors. Perhaps most notably of all, critics and supporters of the banking sector came to occupy opposing positions in a conceptual debate (which was also, at the same time, clearly a political debate) about the *value contributed* by banks – about, in short, banks' economic *productiveness*.

On one side of this argument were lobby groups such as the British Bankers' Association (BBA) (the UK's self-proclaimed "voice of banking & financial services") and American Bankers Association. These bodies essentially peddled the line advanced by Goldman Sachs chief executive Lloyd Blankfein, who described workers at banks (well at least, at his own) as "among the most productive in the world."[2] Such views from within the industry were recirculated by supportive voices in the media. The British libertarian economist Tim Congdon, writing in the influential *Prospect* magazine, described the UK's financial sector as "fantastically productive." Nobel Laureate and America's self-styled "liberal conscience" Paul Krugman, arguing against calls for "narrow banking" (whereby banks would be required to hold all deposits in liquid, short-term assets), insisted that by allowing individuals ready access to their money "while at the same time allowing most of that money to be invested in illiquid assets," banks performed "a productive activity, because it allows the economy to have its cake and eat it too." Others offered similarly forthright claims.[3]

On the other side of the argument were voices such as those of Karel Williams and his colleagues at the UK's Centre for Research on Socio Cultural Change. In their "alternative report" on UK banking reform, Williams and co-authors challenged the image of a "productive" financial sector head-on, arguing that when one considered empirically the sector's *net* contribution to the economy – factoring in costs as well as benefits – the notion of productiveness simply did not stack up.[4] Will Hutton agreed, echoing the comments of the UK Financial Services Authority's chairman Adair Turner by castigating banks for engaging in "economically and socially useless activity"; and so too, apparently, did even the *Financial Times* columnist Martin Wolf. "A large part of the activity of the financial sector," Wolf stated, "seems to be a machine to transfer income and wealth from outsiders to insiders."[5] This, of course, was the very opposite of a depiction of productiveness.

Reading further into this stand-off and thinking about the terms of its engagement prompted two observations. The first was that the protagonists on either side seemed to be talking at cross purposes not just politically but conceptually: using different metrics, different systems of calculative representation, and even, in some senses, different languages. The second observation stemmed from the first. Given the different ways in which "productiveness" could be and was being defined and delimited, fighting fire (banks are productive!) with fire (no they are not!) seemed a powerful yet also *limiting* approach to formulating a radical critique of the economy and "finance's" place within it.

Believing, therefore, that a different way of approaching things might be useful, I began to wonder instead not about whether banks are genuinely productive, but about where and how representations of productiveness – indeed, the very concept *of* economic productiveness – come into being. Through what socio-technical apparatuses are the most potent and pervasive representations manu-factured, and what power relations are implicated in the process? How, moreover, have such technical and social relations of production changed over time: were hegemonic understandings of productiveness created by the same means 50, 100, or 200 years ago as today? Much of this book is ultimately concerned with answering these questions in a historical context; but my immediate interest was, and is, in the mechanisms of manufacture of productiveness specifically in the present.

Two separate experiences led me to what I argue in this book is a – and perhaps even *the* – principal forum for the modern-day "making" of economic productive-ness, by which I mean *the making of accepted representations thereof*: the practice of national accounting. One was returning to Helen Boss's *Theories of Surplus and Transfer*. There she shows that the idea of a distinction between productive and unproductive activities is a longstanding one in economic theory, and that while there *may* be good reasons for avoiding such a distinction intellectually, it cannot be avoided practically, for it is still with us today – not least in national accounts, which, at once, both *depend upon and reproduce* the distinction in question, then releasing it to circulate and do its work amongst, inter alia, "jour-nalists, politicians and voters."[6] The other experience was reading, in the midst of the crisis (June 2009), the then-UK Chancellor Alistair Darling's annual Mansion House Speech to the City. Darling struck what was, given the timing, an extraor-dinarily conciliatory tone.[7] Having read Boss, however, it was the metric Darling used to justify this tone that I found most arresting. "The City of London – and other financial centres such as Edinburgh and Leeds – remain an immense asset to our country. The financial sector makes up 8 per cent of our national economy." He used, as Boss observed politicians so often do, national accounting data – and he did so expressly to substantiate the financial sector's value.

Now, I do not mean to suggest that national accounting metrics, including most prominently the closely-linked gross domestic product (GDP) and gross value-added (GVA) measures, are the only figures mobilized politically to demonstrate the economic value of an activity – or even the only important ones. The BBA, as just one example, often also cites employment or tax figures to prove the bank sector's worth. (Consider the particularly suasive statement that "The corporation tax paid by our financial institutions would pay annually for the building of some 36 hospitals."[8]) I *do* want to argue, however, that there is something singularly important and influential about claims that banking or finance contribute such-and-such a share of national product or value-added. The reason is that they bespeak, precisely, *productiveness*. The very term "value-*added*" asserts augmentation: it conjures a quantum of value that if not generated by the financial sector *would not exist*. The significance of this implication of accretion cannot, in my view, be overstated. For a parasitical industry could equally well employ millions of people and pay millions in tax on its (leeched) profits – but it could not claim to be adding to the national economy; to be *producing*, as opposed to redistributing, wealth. Perhaps, indeed, this unique quality of national accounting data serves in part to explain how and why they have become quite so widely influential, to the degree that "GDP," in particular, in Dirk Philipsen's words now "arguably shapes people's thinking and actions more than any other ideology," and has thus become "the world's key benchmark."[9]

Pondering these issues in the middle of 2009, I decided to look at the only national accounts with which, at the time, I had any familiarity (the UK's), to see what I could learn about how they created and calculated economic productiveness, and especially the productiveness of banks. The most recent release was the accounts for the fourth quarter of 2008. This, I thought to myself, should be interesting, given the recent turmoil in the banking sector. Imagine the shock, then, when I read that while UK nonfinancial corporations' operating surplus had declined by 3.4 percent in Q4, financial corporations' surplus had *risen* – and by *36 percent*![10] Surely this could not be right: Q4 2008 had seen, in the face of enormous losses and write-downs, the state bail-out of the UK banking sector. Searching for an explanation, I turned to the accompanying briefing note, where I immediately found the answer. In relation to the previous quarter (Q3 2008), the operating surplus of financial institutions had been positively impacted in Q4 to the tune of £6.1bn thanks to an increase in the supply of a particular type of service: not a service category I recognized, however, but "FISIM services."[11] What on earth, I wondered, was FISIM? The last two words of the five – "indirectly measured" – were what caught my eye: this baffling increase in financial sector surplus was concentrated in services *defined, at least in part, by their method of measurement*.

Taming the monster in whose midst?

In parallel with these inquiries into the economic contribution of banking and how it was represented, the financial crisis also prompted me to begin thinking about what I presumed was another set of issues altogether: the geographies of finance and banking. In certain respects this was inevitable – I am a geographer by disposition as well as training; and in ways that were both obvious and not so obvious, this was "a very geographical crisis."[12] My own particular thinking around these geographies, however, had quite a specific reference point, in the sense that it crystallized explicitly around the nature of the *political* reaction to what was happening. And although this reaction initially took the form of a "something must be done" clamor from across the political spectrum, it soon cohered in a more tangible sense as a remarkable *absence* of action at any discernible level in any of the major Western nations most impacted by the crisis. As such, the question rapidly became: how, given the depth and breadth of popular support for meaningful reform of the financial sector, do we explain this comprehensive inaction?

I had, and have, a great deal of time for the argument, presented by people like David Harvey, that the limp political response to the crisis can be understood within the broader historical context of the reconstitution of class power under neoliberalism, led by an increasingly consolidated state-finance nexus knitting together, in the case of the US, Wall Street, and Washington.[13] Yet at least two other factors seemed to me to be in play. One was the investment of the state in precisely the envisioning of the financial sector I have just been discussing. Ideas matter, *particularly*, for better or for worse, economic ideas, and the idea that banks are economically productive institutions – an idea rendered palpable in the "8 per cent of our national economy" figure brandished by Chancellor Darling – clearly mattered greatly in the political aftermath of the crisis in the global banking sector. Had banks continued to be seen as economically unproductive in the way that they have, as this book shows, for most of their history, perhaps we could have expected a different political response.

The other factor was the geography of it all. It became increasingly clear that one could not understand the political response, such as it was, unless one took geography seriously. This geography had a number of dimensions, one of which was and is frequently commented upon: the fact that the global banking business is highly concentrated in a relatively small number of global cities such as London, New York, and Hong Kong. Banks and their supporters were only too quick to warn American and British political leaders of the risks of so-called "regulatory arbitrage" – a fancy way of saying that if the US and UK regulators clamped down on banks, then those banks would move their operations to somewhere with lighter, and hence for the banks less costly, regulation, and the US and UK economies would suffer losses in economic output, tax revenues, and employment accordingly. Whether the threat of banks taking business from London or New York and handing it to Frankfurt or Paris was real or not, the *perception* of such a threat almost certainly was.

Thus, I do not want to discount this particular issue. I had a strong sense, however, that there were other, less visible and less discussed geographical factors which needed to be understood. What these were became clear when those nominally in favor of reform began talking, as they increasingly did, of a master-and-servant relationship in the economy. The problem, they said, was that "finance" had become the master of the wider economy; reform should be directed towards making finance the *servant* of that economy.[14] This sounded reasonable enough, but it immediately begged numerous questions, not least of which was how one might distinguish between the financial and nonfinancial economies in the first place, and indeed what sort of work exercises in such boundary-drawing perform – questions closely related, as we will see, to those I ask in this book about the drawing of boundaries between economic productiveness and unproductiveness. The question I began to think about in terms of the evident political inaction, however, was not *what* this wider "nonfinancial" economy was, but *where* it was.

This seemed a particularly important issue, since another thing made very clear by the crisis was not just the heavy concentration of banking institutions in a small number of globally-important financial centers, but international *connectivity* – of financial flows, and of and within the financial institutions that initiate, coordinate and profit from them. The debate around regulatory arbitrage gave the impression that if banks (as institutions) moved offshore from London or New York, the business they did would move them. What was crucially missing from the debate was recognition that much of this business was *already* offshore; had it not been, it is hard to imagine that the crisis would have spread quite as rapidly and powerfully as it did. The extent to which notionally "US banks" or "UK banks" were frequently in fact transnational entities to the very core would later be brought home forcefully to observers in the UK when, in February 2011, it was reported that the UK corporation tax paid by UK-headquartered Barclays Bank in 2009 represented just 1 percent of its global profits for that year.[15]

The pertinent point here is that while the "master and servant" metaphor invoked inter-sectoral relations of power and a desire to rebalance these in favor of the nonfinancial economy, it occluded geographical considerations and thus also *inter-territorial* relations of power. If regulatory action were to be taken in the US or UK to inhibit the self-evident power of the domestic financial sector, who would stand to benefit, and *where*? Would it be French or German consumers and "nonfinancial" companies as well as French or German banking institutions; and with what impact upon precarious Anglo-American balance of payments ledgers? With finance and financial institutions now being *so* transnational, it was hard to believe that such questions were not, at some level, part of the complex political calculus around financial (non)reform.

In view of this particular conjuncture of geography and politics, to understand the regulatory torpor it seemed vital to understand how and when Western banks had *become* so transnationalized, and what the enabling factors in this internationalization had been. But first a basic sense of the scale of contemporary bank internationalization would be necessary, most specifically for the banks of the two countries where the specter of regulatory arbitrage had been raised, namely the US and the UK. The first useful figures I found were for the UK. Published in August 2009, two months after the quarterly national accounts release discussed earlier, these figures were contained in a report by the private-sector body which represents the UK financial services industry internationally: International

Financial Services, London (IFSL).[16] And the numbers were clearly material: net exports by UK banks of £31.1bn for 2008 as a whole; the national accounts, to put this into some sort of context, had reported a total annual operating surplus of £62.0bn for *all* UK financial corporations (including insurance companies). [17] Again, however, it was an apparently technical detail that stood out: comfortably the largest individual bank product or service export category, accounting alone for just under half of all bank net export value, at £15.4bn – FISIM.

There was, then, or at least there *appeared* to be, a link of some sort between my two strands of thinking in relation to the financial crisis. Something evidently central to banks' international reach was also clearly a critical factor in the measurement of their productiveness in the national accounts. I thus began research in and around this nexus – the nexus where the geography of banking encounters ideas about the productiveness of banking and the expression of those ideas in quantitative measures – and this book is the result.

The first thing I discovered was what FISIM actually is, and the answer, as it often is in matters financial, was considerably simpler than the acronym intimated.[18] It is the name given in today's national accounts to the valuation of the output of what most of us see as banks' core business, namely market-making in cash (i.e. the taking of deposits and the provision of loans) and in other financial assets: "financial intermediation services, indirectly measured." Yet I rapidly learned that if the concept is nominally simple, national accountants had seemingly spent the best part of eight decades making it as complicated as it could possibly be. FISIM, and related concepts which preceded it, has long provoked great controversy in national accounting circles, giving rise, as the influential French practitioner-cum-historian André Vanoli once put it, "to perplexity, stress, reversals and memorable rows."[19] In 2010, when people outside of the national accounting community began noticing the disjuncture highlighted above between a practically insolvent UK banking sector and accounts which showed the sector generating more surplus than ever, this controversy seeped out into the wider political arena.

I will return to that particular controversy in the book's Afterword, because it is an extremely salutary one for all manner of reasons. The bulk of the book, however, is about situating FISIM as an outcome not just of a perennial debate on banking and banks' intermediation services within twentieth-century national accounting, but of a centuries-long debate on the economic nature or role of banks within Western economic and social discourse more broadly; indeed, FISIM does not make its appearance until Part III, which covers the past four decades. Equally, the book is about the relationship between this positioning of banks vis-à-vis the pivotal productive/unproductive boundary and their positioning vis-à-vis the geopolitical boundaries that have become a similarly fundamental feature of capitalist society during the long history of this mode of socio-economic production. It links the process of banks being "made" productive to the process of their internationalization which, in the contemporary crisis moment, has appeared to make workable and meaningful reform so politically intractable. It shows, in sum, that how society places banks conceptually and how banks are able to place themselves geographically have become ever more tightly entangled affairs.

The Accumulation of Effective Determinations

Do economists make markets?[20] A consideration of this question, variously conceived, has been fundamental to the process of researching and writing this book. My primary point of reference in this respect has been the burgeoning and very much contemporary literature on the so-called "performativity" of economics. Although it comes in many shapes and sizes, the central gist of the bulk of this literature has been that economics plays an active rather than purely passive role in the economy. Economists and economic statisticians, and the economic ideas, models and measurements they produce, do not merely describe an "external" economic reality; they are always and everywhere part *of* the economy, shaping and reproducing it in the very moment that they attempt to capture it conceptually. In the words of one of the main protagonists in this field, Donald MacKenzie, economics is "effectively performative" since it is "an active force transforming its environment, not a camera passively recording it."[21]

There are both generic and more specific reasons why the literature in question is a touchstone for this book. The generic reason is that one of the main questions posed in the book concerns the effective materiality of economic ideas around the productiveness of banks, especially in relation to the internationalization of finance and banking. Have such ideas, as articulated and quantified both inside and outside the national accounting tradition, served as "mere" representations, or have they influenced political-economic outcomes in one way or another?

The more specific reason for the pertinence of the performative economics literature concerns the special nature of banking. Banking has rarely if ever been seen as a "normal" sector of the economy; the very fact that people so often refer to the "real" economy in contradistinction to the "financial" economy is evidence of this. More than just "different," however, banking has typically been considered politically and economically *vital*, in the sense of both mediating wider rhythms of capital accumulation and serving as a principal site of regulatory leverage within the economy at large. As a consequence of this presumed vitality, banking, as Benjamin Cohen has observed, "is typically subject to more regulation than other sectors of the economy." For Cohen, the key upshot of this, in turn, is that banks need to cultivate "a more active relationship with the public authorities" than many other industries, "not only at home but also outside the nation's borders."[22] While Cohen is undoubtedly right, and this last point in particular is borne out directly by the story told here, banking's perceived "specialness" raises, for me, another key factor. Namely, because it is seen to be uniquely potent and in need of special governance, ideas *about* banking – about the role it plays in the economy – have the potential to be especially efficacious. Eager to ensure that they manage the banking sector in the way that best serves their wider political, social and economic objectives, political authorities will often pay very close heed to prevailing economic ideas about what banks are and how they function. Those ideas thus have a very great capacity to "perform" the economy of the present and the future.

The work of scholars such as MacKenzie, Michel Callon, and Timothy Mitchell on the constructive work of world-making effected by economics has therefore had a deep influence on this book.[23] While it is in some respects invidious to point to just one intervention amongst many, Mitchell's work on housing markets was especially helpful.[24] In it, he shows that the policies championed by the economist Hernando de Soto rely on the notion of a distinct boundary between capitalist and noncapitalist, or market and nonmarket, economic realms. Mitchell suggests that instead of contesting the exact placement of this boundary (and becoming entrapped by the dualisms it sustains), it may be more useful to examine the tools and technologies that validate (mis)placements on one side of the boundary or the other, and to question the nature of the worlds that such placements ultimately help to effect and organize.

With Western political-economic thought having long ago fashioned a "production boundary" separating putatively productive economic activities from unproductive ones, it is, therefore, in precisely the spirit of Mitchell's argument that this book proceeds. Instead of debating specific placements of banking and finance vis-à-vis this boundary, it examines where and how such placements arise and are legitimated and what types of geographical economies they put *in* place; it treats these placements as, à la MacKenzie and Callon, fundamentally performative acts. In doing so it seeks to offer, in the language of Fred Block and Gene Burns, "a sociology of social indicators [through examining] the process by which these particular social facts are created and how the facts are then used by different social actors."[25] It interrogates "*both* the conditions and consequences of metrics and models" precisely because, as Andrea Mennicken and Peter Miller observe, performativity otherwise "can be an empty notion."[26]

To take this approach is not at all to discredit or undervalue the work of scholars who *do* actively contest assignations of certain activities – banking included – as productive or unproductive, for example by deliberately "blurring" those dividing lines.[27] Nor is it to adopt an agnostic position myself on the specific question of the placement of banking. It seems clear to me that some conceptualizations of the productiveness of banking, and the boundary placements underpinning them, *are* indubitably more "accurate" than others – or, as I would prefer to put it, are more adequate to the task of explaining why the political-economic world looks like it does. But that is not the argument I want to make here (although I will take occasion in the Afterword to reflect on the implications of the self-evidently abject inadequacy of national accounting's contemporary conceptualization and methodology for measurement of the productiveness of banks). Rather, I choose to insist that *all* boundary placements – whatever their practical adequacy – have material, socio-historical contexts worth exploring and understanding and, as Callon et al. would have it, perform political and economic work.

Yet although my account is indebted to the work of the above-mentioned scholars on the performativity of economics, I do have reservations about this literature, and my book is in part an attempt to critique and modestly rework it. Some of these reservations are relatively perfunctory, and relate merely to the fact that I am not convinced the work in question is quite as novel and distinctive as it is sometimes held to be. The Callon-edited collection *The Laws of the Markets* was published in 1998, and it shaped in many ways the field which materialized largely in its wake, but by that point critical accounting scholars had been carefully delineating the constitutive function of economic accounting for at least two decades.[28] This earlier work is often neglected in the more recent study of economic performativity by social and cultural theorists – a point also made by one of the key voices in the critical accounting field, the Foucauldian Peter Miller – but it indubitably blazed a conceptual trail and I am keen therefore to acknowledge its influence here.[29] (That said, the critical study of accounting as a performative technology has almost always focused on *company* rather than national accounting, and to this extent it, too, is given a different inflection in this book.[30]) Somewhat comparable arguments about the effectivity of economic ideas, meanwhile, have also been advanced in the field of comparative political economy, especially insofar as ideas are seen to shape institutions, and I have learned from and leaned upon this literature as well.[31]

My more substantive concerns with the plethora of work on economic performativity are twofold. First, there is in some of this work a creeping instrumentalist tendency. By this I mean that because economic theories and ideas are recognized as being effectively performative in one time and place they are assumed to be so both more generically and, even, to the exclusion of *other* material factors. Yet this is clearly not the case. Ideas *can* be effective; but they are not always. Sometimes, as we will see in Chapter 2, they have little or no practical consequences; and even when they do, such effectivity tends to be layered on, or to blend with, the effects of other forces. This last point will be established more concretely in Chapter 5: in arguing that ideas about economic productiveness facilitated the late-twentieth-century internationalization of banking, I am not seeking to contest existing explanations for the latter phenomenon, but rather to add a new dimension to them.

Second, existing work on economic performativity tends to focus on just one side of what is surely economics' *dialectical* implication in the history of capitalism. What do I mean by this? Economics, it is said, shapes the world as well as attempting to describe it. But economics is also shaped *by* – as it is always a product *of* – the world it strives, always imperfectly, to model. From my perspective, this recognition is all too often missing from the otherwise insightful scholarship on the constitutive dimensions of economic ideas, measurements and "machines." The recognition is, moreover, critical, since unless we constantly acknowledge and try to understand the ways in which the economic world envisioned by economics frames the knowledge that *is* economics, we risk obscuring that world's obdurate materiality. In its strongest forms, virtualism can verge on denial of capital or more specifically of, in the work of Daniel Miller, capitalist markets.[32] In more tempered forms, it can still provide the impression that the economy does not in fact add up to much more than the outputs of economics' discrete performative works. Either way, my book is underpinned by an insistence that there *is* a capitalist system, increasingly structured by markets, with a history certainly sculpted *in part* by economic discourses and their instantiation in different calculative technologies, but the dynamics of which are clearly irreducible to those ideas and indeed represent an ineluctable framework for comprehending those ideas and their potential significance.

This insistence speaks to, and actively seeks to problematize, something of a divide in the history of critical or "radical" social-scientific scholarship on money and finance – a divide that is especially marked in my home discipline of human geography. In the 1980s and early 1990s, professedly critical geographers of money and finance worked largely in a radical materialist political-economic tradition, influenced in particular by David Harvey's elucidation of the dynamics of finance capital in *The Limits to Capital*.[33] But from around the mid-1990s, as human geography more broadly underwent a "cultural turn," the emphasis changed and critical work on money and finance headed largely in new directions. Andrew Leyshon and Nigel Thrift's 1997 collection of essays, *Money/Space*, is especially significant in this regard for it both incorporated and catalyzed this shift: the first part of the book assayed a political economy approach; the second an avowedly *alternative*, and now privileged, "discursive" approach.[34]

My quarrel with Leyshon and Thrift here would be that they depicted matters in either/or terms in a comparable way to that in which, I am suggesting, the economic performativity literature has also often tended to do. But surely it cannot be one (political economy) or the other (discourse). We need critically to analyze the material motions of capital, *and* we need to understand the work of ideas in framing and constituting the capitalistic environment. As such this book, while paying due heed to the materiality of economic ideas, is written against the grain of Leyshon and Thrift's apparent implication (as I observed elsewhere) that "adopting such a 'discursive approach' to matters of finance somehow requires 'throw[ing] away' Marxism."[35]

My insistence on treating matters dialectically is rooted in a conception of history which I find fuller and more helpful than that which is implicit in the performative economics literature, but which the latter can undoubtedly help to embellish in a partial fashion. According to this conception, ideas, including economic ideas, must be seen as "both cause and effect," in the words of Stephen Resnick and Richard Wolff, of the social processes that constitute the political-economic world. A change in ideas impacts on this world, whilst "a changed social totality reacts back upon the thinking process to change it."[36] As such, the key question for scholars interested, as I am here, in the nature of the role of ideas in history, becomes, in Harvey's words, the following: "what is it that produces ideas and what is it that these ideas serve to produce?"[37]

Even this, however, is to oversimplify matters somewhat, for it likely draws too firm a distinction between the nature – some would say "ontological status" – of ideas on the one hand and a ("material") world of non-ideas on the other. Ideas *are* material, and thus although I argued in the previous paragraph that they exist in a dialectical relationship with social processes, thinking is of course itself one such process, and thus (after Resnick and Wolff, again) is "an active constituent part" of the social totality rather than something external to it. A crucial implication of this, and one which anticipates many of the insights of the economic performativity shift, is that "a change in thinking *is* a change in a component process of the social totality"; the thought process contributes to the creation of the object of which it is a part.[38] To the extent, then, that we can speak at all of ideas – economic or otherwise – separately from other social processes, we must try to do so in a more sophisticated and nuanced fashion than we may be accustomed to. Economic ideas and economic "reality" are mutually constitutive to an extent that makes any notion of *hierarchical* determination unworkable. This, I think, is at least partly what Louis Althusser had in mind when he asserted that ideas are neither "the essence of the economic" (the Hegelian view) nor "pure phenomena of the economic" (the caricature of the Marxian position). Economic "reality" effects things (including ideas), but ideas also have their own "specific effectivity," and the two are so intimately bound up with one another that we need to conceptualize history ultimately as the "accumulation of effective determinations."[39]

It is such a view of history I try to work with here. The effective determinations are many, and multi-directional; and so while much of the book is about economic ideas shaping economic geographies of finance and banking, its later sections argue that the worlds thus realized have, to use Resnick and Wolff's phrase, "reacted back" upon the ideational process.

The economic ideas I discuss in the book, as already indicated, primarily concern perspectives on the productiveness of banking and finance – the productiveness of, that is, the *providers* of debt, as opposed to the "productivity of debt" per se, to use Janet Roitman's phrase.[40] Two further points of clarification are in order here. First, the focus is on product*iveness*, not product*ivity*. The distinction may seem trivial – and often times, just to confuse matters, the word productivity is used to denote what I am referring to here as productiveness – but it is not. Productiveness is an absolute concept in the sense that it is its own referent: is something or someone (economically) productive, or not? Productivity, by contrast, is a relative concept. In relating a quantum of output to a quantum of one or more inputs into the productive process, productivity is, at heart, a measure of the *efficiency* of production. Productiveness, as we shall see, is a child very much of classical political economy; productivity and efficiency belong more to neoclassical economics. The latter indicators certainly have their own critically important social histories, too, both in terms of how and by whom they have been envisioned and calculated and how and by whom they have been mobilized.[41] But such histories are not the subject of this book, even if they can be usefully read alongside it.

The second vital clarification distinguishes between what we might think of as "direct" and "indirect" productiveness. The question of whether a person, activity or institution is directly productive is a question of whether it or they are productive *in and of themselves*. Indirect productiveness is more a question of facilitation: does the person, activity or institution in question enable or facilitate productiveness *elsewhere* in the economy. This book is about the sources and effects of representations of direct productiveness. The distinction is, as we will see, an important one, particularly insofar as some (though certainly not all) of those who historically have categorized capitalist banking as economically unproductive have simultaneously maintained that, when functioning smoothly, it lubricates economic productiveness more broadly. Adam Smith's thought, perhaps most notably, exemplifies such a conceptual acceptance of banking's indirect productiveness alongside a denial of direct productiveness.

If productiveness is its immediate ideational subject matter, throughout the book there lurks, in the background, an even more fundamental economic concept. This concept, I argue, is materially present in all of the ideas, measurements and representations of productiveness that I discuss, even if such presence is sometimes latent and opaque rather than transparent and explicit. This concept is the basic notion of *value*, and its ubiquity demands a brief upfront consideration of its pertinence.

The question of value is arguably the central and most contentious question in the whole history of economic thought; different economic philosophies can be distinguished from one another to a significant extent by the different theories of value which animate them.[42] Not all such philosophies, it is true, wear their understanding of value on their sleeve. Nevertheless it *is* always foundational, and hence no economic principle can be properly understood except in relation to the value theory that buttresses it. Gunnar Myrdal, long ago, made the same point about economic policy, stating that "value theory is always implicit in the political results, even where it has not figured explicitly among the premises."[43] A recurring theme of my book, in turn, is that the same is true of all qualitative or quantitative representations of a person or institution's economic contribution: since it is ever present, value theory simply cannot be escaped, or at least it *should not be* escapable. This is most plainly the case where the representation in question concerns our key question of productiveness, since value is ordinarily the object of this alleged quality even where – and perhaps, *especially* where – it is not specified as such.

With this inescapability in mind, the significance of the changing historical theorization of value is reaffirmed repeatedly in what follows.[44] I show that as value theory changed, so too did not only the representation of banking's productiveness, but also the very meaning and possibility of such a representation. I also argue that we can much better appreciate what is going on in a "practical" economic valuation calculus such as the national accounts if we think through the relationship of such a calculus to the "theoretical" valuation registers constituted by different economic philosophies. Finally, I suggest that in exploring such relationships, we can learn as much about those economic philosophies themselves – their internal tensions and constraints – as about the techno-political tools which draw upon them.

Meanwhile, my concern with value theory and its generic resonance is one reason why I consciously try to avoid using categories or classifications that make unexamined assumptions *about* value and its creation. The best example of this is the split so often made between banks' "core" and more "risky" activities – between, that is, banking's so-called "utility" and "speculative" or "casino-like" functions. I neither mobilize this split nor, as typically occurs, focus my critique solely on the latter. Aside from the worry that value is uncritically apportioned in the process, I resist these two linked tendencies for three further reasons. First, because said split is another product of exactly the types of boundary envisioning and placement processes I explore in this book; second, because questioning the "casino" tends, without justification, to exempt the "bread-and-butter" from critical analysis; and third, because, with market-making activities and spread-based revenue generation mechanisms being fundamental to both the utility *and* the casino, the two are not in fact as structurally dissimilar as is often presumed to be the case. The book, therefore, is about "banking," in more-or-less all its Western forms. Disaggregation of banking activities into different types is inevitably necessary at various points, but I endeavor to effect such breakdowns on a coherent, critical, meaningful, and transparent basis.

One other question of distinction is important to address here before I turn below, in the final section of the introduction, to a summary of the book's overall argument and a description of each of its ensuing chapters. This distinction is between, broadly speaking, banking and "money." The book, as its title indicates, is first and foremost about the crossing of boundaries by banks rather than by the monies they handle. The term "finance," of course, is frequently deployed with both meanings, and it is almost inevitable that there is slippage between them in my account. I have tried, however, to be as consistent as possible, and as a rule "finance" refers here, *unless explicitly stated otherwise*, to the institutions and operations of finance rather than the assets or instruments thereof.

Having said all that, it would be crass to imagine that one can examine the history of banks' negotiations of geopolitical borders without also telling at least part of the convoluted story of money and *its* territorial geographies, a story which of course encompasses the materialization and growth of financial markets of various kinds. One cannot – not least since multinational banks, as Stefano Battilossi has observed, represent to one degree or another "agents and vehicles of international capital flows."[45] As such, the geographical scope and mobility of money and of other financial assets in their various forms do represent key elements of this study; they are dealt with extensively and directly, not peripherally and indirectly. Yet they are not, I repeat, the main focus: I address such issues only to the extent that it is necessary to do so in order to understand the dynamics of *institutional* financial spatiality. After all, as Brian Scott-Quinn reminds us, "[t]he fact that [financial] markets have become global and integrated does not of itself imply that the intermediaries which offer services to investors and borrowers in these markets need operate in more than one country."[46]

The question remains, however, of *why* banks and not money capital represent the book's primary consideration. There are, again, three main reasons. One I have already foregrounded: the fact that my initial thinking in regard to the financial crisis revolved specifically around the conceptualization of the productiveness *of banking* and the politics of the geographies *of banking*. The second reason is that on my reading, at least, the history of money capital's geographical peregrinations in general, and its negotiation of inter-state boundaries in particular, has been more fully told – and certainly more closely tied by researchers to the development and dissemination of economic ideas – than is the case for financial institutions.[47] And last, but most important of all from my perspective, is a factor relating to the crucial economic concept we have just been dealing with: the concept of value. This last factor requires special attention.

It is my view that the analysis of money in general, and not just of money's geographical configurations and mobilities, too often fetishizes money *as value*. But money is not value; one of its functions is to act as a store of value, of course, and another is to serve as a means of payment for items perceived to *have* some kind of value, but it is not value itself.[48] I have lost count of the number of times that I have read accounts of international finance that invoke the scale and speed of cross-border flows of financial assets of various kinds as if such movements matter sui generis. Yet what surely matters, economically and politically, is how value is redistributed (and, some would argue, created) by means of such flows, and who the beneficiaries of such flows are. It is theoretically possible for large sums of money to flow around the world with no net winners or losers, and in view of this it can never be enough to focus just on the flows themselves. We need to know who gains and who loses, how, where and why, and to this end we need to understand the geographical political economy not only of money but of the banks which create, move, and trade in it; not only of financial markets, but of the banks which construct, feed, and inhabit them. Benjamin Cohen alludes to the vital, sector-specific rationale for this, observing correctly that "with banks, much more is involved than just the issue of capital mobility."[49] But the imperative is actually, I think, a much more generic one. Our analysis of the contemporary global political-economic conjuncture too often elides the critical questions of value production and distribution through its construction of what Colin Crouch describes as a state-market analytical binary that leaves little or no space for large multinational corporations (including, of course, *financial* corporations), even though such corporations are the primary locus of profit generation and circulation. My book is therefore written in the conviction that Crouch is right that it is in the "lack of a distinction [between the market and firms] that several of our problems lie."[50]

The Argument and Structure of the Book

While not exactly born with capital, the idea of someone or something being economically "productive" only became a subject of explicit and sustained reflection with the development and social embedding of market-based capitalism. Much the same is true of what we now think of as banking: money had been lent and borrowed for many centuries, but it was only once markets began to be organized along capitalistic lines that the first instruments of "modern" finance and the first institutions dedicated to the business *of* money came into being. These two products of capitalist history, meanwhile, did not "meet" – in the sense of opinions being proffered specifically as to the economic productiveness, or not, of banking – until the very end of the seventeenth century. But if such a confluence was thus only relatively recent in the long scheme of things, it is a central argument of this book that the envisioning of banking *as productive* was considerably *more* recent. For, within those Western systems of representation of the economic world considered most authoritative at any particular point, it was not until well into the twentieth century that a positive envisioning of banks' contribution came to supplant the negative picture which had long predominated.

It is often thought that internationalized banking is of similarly recent vintage. Indeed, someone born between the two world wars and unaware of financial history prior to the 1930s might reasonably argue that banking was an essentially national phenomenon until the 1960s, and that it took still another 15 to 20 years for anything other than US-based banks to make meaningful inroads into overseas markets. Internationalized banking, from this perspective, would appear the exception to a nationally-circumscribed historical norm. In actuality, however, the reverse is true: the three decades beginning with the onset of the Great Depression in the early 1930s represented a very brief and very anomalous interlude in a capitalist history characterized, for the most part, by open and integrated trans-state financial and monetary markets across which banks operated with typically few inter-territorial restrictions.

Beginning from the beginnings of capitalism, *Banking Across Boundaries* tells these two stories and investigates the relations between them. Arguably its central proposition is that the two "worlds" in question – the conceptual world of the envisioning of banks' economic productiveness, and the material world of banks' spatial anatomy – have edged closer and closer together over time, to the point today where each is thoroughly implicated in the other. To develop and substantiate this proposition, I split the history of capitalism into three periods (corresponding in turn to the three parts of the book), and I argue that each was characterized by a substantially different type of relationship between the conceptual and the material.

Part I, covering the period up to the 1930s, is entitled "Worlds Apart," for the simple reason that the conceptual and the material were more-or-less entirely separate from one another. And because they were effectively separate, they are discussed largely separately, in Chapters 1 (the conceptual) and 2 (the material) respectively. Chapter 1 posits that the idea of economic productiveness was first given substantive form in Western political economy, and that political economy was the primary and certainly most influential Western forum for the envisioning of such productiveness from the seventeenth century through to the late nineteenth century. Political-economic discourse is by no means the chapter's sole focus, however, for it did not emerge out of nothing, and its picturing of the economic contribution specifically of banks clearly built upon a long history of representation within *other* social discourses of money-related activities in general and usury in particular. Though it avowedly stripped such other representations of their normative dimensions, the "science" of political economy uniformly retained the placement of "finance" on the "negative" side of a foundational boundary which in its case divided the productive from the unproductive rather than, for instance, the moral from the immoral.

Chapter 2 explores, over the same extended time span, banks' positioning with regards the book's other key boundary form: the geopolitical boundary between states – states which, by the later stages of this period, had overwhelmingly become *nation*-states. Drawing here more than in any other chapter of the book upon an already vast secondary literature, I show that as a rule banks encountered few obstacles when, as many did, they sought to expand operations beyond their domestic territorial base. I also show that the monies and increasingly diverse and sophisticated financial instruments in which banks dealt were afforded a similar spatial mobility by the authorities who policed states' geoeconomic borders. Again, this much has been substantiated previously in the historical literature. Where I add to that literature is in arguing, against widely-held views to the contrary, that economic concepts – around productiveness or otherwise – played little or no role in the fostering or maintenance of such an open environment, even in the era of the gold standard and Ricardian free trade theory. Banks were able to operate across geopolitical boundaries not so much because economic orthodoxy held that they should be able to, but more in the sense that it was not argued that they should not.

In Part II, which takes us through to the mid-1970s, I demonstrate that by around 1930 the constellation of ideas and practices mapped out in Part I had been totally transformed. The central argument in this middle section of the book is that having previously existed largely independently of one another, the conceptual and material worlds we are concerned with had not only now experienced a rapprochement, but had done so in such a way that they were now, as the title indicates, "Worlds Aligned": they shared a common terrain, and they "fitted" directionally with one another in the sense that each appeared logical in relation to the other. What do I mean by this? Stated simply, I mean that it would be considerably harder to understand why banking assumed the spatial configurations it did without awareness of prevailing conceptualizations of banks' productiveness; and that equally, it would be more difficult to understand those conceptualizations themselves outside of the material context of banks' actual and ventured spatial practices.

This alignment is especially important, I argue, in terms of the "framing" work of economic ideas. Such ideas, in the fraught international political economy of the 1930s and 1940s in particular, were more impactful than ever before, not least in relation to questions of finance. Where the concept specifically of *productiveness* was concerned, the key technology of representation now became the new calculus of national accounting, the neoclassicization of economics having avowedly – if not, I claim, in practice – buried this question as a worthy theoretical issue. With notable exceptions (the key one being in the context of the discussion of the issue of capital controls prior to and at the Bretton Woods conference in 1944), notions of productiveness typically were not actively invoked in the politics of finance and banking. But they were now, I insist, *right there, defining the feasible*: informing, infusing and molding the decision-making milieu, if not yet demonstrably "performing" the political economy in a directly and visibly constitutive sense. I flesh out this claim in part by emphasizing the "alignment of worlds" in and through key individuals – persons implicated in the envisioning of both economic productiveness *and* the geopolitical possibilities of finance. Such alignment was nowhere more apparent, we shall see, than in the persona of John Maynard Keynes: Keynes the economist, Keynes the national accountant, and Keynes the government advisor and official Bretton Woods negotiator.

Crucially, it is posited in Part II that the alignment of our conceptual and material worlds from the 1930s through to the mid-1970s displayed an opposite "polarity" on either side of the Atlantic; and the chapter structure flows directly from this proposition. Chapter 3 focusses on developments in Europe, and in particular in France and the UK. Here, it is claimed, the historically negative envisioning of banks' economic contribution persisted, and was cemented in the new discipline of national accounting. In both the UK and France, the official accounts would show the financial sector as effectively unproductive – as adding marginal, zero, or often *negative* value to the national economy – throughout this period. At the same time, British and French banks, which had been at the forefront of cross-border expansionism in earlier times, remained largely domestically-constrained. Pointing to the seminal role played by Keynes within this particular historical-geographical conjuncture – what we might, after Gramsci, call a "historic bloc" – of ideas and practices, I argue that a negative view of banks' productiveness "fitted" with the sector's conservative geopolitical posture, and vice versa.

In the US, meanwhile, events took a wholly different course, and Chapter 4 explains the conjuncture/"bloc" which materialized there. The material and conceptual were, once more, aligned, but the boundary positionings were the *obverse* of those which obtained in the UK and France. American banks were agitating to re-colonize international markets as soon as The Great Depression and World War II were behind them; and they were the first successfully to do so, from the late 1950s onwards. At the same time, the US national accounts presented the financial sector in a wholly different light. They were the first, anywhere in the world, to show banks as definitively productive and to offer a range of methodologies for quantifying this productiveness. The chapter encourages us to understand this envisioning in the light of the contemporary geopolitics of US finance, and to see such geopolitics, in turn, in light of the supportive picturing afforded by the national accounts.

The third and final part of the book takes us from the mid-1970s through to the present-day. It focuses upon three interrelated sets of changes that distinguish this period from the preceding one. First, banks from the UK and France, as well as from Germany and Japan, increasingly joined American banks in colonizing foreign markets. Second, the envisioning of banks as directly productive economic agents not only became the consensus representation within national accounts worldwide, but *also* began to permeate the contemporary incarnation of the field of scholarly political economy – a field which, since its halcyon days with Smith, Ricardo, and Marx, had until this point continued to place finance on the negative side of the production boundary (albeit in the barely-discernible intellectual shadows cast by the dominant neoclassical economic paradigm). Last but by no means least, these conceptual and material developments became ever more tightly enmeshed; indeed, they did so to such an extent that they were now, I claim, "Co-constituted Worlds."

To avoid misinterpretation, it is worth being precise here about what exactly I mean by the notion of co-constitution. The first thing to say is that it entails bi-directionality: ideas constituting practices *and* practices constituting ideas. The second is that the meaning is obviously stronger than the notion of alignment mobilized in Part II: constitution involves, to use MacKenzie's phrase, effective performativity; it means a *material* contribution, without which the outcome would look materially different. Third, however, it does not equate to causation. In arguing, as I do, that the moving of banks across the conceptual production boundary contributed to their ability physically to cross international boundaries, and that the latter crossing contributed in turn to the former – hence the virtuous/vicious circle image invoked above – I am not suggesting that one *caused* the other. I am arguing, rather, for a dynamic of *enablement*. Clearly other contributory factors were, and are, at work.

Given the different nature of the argument compared with those advanced in Parts I and II, an alternative chapter structure is again called for. While recognizing their mutually-constitutive nature, the two "directions" of impact are assessed in the two chapters respectively: ideas on practice (Chapter 5), and then practice on ideas (Chapter 6). In Chapter 5, I show how ideas about the productiveness of banking were explicitly put to work in the service of opening up international markets to Western financial institutions. Despite the fact that US banks were no longer the only meaningful actors in the internationalization of banking, it was they – unsatisfied with the significant unilateral advances already made – who nonetheless led the push, which crystallized in the vigorous insertion of financial services into international trade liberalization treaties. As I demonstrate, such insertion required lobbying at two levels (within the US, and externally), and concepts of productiveness were actively leveraged in each case.

The book's final chapter considers the somewhat more elliptical question of material economic realities "reacting back" on the selfsame ideas that shape those realities. Its central claim is that as the banking businesses of the US, the UK and other major Western powers became increasingly internationalized from the late 1970s through to today (a trend the chapter describes and, to the extent possible, seeks to quantify, particularly for the US and UK banking sectors), so the principal technologies of envisioning of economic productiveness – the national accounts and scholarly political economy – increasingly validated the notion that banks *are* indeed productive. In other words, the globalization of banking and finance impacted on fundamental perceptions and representations of finance, as well as on financial services practices and policies.[51] But those perceptions and representations changed, I submit, not so much in recognition as in *neglect* of banking's remodeled spatial anatomy: the material world thus shaping ideas about it precisely through its *mis*apprehension. I make this case most explicitly with regard to contemporary political economy (the case being less clear, I think, with national accounting). As US and UK banking profits swelled in both absolute terms and as a proportion of total "national" corporate profits from the 1970s, the vital, growing contribution of international expansion was conspicuously underplayed. Instead, it was inferred that such growing profit shares were evidence of a "financialization" of Anglo-American capitalism – and that financialization was only possible if the classical political economists (Marx included) had been wrong, and finance is not, after all, unproductive.

With the story pursued to the present and the circle, so to speak, squared, all that then remains is to return to where the book started, with the financial crisis which began in 2007. This I do in a short Afterword where, informed by the book's findings, I reconsider the two overarching, intertwined, and crisis-provoked questions which prompted the book's emergence: the question of the conceptualization of banks' economic productiveness, and the question of the politics of banking geographies. I take the latter first, and argue that if the post-1970s round of internationalization of banking has impacted representations of the productiveness of finance within political economy and national accounting, then it has *also* done so in Anglo-American politics – for which, in a curiously mercantilist twist, the banking sector's trade surplus appears to *make* it, almost by definition, productive.

Meanwhile I argue that, as has seemingly been the case in so many other realms, predictably unhelpful conclusions have been drawn from the crisis in terms of its implications for the official assessment and measurement of banks' productiveness. As noted above, the UK national accounts threw up wholly incongruous measures for the economic contribution of banks during the depths of the banking crisis; other countries' accounts, including America's, did likewise. The reaction, inevitably, has been practitioner soul-searching, rejoining of the long battle over the treatment of banks' "intermediation services," and a renewed search for a "better" statistical solution. Yet this comes after 80-odd years have *already* been invested in such a search; and more than 50 after George Jaszi, later a head of the US Bureau of Economic Analysis, reflected that "it seems to me unlikely that a really satisfactory solution will ever be found."[52] Only, I suggest, once we accept that Jaszi was right, and understand *why* he was right, can we begin directing our intellectual energies in – dare I say it – more "productive" directions, and contemplate a different political-economic future with a potentially different place, in all regards, for finance and banking.

Notes

1   J. Kirshner, "The inescapable politics of money," in his (ed), *Monetary Orders: Ambiguous Economics, Ubiquitous Politics* (Cornell University Press, Ithaca, 2003, 3–24), p.12.

2   G. Farrell, "Blankfein defends pay levels for 'more productive' Goldman staff," *Financial Times*, 11 November 2009.

3   Respectively: T. Congdon, "Tobin tax is national economic suicide," *Prospect*, 2 September 2009; P. Krugman, "Don't Be Narrow-Minded," *New York Times*, 29 March 2010. See also Allister Heath's (the editor of *City A.M.*) recent insistence,

in an article significantly titled "How to reverse Britain's slow decline" (*City A.M.*, 21 March 2011), that financial services are "the most productive sector of the UK economy."

4 CRESC, *An alternative report on UK banking reform*, 2009, available at http://www.cresc.ac.uk/sites/default/files/Alternative%20report%20on%20banking%20V2.pdf.

5 W. Hutton, "This tax on the City is a bonus," *The Guardian*, 9 December 2009; M. Wolf, "The challenge of halting the financial doomsday machine," *Financial Times*, 20 April 2010. Turner had provoked fury in the banking community by calling many banking activities "socially useless" in an interview in *Prospect* magazine ("How to tame global finance," 27 August 2009).

6 H. Boss, *Theories of Surplus and Transfer: Parasites and Producers in Economic Thought*, Unwin Hyman, Boston, 1989; the quotation is from p.4.

7 "Now, it is traditional at this point in the speech to compliment the UK's financial services sector. There may be some who think, given the role of some banks in the global economic turmoil, that this tradition should be broken tonight. I intend to keep to that tradition." HM Treasury, *Speech by the Chancellor of the Exchequer, the Rt Hon Alistair Darling MP, at Mansion House*, 17 June 2009, available at http://www.hm-treasury.gov.uk/press_57_09.htm.

8 BBA, "Focus on finance," *Research Bulletin 1*, 15 June 2007. Available at www.bba.org.uk/content/1/c4/96/51/Focus_on_Finance.pdf.

9 D. Philipsen, "Rethinking GDP: Why We Must Broaden Our Measures of Economic Success," *The Nation*, 8 June 2011.

10 ONS, *Quarterly National Accounts, Quarter Four, 2008*, p.4.

11 ONS, *Quarterly National Accounts briefing note, Quarter Four*, 2008, pp.6–7.

12 S. French, A. Leyshon and N. Thrift, "A very geographical crisis: the making and breaking of the 2007–2008 Financial Crisis," *Cambridge Journal of Regions, Economy and Society*, 2, 2009, pp.287–302.

13 D. Harvey, *The Enigma of Capital and the Crises of Capitalism*, Profile Books, London, 2010. See also, for a different slant on the same nexus, S. Johnson and J. Kwak, *13 Bankers: The Wall Street Takeover and the Next Financial Meltdown*, Pantheon, New York, 2010; and the work of Karel Williams and collaborators, mainly in the UK context, on the latter's own "distributive coalition." The nature and operation of this nexus/coalition as it has historically pertained explicitly to the field of *international* finance addressed in this book is discussed most expansively by L. Seabrooke, *US Power in International Finance: The Victory of Dividends*, Palgrave Macmillan, London, 2001, and B. Cohen, *In Whose Interest?: International Banking and American Foreign Policy*, Yale University Press, New Haven CT, 1988.

14 Cf.J. Quiggin, "Financial Markets: Masters or Servants?," *Politics & Society*, 39, 2011, 331–45; J. Froud, S. Johal, J. Law, A. Leaver and K. Williams, "Rebalancing the Economy (Or Buyer's Remorse)," *CRESC Working Paper* 87, 2011.

15 J. Treanor, "Barclays bank forced to admit it paid just £113m in corporation tax in 2009," *The Guardian*, 18 February 2011.

16 IFSL was merged into a new body, TheCityUK, in 2010.

17 IFSL, *UK financial sector net exports 2009*, August 2009, available at http://www.thecityuk.com/assets/Uploads/UK-Financial-Sector-Net-Exports-2009.pdf; p.1.

18 On the politics and poetics of "complexity-speak" in modern finance, see my "Complexity, finance, and progress in human geography," *Progress in Human Geography*, 33, 2009, pp.807–824.

19 A. Vanoli, *A History of National Accounting*, IOS Press, Amsterdam, 2005, p.154.

20 D. MacKenzie, F. Muniesa and L. Siu (eds), *Do Economists Make Markets?: On the Performativity of Economics*, Princeton University Press, Princeton NJ, 2008.

21 D. MacKenzie, *An Engine, Not a Camera: How Financial Models Shape Markets*, MIT Press, Cambridge MA, 2008, pp.18,12.

22 Cohen, *In whose interest?*, p.12.

23 The literature is now very large (and getting bigger), but key contributions include: M. Callon (ed), *The Laws of the Markets*, Blackwell, Oxford, 1998; MacKenzie, *An Engine*; MacKenzie et al. (eds), *Do Economists Make Markets?*; and the special issue "Performativity, Economics and Politics" of the *Journal of Cultural Economy*, 3(2), 2010.

24 T. Mitchell, "The properties of markets," in MacKenzie et al. (eds), *Do Economists Make Markets?* (244–275).

25 F. Block and G. Burns, "Productivity as a social problem: the uses and misuses of social indicators," *American Sociological Review*, 51, 1986, pp.767–780, at pp.767–768.

26 A. Mennicken and P. Miller, "Accounting, territorialization and power," *Foucault Studies*, 13, 2012, pp.4–24, at p.4; original emphasis.

27 E.g. K. Mitchell, S. Marston and C. Katz (eds), *Life's Work: Geographies of Social Reproduction*, Blackwell, Oxford, 2004.

28 For an excellent introduction, see P. Miller, "Accounting as social and institutional practice: an introduction," in A. Hopwood and P. Miller (eds), *Accounting as Social and Institutional Practice* (Cambridge University Press, Cambridge, 1994, 1–39), in which he argues that "the 'economic' domain is *constituted and reconstituted* by the changing calculative practices that provide a knowledge of it" (p.4, original emphasis) – a claim that is difficult to distinguish substantially from those later made by those working in the "new" field of performative economics.

29 P. Miller, "Calculating economic life," *Journal of Cultural Economy*, 1, 2008, pp.51–64.

30 Of particular importance here, see the work of James Perry and Andreas Nölke, especially J. Perry, and A. Nölke, "The political economy of international accounting standards," *Review of International Political Economy*, 13, 2006, pp.559–586, and A. Nölke and J. Perry, "The power of transnational private governance: financialisation and the IASB," *Business and Politics*, 9, 2007, no. 3.

31 See especially M. Blyth, *Great Transformations: Economic Ideas and Institutional Change in the Twentieth Century*, Cambridge University Press, Cambridge, 2002.

32 D. Miller, "Turning Callon the right way up," *Economy and Society*, 31, 2002, pp.218–233.

33 D. Harvey, *The Limits to Capital*, University of Chicago Press, Chicago, 1982. See especially the collection: S. Corbridge, R. Martin and N. Thrift (eds), *Money, Power and Space*, Blackwell, Oxford, 1994.

34 A. Leyshon and N. Thrift, *Money/space: Geographies of Monetary Transformation*, Routledge, London, 1997.

35 B. Christophers, "On voodoo economics: theorizing relations of property, value, and contemporary capitalism," *Transactions of the Institute of British Geographers, NS* 35, 2010, 94–108, at p.95, citing Leyshon and N. Thrift, *Money/space*, p.xv.

36 S. Resnick and R. Wolff, *Knowledge and Class: A Marxian Critique of Political Economy*, University of Chicago Press, Chicago IL, 1987, pp.56–62.

37 D. Harvey, "Population, resources and the ideology of science," *Economic Geography*, 50, 1974, pp.256–277, at p.268.

38 Resnick and Wolff, *Knowledge and Class*, p.56 (original emphasis).

39   L. Althusser, *For Marx*, Verso, London, 2005, pp.107–113.

40   J. Roitman, "Unsanctioned wealth; or, the Productivity of Debt in Northern Cameroon," *Public Culture*, 15, 2003, pp.211–237.

41   E.g. Block and Burns, "Productivity"; C. Maier, "The politics of productivity: foundations of American international economic policy after World War II," *International Organization*, 31, 1977, pp.607–633.

42   See especially K. Cole, J. Cameron and C. Edwards, *Why Economists Disagree: The Political Economy of Economics*, Longman, London, 1983.

43   G. Myrdal, *The Political Element in the Development of Economic Theory*, Transactions Publishers, New Brunswick NJ, 1990, p.15.

44   In this respect I have been influenced in particular by the important collection *Value and the World Economy Today* (Palgrave Macmillan, London, 2003) edited by Richard Westra and Alan Zuege, and my book is written with the same underlying conviction – that value theory *matters* – as those essays.

45   S. Battilossi, "Financial innovation and the golden ages of international banking, 1890–1931 and 1958–81," *Financial History Review*, 7, 2000, pp.141–175, at p.141. On the analytical inextricability of international banking and international finance, see also R. Aliber, "International banking: a survey," *Journal of Money, Credit, and Banking*, 16, 1984, 661–678.

46   B. Scott-Quinn, "US investment banks as multinationals," in G. Jones (ed), *Banks as Multinationals* (Routledge, London, 268–293), p.275.

47   As recently as 2002, Stefano Battilossi and Youssef Cassis were still able to describe "the internationalization of banking in industrialized countries and the rise of a new global financial order" as "a new and important subject which has so far been neglected by historians." "Preface," in their (eds) *European Banks and the American Challenge: Competition and Cooperation in International Banking under Bretton Woods* (Oxford University Press, Oxford, 2002), p.vi. Recent examples of work which explicitly considers the history of geographical capital mobility in relation to the power of economic ideas include M. Watson, *The Political Economy of International Capital Mobility*, Palgrave Macmillan, London, 2007, and many of the essays in J. Kirshner (ed), *Monetary Orders: Ambiguous Economics, Ubiquitous Politics*, Cornell University Press, Ithaca NY, 2003, in particular those by Mark Blyth and Kirshner himself.

48   See G. Ingham, *The Nature of Money*, Polity Press, London, 2004, for a useful introduction.

49   Cohen, *In Whose Interest?*, p.14.

50   C Crouch, *The Strange Non-Death of Neo-liberalism*, Polity Press, London, 2011, pp.ix-x.

51   On the latter type of impact, see especially W. Coleman, *Financial Services, Globalization and Domestic Policy Change: A Comparison of North America and the European Union*, Palgrave Macmillan, London, 1996.

52   G. Jaszi, "The conceptual basis of the accounts: a re-examination," in National Bureau of Economic Research, *A Critique of the United States Income and Product Accounts* (Princeton University Press, Princeton NJ, 1958, 13–148), p.63.

Part I
Worlds Apart
Before Keynes

1

The Birth of Economic Productiveness

> It is of no little interest, and importance, too, to observe how economists have denied productivity now to this class, now to the other.
>
> Lewis H. Haney (1911)[1]

What is the contribution of banks, and in particular their services of financial intermediation, to the production of wealth? It is the answers that have been given to this question, and the various representative technologies through which such answers have been crafted, that I begin to probe in this chapter. Doing so will, I hope, offer already at this early stage a clear demonstration of what later develops into a central theme of the book as a whole: the importance of boundary placement in regimes of economic representation. Thus we will see, amongst other things, that opinions as to banking's "worth" have very often been based upon the assignation of banking activities to one side or other of the productive/unproductive boundary – and, indeed, to either side of various other closely-related conceptual borders.

The period covered in this chapter is a formidably vast one, starting in the pre-Christian era and leading all the way up to the 1930s and the key figure of John Maynard Keynes. There are three important reasons for casting the net this expansively. First, and most obviously, it is vital to forestall the tendency to presume "it was ever thus." The representations most familiar to us today are almost inevitably those of most recent vintage and those granted the most substantial and sustained public exposure. As I will go on to argue in Parts II and III, the representations of productiveness emanating from national accounts have, over the past 70 or 80 years, assumed a particular and heightening significance. But, vitally, they are far from being the *only* representations that history has bequeathed to us.

Banking Across Boundaries: Placing Finance in Capitalism, First Edition. Brett Christophers.
© 2013 John Wiley & Sons, Ltd. Published 2013 by John Wiley & Sons, Ltd.

On the contrary: all manner of different perspectives on the contribution of banks and financial intermediation have been offered up at different times and in different places, and it behooves us to treat these with the same seriousness as those which happen to enjoy pre-eminence in the narrow historical-geographical conjuncture that is the early twenty-first century here-and-now.

Second, and related to this point, is a question of understanding. Not only would a restricted focus on more contemporary representations risk endowing such representations with a veneer of naturalness or universality, it would also make the task of understanding those representations *themselves* a difficult if not impossible one. We cannot understand without context. Representations developed and propagated in the post-war era may be different in various ways from those that have come before, but they are not independent of them: they build upon them, even if sometimes through opposition. To enrich our comprehension of what national accounts and other contemporary fields of representation say about economic productiveness, therefore, it is necessary to identify and interrogate their long-term conceptual lineage.

Third, and most important of all, there is the matter not just of boundary placements, but of boundaries per se. The "production boundary," as we will see, is one of the most fundamental theoretical concepts in the national accounting canon; where activities are placed in relation to this notional boundary essentially determines, for national accountants at least, whether such activities are deemed "productive" or not. But this boundary, we should be clear, is not something with an objective, pre-existing substance of its own – something simply waiting "out there," as it were, to be discovered, and then to have economists, politicians and other "authorities" place different activities on either side of it. Placements can only be made once the boundary underpinning such placements has itself been conceptualized into existence; and the "production boundary," in turn, depends upon the prior construction of something *called* "productiveness." Where does this concept come from? Who created it, and why? What will become clear in this chapter is that twentieth-century national accounts created neither productiveness nor the boundary separating it from the unproductive.

While my emphasis in this chapter is very much on the *economic* dimensions of historical representations of banking (and especially the core question of economic productiveness), the emphasis is not an exclusive one. I also consider what might be termed moral or social perspectives on what it is that bankers are perceived to do. Part of the reason for this is that, particularly the further back in time one goes, it is often hard to disentangle purely "economic" considerations from "non-economic" ones. Indeed, one could argue, as both Max Weber and, latterly, Jürgen Habermas have famously done, that modernity is defined precisely by the gradual processes of differentiation between such "spheres."[2] Another part of the reason for looking beyond the economic is that economically-oriented representations, with a few notable exceptions, barely existed in the form we tend now to understand them prior to the birth in the eighteenth century of the tradition of political economy and its central inquiry into the sources of wealth creation; yet the "economic" representations of banking that did then begin to proliferate called upon, in various ways, different representative themes that had been evolving since long before – not least the centuries-old excoriation of usury.

This last observation leads directly on to a final, related point I need to make here. If, as I argue later in the book, national accounting became over the course of the twentieth century a primary forum for the "making" of economic productiveness – and thus, one might even suggest, of an activity's deemed inherent worth more generally – it is clear that other representative "technologies" served such purposes in earlier times. Certainly, from the mid-eighteenth century, political-economic theory was one such; but it was not alone. Assessments of banking and the activities of bankers, loan brokers and other financial intermediaries have featured prominently, for many centuries, not only in avowedly "factual" discourses (like, from the eighteenth century, political economy), but also in professedly "fictional" traditions (literature, for example) and in those discourses widely seen to mix fact and fiction, such as religion and philosophy. Tracing the genealogy of contemporary "productive finance" hence necessitates engagement with all these fields. Indeed, a compelling reason for *not* limiting our research to putatively fact-based discourses has been persuasively put forth by Mary Poovey: namely, that while prior to the eighteenth century there existed a range of different types of writing on money and finance, these neither were consistently differentiated from one another in format or function, nor did they distinguish clearly between what *was* fiction and what was fact.[3]

With these preliminary observations in mind, the chapter begins with a relatively brief overview of the evolution in perspectives on "banking" in the centuries prior to the formal development of what we understand, today, as a *banking system*. The relatively narrow focus in this first section is on the practice of lending money at interest: what was written about it, and what kinds of dichotomies were erected to demarcate positive assessments from negative ones. The second and third sections of the chapter then move onto the "modern" era. Section two is given over to perspectives on banking formulated in literature, in philosophy, and – to the extent that it can be segregated from either of those two, or from political economy – in politics (Western religion had, by this point, effectively put to bed its own quarrels on such matters). Section three explores in turn the conceptual placement of financial intermediation in European, and largely British, political economy: the tradition of the Physiocrats, of Adam Smith, and of Malthus, Ricardo and Marx. Together, these two discussions take us up to the late nineteenth century. The fourth and final part of the chapter is intended to bridge the gap between where section three leaves off (with Marx) and Chapter 3 later picks up (with Keynes): a gap most notable, in the context of this book, for the emergence of neoclassical economics.

Scourging the Money Lenders

There exists in the historical literature considerable debate over the origins of modern banks. Yet upon gaining only a modest level of acquaintance with that literature, one thing becomes readily apparent: the identification of origins depends very much on the definition of "banks" being used. Some authors, thus, argue that what we can think of as banks appeared as early as the fourth century BC, in ancient Greece.[4] Others, greater in number, point to twelfth-century Italy, or to the Low Countries in the fourteenth century.[5] But if we are interested in the systemic emergence of the type of fractional-reserve deposit banking and associated nexus of credit creation that has come to define modern banking, most scholars would agree that late-seventeenth-century England was the key crucible. Even Raymond de Roover, the author of two brilliant, seminal books on early banking in Italy and Belgium, concedes as much:

> It is true that the modern banking system based on the circulation of notes and the discounting of commercial paper was evolved in England during the seventeenth century. This development originated in the exchange, deposit, and lending activities of the London goldsmiths under Elizabeth and James I and culminated in the foundation of the Bank of England in 1695, during the reign of William and Mary.[6]

In this chapter, therefore, when I turn in the two following sections to discuss social perspectives on the contribution of modern banks per se, England, and the period from the 1650s onwards, becomes my main focus.

Here, meanwhile, we will deal with the much longer historical period leading up to and including the sixteenth century, with our spotlight trained upon the one activity that can be traced with some consistency all the way back into the classical era which *does* remain central to what banks still do today: issuing credit, which is to say lending money at interest. And while, as we will see, a series of powerful conceptual couplets emerged over time to frame dominant perceptions of profit-oriented money-lending, perhaps the most pertinent observation to make of this period concerns a couplet that did not substantively materialize until *later*: the productive/unproductive distinction. Indeed, not only was the activity of credit provision not couched explicitly in such terms; but in the English language, at any rate, the word "productive" *itself* did not enter common parlance, in any of its various meanings, until the early seventeenth century.[7]

Before examining those representative tropes that *were* widely mobilized in the representation of money-lending through antiquity and the Middle Ages, however, we must first pause to consider a towering historical figure who discoursed stridently on this activity, and whose words have, in some readings, been taken as a commentary on economic "productiveness." This figure is the Greek philosopher Aristotle. As the English economic historian William Ashley once remarked, it had become, by the late-nineteenth century, more-or-less accepted scholarly wisdom that Aristotle saw money as "barren" and thus held that "interest cannot justly be demanded for use of it."[8]

That Aristotle's famous monetary critique in his *Politics* is often seen as a statement on the nonproductiveness or economic "sterility" of credit is understandable. For one thing, his commentary was indeed based at least in part on economic – rather than purely ethical – considerations.[9] Moreover, his thoughts on money clearly influenced many of the great modern political economists for whom, as we will see below, banking in general – and lending at interest in particular – *was* an economically unproductive activity. Not least among these was Marx, and particularly his arguments in Volume 3 of *Capital* about capital achieving "its most superficial and fetishized form" in the shape of credit money. (Compare, for instance, Aristotle's "birth of money from money" with Marx's "money breeding money.")[10]

But two caveats are in order here. First, a case can be readily made that the "productiveness" reading was one that came to be imposed on Aristotle retrospectively, in an era when the conceptual distinction between economic productiveness and nonproductiveness *had* become both meaningful and germane.[11] This case is buttressed by the fact that Aristotle himself did not use the word "barren"; what he said was that "of all modes of making money," charging interest on loans "is the most unnatural" (suggesting a moral, not economic, judgment); "barren" was only attributed to Aristotle later, implicitly by Shakespeare in *Merchant of Venice* (Antonio asking "when did friendship take | A breed of barren metal of his friend?"), and then explicitly by arch-critic Jeremy Bentham (claiming Aristotle had alleged that "all money is in its nature barren").[12] Second, and more importantly in my view, if there was, in Aristotle, an argument about interest and "economic productiveness," or more generically about the role of credit in value or wealth creation, it was one that was comprehensively missed by Aristotle's chief interlocutors for over two thousand years.

Instead, from the time of Aristotle essentially up until the time of Adam Smith, hegemonic social perspectives on money-lending were overwhelmingly moralistic or legalistic in nature; and very often, in societies pervaded by natural law conventions, they were both, as was quintessentially the case with Christian canon law. James Ackerman, in fact, in an excellent overview article, argues that for Aristotle himself, interest was "inherently unnatural *and unjust*."[13] And like so many in the centuries after him, Aristotle used, when speaking about interest, the familiar term that by his time had already become, and which still remains, deeply pejorative: usury.

But what exactly is this "usury" about which so much has been said and written? Today, we typically think of usury as the charging of "excessive" interest – this loan rate is usurious, that one is not – but this definition and understanding is actually a relatively recent one. For the bulk of the history of money and of its lending practices, usury meant *all* interest, "whether high or low, excessive or moderate."[14] It was only in the early modern period, as Margaret Atwood observes in her fascinating and accessible history of debt, that "usury changed its meaning from mere interest-charging to exorbitant interest-charging."[15]

This change came about slowly, and certainly not without struggle: Jacques le Goff appropriately describes the controversies and battles over usury as constituting one of the great "labour pains" of early, merchant capitalism.[16] Such pains were experienced most acutely of all by the Church. It was the Catholic Church that, since its very inception, had consistently led the campaign against interest in the Judeo-Christian world; and it was the nonconformist churches and their leading theologians that, from the early fifteenth century, decisively reshaped the meaning of usury and, more importantly, the underlying moral economy of lending money at interest. While, in early tracts, Martin Luther had "condemned interest energetically," he later changed his position; and even more influential in legitimizing interest were John Calvin's teachings.[17] The upshot, in any event, was a rewriting of usury laws in major Protestant (and proto-capitalist) countries to permit the charging of interest up to specified ceilings, most notably in the Netherlands (in 1543, to 12%) and England (1545, to 10%).[18] The rest of the Western world gradually followed suit. And while debate continued, "the battle was over. Interest became a permanent fixture in Western civilization. The usury debate began to assume its present proportions – discussion of when interest becomes excessive."[19]

While a thorough overview of the longstanding, pre-1500s critique of usury – usury *as interest* – is neither viable nor necessary here, it is important nevertheless to grasp that critique's main lineaments. For it was not homogeneous, and nor did it remain stable over time. Moreover, the ethico-intellectual critique was often thoroughly wrapped up with decidedly worldly considerations: the Church's overt association of usury with Jewish moneylenders being perhaps the most noteworthy example of such.[20] If we were to try to extract and highlight some key trends in discourses on usury – from their origins in the ancient world (witness the frequent denunciations in the Old Testament), through the early teachings of the Church Fathers, the later analyses of St. Thomas Aquinas and fellow Scholastics, the influential-if-idiosyncratic interventions such as those famously offered by Dante in his *Divine Comedy* (which consigned usurers to the Seventh Circle of Hell) and the Shakespeare of *Merchant of Venice*, and all the way up to the final flickerings of those discourses-proper in the fires of the Protestant Reformation – perhaps three would stand out.[21]

First, there was a hazy but ultimately definitive shift from the condemnation of charging interest on loans specifically to the poor, to the condemnation of interest per se. The former type of critique, seemingly most concerned with the social consequences of lending at interest, is particularly noticeable in the various books of the Old Testament; by the time of Aquinas (1225–1274), by contrast, emphasis had shifted to "the intrinsic 'immorality' of interest itself."[22] Second, and as recounted by, among others, Le Goff, the *degree* of immorality or sinfulness that usurious acts were seen to represent also changed over time: hence Le Goff's telling of how usurers came to be condemned to Purgatory rather than, as was previously the case, to Hell.[23] Third, and also related in various complex ways to the Church's growing need to reconcile itself to a world in which money and its lending and borrowing were simply facts of economic life (not least in terms of the economy of the Church itself), historians have documented the numerous methods dreamed up – and sanctioned, explicitly or implicitly, *by* the Church – effectively to circumvent usury laws. These included so-called "triple contracts" (forms of partnership) and *rentes* (also referred to as annuities). A whole series of fraught conceptual distinctions – based on ownership or, as in Aquinas, on the differentiation of "fungible" from "nonfungible" goods – were inevitably invoked to legitimate such financing instruments and, in the process, to distinguish "licit rents and profits" from "mortally sinful" or "unlawful" usury.[24] Perhaps the most famous of such instruments were the bills of exchange that came to be used extensively by the dominant Italian "bankers" of the fourteenth century such as the Medici family. These bills, which we shall encounter again shortly but will only consider in any depth in the following chapter, essentially served as personal checks for use as means of payment in foreign trade transactions.[25]

What, therefore, in summary, are we to make of the centuries-long critique, emanating centrally from the Church but also circulating widely outside it, of historic practices of lending money at interest? What is arguably most striking about those discourses in which money-lending figured prominently is their over-whelmingly *normative* nature. These were worldviews with very clear principles about the way the world *should* be, not just the way it temporarily was. And within this overall framework of normativity, interest invariably fell on the wrong side of the moral-legal boundaries through which the world was to be navigated, policed, and reconfigured: which is to say that what was said about it was not only normative in nature, but was overwhelmingly *negative* in content.[26]

If this was the case, then, how should we approach the somewhat contrary argument recently made by the historian Niall Ferguson in his widely-read *The Ascent of Money*? Ferguson agrees that for much of human history usury had been condemned, but claims that by the mid-fifteenth century a different view of money-lending, and of the "banks" who practiced it, had crystallized. "Having once been damned," he writes, "bankers were now close to divinity."[27] Given both Ferguson's profile and the direction of the arguments I have offered here, this contention requires our consideration before we move on to the era of modern deposit banking in the next section.

Ferguson's "divinity" assertion is made, critically, in the context of a discussion of Italy's Medici dynasty and their methods of monetary circulation. Because the Medici did not fall foul of social or religious censure, Ferguson's conclusion is that attitudes to "banking" and money-lending had somehow changed. And, in one sense at least, he is right: the Medici, as de Roover remarks, *did* for the most part live as "respected citizens" rather than ostracized usurers. But what Ferguson fails to acknowledge is that they were able to do so only by dressing up the (forbidden) interest payment mechanism as something else entirely. The bill exchange transaction, it was argued, was not an interest-bearing loan but instead either a mere "commutation" of – by definition – moneys of equal value, or a buying and selling of foreign currency. As de Roover writes, "speculative profits on exchange served as a cloak," with "the presence of concealed interest" nonetheless being "undeniable." [28]

To Ferguson's hypothesis, therefore, we can rejoin that the Medici can scarcely have made banking "divine," for in the sense that banking was and (assuredly) is today centrally associated with credit provision, they were not regarded *as* bankers. The explicit charging of interest remained, at least until Luther's *volte face*, unlawful and immoral; indeed "many a [Medici] banker," privy to the exchange bill machinations that were hidden from public view, appeared to internalize social censure in the form of "an uneasy conscience about his unholy deals."[29] And where banking and bankers *were* explicitly associated with the buying and selling of credit, reproval was never far away – hence, for example, the repeated prohibition of emergent deposit-banking practices in the fifteenth-century Low Countries.[30] There, as James Murray has recently demonstrated, "the profession of banking" continued to be seen "as morally ambiguous at best, and as evil and corrupting at worst," until well into the sixteenth century.[31] For the bankers of such worlds, it would be fair to say, the endowment of "divinity" would still have seemed a very distant prospect indeed.

Deposit Banking and Wealth Destruction

In this section and the remainder of the chapter, I move on to discuss much more directly representations of banking, and of bankers, than of the processes of lending money at interest that were to become, of course, a central component *of* the modern banking system. To be sure, in the early years of the emergence of deposit banking in England in the late-seventeenth century, and for much of the eighteenth century, representations of banking remained closely tethered to – and were often indistinguishable from – discourses on such varied financial matters as usury, money, debt, and financial speculation (the last of these attaining a much higher public profile in the years following the inflation and bursting, in 1720, of the South Sea Bubble). Influential mid-seventeenth-century tracts such as David Hume's "Banks and Paper-Money" (1752) and the 5th Lord Elibank's "Essay on Paper-Money and Banking" (1755), both of which we shall consider below, were emblematic of this enduring coupling. And in this sense, it is clearly imprecise to speak of representations of banking as if a discrete, separable discourse existed as such. Yet during this period, significantly, what was said and written about banking *did* come to be increasingly detached from commentary on other financial issues. Nowhere, perhaps, is this clearer than in Charles Dickens, from whose "assaults on financial speculation" in novels such as *Little Dorrit* (1855–1857) "banking and the Bank of England are clearly exempt."[32]

Dickens's era is located at the very end of the period covered in both this section and the next: broadly-speaking, the mid-to-late seventeenth through nineteenth centuries. Here, I consider representations of banking in literature, philosophy and politics, whilst political economy is the explicit focus in the following section. Even this, though, is a problematic and hence somewhat unsatisfactory division. Some of the figures I consider presently under the broad umbrella term "politics" – pamphleteers such as John Briscoe, noblemen such as Patrick Murray (the 5th Lord Elibank), and mavericks, such as John Law, who ultimately elude all pigeon-holing – would possibly have seen themselves *as* economists. Moreover, the two political philosophers whose work I cite here, David Hume and John Locke, both wrote trenchantly on economic issues, and are recognized not only as having presaged some of the foundational arguments of Smithian political economy, but (in Hume's case) as having explicitly influenced Smith himself.

It is also particularly striking, in my view, how central money in general, and money-related matters such as banking in particular, were to the various literary genres of the age.[33] It took until deep into the nineteenth century for literary writing and political-economic writing to become clearly distinguishable from one another in terms either of their style or, more pertinently, of the forms of "value" they sought to mediate for their audiences.[34] Indeed, it is no coincidence that historians often feel compelled to reach for putatively *literary* texts in order to recompose the factual particulars of seventeenth and even eighteenth-century financial worlds: many of the literary "greats" had an impressive, almost uncanny, grasp of the workings of contemporary financial instruments, institutions, and markets. As Frank Melton has noted, for example, Daniel Defoe's *Roxana* (1724) "comes closer than any other contemporary description to an accurate perception of the scrivener's business."[35]

Melton's book on the origins of fractional-reserve deposit banking in late-seventeenth century England offers, on my reading, the best available discussion of how this system gradually emerged from out of a disparate set of existing, "quasi-banking" activities.[36] A headline familiarity with this narrative, and with the nature of those pre-existing activities, will stand us in good stead for what follows, so I will rehearse it briefly here. In Melton's telling, there were two primary institutional antecedents in England to modern banks proper: scriveners (or loan brokers) and money-lenders. While there were certain similarities between the two, and both sets of activities were regulated by the terms of seventeenth-century usury laws (usury, of course, by this stage having taken on its "newer" meaning pertaining to interest rate ceilings rather than the charging of interest per se), there were nonetheless key differences of both business model and means of income generation. Scriveners received money from their clients and placed it out on loan in those clients' names; for doing so, they received purely a brokerage fee set at 0.25% of the value of the loan. Lenders, by contrast, placed out at interest their *own* capital, and "were entitled to the maximum legal rate of interest" – an activity that, Melton says, was "far more profitable" than simple money broking.[37]

Deposit banking, in turn, effectively developed in the late seventeenth century through a merging of these two existing activities. Key figures such as Sir Robert Clayton – the main protagonist in Melton's book – realized that the usury laws contained manifest loopholes, most especially the patent inability to stop scriveners from acting *as* money-lenders *with depositors' capital.* "In the time before their [broking] clients recalled their deposits," writes Melton, "these financiers were free to speculate with their capital." In short, they began to loan *others'* money in their *own* name, and at a greater rate of interest than that paid to depositors. Here, again, is Melton:

> In one instance a banker might act as a loan-broker for his clients in an outward and honest way, putting out a loan on a portion of the deposit. In another instance – the private role of the banker in lending capital in his own name – he surreptitiously expropriated another part of the same deposit.[38]

What, then, did contemporaries, and those who witnessed the proliferation of such practices in the two centuries following these early developments, make of this newfangled "banking" business? Perhaps the most important observation we can make to begin with is that the long-held suspicion of and negativity towards the still-fundamental practice of lending money at interest remained. Only, now, it was redoubled, by virtue precisely of banks' very modus operandi: the highly-visible opening up and maintenance of an interest rate *differential* between their borrowing and lending activities. Thus, towards the end of the period under consideration here, the tenor of most political, philosophical, and literary commentary on banks' perceived role and contribution is remarkably consistent not only with that characterizing the commentary which emerged in the *early* years of deposit banking, but also with that familiar from the centuries-long critique of pre-"banking" usury which was summarized above. Whatever conceptual boundaries were assembled and invoked to distinguish positive from negative, banks still typically found themselves placed on the "wrong" side. Hence even nineteenth-century apologists such as George Warde Norman – a timber merchant and, more importantly, a director of the Bank of England from 1821 to 1872 – were forced to acknowledge that banks still fought a constant battle of minds against "the opprobrium cast upon them."[39]

Yet, more supportive voices did, indubitably, emerge; and not only among obvious constituencies such as Norman and fellow banking practitioners. Dickens, I have intimated, was one such, although his conciliatory gestures towards bankers were generally drowned out amidst the cacophony of his generic offensives against greed and speculation. There *was*, nevertheless, something of a shift in representations of money and banking within sections of the Anglophone literary establishment during the period with which we are concerned. A set of more accommodating, accepting and even – on occasion – affirmatory attitudes crystallized. Patrick Brantlinger traces this shift to "the waning of romanticism and the rise of realism"; and certainly there is a healthy dose of the latter in the nineteenth-century Irish essayist William Lecky's arguments in favor of credit, which postulated that "nothing can appear more simple than the position that interest occupies in pecuniary arrangements. We know that, in a society in which great works of industry or public utility are carried on, immense sums will necessarily be borrowed at interest, and that such transactions are usually advantageous both to the lender and the borrower." Echoing, Brantlinger notes, comparable, earlier reflections by the poet-philosopher Samuel Coleridge and the poet-politician Thomas Macaulay, Lecky's realism reads as the very antithesis of Aristotle's critique of money's affectations. Thus, if credit, for Lecky, is explicitly not "unnatural," neither is it immoral. "This remarkable agency," Lecky opined, "has long proved one of the great moralising influences of society."[40]

For those who subscribed to this "naturalization" of credit, it became of course increasingly difficult to oppugn the bankers who specialized in the circulation of that credit. This more positive outlook on the contributions of banking that I am keen to foreground here began to materialize in the eighteenth century, and then gathered pace in the nineteenth. To be sure, the still-marginal community of banking advocates shrunk to the point of almost disappearing entirely in the wake of each successive banking crisis, such as those of 1772, 1797–1798, 1825, 1836–1837, 1847, and 1857. Even in the midst of such challenging circumstances, however, a discursive and political space was newly opening up for criticism to be directed *elsewhere*. Hence the ability of Bank of England director Norman, in the "fallout" year that was 1838 – and in a tactic that will be familiar not just to historians of the stock market crash of 1929, but to all contemporary observers of the types of responses that our most recent financial crisis has elicited from figures in authority – "to blame the Legislature, which has forborne to prescribe or enforce any particular line of action," rather than private bankers for seeking to obtain "the largest possible profit."[41]

Where commentators in political, philosophical, and literary circles were now making more positive noises about the contribution made by banks, however, such affirmations almost never alluded to something called, or even bearing close resemblance to, economic "productiveness." The deemed benefits of the banking system lay, it was claimed, elsewhere. As early as 1705, the infamous Scotsman John Law (gambler, convicted killer and prison escapee, but later Controller General of Finances for France, and then chief architect of the so-called Mississippi Bubble), claiming that the "certain good [the banking system] does, will more than balance the hazard," pointed specifically to "conveniences, [such] as quicker and easier payments." Born into a banking family, Law nonetheless scotched the notion of more fundamental contributions: "the nation had no benefit by the addition the bank makes to the money; nor the people by being supplied with money when otherwise they could not, and at less interest."[42] Others, writing later and thus at a more mature stage of development of the banking system, were slightly more generous. An influential essay of 1758, officially anonymous but believed to be the work of the Reverend Robert Wallace, an eminent figure in the intellectual life of seventeenth-century Edinburgh, posited banks as critical *enablers* of the wider economy:

> By giving credit, [banks] furnish men of substance with the means of giving greater employment to the industrious, and enable merchants to carry on a more extensive trade. The more notes the Banks can circulate in this way, the more will industry and trade be promoted.[43]

But there was still no suggestion in such supportive tracts that banks were *themselves* directly productive economic agents.

Within the English literature, the only exception to this rule I have come across is in another anonymous essay, this time published in 1802. The author is evidently a strident champion of banks, arguing that "the multiplication of banking companies, so far from being an evil, is itself a good." Some of his (or perhaps, her) arguments closely parallel those made elsewhere: as in the aforementioned text, it is claimed that banking *stimulates* "trade, commerce, manufactures and agriculture" and thus it "must be considered as a mine to the kingdom and the bankers as the workers of this mine for the public good"; there is something, too, of Lecky's (later) "moralising influences" in the suggestion that a banking system "increases the security of the public, by obliging all of them to be very circumspect in their conduct, and not extend their issues beyond a due proportion of their cash." Where the author materially departs from other proponents is in the advancement of a much bolder hypothesis as to banks' economic contribution. "The operations of banking," it is bluntly stated, "are creative of wealth."[44]

Yet we need to be clear that in making this assertion the author was an apparently solitary voice, and was demonstrably swimming against powerful contemporary currents. James McCulloch, the editor of the important 1857 collection of essays on "paper currency and banking" in which this piece appeared – and who, as a leading economist and editor of the 1828 edition of Smith's *Wealth of Nations*, was very much *au fait* with prevailing political-economic theories on such matters – clearly thought it made some interesting points about turn-of the-century banks; but he signaled to readers that it gave "rather too favourable a view of these establishments."[45] Moreover, the author himself had intimated that the piece constituted political polemic, or lobbying document, as much as academic treatise, written as it was to "enhance [banks'] value in a political point of view." And while our task here is admittedly not to judge such commentaries on the role of banks, but rather to provide an overview of their contents, it would I think be remiss not to observe that this author's brief explanation of *how* banking created value – "for wherever a bank can flourish, it will convert the product of industry into money" – is not one that would have inspired confidence among contemporaries, economists or otherwise.[46]

Meanwhile, if allusions to productiveness were thin on the ground in positive eighteenth- and even nineteenth-century accounts of the banking system, the (greater number of) critical commentaries on banking that emanated from the spheres of politics, philosophy, and literature *were* now beginning to deploy a variant of the productive/unproductive conceptualization which, as we will see below, was simultaneously being more formally developed by political economists. But in many respects writers in these spheres, perhaps more given to hyperbole and rhetorical flourish, went even further. Banks, they suggested, were not merely "unproductive" of wealth; they were *destructive* thereof, both in absolute terms and relative to those sectors of the economy that were, by contrast, considered productive. A vigorous, early and influential version of this argument was set out by the Enlightenment philosopher Locke in 1692, in the period when English deposit banking was experiencing its first phase of significant growth. A consideration nominally of "the consequences of a law, to reduce interest to four per cent," and one in which Locke explicitly discusses "brokers" but *includes* within this category "bankers and scriveners" (sitting these two alongside "other such expert brokers"), it bears quoting at length:

> But however these measures may be mistaken, this is evident, that the multiplying of brokers hinders the trade of any country, by making the circuit, which the money goes, larger, and in that circuit more stops, so that the returns must necessarily be slower and scantier, to the prejudice of trade: Besides that, they eat up too great a share of the gains of trade, by that means starving the labourer, and impoverishing the landholder, whose interest is chiefly to be taken care of, it being a settled unmoveable concernment in the Commonwealth.[47]

Such a downbeat assessment of banks' role in the economy rapidly became the consensus view among England's educated, literary classes. Here, for example, just two years later, is the prolific pamphleteer John Briscoe, making his case *against* banks by arguing *for* those economic agents considered productive: "Trade therefore being the only medium whereby riches can be conveyed to us, we ought to exert the utmost of our abilities to encourage it, and to take care that nothing be done which may prove injurious, much less destructive to it."[48] Briscoe and his fellow critics held *any* expansion of the banking system as being likely to fall squarely within this latter, destructive category. And in 1695, the year following the appearance of Briscoe's pamphlet, an anonymously-authored piece published and distributed in London spelled things out in even starker terms: since banks were clearly not generating wealth, they must, by definition, be extracting it in the manner of leeches from the rest of the national economy:

> [One] part of the nation preys upon t'other; the mighty gains that have arisen to [banks], since their establishment, being no less than twenty percent must be a loss somewhere, for 'tis all within our selves; and though banks may very well be compared to ravenous birds, yet in this they exceed them, the vultures themselves not preying upon each other.[49]

Until the second half of the eighteenth century, when there began to materialize in the public sphere a more critical mass of banking patrons, very few voices dissented from this overtly negative position. Hence, around mid-century, the consensus remained that of the critics, and was now articulated most forcefully by the likes of Hume and Patrick Murray (to whose respective claims, it is worth noting, the contrary 1758 essay attributed to Reverend Wallace and cited above represented a direct response). For Hume (1752), the endeavour "artificially to increase" credit monies, which was what he saw as private banks' doing, "can never be the interest of any trading nation."[50] Murray, in turn, extended this argument, stating that bankers' "pursuits after gain" were not only "inconsistent with" but "destructive of all trade, industry, and manufactures."[51]

One of the most interesting and important features of this incipient *economic* critique of banking that emerged in England from the late seventeenth century (and thus prior to the birth of political economy proper), is that it remained in most cases a thoroughly *moral* discourse as well. The moral and economic arguments were not only entwined, but were often barely distinguishable from one another. Vivid examples of such hybrid critique can be found in what Colin Nicholson has described as Alexander Pope's attacks on "wealth variously generated by fraud and by usury," not least in the "Epistle to Bathurst" (1733).[52] Similarly, Jonathan Swift's "Run upon the Bankers" (1720) included this memorable line: "For in that universal call, Few bankers will to heaven be mounters." But perhaps the two most arresting and influential of mixed moral-economic indictments of banking from this period are found in an anonymous – but still widely cited – early tract on "The Mystery of the New Fashioned Goldsmiths or Bankers" (1676) and in a 1701 essay by Daniel Defoe. The former, blending the rhetoric of natural law with that of a type of "natural economy," railed at bankers' "mischievous trade" and "unlawful practices and profits," their "prodigious unlawful gain" being generated "in contempt of law and justice" through "usurious unlawful bargains, and oppressive exactions from the needy and men in straights."[53] Defoe, meanwhile, spoke of bankers as "vile people" and condemned them thus:

> Nay, the war they manage is carried on with worse weapons than swords and muskets; bombs may fire our towns, and troops overrun and plunder us. But these people can ruin men silently, undermine and impoverish by a sort of impenetrable artifice, like poison that works at a distance, can wheedle men to ruin themselves, and *fiddle them out of their money*, by the strange and unheard of engines of *interests, discounts, transfers, tallies, debentures, shares, projects*, and the *devil and all* of figures and hard names.[54]

Only very rarely, within this broadly-based critique of the emergent deposit banking system, was normativity dispensed with altogether. Of the many from which I have extracted opinions here, the two essays that arguably came closest to offering "purely" economic assessments were – perhaps not surprisingly – those of the two great British empiricists, Locke and Hume. In all other instances, the economic remained heavily freighted with the ethical and judgmental. It took until towards the end of the eighteenth century, in Britain at least, for a "new" discursive field to crystallize, in which the study of "the economy" for the first time became the discrete object and end in itself, rather than being merely part of a wider terrain of investigation into the constitution of society.[55] Only with the materialization of this new field did it become consistently possible for the economic and ethical critiques of money and (later) banking, which had been welded together since the days of Aristotle, to subsist largely independently of one another, and for the former to shed the vernacular and mood of the latter. This new field, of course, was the professionalized discipline – and, in the vision of Smith and Ricardo if not always Malthus and Marx, the positive "science" – of political economy.

Productive and Unproductive Labor

Eighteenth- and nineteenth-century political economy represents a formative set of intellectual and social developments in the story of primarily *twentieth*-century boundary crossings that this book attempts to relate. It does so for numerous reasons that will become increasingly apparent as the story unfolds, but the main one can be foregrounded and partially fleshed out here. This is that the tradition of "classical" political economy associated with figures such as Adam Smith was responsible for the fashioning of concepts that not only came to underpin twentieth-century national accounting practices, but which remain fundamental to the way the "economic world" is popularly and politically envisioned and narrated today. The most important such concept, in the present context, is that of economic "productiveness": the capacity for creation, that is to say, of economic value or "wealth." What such productiveness is; why it is important; where it derives from; and how it can be differentiated from nonproductiveness – all these questions continue to pervade contemporary debates about various different economic activities and actors (not least, of course, banking and bankers); and all effectively originated with eighteenth-century political economy. Indeed, I take, in this book, the centrality of questions of wealth, its production, and the sources thereof to be the defining feature *of* classical political economy.[56]

The political economists whose ideas and writings came to dominate this new intellectual field in the English-speaking world proceeded to provide answers to these particular questions of wealth creation at two separate levels. The first level was that of what came to be called the "factors of production": the inputs or resources implicated in the economic processes which *led* to wealth creation. These factors invariably included – variously categorized – such things as tools, land, machinery, buildings, and labor. At this first level, the question posed was essentially this: which factor, or factors, are responsible for the creation of value; for, in other words, *increases* in the wealth of societies or of nations? Now, there is a long and ongoing history of controversy over what the likes of Smith, Ricardo, and Marx did or did not say about these matters, but for our purposes here one particular – and unarguable – feature of their respective theorizations is pertinent. Specifically, all three subscribed, to one degree or another, to a labor theory of value, according to which human labor was deemed to be the sole or at least main source of value creation.[57] And it was this common answer to the headline question of factor productivity that opened up, for all three theorists, the second level of questioning around economic productiveness that I noted above. For if labor, generically, was the source of new (or "surplus") value, it seemed necessary to ask whether *all* labor was so productive, or whether only *certain types* of labor generated this incremental wealth. It was in offering answers to this second question that the classical political economists developed the key concepts of *productive* and *unproductive labor*.

The bulk of this section of the chapter is thus taken up with a consideration of the various perspectives of the great political economists, from Adam Smith onwards, on productive versus unproductive labor, and on the "placement" of banking in this particular respect. (*Was* it productive, or not?) But while Smith was the first to frame the matter of wealth creation *explicitly* in terms of this dichotomy, earlier economic theorists had certainly hinted at such a distinction, and Smith's arguments – equally certainly – were pitched in part as rejoinders to those existing theoretical assemblages. Two were critical, and both merit recognition here for what they had already contributed to the "productiveness" debate.

The first was the "mercantilist" theory that largely dominated European economic thought in the early modern period, and associated with writers such as Thomas Mun and James Steuart. Although it came in various strains, mercantilism ultimately posited that economic value was a zero-sum game between different nations. Wealth consisted primarily of precious metals, and, other than through mining thereof, could only be materially increased by running a positive balance of trade, meaning an excess of exports – paid for in gold or silver – over imports. "Mercantilist literature," Vaggi and Groenewegen confirm, "largely emphasized the role of exchange and circulation of commodities in the process of the creation of wealth."[58] As such, the merchant, or goods trader, was accorded pride of place by those mercantilists who sought to calibrate relative contributions to wealth creation. Charles Davenant, writing in 1695, expressed this view most concisely, claiming that the merchant "deserves all favour as being the best, and most profitable member of the Commonwealth."[59]

But it would be wrong to suppose that mercantilism was always this crude and singular. A more subtle perspective was offered by another Englishman, Josiah Child, who, while agreeing that all incremental wealth must be derived through international trade, maintained that not only merchants were productive participants in this particular drama. Rather, "merchants, artificers, farmers of land" were considered by him "the three sorts of people who by their study and labour do principally, if not only, bring in wealth to a nation from abroad." Moreover, and directly foreshadowing Smith's formal theorization of the category of *unproductive* laborer, Child continued: "other kinds of people, viz. nobility, gentry, lawyers, physicians, scholars of all sorts, and shopkeepers, do only hand [wealth] from one to another at home." Granted, Child did not explicitly include bankers in either list; but for a book first published in the 1660s, this is to be expected; and in any case, Child leaves us in little doubt as to where scriveners and money-lenders, in his view of things, belonged. The "abatement of interest," he submitted, would benefit all economic actors except for the "griping dronish usurer"; it would, he argued, along lines very similar to those later trodden by Johns Locke and Briscoe and by mid-eighteenth century critics such as Hume and Murray, be "the cause of the increase of the trade and riches of any kingdom."[60]

Very different to the trade- and merchant-focused theorization of wealth creation developed by the mercantilists was the second corpus of economic theory, and the second existing perspective on economic productiveness, upon which Smith trained his critical sights: Physiocracy. For where the mercantilists identified the source of wealth creation in cross-border trade, the eighteenth-century French Physiocrats, led by François Quesnay and Anne-Robert-Jacques Turgot, located it in "nature" and the cultivation thereof. Recalling our factors of production, then, surplus value was held to be a product, ultimately, of the land; but since *realization* of this value always required the application of human labor, it was those who worked on the land that were held to be uniquely productive. "Quesnay remarked on agriculturalists as the 'productive class' of society and other groups as 'sterile classes'. Turgot called farmers the 'unique source of all wealth'."[61] And note that the "sterile classes" evoked in Quesnay's *Tableau économique* (1759), which was later to have a profound influence on Marx, did indeed extend to encompass *all* laborers other than those engaged in agriculture, including those in France's incipient manufacturing industries. "Industry," it was argued, "only reshaped the products of nature from the primary sector without adding anything to their value."[62] It merely moved wealth around, without adding to its quantum.

As we will see, the crude theories of the mercantilists and Physiocrats as to productive versus unproductive labor – and, thus, regarding the nature and location of the "production boundary" which separated them – were substantially advanced and reshaped by, most especially, Smith and Marx, in the context of their respective labor theories of value. (And it is important to emphasize that notwithstanding their identifications of productive "classes," neither mercantilism nor Physiocracy *were* labor theories; labor could only ever be productive in a strictly derivative sense, through serving as a catalyst of the a priori productivity of trade and nature respectively.) Before turning to those theories, however, it is vital to clear up some of the confusions that often surround their considerations of the "productive labor" issue.

Four particular – and closely related – confusions remain both common and, in my view, extremely significant. The first is the confusion of use value with *economic* value. Where the political economists sought to distinguish productive from unproductive labor, it was the latter type of value that interested them; so, it remained perfectly possible for "unproductive" laborers to generate considerable use values. The second confusion concerns the mistaken assumption that the likes of Smith and, perhaps most especially, Marx, were making normative or moral assessments. They were not. In neither author is there any conflation of "productive" with "good" and "unproductive" with "bad."[63] This, in turn, reflects the fact that, thirdly, neither are they – as is often assumed to be the case – making *social* judgments: suggesting that this activity is "productive" for society, and that one "unproductive." Today, as I discussed briefly in the introduction to this book, we often hear critics bemoaning the fact that certain banking activities are "socially unproductive." Yet such statements beg the question: unproductive in *what* society? More often than not, there is an implicit appeal here to a social utopia that simply does not exist.[64] Smith and Marx never did this. Thus although Marx did consider the social *necessity* of various types of labor, the question was always posed in material historical context – was this labor necessary, in other words, specifically for the maintenance of the capitalist mode of production?[65] And the same was true, for both Marx and Smith, of their assessments of economic productiveness. Hence the error of the fourth misconception: namely, that the concepts of "productive labor" offered by these political economists were somehow free-floating; this type of labor *always and everywhere* being productive, and that one not. Again, this is clearly not the case. Both for Marx and, Marx credited, for Smith – "Smith here got to the very heart of the matter, hit the nail on the head" – labor was only considered productive if it produced surplus value *for capitalists.*[66] The very same types of laboring activity could therefore be productive in one economic context but not in another; it depended on the given relations of production.

It was, then, with Adam Smith's *The Wealth of Nations*, first published in 1776, that the categories of productive and unproductive labor were formally introduced into Western political economy. Smith gives his fullest articulation of this dualism in Chapter 3 of Book II, which begins thus:

There is one sort of labour which adds to the value of the subject upon which it is bestowed: there is another which has no such effect. The former, as it produces a value, may be called productive; the latter, unproductive labour. Thus the labour of a manufacturer adds, generally, to the value of the materials which he works upon, that of his own maintenance, and of his master's profit. The labour of a menial servant, on the contrary, adds to the value of nothing. Though the manufacturer has his wages advanced to him by his master, he, in reality, costs him no expense, the value of those wages being generally restored, together with a profit, in the improved value of the subject upon which his labour is bestowed. But the maintenance of a menial servant never is restored. A man grows rich by employing a multitude of manufacturers: he grows poor by maintaining a multitude of menial servants.[67]

This excerpt is widely-cited, and for good reason: it provides an excellent synopsis of Smith's overall views on this issue. For him, the world of capitalist economic activities really could be simply bifurcated thus: into productive labors that produced economic value, and unproductive labors that shifted such value around.

But there is one key feature of Smith's argument that is not captured here: the claim that productive and unproductive labors could be distinguished from one another not only in regard to their capacity to produce surplus for capitalists, but also in terms of the *materiality of their outputs*. In short, for labor to be productive it had to involve the creation or transformation of physical goods; anything that did not – including, of course, all service activities – was, by definition, unproductive. For Smith's clearest statement of this position, we need to turn to Book IV:

[The work of menial servants] consists in services which perish generally in the very instant of their performance, and does not fix or realize itself in any vendible commodity which can replace the value of their wages and maintenance. The labour, on the contrary, of artificers, manufacturers, and merchants naturally does fix and realize itself in some such vendible commodity. It is upon this account that, in the chapter in which I treat of productive and unproductive labour, I have classed artificers, manufacturers, and merchants among the productive labourers, and menial servants among the barren or unproductive.[68]

In his various enumerations of different productive and unproductive activities, Smith does not explicitly "place" banking (though he does "out," as unproductive, lawyers and various other members of "the most respectable orders in the society"). Indeed, one of the curiosities of *The Wealth of Nations*, seen from a contemporary standpoint, is how little Smith has to say about banking, and indeed money. But with *all* services deemed unproductive of wealth, it is a given that banking, from Smith's perspective, belonged on the "negative" side of the production boundary. And where he does talk more generically about the relative contributions and costs of the banking system, in his discussions particularly of Scottish private banks, The Bank of Amsterdam, and the Bank of England, Smith makes it clear that the economic capacity of banks is a strictly circumscribed one. Hence his lauding of the "great and general utility of the banking trade"; a utility evoked most colorfully in the following passage:

The judicious operations of banking, by providing, if I may be allowed so violent a metaphor, a sort of waggon-way through the air, enable the country to convert, as it were, a great part of its highways into good pastures, and corn fields, and thereby to increase, very considerably, the annual produce of its land and labour.[69]

Banks, operating judiciously, were important facilitators of wealth creation; but they, and the bankers who worked for them, were not directly productive as such.[70]

Though it took much longer than is often assumed for Smith's *Wealth* and the arguments it contained explicitly to penetrate the wider collective consciousness of British literate society, it soon came to frame and inform debate among those who *were* writing about finance and the economy for broader audiences and often with specific policy questions in mind – writers who belonged to what Poovey refers to as the "economic establishment."[71] Debate on banking represents a very good example of this rapidly percolating Smithian influence, and Smith's fellow Scot William Howison an individual case in point. Writing in 1803, Howison envisioned society in terms of two main economic classes, labeled "productive" and "consuming" respectively. Banks, meanwhile, were part of a "middle class" sandwiched between these two. Like Smith, Howison believed that under capitalism banks were "necessary to society," being part of a middle class that was "essential to both the other two" classes. But necessity did not equate with productiveness. Far from it: as part of the middle class, banks functioned "at the expense of the other classes," and were thus "supported by" them and constituted "a burden upon the[ir] productive and useful labour." In so doing, banks were held to "absorb, in a great degree, the floating wealth of the country, by a species of labour unproductive to society."[72]

Smith's and, later, Marx's views on productive and unproductive labor have come over time to exert a significantly greater and more enduring influence in popular, political, and scholarly discourses of the economy than those of the other great political economists of the eighteenth and nineteenth centuries. But the production boundary which Smith erected also constituted a crucial infrastructure in the theorization offered by, most especially, Thomas Malthus – whose writings on such matters informed, in turn, Marx's own refinements – and we need therefore to attend to his arguments here. We can do so, however, in much less depth than accorded to either Smith or Marx.

The one important political economist, meanwhile, whose work we do *not* need to consider in this regard – but who comes much more centrally into focus in Chapter 2 – is David Ricardo. Various writers, including Marx himself, have sought to argue that the distinction between productive and unproductive labor was an important one for Ricardo.[73] But it is hard to see, on almost any reading of Ricardo's political-economic opus (*On the Principles of Political Economy, and Taxation*, first published in 1817), that this was actually the case. Granted, he does refer to these concepts at various points. But he refers to them *as Smith's*, and he makes no attempt critically to assess or substantively to rework them.

Malthus, however, was an altogether different fish. The question of productive and unproductive labor was, for him, pivotal. He invested even more theoretical capital in the distinction than Smith had done, placing his discussion of the subject close to the very front of his own *Principles of Political Economy* (first published in 1820). He insisted that "some such classification of the different kinds of labor is really called for in an inquiry into the nature and causes of the wealth of nations," for without it "a considerable degree of confusion would be introduced into the science of political economy." Yet for all the rhetorical emphasis, Malthus ultimately came down in effective agreement with Smith, which is why we can dispense with him relatively briefly. His rather long discussion of the subject of labor productivities boils down, in essence, to a rationalization "for adopting [Smith's] opinion," even on such controversial matters as the materiality of "the difference between material products and those which are not matter." Perhaps the one area in which Malthus does deepen Smith's position is in his explanation of why, for him as for Smith, it is important to distinguish between laborers – such as bankers – who *facilitate* wealth creation, and those who create it themselves: "if we were to include under the head of productive labour, all the exertions which may contribute, however indirectly, to the production of wealth, the term would cease to have any definite and useful signification, so as to admit of being applied with advantage to an explanation of the causes of the wealth of nations."[74]

In the 1830s and 1840s, which were the two decades separating the publication of the major economic works of Malthus on the one hand and Marx on the other, the Smithian perspective on productive and unproductive labor, and thus on the productiveness of banks, continued to hold sway within the British "economic establishment." Yes, banks played a crucial facilitative role in the economy; few now disputed this. ("The utility of banking is now become so generally known," the financial writer William John Norfolk remarked in 1845, "that little requires to be said upon this point."[75]) Yet as William Howison had argued, utility and productiveness were not equivalent, and one did not imply the other: an argument which, as we shall see, neoclassical economics would later confront and contest head-on. Hence, during this period Smith's conceptual architecture remained the touchstone, and influential periodicals such as the *Quarterly Review* periodically "point[ed] the attention of the public" to, in the words of the geologist-turned-political-economist George Poulett Scrope, "the vicious banking system of England, as the one main cause of the distress against which all the productive interests of the country have been mainly struggling for many years past."[76]

Which brings us, finally, to Marx. Marx considers the question of productive and unproductive labor at numerous points in numerous texts, and yet one never gets the sense that it is as important for him as it was for either Smith or, certainly, Malthus. In Volume I of *Capital*, for instance, the matter is largely relegated to an appendix. And while the pertinent chapter (Four) of *Theories of Surplus Value* is a long one, Marx's *main* concern there is with preceding debates, not with formulating his own arguments. Not only, furthermore, are Marx's various writings on this subject scattered; they are also, at points, rather contradictory, with differences in interpretation emerging in different places.[77] Such differences explain, in part, the emergence over the past 40 years of a vast and ongoing debate – one variously and, I think, aptly described as "tedious" (David Harvey) and "confused" (Ernest Mandel) – among contemporary Marxian scholars as to what Marx did or did not claim.[78]

I have no intention or need to enter into those debates here. Instead, I will focus on the basic contours of Marx's arguments, at which level he *is*, in my view, broadly consistent throughout. His basic position, we can begin by recognizing, accords very closely with Smith's: productive labor is quite simply labor which is productive *for capital*. Michael Webber and David Rigby summarize this foundational claim nicely: "that laborer alone is productive who produces surplus value for the capitalist and who thus works for the self-expansion of capital."[79] But beyond this basic point of agreement, Marx advances a series of modifications of, and extensions to, the positions previously set out by Smith and Malthus. Three are critical.

First, Marx does away entirely with the matching up of physical goods with productive labors and "immaterial" services with unproductive labors. The Smithian fallacy that labor is productive "only if it results in ... a material product" stems, Marx argues, from the "fetishism peculiar to the capitalist mode of production from which it arises": that which consists "in regarding *economic* categories, such as being a *commodity* or *productive* labour, as qualities inherent in [their] material incarnations."[80] Thus services *can* be productive; labor is productive not because it produces things, but because it produces surplus value. The great irony of Marx's departing from Smith on this point, of course, is that when contemporary commentators castigate the historic tendency to regard service activities as unproductive, they very often identify Marx, and *not* Smith, as the culprit![81]

Second, the distinction in Marx between productive and unproductive labor is intimately bound up with another conceptual distinction, in this case one that was not present in Smith: that between production and circulation. Now, just to complicate matters, Marx uses the term "circulation" in two different senses, so it is important to be clear about which one applies here. First, and perhaps most familiarly, he writes about the circulation of capital at the broadest level: capital, indeed, *as* a perpetual process of movement or circulation through different "forms" (money, production, commodities); the "capital flow" which, Harvey recently argued, we need to understand to understand capitalism.[82] Second, Marx writes about circulation in a more restricted sense: as the specific phase in the overall circulation of capital concerned with the realization of the outputs of productive processes *as money*. And it is this second definition that is pertinent here. Circulation, Marx claims, does not generate value; and thus labor bought by capitalists focused on circulatory activities is not considered productive.[83] This, as we shall shortly see, is an important distinction where banking is concerned.

Third, and lastly, Marx offers a trenchant disabusal of what he regards as the existing tendency to see "productive labor" through rose-tinted spectacles. His only forebear to overcome this tendency, he claims, is Ricardo. According to Marx, Smith had intimated that to be a productive laborer was a privilege, thus investing the role with a certain "tenderness." But this tenderness, as Ricardo had seen, was nothing but an "illusion." Marx went on:

> It is a misfortune to be a productive labourer. A productive labourer is a labourer who produces wealth *for another*. His existence only has meaning as such an instrument of production for the wealth of others. If therefore the same quantity of wealth for others

can be created with a smaller number of productive labourers, then the suppression of these productive labourers is in order.[84]

Having delineated Marx's reformulation of the productive/unproductive dualism, therefore, it remains only to see where the activities of banking "fitted." And Marx, unlike Smith, *did* explicitly place those activities. For him, there was no doubt that they were unproductive – that they entailed a mere redistribution of surplus value that had *already* been produced, elsewhere in the economy, by productive labors. The labor of bankers was excluded from the productive sphere not because it was a service, however, but because it was perceived to be exchanged in the realm of capitalist circulation rather than production. "This work," Marx insisted, "is a cost of circulation and not value-creating labour."[85]

The consignment of banking to the unproductive realm has, interestingly, been highlighted by critics as one of the most significant consequences of Marx's separation of circulation from production; and is seen as one of the main reasons why Marxian scholars continue to cling to that particular dualism. As Helen Boss writes: "What would Marxian economics lose were it to drop the production circulation dichotomy? Possibly the hardest pill to swallow would be the implied inclusion within the productive domain of financial services."[86] Be that as it may (and many Marxists would, I suspect, contest the argument that the latter would necessarily result from the former), the most important learning, in the present context, is clear: Marx saw banking as unproductive. Nowhere is this conviction more forcefully and concisely articulated than in the following, famous quotation, with which I will end this section of the chapter:

> Talk about centralization! The credit system, which has its focal point in the allegedly national banks and the big money-lenders and usurers that surround them, is one enormous centralization and gives this class of parasites a fabulous power not only to decimate the industrial capitalists periodically but also to interfere in actual production in the most dangerous manner – and this crew know nothing of production and have nothing at all to do with it.[87]

Dissolving the Production Boundary

What happened in the realm of economic thinking in the half-century between Marx's death in 1883 and the rapid rise to prominence in the mid- to late 1930s of the English economist John Maynard Keynes? How did the key developments of this period play out in terms of the theorization of the production of wealth? And with what implications for perspectives on the place of banks among the respective ranks of the productive and unproductive? These are the questions addressed in this final section of Chapter 1.

What happened was, in short, no less than a theoretical revolution: the "neo-classical" or "marginalist" revolution. This was a paradigmatic shift of enormous and ongoing consequences: from a (political) economy tradition focused on macro questions of wealth generation, to an increasingly mathematized "neoclassical" economics – now cleaved *off* from new, distinct disciplines such as sociology and political science – preoccupied with interlinked questions of market exchange, pricing, and supply and demand.[88] And it was a revolution which, as we will see, had direct and profound implications not just for thinking about economic productiveness generically, but for the very notion of a "production boundary" per se. For, in the hands of its leading developers such as William S. Jevons and Alfred Marshall in England and Carl Menger and Leon Walras in continental Europe, neoclassical economics effectively sought to dispense with hard-and-fast distinctions between productive and unproductive economic processes and labors.

Yet just as the man to whom the concept of the "production boundary" is typically traced – Adam Smith – built upon and formalized existing work that already gestured in the direction he was heading, so too the neoclassicists followed signposts previously erected. Two figures were key in this respect. The first was Jeremy Bentham, best known perhaps as a social reformer and philosopher, but also a prolific writer on economic issues.[89] The concept of "utility" that underpinned his philosophy also guided his economics, including the landmark *Defence of Usury* (1787), which contained attacks on, inter alia, Smith himself.[90] Bentham's economic ideas strongly influenced neoclassical economists of the late nineteenth century, Jevons among them.[91] The second writer often thought of as a classical political economist, but whose ideas arguably sit closer to those of the neoclassicists than to those of Smith et al., was John Stuart Mill: adroitly labeled "the last of the classics and, simultaneously, the first of the moderns" by Vaggi and Groenewegen.[92] Again, for Mill, as for Bentham, the emerging concept of *utility* was critical.

Significantly, it is in their writings on value theory, labor, and the productiveness *of* labor that the tensions exhibited by Bentham and Mill – hanging, as it were, between an existing classical paradigm with which they did not fully concur, and a coming neoclassical paradigm that had not yet been born – are most apparent. Let us look briefly at Mill and his *Principles of Political Economy*, first published in 1848, for an example of this. Thus, on the one hand, Mill is seen to be striving to break away from, in particular, Smith, by re-theorizing what it is that "production" produces and where it is that value lies. "Labor," he asserts, in a direct foreshadowing of the neoclassicists, "is not creative of objects, but of utilities." But still he could not quite bring himself to relinquish the labor theory of value, and nor therefore the classical notion of productive labor as "labor productive of wealth." Indeed, so embedded in the classical way of thinking does Mill remain that he feels obliged to offer yet another painfully-contorted definition *of* productive labor – reducing it to exertions "which produce utilities embodied in material objects," or at least to those exertions which have "an increase of material products [as their] ultimate consequence."[93]

Where the neoclassicists departed substantively from Mill and Bentham was to reject unreservedly the labor theory of value, thus strengthening and formalizing the equation of value with utility that those two had struggled to configure. The utility – or "subjective preference" – theory of value that frames neoclassical economics posits that the value of a good or service is based not on the labor expended in its realization, but is simply a function of relative utility, with each individual's desire to maximize personal utility or "welfare" driving their own preferences between alternative consumption options. In effect, traditional value theory is reversed: value is seen now to be based not on what goes in (labor), but on what comes out (market price). The reason for emphasizing this here is that it was *precisely* in effecting this reversal that the neoclassicists put paid, at least nominally, to the productive/unproductive dichotomy.

This formal rejection of a distinction between productive and unproductive labor is particularly striking in the work of Jevons. In his *Theory of Political Economy*, first published in 1871, Jevons nods to the notion of "productive labor" on just one solitary occasion; and in doing so, he summarily discards it. "I hold labour," he says, "to be *essentially variable*, so that *its value must be determined by the value of the produce, not the value of the produce by that of the labour.*"[94] One could hardly imagine a clearer statement of the distance between the two schools, or of the redundancy of "productive labor" as an active theoretical principle under neoclassicism. The implications are spelled out by Geoffrey Pilling:

> [N]ot least amongst the consequences of the victory for the 'marginal revolution' during the last three decades of the nineteenth century was the loss of any critical distinction between productive and unproductive labour. The triumph of a [utility] theory of value ... necessarily precluded any separation of productive from unproductive labour. Indeed, the latter term could have no meaning. Any labour embodied in a good finding a purchaser on the market was by definition productive labour. Under capitalism there is no exploitation.[95]

What was the upshot of this sea-change in economic theory for commentary on the inherent "productiveness," or otherwise, of different economic sectors and of laborers in those different sectors – including banks and bankers? In mainstream economics such commentary inevitably, and rapidly, disappeared. Joseph Schumpeter dismissed it as "meaningless," a "dusty museum piece."[96] Gone for good were the painstaking, Manichean enumerations of productive laborers and unproductive laborers which we find in the works of Smith, Malthus, and Marx. The Smithian productive/unproductive dichotomy which underpinned such enumerations came to be regarded as no more than "an unfortunate error from the past." It might occasionally still "seduce the uninitiated," but it was clearly far "too value-laden and crude for scientific discourse" – which, of course, professional economics now claimed to be.[97] In terms of scholarly discourse more broadly, therefore, it was only in fields deemed arcane, "ideological" and *non*-scientific – such as radical, and especially Marxian, political economy – that the notion of a substantive production boundary separating productive from non-productive capitalist activities lived (and lives) on; and we shall return, much later in the book, specifically to consider recent trends in the "placement" of banking and financial services by scholars within those particular fields.[98]

Yet in terms of its wider purchase, it would, I think, be accurate to say that the productive/unproductive dichotomy had entered the popular lexicon to stay by the time Keynes arrived on the scene. For the entire twentieth century and, as highlighted in the introduction to this book, *palpably* in the first decade of the twenty-first, the drawing of distinctions between productive and unproductive capitalisms has been an important feature of the discourses of "journalists, politicians and voters" alike.[99] The visibility and potency of such distinctions is only heightened in times of economic recession or "crisis," when questions of blame and of relative levels of positive contribution – of who is and is not "pulling their weight" – take on renewed salience. And while these distinctions often pertain to matters of perceived *social* rather than explicitly economic contribution, it is typically very hard to disentangle the two in terms either of intended usage (social contribution so often being deemed to be a function *of* economic contribution) or, assuredly, of terminological and philosophical genealogy.

It is a central claim of this book, however, that while it is possible to find examples of the productive/unproductive dichotomy being invoked across a wide range of twentieth and twenty-first century socio-economic discourses, its mobilization within one particular domain of representation has been especially – indeed, profoundly – material: the domain of national accounting. As Chapter 3 recounts, national accounting evolved from relatively modest origins rapidly to become, in the space of a few short years in the immediate post-war era, a pivotal technology of economic calculation and visualization; which is exactly what it remains today. In fact we can say, without overstating the case, that national accounting now constitutes a core calculus in both the representation and reproduction of contemporary capitalist society itself. Moreover, the "production boundary" theorized into existence by Adam Smith and the other great political economists does not just live on in the national accounting calculus; it frames, rather, its very ontology. The cumulative envisioning of banking vis-à-vis this boundary afforded by those political economists before turn-of-the-century neoclassicism moved to shut down the boundary question was, this chapter has demonstrated, categorically unproductive. As such, any substantive boundary crossing was yet to take place.

Notes

1   L. Haney, *History of Economic Thought: A Critical Account of the Origin and Development of the Economic Theories of the Leading Thinkers in the Leading Nations*, Macmillan, New York, 1911, p.104.

2   M. Weber, "Religious rejections of the world and their directions," in *From Max Weber: Essays in Sociology* (eds. H. Gerth and C. Wright Mills, Oxford University Press, New York, 1946, 323–359); J. Habermas, *The Theory of Communicative Action, volume 1: Reason and the Rationalization of Society*, Polity Press, Cambridge, 1984.

3   M. Poovey, *Genres of the Credit Economy: Mediating Value in Eighteenth-Century and Nineteenth-Century Britain*, University of Chicago Press, Chicago, 2008.

4   R. Bogaert, "Banking in the ancient world," in R. Bogaert, H. Van der Wee and
    G. Kurgan-Van Hentenrijk (eds), *A History of European Banking* (Mercatorfonds,
    Antwerp, 1994, 13–70).
5   H. Van der Wee, "European banking in the Middle Ages and Early Modern Times
    (476– 1789)," in R. Bogaert, H. Van der Wee and G. Kurgan-Van Hentenrijk (eds),
    A History of European Banking (Mercatorfonds, Antwerp, 1994, 71–264); R. de
    Roover, *The Rise and Decline Of The Medici Bank, 1397–1494*, Harvard University
    Press, Cambridge MA, 1963, and *Money, Banking and Credit in Mediaeval Bruges*,
    The Mediaeval Academy of America, Cambridge MA, 1948.
6   De Roover, *Money, Banking and Credit*, p.3.
7   http://dictionary.oed.com/cgi/entry/50189374.
8   W. Ashley, *An Introduction to English Economic History and Theory, Part 1*,
    G.P. Putnam's Sons, New York, 1888, p.152.
9   T. Divine, *Interest: An Historical and Analytical Study in Economics and Modern
    Ethics*, Marquette University Press, Milwaukee, 1959, pp.17–18.
10 K. Marx, *Capital*, Vol. 3, Pelican Books, London, 1981, pp.515–516. The quotations
    from *Politics* are from Benjamin Jowett's translation, available here http://classics.mit.
    edu/Aristotle/politics.html.
11 Cf. E. Cannan, W. Ross, J. Bonar and P. Wicksteed, "Who said 'Barren Metal'?:
    A Symposium," *Economica*, 5, 1922, pp.105–111, and S. Meikle, *Aristotle's Economic
    Thought*, Oxford University Press, Oxford, 1995, pp.63–64.
12 J. Bentham, "Defence of usury," in *Jeremy Bentham's Economic Writings, vol. 1*
    (ed. W. Stark, Allen and Unwin, London, 1952), p.158.
13 J. Ackerman, "Interest rates and the law: A history of usury," *Arizona State Law
    Journal*, 61, 1981, pp.61–110, at p.69 (emphasis added).
14 De Roover, *Rise and Decline*, p.10.
15 M. Atwood, *Payback: Debt and the Shadow Side of Wealth*, Bloomsbury, London,
    2008, p.97.
16 J. Le Goff, *Your Money or Your Life: Economy and Religion in the Middle Ages*, Zone
    Books, New York, 1998, p.9.
17 Ackerman, "Interest rates," pp.77–79.
18 J. Munro, "The medieval origins of the financial revolution: Usury, rentes, and nego-
    tiability," *International History Review*, 25, 2003, pp.505–562, at p.554. Note that in
    England the 1545 law permitting interest was repealed in 1555, before being restored
    by under Elizabeth I in 1571. Ibid.
19 Ackerman, "Interest rates," p.79.
20 J. Shatzmiller, *Shylock Reconsidered: Jews, Moneylending, and Medieval Society*,
    University of California Press, Berkeley, 1992.
21 I found the overviews offered by Ackerman, "Interest rates" and Munro, "Medieval
    origins," especially helpful here.
22 Ackerman, "Interest rates," p.74.
23 Le Goff, *Your Money or Your Life*.
24 "Licit rents and profits" and "mortally sinful" are from Munro, "Medieval origins,"
    p.510; "unlawful usury" is from Le Goff, *Your Money or Your Life*, p.10.
25 See especially de Roover, *Rise and Decline*.
26 See, for instance, the essays collected together by J. Vitullo and D. Wolfthal (eds),
    Money, Morality, and Culture in Late Medieval and Early Modern Europe, Ashgate,
    Farnham, 2010.
27 N. Ferguson, *The Ascent of Money: A Financial History of the World*, Penguin,
    London, 2008, p.47.

28   De Roover, *Rise and Decline*, p.11.

29   Ibid, p.12.

30   Munro, "Medieval origins," p.548.

31   J. Murray, "The Devil's evangelists? Moneychangers in Flemish urban society," in Vitullo and Wolfthal (eds), *Money, Morality, and Culture* (53–67), p.53.

32   P. Brantlinger, *Fictions of State: Culture and Credit in Britain*, Cornell University Press, Ithaca, 1996, p.159.

33   See especially C. Nicholson, *Writing and the Rise of Finance: Capital Satires of the Early Eighteenth Century*, Cambridge University Press, Cambridge, 2004.

34   Poovey, *Genres*.

35   F. Melton, *Sir Robert Clayton and the Origins of English Deposit Banking, 1658–1685*, Cambridge University Press, Cambridge, 1986, p.8. As we will see shortly, scriveners, as understood here by Melton, were eighteenth-century English loan-brokers.

36   Ibid. But see also the classic, 1929 account by R. D. Richards, *The Early History of Banking in England*, P. S. King & Son, London.

37   Melton, *Sir Robert Clayton*, p.38.

38   Ibid, pp.18, 39. Interestingly, and not immaterially, the key distinction that the usury laws drew – but could not ultimately police – between bankers' *own funds* and *deposited funds* is one that, as we will see much later, is today also central to (but equally problematic for) the treatment of banks and their various revenue streams in national accounts.

39   G. Norman, "Errors with respect to currency and banking," in F. Capie (ed), *History of Banking, vol. I: Money* (Pickering & Chatto, London, 1993, 265–369), p.346.

40   Brantlinger, *Fictions*, 136–144; the quotation is from p.139. W. Lecky, *History of the Rise and Influence of the Spirit of Rationalism in Europe, vol.II*, Appleton, New York, 1890, pp.241, 331.

41   Norman, "Errors," p.347.

42   J. Law, "Money and trade considered," in Capie (ed), *History of Banking, vol. I* (97–121). The quotations are from pp.99–100, 103. See also R. Murray, "A proposal for a national bank," in F. Capie (ed), *History of Banking, vol. III: Financial Revolution* (Pickering & Chatto, London, 1993, 19–28), for a similar example – from the same turn-of-the-century era – of the championing of the "great conveniences attending banks" (p.22).

43   Anon, "Essay of banks and of paper credit," in J. McCulloch (ed), *Classical Writings on Economics, vol. 3* (Pickering & Chatto, London, 1995, 75–91), p.79. The identification of Wallace as the most likely author is provided by McCulloch, "Preface," in his (ed), *Classical Writings on Economics, vol. 3*, p.x.

44   Anon, "The utility of country banks considered," in McCulloch (ed), *Classical Writings on Economics, vol. 3* (99–135). Quotations from pp.109–110, 119, 128. Around the same time, a similar argument emerged from a most unlikely French source: the socialist Henri de Saint-Simon (1760–1825), whose ideas would later have a considerable impact on the likes of Marx and John Stuart Mill. Saint-Simon, as Eric Hobsbawm, *How to Change the World: Tales of Marx and Marxism*, Little Brown, London, 2011, p.28, has recently remarked, "notably" included bankers amongst the ranks of those he saw as "productive entrepreneurs."

45   McCulloch, "Preface," p.x.

46   Anon, "The utility of country banks considered," pp.119–120.

47   J. Locke, "Some considerations of the consequences of the lowering of interest and the raising the value of money," in *The Works of John Locke, vol. IV*, 12th edition (Rivington, London, 1824, 1–116), p.28.

48 J. Briscoe, "A discourse of the late funds of the Million-Act, Lottery-Act, and Bank of England," in Capie (ed), *History of Banking, vol. I* (9–68), p.17.

49 Anon, "Angliae tutamen, or, The safety of England. Being an account of the banks, lotteries, & c tending to the destruction of trade and commerce," in Capie (ed), *History of Banking, vol. III* (105–140), p.111.

50 D. Hume, "Banks and paper-money," in Capie (ed), *History of Banking, vol. I* (203–210), p.205.

51 P. Murray, "Essay on paper-Money and Banking," in Capie (ed), *History of Banking, vol. I* (211–220), pp.214, 218.

52 Nicholson, *Writing*, p.143. See also H. Erskine-Hill, "Pope and the financial revolution," in P. Dixon (ed), *Writers and Their Backgrounds: Alexander Pope* (G. Bell & Sons, London, 1972, 200–229).

53 Anon, "The mystery of the new fashioned goldsmiths," in Capie (ed), *History of Banking, vol. I* (1–8), pp.4–7.

54 D. Defoe, "The villainy of stock-jobbers detected," in Capie (ed), *History of Banking, vol. I* (69–96), pp.91–92; original emphasis. Patrick Murray's later critique can be slotted into broadly the same ethico-economic register, castigating as it did "the pernicious practices of bankers" – practices he envisioned as "rapine and violence" that were "swallow[ing] up" the "industry and frugality" associated in England with "agriculture, trade and manufactures." So, too, can the powerful critique presented a century later by the Chartist pamphleteer R J Richardson: "The curse of paper money and banking new blasts the constitution of society, and its attendant curse, the practice of usury, has not only been productive of an incalculable deal of mischief, but it still fosters the evils it has engendered, and holds the whole nation in a state of subjugation." See, respectively, Murray, "Essay," pp.214, 217; R. Richardson, "Exposure of the banking and funding system," in M. Poovey (ed), *The Financial System in Nineteenth-Century Britain* (Oxford University Press, New York, 2003, 238–242), pp.238–239.

55 A development brilliantly analyzed by Michel Foucault in *The Order of Things*, Tavistock, London, 1970, and Susan Buck-Morss in "Envisioning capital: political economy on display," *Critical Inquiry*, 21, 1995, pp.434–467.

56 It is for this reason that I do not discuss in this section certain important eighteenth- and nineteenth-century writers on the economy who often are characterized as, to one degree or another, political economists. Perhaps the most important consequent absentees are the utilitarians, most notably Jeremy Bentham and John Stuart Mill (whose work did not, on my reading at least, privilege the question of wealth creation in the manner of those writers whose work I *do* address here). Both are, however, discussed briefly in the final section of the chapter.

57 There is absolutely no need here to delve into the vast debates over the similarities and differences between the value theories of the leading eighteenth- and nineteenth-century political economists. The consistent centrality of labour – and, thus, of its deemed productiveness – is the pivotal point here. As Duncan Foley writes: "Smith, Ricardo and Marx each used the labor theory of value in his own way and to his own purposes. Each emphasizes, therefore, the facet of the theory most relevant to his own vision. As a result we have recognizably different, but not inconsistent, 'labor theories of value' in these three authors." See: "Recent developments in the labor theory of value," *Review of Radical Political Economics*, 32, 2000, pp.1–39, at p.2.

58 G. Vaggi and P. Groenewegen, *A Concise History of Economic Thought: From Mercantilism to Monetarism*, Palgrave Macmillan, Basingstoke, 2003, p.6.

59 C. Davenant, *An Essay upon Ways and Means of Supplying the War*, 3rd edition, Jacob Tonson, London, 1701, p.57.

60 J. Child, *A New Discourse of Trade*, 5th edition, Robert and Andrew Foulis, Glasgow, 1751, pp.18–19.

61 R. Bleischwitz, "Rethinking productivity: why has productivity focused on labour instead of natural resources?," *Environmental and Resource Economics*, 19, 2001, pp.23–26, at p.25.

62 Vaggi and Groenewegen, *Concise History*, p.61.

63 As John Stuart Mill confirmed: "the term unproductive does not necessarily imply any stigma; nor was ever intended to do so." *Principles of Political Economy*, Prometheus Books, New York, 2004 [1848], p.70.

64 The same problem arises in certain neo-Marxian attempts to rework Marx's notion of "productive labour." This is perhaps most obviously true, as Michael Webber and David Rigby, *The Golden Age Illusion: Rethinking Postwar Capitalism*, Guilford Press, New York, 1996, p.111, note, of Paul Baran's argument in *The Political Economy of Growth* that labor is only productive if it creates goods or services that would be required in a "rationally ordered society."

65 Marx's consideration of the social necessity as well as economic productivity of different categories of labor leads E. Hunt, "The categories of productive and unproductive labor in Marxist economic theory," *Science and Society*, 43, pp.303–325, to argue that Marx maintained two different definitions of "productive labour." I prefer the distinction between economic *productiveness* and social *necessity*.

66 The quote is from K. Marx, *Theories of Surplus Value*, Part 1, Progress Publishers, Moscow, 1963, p.157.

67 A. Smith, *The Wealth of Nations: I–III*, Penguin, London, 1982, pp.429–430.

68 A. Smith, *The Wealth of Nations: IV–V*, Penguin, London, 2004, p.261.

69 Smith, *Wealth: I–III*, p.420.

70 That Smith was widely regarded as having denigrated as "unproductive" *all* types of professional services was clear from the howls of indignation that the book elicited from society's great and good – howls that Marx, for one, found highly amusing. Discussing these "polemics against Adam Smith's distinction between productive and unproductive labour," Marx observes that the "great mass of so-called 'higher grade' workers—such as state officials, military people, artists, doctors, priests, judges, lawyers, etc. ... found it not at all pleasant to be relegated *economically* to the same class as clowns and menial servants and to appear merely as people partaking in the consumption, parasites on the actual producers." *Theories of Surplus Value*, Part 1, pp.174–175; original emphasis.

71 Poovey, *Genres*, p.180.

72 W. Howison, "An investigation into the principles and credit of the circulation paper money, or bank notes, in Great Britain," in F. Capie (ed), *History of Banking, vol. IV: English Banking* (Pickering & Chatto, London, 1993, 131–204), pp.188–189.

73 Marx, *Theories of Surplus Value*, Part 1, pp.176–177; R. Chernomas, "Productive and unproductive labor and the rate of profit in Malthus, Ricardo, and Marx," *Journal of the History of Economic Thought*, 12, 1990, pp.81–95.

74 T. Malthus, *Principles of Political Economy*, 2nd edition, William Pickering, London, 1836, pp.36, 45, 47.

75 W. Norfolk, "The general principles of banking, bills of exchange, British funds, and foreign exchanges," in Capie (ed), *History of Banking, vol. IV* (337–362), p.349.

76　G. Scrope, "The rights of industry and the banking system," in Capie (ed), *History of Banking, vol. IV* (205–256), p.218.

77　As demonstrated and discussed by, for instance, Ernest Mandel in his "Introduction" to K. Marx, *Capital, Vol.* 2, Penguin, London, 1992, at pp.40–46.

78　D. Harvey, *The Limits to Capital*, University of Chicago Press, Chicago, 1982, p.105; Mandel, "Introduction," p.40.

79　Webber and Rigby, *Golden Age Illusion*, pp.110–111.

80　Marx, *Capital, Vol. 1*, Penguin, London, 1990, p.1046, original emphasis.

81　E.g. R. Bootle, *Money for Nothing: Real Wealth, Financial Fantasies and the Economy of the Future*, Nicholas Brealey Publishing, London, 2003, p.134.

82　D. Harvey, *The Enigma of Capital and the Crises of Capitalism*, Profile Books, London, 2010.

83　See especially *Capital, Vol.* 2, pp.209–211.

84　Marx, *Theories of Surplus Value*, Part. 1, p.225; original emphasis.

85　Marx, *Capital, Vol.* 3, p.432.

86　H. Boss, *Theories of Surplus and Transfer: Parasites and Producers in Economic Thought*, Unwin Hyman, Boston, 1989, p.103.

87　Marx, *Capital, Vol.* 3, pp.678–679.

88　See, for example, D. Milonakis and B. Fine, *From Political Economy to Economics: Method, the Social and the Historical in the Evolution of Economic Theory*, Routledge, New York, 2008.

89　W. Stark (ed), *Jeremy Bentham's Economic Writings*, Allen and Unwin, London, 1952.

90　Ackerman, "Interest rates," pp.83–85.

91　J. Dinwiddy, *Bentham: Selected Writings of John Dinwiddy* (ed. W Twining, Stanford University Press, Stanford, 2004), p.104.

92　Vaggi and Groenewegen, *Concise History*, p.xiv.

93　Mill, *Principles of Political Economy*, pp.71, 74. John Ruskin ridiculed Mill for these "inconsistencies" in his magisterial "Unto this last," in *Unto This Last and Other Writings* (Penguin, London, 1985, 155–228), pp.204–205.

94　W. Jevons, *The Theory of Political Economy*, 4th edition, Macmillan and Co., London, 1911, p.166; original emphasis. Another, very similar statement was provided by another of neoclassicism's architects, Alfred Marshall, who wrote in his *Principles of Economics* (9th, variorum, edition, ed. C. Guillebaud), vol. 1, Macmillan, London, 1961 (first published in 1890): "We may define labour as any exertion of mind or body undergone partly or wholly with a view to some good other than the pleasure derived directly from the work. And if we had to make a fresh start, it would be best to regard all labour as productive except that which failed to promote the aim towards which it was directed, and so produced no utility" (p.65).

95　G. Pilling, *The Crisis of Keynesian Economics: A Marxist View*, Taylor & Francis, London, 1986, p.109.

96　J. Schumpeter, *History of Economic Analysis*, Routledge, New York, 1987, pp.599, 597.

97　The quotations are from Boss, *Theories*, p.4.

98　"Coincident with demise of growth as the central question for orthodox political economy," observes W. Gramm ("Unproductive labour and unproductive consumption: historical review, contemporary relevance," *International Journal of Social Economics*, 14, pp.154–166), at p.157, "the concepts — the relationships — of unproductive labour and consumption became relegated to the new 'underworld' of institutional, sociological economics."

99　Boss, *Theories*, p.4.

2

Instrumental Internationalism

Mankind, in following the present sense of their minds, in striving to remove inconveniences, or to gain apparent and contiguous advantages, arrive at ends which even their imagination could not anticipate ... and nations stumble upon establishments, which are indeed the result of human action, but not the execution of any human design.

Adam Ferguson (1767)[1]

One of the great curiosities of the large-scale internationalization of banking and finance in the latter decades of the twentieth century is the fact that the phenomenon appeared novel, but in most respects was not. The appearance of novelty related to what came immediately before this period of internationalization: for three decades beginning in the early 1930s the world of finance was a highly territorialized one. The provision of banking services occurred chiefly on a national basis. So, too, did the provision of finance: with the majority of nations imposing capital controls of various sorts, the lending and borrowing of money and the circulation of financial assets was restricted to within national borders to a degree almost unimaginable to inhabitants of most capitalist countries today. When, at different speeds and from different moments in time, these bounded national financial spaces began to open up from the 1960s onwards, it seemed like a very new and very original socio-economic experience.

Yet there was, in reality, little that was genuinely novel about the more open financial world that soon came into being. An appearance of newness was only possible in the context of a very limited historical framing, for the decades immediately preceding the 1930s were characterized by an international financial openness that contrasted just as sharply as late-twentieth century capital and

Banking Across Boundaries: Placing Finance in Capitalism, First Edition. Brett Christophers.
© 2013 John Wiley & Sons, Ltd. Published 2013 by John Wiley & Sons, Ltd.

banking freedoms did with the 30-year window of enclosure that was wedged
between the two. Before enclosure became the norm in the 1930s, banks operated
widely overseas and monies moved largely unhindered across national borders.
Not for nothing, therefore, has the period from 1890 to 1931 been called the first
"golden age" of international banking.[2] Indeed so widely-recognized is this
accordion-like historical progression of international finance – re-expansion following a limited period of compression – that much of the ongoing debate about
the two respective eras of "open" finance has come to focus specifically on the
question of which of the two should be considered the *more* globalized.

In this book, I am not interested in examining metrics of relative globalization
or internationalization. We will, to be sure, have occasion to assess in some depth
the degree to which banking in the late-twentieth and early-twenty-first centuries
became a truly cross-border phenomenon. Chapter 6 takes up this particular
empirical theme. But when it comes to considering the post-1950s internationalization of finance in a comparative light, which is to say alongside the internationalization exhibited prior to the 1930s, our concern is less with the quantitative
extent of this phenomenon than with the factors which facilitated it. Did the same
sets of forces account for the openness of global finance in the past – before the
international financial system abruptly fragmented in the interwar years – as in
the contemporary globalized period beginning in the 1960s?

This book offers only a partial answer to this question. It does so for two main
reasons. The first is that all manner of persuasive answers have already been
advanced by a wide range of scholars and it is not one of the book's objectives
explicitly to challenge these, even if it does highlight concerns with some of them.
Understanding the political powers and economic realities which encouraged the
opening up of international finance in the latter decades of the twentieth century
has become, in fact, almost a sub-discipline in itself.[3] Meanwhile, the literature
devoted to exploring the factors underpinning financial globalization in the decades and, indeed, centuries preceding interwar protectionism, is only marginally
less extensive (and I rely on it extensively in this chapter). It is clear from these
literatures that the causes of the internationalization of finance at different historical junctures have been many, and that there were considerable differences
between the forces at work in the two periods in question. My hope is that the
arguments offered in this book will add merely an incremental and essentially
complementary perspective to this body of existing scholarship.

The second reason for offering only a partial answer to the question of the
differences between the two eras is that the book is not really about *causes* of
boundary crossing. It is about technologies of enablement. As I noted in the
introduction, one of the book's main propositions is that in the second half of the
twentieth century, representations of the productiveness of finance changed in
such a way that it is hard to imagine the financial world internationalizing in the
way it did, and to the degree that it did, *without* those representative shifts. In
other words, the book is concerned to elucidate how it is that the constellations
of forces that other scholars have identified as causes of this internationalization
crystallized historically *as causes*. Such forces derived their powers of causation

in part, I argue, from the shifts in economic discourse that were occurring in the background, but which periodically came to the foreground when actively mobilized by the political and corporate champions of internationalized finance.

It is in this particular respect, then, that the book aims to contribute to the "what is different" debate; and it is in this particular respect that the late-twentieth-century globalization of finance *did* display genuine novelty. It differed from financial globalization in earlier eras, I claim, in the sense that it was animated, buttressed, and ultimately enabled by economic principles – by, more specifically, technologies of representation of economic categories and dynamics. The literature on financial globalization in different eras has not recognized this distinguishing feature of the phenomenon in its latter-day guise. Chapters 4 and 5 therefore present this case in detail by analyzing the various ways in which such technologies of economic representation were implicated in the processes of post-1950s banking internationalization charted in those two chapters and in Chapter 6.

To appreciate and understand the novelty of this intertwining of economic representations and economic materialities, however, we need to go back first to the internationalized financial system, or systems, which existed before the 1930s. That is the task in the present chapter. In doing so, we will see that there was no comparable appeal to economic doctrines to justify internationalization. Demonstrating this is important in a twofold sense. It is important most obviously because it sharpens our understanding of the particularity of the internationalization of finance in different eras. But it is also important because there exists a historical literature within which it is intimated, contrary to my own argument, that two interrelated conceptual economic models *did* play an active part in fostering financial internationalism, specifically in the nineteenth century. Those two models were the so-called "price-specie flow" model (a clunky term often substituted simply by the "gold standard" which it presumed to operate) and a more generic model of free capital mobility. Contra the intimations of the literature in question, I will argue that the former model, while "available" for mobilization, was not actively invoked; and that the latter simply did not exist during the era in question. In point of fact, prior to the twentieth century, the only credible economic arguments systematically invoked in relation to the cross-border dimensions of banking and finance were actually directed *against* the openness of geopolitical borders.

The chapter's analysis of the macro-spatiality of banking and finance runs up to the period when national financial systems widely turned in on themselves in the 1930s, and contains three sections. The first tells a chronological story of this spatiality, beginning with the medieval period characterized by primarily metal monies and, in the form most notably of the financial institutions of the Italian city-states, by the first real harbingers of modern international banks. The story proceeds through to the modern heyday of industrial capitalism in northern Europe and North America, taking in the development of paper monies and of modern financial markets along the way. Throughout, the emphasis is on charting in basic terms the nature and extent of geopolitical boundary crossing by financial flows and institutional operations. The second, much shorter section, indebted like the first to substantial existing secondary literatures, aims to capture the main factors that *explain* the crossings that occurred in these various periods. The final section turns to the question of economic theory and demonstrates that in contradistinction to the late-twentieth-century incarnation of globalized banking and finance, earlier examples of open and integrated cross-border financial systems not only lacked explicit grounding in supportive conceptual economic frameworks, but, equally importantly, scarcely required their legitimating authority in the first place.

A Brief "Pre" History of the Geographies of Money, Finance, and Banking

The Early and High Middle Ages

From the final years of the Roman Empire in the fifth century through to the early years of European merchant capitalism in the twelfth century, the Western world was characterized by a striking financial openness. To the extent that one can speak meaningfully of a financial "system" existing during that period, it comprised a number of key features: the use of primarily metal, coin-based monies; very little by way of either noncash financial assets or what we would now think of as geographically-oriented capital controls (volume limitations or financial levies on movements of capital across territorial borders); and, royal mints aside, practically nothing in the way of formal financial institutions.

Money, in the shape of gold, silver, and copper coinage of varying weights and degrees of sophistication, flowed relatively unhindered across borders for most of this long period. The overwhelmingly dominant coin from the fifth to the seventh century was the Byzantine nomisma (in Greek) or solidus (in Latin), famously depicted as "the Dollar of the Middle Ages" by Robert Lopez.[4] But for the following five centuries, across the whole breadth of what is now Western Europe, the silver penny or (in French) denier was, as Peter Spufford has demonstrated, "not merely the characteristic coin" but "virtually the only coin in use." This is not to say, we should immediately note, that only one type of physical coin was actually minted and circulated. Far from it: there were literally hundreds of different varieties of denier, struck at mints scattered throughout the continent and under the authority of a wide range of monarchs. But, critically, these various deniers "were apparently interchangeable throughout Frankia" and "could and did travel very long distances from the places in which they were minted."[5] Perhaps the key point to note here is that to the extent that contemporary relations of state and sovereign power were spatialized, money typically was not regarded as either symbolically or materially expressive of such geographical framings. As Benjamin Cohen writes: "the sovereign right of coinage was hardly ever interpreted in exclusively territorial terms. Few states expected – or even, in principle, claimed – a monopoly for their own coins within their own frontiers."[6]

There were, however, isolated exceptions to this overall picture of freedom of monetary flows, and it is important to register their existence. Perhaps the most notable example was that of England from the early tenth century. England minted its own silver pennies, and while these – as we shall see below – would at various points come to circulate widely overseas, foreign pennies faced significant barriers to incursion in the other direction. In 930, King Athelstan famously stipulated that forthwith "there shall run one coinage throughout the realm"; and while its borders were always somewhat porous, this proscription served "for centuries as an effective barrier to the circulation of foreign coin in England."[7] It was not the first instance of the attempted imposition of capital controls (Byzantine merchants had, for instance, theoretically been forbidden from using the solidus outside of the Empire). But for the long period of the Early and High Middle Ages, it appears to have been the most successful.

Nor, we should be clear, was money just a matter of coins and bullion in this era. It was *primarily* an age of metal, but credit instruments did exist. Indeed, as David Graeber has most forcefully argued, our conventionally-pictured sequencing – of virtual or credit monies historically succeeding metal monies – does not stand up to close scrutiny. Virtual monies, in the form of debt, long preceded coin in most parts of the world. Yet such monies were, in the European territories of the Early and High Middle Ages, limited both qualitatively and quantitatively. Especially where one was dealing with strangers, and certainly for anything but the smallest transactions, people "expected money that would be acceptable anywhere." And that, Graeber concedes, meant coin.[8]

The Late Middle Ages

The thirteenth, fourteenth, and fifteenth centuries witnessed a series of novel developments in money and finance that would be of enduring and profound significance for the evolution of Western society as a whole. For the most part, these developments served to maintain, and in some cases even deepen, the geographically integrated and open nature of existing financial "systems" – although as in the preceding era there were some notable exceptions to this rule. And intriguingly, pressures towards openness *and* closure were arguably both experienced most strongly in the same region, which was the region where most of the more important financial innovations of the age happened to originate: Italy, and its leading city-states. For Graeber, in fact, the "history of modern financial instruments" begins with "the issuing of municipal bonds – a practice begun by the Venetian government in the twelfth century."[9] Meanwhile Giovanni Arrighi, another wonderful chronicler of financial history, regards "finance in its modern capitalist form [as] a Florentine invention" in the "late thirteenth and early fourteenth centuries," with "mid-fifteenth-century Genoa" subsequently becoming "the real birthplace of modern financial capitalism in all its forms."[10]

Following directly on from the preceding discussion, we can begin by considering developments in coinage. The thirteenth century was significant in this regard for it saw a continuation and intensification of a process of currency proliferation that had begun, stutteringly, in the twelfth century. Traced by Spufford to a range of factors, not least of which was a gradual fragmentation of rights to mint, the idea that coins could be variously denominated took hold and spread rapidly. "No longer was a denier in one place equal to a denier in another." As the uniformity of coinage disintegrated, it became increasingly necessary to specify the currency in which a sum was being expressed, as in "money of Pavia, or Cologne, or Toulouse."[11] And with this fragmentation was born, of course, the phenomenon of foreign exchange, at flexible rates, among various coinages.

Despite the increase in the types of deniers and shillings and so forth, the metallic monetary world remained an extremely open and fluid one. "The principal national currencies easily crossed political frontiers," John Day confirms in relation to this period.[12] Consider, for example, the reciprocal relationship between coinages in England and the Low Countries in the late thirteenth century. First, English pennies were imported into the latter region, where they were given the name esterlins. They were then imitated locally – produced in large numbers, and subsequently used freely as payment internationally, including in England itself. Indeed, Nicholas Mayhew suggests that by 1301, half of the esterlins struck in the Low Countries in the 1290s had ended up in England.[13] (Equally strikingly, more than 90 per cent of new English coinage in the 1310s and 1320s is estimated to have been struck from resmelted foreign coin.[14]) Consider, also, the situation some two centuries later in France, where, in the wake of the silver "famine" of the mid-fifteenth century, no fewer than 21 different varieties of non-French coin were permitted to circulate in 1471, up from nine just five years earlier.[15]

There were, to be sure, important examples of attempts being made to restrict coin and indeed bullion movements across territorial boundaries. As Raymond de Roover has documented, Flanders largely prohibited the export of domestic coins in the fourteenth and fifteenth centuries. But such attempts, provoked in part by recurrent silver and gold famines – real or perceived – of the kind mentioned above for France, met with little success, running against real-world economic and financial circumstances that the ordinances in question, de Roover notes, "disregarded completely."[16] These restrictive attempts were also in the minority. At the other extreme were places such as Venice, where for much of the thirteenth through fifteenth centuries the volume of coin and bullion exported was regarded rather as a primary measure of economic success.[17]

Alongside these trends in coinage creation and circulation, however, the Late Middle Ages also saw innovations in paper money that precipitated a relative *decline* in the shipping across space of metal-based monies. The most vital of these was the introduction in the fourteenth century of the bill of exchange.[18] We have already come across this instrument in Chapter 1, in its implication in the circumvention of usury laws. But its most visible role, at least initially, was in lubricating commodity trade between places – including across geopolitical borders – in such a way that coins did not always need to be transported to the full value of the transactions involved. The bill, as a money substitute, "reduced to a minimum the shipments of specie which were necessary in order to make international payments."[19]

How did the bill of exchange function? It is not necessary here to go into great detail, but the essential dynamics are important. In its simplest form, the bill was a promise: by one merchant (the drawer) to another (the payee) to make a cash payment at a later date. This simple situation was made more complicated, however, by three extensions; and it was these same extensions that made the real difference in terms of stimulating long-distance commodity trade and reducing the associated coin circulation. First, bills could be drawn in one place to be payable in another, and in the currency of the latter. Second, bills increasingly were rendered negotiable, meaning that the original payee could transfer to a third party – another merchant, for example – the monetary claim on the drawer that the bill represented. Third, dedicated financial "intermediaries" soon got involved; and it was these intermediaries, as we shall shortly see, that emerged as the most prominent forerunners of modern banks. They assumed two key roles vis-à-vis such bills. They bought (negotiable) bills for cash from payees, but at a discount to face value; and they *effectively* extended credit to the drawers of bills by acting as the drawee who would ultimately pay it off. The cumulative result of these innovations was rapid growth, in the Europe of this era, in the circulation of paper-denominated credit claims. Coins now needed to be shipped not to fund all individual commodity transactions, but only the *net* amounts owing when merchants and their "bankers" periodically settled outstanding claims, typically at the international fairs held in the great trading duchy of Champagne and at other key merchant hubs.

One critical recognition here is that not only did the bill of exchange serve to stimulate trade, but was itself of course a creature of a trade-oriented economy: of, in other words, merchant capitalism. The nature and geography of contemporary trade relations gave rise to the need for – or at least, underwrote the use value of – a financial instrument of this form. To appreciate this is to appreciate also, in the same moment, why Italy was the "natural" seedbed for such innovations, for by the end of the thirteenth century the Italian city-states, and most particularly Venice and Genoa, had taken an iron grip on European trading relationships with non-European societies. They were *the* gateways to trade with the Eastern Mediterranean and further east, and would maintain this dominance until into the sixteenth century. As historians such as de Roover and Day have shown, it is only in the context of this external trade, and its knock-on implications for Italy's role in trading relationships *within* Europe, that we can understand the concentration within the Italian states of Genoa and Florence of early innovation in paper financial instruments.[20] Florence's prominent role, for instance, was intimately bound up with its control of the wool trade.[21]

The more immediately pertinent recognition, however, is that except in their most rudimentary forms, or where explicitly restricted from doing so, bills of exchange circulated freely across borders. As lubricants of trade, this was their raison d'être; without such mobility, they were largely shorn of purpose. Some states did attempt to stymie this mobility and thus neuter the bill, often in the belief that its use contributed to the depletion of metallic reserves.[22] But such states, England among them, were in the minority and were mainly peripheral to the development of merchant capitalism during this period.

If bills of exchange were, almost of necessity, an integrative inter-territorial phenomenon, so too were another of the novel financial innovations to which the Late Middle Ages gave rise, and which we therefore need to consider here. These were the intermediary institutions, or "banks," whose birth and early growth were so fundamentally bound up with the bill of exchange, and whose origins are also therefore located in Italy. As we noted in Chapter 1, bills were such institutions' stock-in-trade (making the epithet "merchant banks" an entirely appropriate one); deposit banking proper did not come until later, and elsewhere in Europe. These early financial institutions, while headquartered in Italy, and most commonly in Florence, were international entities from the very start. Their international presence was initially relatively mobile, closely tied to the fairs of Champagne, and relied, as Arrighi has noted, "on a network of correspondents that spanned the entire European world-economy."[23] But from the late thirteenth century the leading houses began to put down roots overseas in the shape of more organized and sedentary branches or partnerships. Among the leading fourteenth-century financial companies, the Peruzzi had permanent foreign establishments in Bruges, Paris, and Avignon; the Medici, who dominated the fifteenth century, added Lyons, London, Basel, and Geneva to Bruges and Avignon, though lacked a foothold in Paris.[24]

In the coupled emergence of "merchant banks" and bills of exchange, together with the trend towards currency proliferation and foreign exchange of coinages, we have covered all but one of the key developments in money and finance of the Late Middle Ages – and all reinforced, rather than reduced, the territorial openness prevailing at the beginning of the period. The final critical development, however, was of a more locally-ringfenced nature, and it too was centered on Italy. This was the emergence of state debt through the issue of bonds by the city-states of northern Italy in the fourteenth century, with Venice and Florence leading the way. As Michael Veseth observes: "The government of the Italian city-state of Florence created history's first funded public debt through legislation enacted in 1344 and 1345."[25]

The debt issued in this period by the Florentine and other Italian city-states did not travel far-and-wide in the manner of contemporary coinages and bills of exchange. This is not to say that there was no secondary market in such debt: there usually was. But the buyers of this debt both on original issue *and* from existing investors were almost invariably wealthy citizens of the city-states themselves. There are two main explanations for this initial local circumscription of bond markets. First, the purchase of such bonds was in many cases forced – Veseth describes the Florentine *prestanze* loans as effectively "interest-bearing tax payments" – and such compulsion could only be effected within local political territories. And second, much of the finance was required for the fighting of wars: wars waged against other Italian city-states or towns that could not, of course, be expected to contribute money towards their own antagonists. The upshot, as Niall Ferguson remarks, was that since it was wealthy local citizens that typically populated the governments of city-states like Florence, "the people who issued the bonds ... were in large measure the same people who bought them."[26] As we shall see below, however, this highly localized public financing was a short-lived phenomenon within the longer, ongoing history of state debt creation and circulation.

The Early Modern era

The period of time stretching from the beginning of the sixteenth century to the late eighteenth century has received considerably less attention than the mid- to late nineteenth century in the recent literature devoted to historicizing modern-day globalized finance. In at least two respects, I want to suggest here, this is unfortunate. For one thing, the financial world of the Early Modern era was arguably no less spatially open and integrated than the more familiar international financial system of the Victorian age. And for another, it was unarguably *more* important in terms of the range and significance of the financial innovations it spawned.

The Middle Ages, as we have seen, bequeathed a Western world in which money *qua* money flowed, for the most part, relatively freely across state boundaries. "The general rule," as Boyer-Xambeu and colleagues have noted of the sixteenth century, "was that coins circulated everywhere without consideration for frontiers."[27] The next two hundred years served only to make things even more open than they already were, for the few remaining examples of large-scale attempts to contain monetary flows were finally dispensed with. England led the way in this regard, removing its remaining prohibitions to the export of bullion in 1663, in what the economic historian William Shaw has called "one blow of astounding boldness." Various English governments subsequently "retraced their steps in uncertainty," but the die was effectively now cast, and other historically interventionist states followed suit.[28] France was a relative laggard, waiting until 1755 to free up commerce in money, and doing so against the backdrop of growing support for mobile capital as a check on sovereign power among intellectuals such as Montesquieu (who died that year) and Turgot.[29] This, it is important to note, essentially marked the end of substantive efforts to control the flow of monies across borders until the broadly-based retrenchment of the twentieth century's interwar era. And at this point, in the mid-eighteenth century, such monies still consisted mainly of metallic coins. Paper banknotes – which, unsurprisingly, circulated primarily locally in their early incarnations – were a relatively new innovation, and formed only a small part of the money supply where, as in England, they did now exist.[30]

The solitary more territorially-constrained financial artifact of the Late Middle Ages – state debt – also began during the Early Modern period to assume a much more spatially-distributed guise.[31] With wars raging periodically throughout, the leading modernizing Western states all borrowed prolifically to replenish military coffers. "By the eighteenth century," as Bonney observes, "'mountains of debt' ... had become the norm in western Europe."[32] Much of this debt, it is true, continued to be sourced locally. Certainly this was the case in the Netherlands, where wealthy Dutch families contributed the lion's share of "national" public credit.[33] And even where debt *was* sourced from further afield, it would in some cases be inappropriate to envision such financing as "external" in the sense of crossing meaningful geopolitical boundaries. The derivation of massive Spanish public debts in the sixteenth century by regents such as Philip II is a case in point: while the bulk of this debt was provided by power-ful banking families based outside Spain itself (in, most materially, Germany, Genoa and Portugal), almost all were located within the purview of the Spanish Empire.[34]

It was, therefore, elsewhere in Europe that the trend towards truly external state debt financing was most observable. Funding of the French public debt displayed important elements of this tendency, particularly in the middle decades of the eighteenth century. For most of the Early Modern era, domestic sources had been far-and-away the dominant providers of government debt finance.[35] But after the bubble years of 1719–1720, the French developed a market for government debt "in the form of life annuities that were very attractive to foreign investors by virtue of paying a very high rate of return." Foreigners appear to have acquired these *rentes* through their banking representatives or other agents in Paris.[36] Meanwhile, one other country whose state debt was bought and held widely overseas, from the seventeenth century onwards, was Austria. In this case, the Dutch were especially significant investors; and in the eighteenth century, Dutch "loan contractors" would take on a key role in retailing the national debt of numerous countries, doing so not only within the Netherlands but throughout Europe.[37]

Yet it was in England that a model of state deficit financing explicitly incorpo-rating cross-border investment – a model that would later be widely replicated elsewhere – was first formalized. In many respects this was unforeseeable, since prior to its financial reforms of the 1690s England, unlike many other leading European states, had no regularized system of state borrowing: a state of affairs reflecting in large part a history of conflict over finance between the Crown and Parliament.[38] (While many English monarchs had been serial [and indeed notori-ously unreliable] debtors, often raising their loans overseas – defaults by the first three Edwards are all commonly held to have ruined Italian financing houses – such borrowing was never systematic, nor always backed by the government.[39]) But with various proposals for systematized long-term government borrowing already in circulation, and with the declaration of war against France in 1689 providing an immediate impetus, the next decade saw a revolution in English state financing.[40] The first long-term government loan was raised in 1693, for £1m at an interest rate of 10 percent per annum; and in what was perhaps the seminal moment in the history of the national debt, the Bank of England was founded the following year.

Because its creation and structure were so intimately bound up with another key financial innovation of this era, the private joint-stock company, we will look below in more detail at the Bank of England, and particularly its provisions for receiving investment from abroad. Before doing so, however, it is critical to high-light just how internationalized the English national debt – and not just that element provided through the Bank of England – soon became.[41] J. F. Wright has provided the most comprehensive analysis of this internationalization. Drawing on the work of several earlier historians, he shows that overseas investors had grown their holdings to 13.8 percent of the funded (long-term) national debt by 1750 and 16.6 percent by 1762. Even these figures, however, are, Wright suggests, probably underestimates, since some overseas owners preferred to hold their assets in the names of English agents or nominees.[42]

To understand more fully the early configuration of the English national debt, we also need to understand the parallel development in England of the joint-stock company (meaning a company in which owners hold equity represented by company stock, or shares), for the two were indissoluble; and thus like the national debt, the English joint-stock company was an internationalized phenomenon from its very beginnings. The Bank of England was, in its original incarnation, one such company: it was, despite its public purpose, a private institution, one funded by subscriptions to its company stock, which in turn funded the government through the provision of loans. The subscribers were incorporated under the title of "Governor and Company of the Bank of England," and the invitation to subscribe was a remarkably catholic one, pitched to "all and every Person and Persons, Natives or Foreigners, Bodies Politick and Corporate."[43] This invitation was taken at its word, and by 1762 fully 43 percent of Bank stock is estimated to have been held overseas.[44]

Alongside the Bank of England, there were two other major joint-stock companies "whose shares were to constitute the first part of the perpetual debt of the British government."[45] They were the East India Company and the South Sea Company, and they too allowed, encouraged, and attracted foreign ownership. The three, together, held "nearly all" of the government's funded debt until the War of Austrian Succession (1739–1748).[46] From the 1720s shares in these companies could be purchased and traded in Amsterdam as well as in London, which partly helps to explain why of all overseas investors in the English public debt in the first half of the eighteenth century, the Dutch were comfortably the most active and most material, with Bank of England and East India stock their preferred holdings.[47]

Not all early English joint-stock companies were directly implicated in the raising and management of the national debt, of course. It has been estimated that there were already 150 joint-stock companies in existence in England in 1695.[48] Nor, equally importantly, was the joint-stock company of the late seventeenth and early- to mid-eighteenth centuries exclusive to England. Comparable models of business ownership and investment were utilized with varying degrees of success in France, Prussia and, most notably, the Netherlands itself. Nevertheless, it *was* the corporations specifically embodying English public credit – and whose shares were owned widely overseas – that, in value terms, dominated the early decades of the joint-stock company era in Europe. The number of such companies remained small outside of England. And within England, as Philip Mirowski has shown, "securities not linked to the government or the three big companies" were of "relative insignificance" for the bulk of the eighteenth century.[49]

This situation would of course change over time, especially as the age of merchant capitalism segued in the late eighteenth century into that of industrial capitalism, and companies sprung up en masse with substantial needs for upfront equity investment to fund fixed capital expenditures. Much of this new investment, in these new types of companies, would inevitably also be centered initially in England; but industrial capital requirements soon expanded dramatically in mainland Europe too, and indeed in North America. Most such investment contained sizeable cross-border components. (Already by the late eighteenth century private bankers in Basel, Geneva, and Zurich were investing substantial sums directly into foreign industry, including in Alsatian cotton printing.[50]) For almost the whole of the Early Modern age, however, this shift into equity-financed industrial capitalism was a marginal phenomenon. As a product primarily of the nineteenth century, we will deal with it more fully below.

Having reviewed all key developments in money and financial assets, and in the inter-state geographies thereof, it remains only to address two further subjects for the period under consideration: first, banking institutions; and second, the financial markets in which such institutions were, by now, increasingly operating. I will treat merchant banking and deposit banking separately here. The former business was, by the beginning of the Early Modern age, already well-established, and already highly internationalized; it would retain both characteristics. The latter, meanwhile, only emerged substantively *during* this period, and then as a primarily national phenomenon. These differences, however, are not the only reason for reviewing the two forms of banking activity separately from one another. It makes sense to do so because, as numerous historians have shown, these activities *existed* largely separately from one another, both operationally and geographically, until considerably later in time.[51]

Merchant banks, as we have seen, had been thoroughly entwined from the start with commodity trade and the facilitation of foreign exchange and trade-related payments. Indeed, so close did this relationship between the two spheres remain that, as Martin Körner helpfully reminds us, "during the whole early modern period [merchant] bankers were generally merchants too."[52] They also came now increasingly to invest proprietary funds in foreign territories, in both public and private financial assets. They were, therefore, in each of these main respects, fundamentally cross-border entities.

In the case of the Italian bankers who dominated European merchant banking in the Late Middle Ages, this multi-territorial configuration had taken fixed physical form in the shape of out-of-state branches. By the beginning of the Early Modern era, with the Italian banks having declined as an international force, it was the turn of others to replicate their model of a "networked" cross-border presence. They did not do so, however, in exactly the same form. The multi-state merchant banking "groups" which characterized the sixteenth, seventeenth, and eighteenth centuries were typically not unitary firms holding a series of subsidiary branches, but more often networks of bankers connected by close personal or family connections – often of an ethnically-specific nature – if not always by legally-formalized financial and organizational ties.

The geographical center of gravity of these networks shifted over time, as did their constituent elements. In the sixteenth century it was merchant banking firms headquartered in Augsburg and south Germany that dominated. Arguably most notable in this regard was the Fugger banking dynasty established by Jacob "the Rich," who, by the time of his death and bequest of assets in 1525, "had extended over the whole of Europe" a "net of branches" in a fashion not in fact dissimilar from that which we saw with the Peruzzis and Medicis.[53] Such explicit empires became less and less common, however. More typical of the era were the much-discussed international "Protestant banking networks," often but not always Huguenot-based, that proliferated across large parts of Europe in the seventeenth and eighteenth centuries.[54] Prompted to leave France by religious persecution, the Huguenots were serial founders of banks in towns of refuge including Geneva, Lausanne, Frankfurt, Amsterdam, and London. From these bases, they then spread abroad, including back to France, to open banks – some of which were branches, but many of which were not – in places such as Lyons, Paris, Genoa, and Vienna. Bankers working in these new centers "remained in direct and close relationship with their homelands."[55] And thus was crystallized "a network of contacts which grew and developed among the Huguenot settlements": a Protestant banking "system."[56] Similar networks, likewise predicated on ethnic and family relations, came specifically to link the increasingly-pivotal banking centers of Amsterdam and London to one another; the Huguenots played a part in this networking, but so also, from the second quarter of the eighteenth century, did Dutch Jews.[57]

In contrast to this febrile internationalization of an established set of business activities, "deposit" banking was, as noted in Chapter 1, a novel concept in the Early Modern era – emerging only relatively late on, and centered very much on England, particularly in London. Meir Kohn has this to say of the spatial scope usually displayed by this new type of banking: "Deposit bankers often did not engage in international banking – in foreign exchange and remittance. In Venice and Bruges, as in most other cities, deposit banking was a purely local business and deposit bankers lacked the network of branches or agents in foreign cities required for international banking."[58] What Kohn observes of early deposit banking in general was certainly true of its incarnation in the country where it experienced the strongest initial commercial development (and where, not coincidentally, indigenous *merchant* banking lacked the depth and sophistication that it enjoyed on the continent until very late in the eighteenth century). England's early eighteenth-century national banking system, consisting of a network of country banks tied by partnerships into private banks in London, was indeed *national*. Notes Eric Kerridge: "the specifically English type of banking originated in domestic trade in mainly domestic produce; its roots were not in foreign trade, not in commercial arbitrage between separate markets."[59] "English banking" did of course ultimately internationalize, to a profound and arguably unprecedented degree – but not until the Early Modern era had given way to the age of industrialization.

Just as deposit banking did not emerge *only* in England at this time, neither was it always a private-sector activity. Where it blossomed elsewhere it was frequently as a state enterprise, and nowhere was this more apparent, and more important, than in seventeenth-century Amsterdam. The Netherlands had been a major trading hub since the fourteenth century, and its late sixteenth-century rise to a position of pre-eminence in this sphere – and particularly its domination of the Baltic trade – underpinned its burgeoning parallel role in monetary circulation.[60] This role was secured by, most critically, the founding of the Bank of Amsterdam in 1609.[61] With merchants working in and around Amsterdam struggling with a profusion of currencies, the Bank arrogated to itself the role of a disparate array of money-changers and cashiers. It converted all specie into guilder deposits; and perhaps most importantly, all bills of exchange valued at over 600 guilders had to be paid through the bank. The latter directive compelled all major merchants to set up an account with the Bank, which in turn catalyzed the Bank's pivotal transfer and clearing function. Through its centralized payments system, the Bank effectively controlled the money market.[62] And despite its many perceived limitations – it did not discount bills of exchange, it did not issue banknotes, it did not practice fractional-reserve banking, it did not pay interest on deposits (though it did guarantee them), and it did not lend money to private individuals (though it did to public bodies and, indirectly, to small businesses) – its prudence saw it become *the* bank of trust internationally: in the Baltic and in Russia, for instance, only Amsterdam bills of exchange were accepted. The Bank did not, in itself, *operate* internationally, except insofar as it lent to foreign governments; but it assuredly facilitated ongoing economic internationalization, both financial and nonfinancial.[63]

Stimulation of economic internationalization was also a cardinal feature of the final important financial innovation of the Early Modern era: namely financial markets, by which we mean markets where financial claims, or "securities," could be bought and sold.[64] Such markets developed in parallel, of course, to the joint-stock companies and government debt instruments discussed earlier, for it was primarily the ownership of, respectively, company shares and debt servicing/repayment entitlements that was traded on such markets. Albeit initially in crude forms, these markets began therefore to crystallize in the seventeenth century.

The first active market of any meaningful scale for financial securities was, perhaps not surprisingly, the Amsterdam *Beurs*, which also offered trading in commodities.[65] Here, encouraged and assisted by hundreds of sworn brokers, both retail and institutional investors traded in significant numbers from early in the seventeenth century.[66] The other main financial market in the Early Modern era was in London. Originating later in the seventeenth century and initially operating out of a series of coffeehouses, most notably on Exchange Alley, the London market was dominated by a smaller circle of brokers and dealers, called jobbers.[67] But, critically, and despite the differences between the two, the London market and the Amsterdam *Beurs* were closely linked to one another.[68] And between them, they rapidly came to constitute a hub of deeply internationalized investment flows: as we saw above, not only were foreign entities able to issue securities on such markets (as many international governments did in Amsterdam), but foreigners were able also to buy the securities traded there (as many individuals and institutions, including from the Netherlands itself, did in London).

The ongoing story of financial markets and their international dimensions is explored more fully below. But we can conclude here by briefly tracing the geographical evolution of those markets through to the end of the period we are presently concerned with.[69] As noted, London had, by the end of the seventeenth century, joined Amsterdam as a dominant force. The only other market approaching these two in scale and influence at that time was in Paris. But the Paris market never quite recovered, in the short or even medium term, from the infamous Mississippi Bubble episode of 1719–1720. (The French Revolution and subsequent Napoleonic Wars would deal a further hammer-blow to investor and investee confidence as the century drew to a close.) And over the next half-century Amsterdam's influence also, slowly, waned. The upshot was that as the industrial age dawned, London had assumed the position of unrivalled centre of global financial markets.[70]

The Industrial Age

The period from the late eighteenth century through to the interwar years of the early twentieth century was generally marked by further deepening of the existing internationalism of finance and financial institutions. This is visible in respect of each of the three main, interlocking elements of the developing financial system: money, investment, and banking. I shall now consider each in turn, summarizing selectively from the mammoth literature now available on those topics.

It is helpful to start with money, for money displays what appears to be the single greatest exception to this general trend towards the reproduction of international financial integration. That exception concerns the more widespread materialization in the nineteenth century of concerted state attempts to create and police truly national monies.[71] As many authors have noted, exerting control over money was part-and-parcel of the much broader contemporary project of consolidating political authority within the borders of the nation-state. Such enhanced monetary control typically took the form both of standardizing all domestic money forms, including paper notes as well as coinage, and of restricting the domestic circulation of foreign currencies.[72]

Yet despite this increasing territorialization of money forms and of their ability to circulate freely, it would be wrong to assume that the international monetary system became materially more fragmented, and materially less open, in consequence. Certainly, more minor national currencies not only were prohibited from circulating abroad, but were increasingly denied conversion at the national mints of other countries and were usually not quoted on international foreign exchange markets. The leading currencies, however, were a different matter. As Marc Flandreau and Clemens Jobst have shown, at the end of the nineteenth century the French franc was quoted almost everywhere, and the German mark in most places. The British pound sterling, meanwhile, was quoted on all 40 of the national markets they studied.[73] Sterling was, moreover, accepted "nearly everywhere for both transactions and investment purposes," and is estimated to have accounted for approximately 40 percent of all global foreign exchange reserves at the time of the outbreak of World War I.[74] In other words, a more formal and more concentrated hierarchy of currencies had become established, and as long as there was willingness to deal in sterling there were few cross-border obstacles to money's movement. The global monetary system thus remained highly integrated but, at the same time, demonstrably less *equal* than it had been.

Sterling's growing dominance during this period was clearly closely bound up with Britain's nineteenth-century leadership in both international trade and, as we will discuss in more detail below, international finance. And it was cemented, in the latter part of the nineteenth century, by the international consolidation of the gold standard.[75] Accorded pride-of-place by Karl Polanyi among the technologies of nineteenth-century laissez-faire liberalism, the gold standard was the defining feature of the international monetary system in the four decades prior to World War I.[76] Britain was the first to adopt the gold standard, unilaterally and much earlier than any other nation, with silver coin's legal-tender status finally being revoked in 1821.[77] Other countries remained on silver (e.g. Russia) or bimetallic standards (e.g. France) for considerably longer. But the pull to gold increased in line with Britain's financial and commercial power – Britain's monetary practices becoming more and more expedient for countries trading with or borrowing from it, or seeking to do so. Portugal, whose strong trade links with Britain were immortalized by David Ricardo in his theory of comparative advantage, was the first to join Britain on gold in 1854; most other European nations followed suit in the 1870s, led by Germany in 1871; and by the end of the nineteenth century, only Spain, in Europe, was not on the gold standard.[78]

The key principle of the gold standard was that currencies were convertible into gold on demand at fixed ratios by central banks. It was by no means a perfectly-functioning system, nor without dissension – a number of southern European and South American nations repeatedly suspended convertibility, for instance.[79] But, for the most part, the gold standard succeeded in preserving exchange rate stability during the last decades of the nineteenth century and the first of the twentieth, particularly amongst the world's industrialized countries. And it did so largely without the need for explicit capital controls.[80]

The integrated international monetary system that the gold standard came to underpin was conducive, in turn, to continuing cross-border openness in the second financial realm we are interested in: investment. Throughout the period that concerns us here, huge amounts of money flowed from one country to another in pursuit of profitable financial investment opportunities. Capital mobility, quantified through such measures as national current-account-to-output ratios, was extremely high; so too were levels of capital market integration, as revealed by trends in the relation between domestic savings and investment (a low correlation indicating a high degree of international integration) and by comparison of yields across markets (convergence indicating integration). Indeed research suggests that the levels of mobility and integration achieved in the late nineteenth century, when the adoption of the gold standard substantially increased what were already large international investment flows, were unparalleled – certainly before and perhaps even since.[81]

Much of this voluminous international investment continued to be channeled into state debt. The supply of capital to finance government borrowing was, by the late eighteenth century, "more international than ever before."[82] It became no less so in the nineteenth century. Alongside public debt securities, however, a proliferating array of international corporate debt and equity securities also now became increasingly available. There were opportunities to invest in companies building railroads, in companies running utilities, in companies prospecting for and exploiting natural resources, and plenty of others besides.

Where in the world were these funds targeted? The short answer to this question is: more-or-less everywhere, given that investment was sought, inter alia, in countries where industrialization and urbanization had begun to take root, in countries engaged in external or internal wars, and in European imperial possessions whether settled or not. In the early part of the industrial age, Britain remained a substantial external debtor, its national public debt increasing three-fold from 1793 to 1815 as a result of its exertions in the Napoleonic Wars.[83] At the same time, capital was also beginning to flow in significant volumes to America. Foreign loans helped Americans finance the War of Independence, and by 1789 around a third of the nominal national debt was owed to foreigners. From that point through to the 1870s, America was the largest international borrower. As elsewhere in the world, the *composition* of foreign investment in the US constantly shifted over the course of the 150-odd years we are looking at: before the 1830s, the main holdings were national debt securities and equity shares of the two Banks of the United States; by the end of that decade, money had largely shifted into US state securities; and by the mid-1850s, these, together with the securities of American railroad corporations, made up three-quarters of all foreign holdings.[84]

By the early twentieth century, there was essentially no major territory in the world whose government or private corporations were not – or had not in the recent past been – recipients of substantial foreign investment. Whether it was governments in the Middle East, mining operations in South America, or railway companies in China: all sought and received finance from overseas investors. And while it is hard to draw any conclusions as to the overall geography of these investment receipts and their changing destinations over time, two key observations are important. First, while external funding requirements in the north-western European heartlands of industrial capitalism dipped in the final decades of the nineteenth century and the first decade of the twentieth as indigenous surpluses and savings increasingly became available, they rose again in the aftermath of World War I with the need for reconstruction. Second, recent research, particularly by Moritz Schularick, has demonstrated that less-developed countries were proportionally much larger recipients of international investment in the Victorian era than they have been in recent decades. Schularick estimates, for instance, that in 1913 countries with a per-capita income of less than one-third of the "core" economies accounted for approximately half of total international investment; in the years 2000 and 2001, by contrast, the share of such countries was just 12.5 percent.[85]

The question of where international investment capital flowed *from*, rather than to, is much easier to answer since its sources were much more circumscribed. Until the very end of the eighteenth century, the Dutch remained important capital suppliers; as late as 1791, for example, one-sixth of owners of Bank of England stock still had addresses in the Netherlands.[86] But already by this time Dutch leadership was waning, as Britain rapidly assumed the mantle of predominant global financier – a role it was to retain until early in the twentieth century. In relative terms early nineteenth-century British capital exports were quite small, with almost all domestic savings required for the construction of domestic railways and towns, but from the 1860s the "trickle" of capital overseas, remarked Alec Cairncross in a landmark work, "began to assume really formidable proportions."[87] Thus in the half-century from 1865, capital exports accounted for a third of British savings; and less than a third of all capital raised in Britain through the public issue of securities remained in the UK itself.[88] Of the investment funds exported from Britain during this period, around half went to Argentina, Australia, Canada, and the US.[89]

One often-overlooked feature of this UK-centred geography of capital origination should be mentioned before we consider briefly where else funds were exported from. This is the fact that while the capital discussed in the previous paragraph was exported *from* Britain, it did not necessarily always constitute *British* savings. The lion's share, assuredly, did. But just as there were few restrictions on where Britons were able to invest their money – hence Keynes's famous observation that in the aforementioned half-century the "inhabitant of London" could readily "adventure his wealth in the natural resources and new enterprises of any quarter of the world, and share, without exertion or even trouble, in their prospective fruits and advantages" – so the London Stock Exchange on which domestic and foreign debt and equity securities were listed and traded welcomed investors from all around the world.[90]

Alongside Britain, but lagging well behind it, Germany and France were the other main sources of international investment in the nineteenth century. In the first half of the century, for instance, foreign government loans were frequently marketed in Berlin and Frankfurt; and in the late nineteenth century US railroad companies were a popular German investment. Foreign investment from Germany tended to occur in waves, but was material throughout; and by 1913 Germany was still the third largest source of international investment capital (behind Britain and France).[91] The French, meanwhile, tended to lend to places where they had strong political influence and close cultural ties such as Italy, Spain, and Russia.[92] But by the end of the nineteenth century French investors had become less restricted in their geographical selection and were investing much more widely – including, alongside British and German investors, in Latin America.[93]

If French and German investors began in the late nineteenth century to loosen Britain's grip on the Latin American market – Britain had been the main source of finance for Latin America in general, and more particularly for Argentina, Brazil, Mexico, and Peru, since the 1820s – it was the US that ultimately emerged as its main rival in the region, and which, in the first two decades of the twentieth century, rapidly came to eclipse it.[94] And this emergence of America as a leading source of investment funds was, of course, a much wider phenomenon, Wall Street's other major turn-of-the-century investments including two with an African focus: Cecil Rhodes's African diamond mines and Britain's costly fighting of the Boer War. It was also, perhaps most notably, US capital that underwrote much of Europe's post-World War I reconstruction.[95] More broadly, as the UK's role in providing international investment finance began what appeared to be an inexorable decline, "the United States became," in the interwar years, "the chief capital supplier to the world."[96]

Britain's earlier rise to ascendancy in the provision of international investment finance had been closely tied up with an equivalent achievement of hegemony in the final realm we shall address here, and the one that is of most central concern throughout the book: banking. We can see this first of all in the field of international merchant banking, which, through to the late 1700s, had been largely dominated by continental European bankers, but which came to be heavily centered on London from the early nineteenth century – although, once again, "British" banking was no more homogeneously "British" than "British" investment. Take, as a prime example, the Rothschild bank that, alongside its great rival Barings, towered above all competitors for most of the nineteenth century.[97] The founder of the London headquarters of the bank, Nathan Mayer Rothschild, was a German who moved to England in his early twenties.

In any event, London had by 1800 become the acknowledged center of the merchant banking world. Issuing and trading bills of exchange remained, in this period, such banks' bread-and-butter business: they were still, in other words, oriented largely towards international trade finance.[98] But for the market leaders such as the Barings and Rothschilds, managing and underwriting the issue of international – and particularly sovereign debt – securities was also becoming a significant source of revenue; Barings led the market up to around 1815, but by 1820 Rothschilds was dominant.[99] The latter firm was also highly significant for being the first substantial merchant bank without a significant interest in commodity trade per se, as opposed to solely the financing thereof. Whereas Barings retained such an interest until well into the nineteenth century, Rothschilds was already a bank sui generis.

The largest British-based merchant banks of the nineteenth century not only managed and generated substantial international capital flows, but were international operational entities themselves. As with their prominent continental European forebears, however, it remained the case that in most instances theirs was not a model based on permanent, wholly-owned overseas subsidiaries or branches. Rather, such banks tended to rely on networks consisting of interlocking partnerships, "correspondent" banks, and agencies – often, as before, glued together by family connections. It is in view of this less formalized international structure that Geoffrey Jones refers to such banks as "international" rather than "multinational."[100] Their networks extended across much of continental Europe, with the Rothschilds' being emblematic: "Nathan in London, Amschel in Frankfurt, James (the youngest) in Paris, Carl in Amsterdam and

Salomon roving wherever Nathan saw fit."[101] The Barings and Rothschilds also created agencies and partnerships in the US, such as the Rothschild representative August Belmont, as that market's thirst for capital relentlessly grew.[102] As Karl Polanyi would later remark with piercing insight, the Rothschilds "were subject to no *one* government; as a family they embodied the abstract principle of internationalism."[103]

The British-headquartered international merchant banks were complemented from the 1830s onwards by a group of what Jones does consider to have been truly *multinational* banks: the Anglo-Imperial and Anglo-International banks described in famous studies by A. S. J. Baster.[104] It is in direct reference to these banks that Jones submits that the nineteenth century "saw the birth of modern corporate multinational banking."[105] Typically offering both investment *and* retail banking services to local clients in the territories in which they operated, such banks had head offices in London but were not the outgrowth of domestic banks and, with no domestic business, they were essentially independent and freestanding. By 1870 there were 17 such banks, with branches spread mainly across Europe, Asia, and both South and North America.[106] This number had swelled to 30, and over 700 branches, by 1890.[107]

While British-headquartered banks of these various forms indubitably dominated international banking in the nineteenth century, it would be wrong to imagine that they had things entirely their own way, either overseas or, indeed, domestically. Taking the latter space first, German banks were present in London in one form or another throughout the century, although until 1895 Deutsche Bank was the only first-tier German bank with a permanent London branch as such.[108] More material was the incursion of US merchant banks from mid-century.[109] These, note, were exclusively private, unincorporated banks, for public national banks were banned by US regulations from opening overseas branches until 1914. The first significant entrant to London (and, in the case of this particular firm, also Liverpool) was Brown, Shipley & Co, a branch of the US bank Brown Brothers.[110] Among later arrivals, from the 1860s and 1870s, J. S. Morgan & Co was among the most influential.

Outside of Britain, the main competition to British banks, aside from indigenous operators, came from French and German institutions, just as French and German investment finance constituted the main competition to British capital exports. Such institutions only really began to develop an overseas presence in the second half of the century, however. When they did so, one key difference from the British "multinational" banks discussed above was that these French and German overseas banking entities typically *were* formally linked to domestic banking institutions.[111] And while some French banks were active in retail markets, most of these overseas banks focused on trade finance (offering credit and payment services to local merchant communities) and the facilitation of international investment. Amongst the German operators, Deutsche and Dresdner Banks were overwhelmingly dominant, using both branches and arm's-length partnerships, and securing a presence in "most of the world's important commercial centers" by the eve of World War I.[112] This included the US.[113] French banks, with the Sociétié Générale twins (Crédit Foncier and Crédit Mobilier) to the fore, were particularly strong in Spain, Russia, and Turkey.[114] Between them, it has been estimated that French and German banks had accumulated some 500 foreign branches by 1914 – by which time the overseas branches of the British multinational banks numbered "well in excess of 1,000."[115]

Up to the time of the outbreak of world war, significantly, the US remained only a bit player in overseas banking. With the exception of the few private merchant banks with branches in London discussed above, which existed mainly to facilitate the flow of foreign investment capital back to America, nineteenth-century US foreign trade was financed largely by foreign banks (which themselves often had a US presence). American bankers only began to develop a significant interest in establishing a presence overseas in the late 1890s, which was when American capital began flowing abroad in significant sums. And then, of course, there were the regulations which prevented national commercial banks from opening foreign branches until 1914. The upshot was that such banks were limited to the types of strategies pursued by Citibank, which opened a foreign exchange department in 1897 to provide international payment and collection services and foreign trade financing facilities to US multinational corporations, supplementing this domestically-situated business with the establishment of an international network of correspondent banks such as London City and Midland and, in Germany, Deutsche Bank.[116] Only in the interwar years were US commercial banks able to begin opening foreign branches, many of which were in Latin America; and even at the "zenith" of such activity in the late 1920s, as identified by Yoon Park and Jack Zwick, only 81 overseas branches were operational.[117]

How, in concluding this section, might we briefly summarize the overall geographical landscape of international banking in the industrial age up to the 1920s and 1930s? Once more, Jones is a helpful guide. He makes two important and connected observations that are worth stressing. The first is that where banks developed a permanent overseas presence in the form of branches, these were "overwhelmingly concentrated on developing economies." Thus, and second, apart from establishing footholds in the international financial centers of London, Paris, Frankfurt, and New York, "foreign penetration of the domestic banking systems of Britain, continental Europe or … the United States was virtually nonexistent."[118] This was how things broadly stood up to the point when, for the first and only time in history, global financial protectionism abruptly arrived on the scene in the 1930s.

Logics of Boundary Crossing

The preceding overview focused primarily on a simple mapping of inter-territoriality in monetary and financial affairs through history, but in providing this mapping it also offered plenty of indications as to causality – as to how we might seek to *explain* both the generic cross-border openness and integration displayed by such history, and, more visibly and specifically, discrete bursts of intensified cross-border activity. The objective of the present, much shorter section is to try to impart some structure and coherence to this explanatory side of things. What, over the (very!) *longue durée*, were the main reasons firstly for monies spreading far-and-wide and for banks increasingly doing likewise; and secondly, for the relative freedoms with which both, on the whole, were able to do so?

The reality, of course, is that there are almost as many individual explanations for banking or monetary systems having been open and integrated as there have been individual economic-geographical constellations of open-and-integrated finance itself. Religion, for instance, has often been a material factor, with examples ranging from the medieval systems of papal taxation that saw Italian bankers gain footholds across Europe and corresponding flows of silver back to Rome, to the Crusades of the same era and their effect of sucking substantial quantities of bullion out of Europe and eastwards.[119] Similarly, and indeed often connected to religious concerns, we can recognize the importance of migration: large-scale movements of people for religious, political or economic reasons have often been linked to large-scale movements of money and of financial institutions.[120] Amongst other factors frequently highlighted as forces for geographical integration are various communicative technologies, and particularly those that proliferated from the mid-nineteenth century: the railroad, the steamship, transatlantic cabling, the telegraph, and so forth.[121] The list of enabling and formative influences could go on almost ad infinitum.

Nevertheless, by stepping back from the detail and adopting a high-level perspective, we are able to extract some order from this overall complexity. Five core sets of factors stand out from the above history as overwhelmingly and consistently vital in underpinning the open and integrated nature of international finance and banking up to the time when that history draws to a close in the 1920s. I will briefly discuss each of these separately, although in reality they have very often been linked and mutually constitutive.

Before doing so, however, I want to place this schema firmly in the context of the argument of the book as a whole. For what I will emphasize in the final section of this chapter, and in later parts of the book, is that this inventory is instructive as much for what it does *not* include as for what it does. The one thing conspicuously missing from this list, but which would by contrast be central to any enumeration of the factors underlying internationalization of banking and finance over the past half-century, is economic doctrine. There was, in other words, nothing consistently normative about the integrated openness that largely characterized international finance in the centuries leading up to the brief twentieth-century interlude of national enclosure. Borders were open not because that is the way economic theory and its distributors said things *should* be. Their openness resulted from a history that economics may be able to help rationalize *ex post facto*, but which it did not design and summon into being *ex-ante*. As Gerald Dwyer and James Lothian have astutely observed, along somewhat similar lines, of the international coinages of the Late Middle Ages more specifically:

All of them were simply adopted. None of these international monies arose due to anyone's initial intention to create a new international money. Rather, in each instance their roles as international monies evolved due to their becoming generally acceptable to others over time. They thus achieved their status without any laws being passed, any official monetary conferences being held, or any foreign ministers issuing joint communiqués.[122]

Trade

The first and arguably most unceasingly important reason for open cross-border banking and finance through the ages is trade. From the moment trade across geopolitical borders took anything other than crude barter form, there existed a hugely powerful stimulus to integrated monetary relations. How, after all, could strangers trade commodities through anything other than barter if they did not use the same money form or at least have ways of readily converting one money into another? It is significant in this respect that during the mid-twentieth-century heyday of inter-state capital controls, the one employment of foreign exchange that enabled it to be secured relatively painlessly and cheaply was commodity trade. Open finance has always been a handmaiden of international trade.

As such, one can point to all sorts of histories, pertaining to almost any era of merchant or industrial capitalism, to illuminate this close connection. It applies to both money and banking. In the case of the former, here, for instance, is Peter Spufford explaining the free flowing of monies in medieval times: "Trade balances provided the basic and overwhelming reasons for normal and continuous flows of specie both within thirteenth-century Europe and outside it."[123] Meanwhile, William Shaw, though undoubtedly overstating the case, spoke to the same vital coupling when describing the "modern system" of integrated international monetary circulation that emerged after restrictions on bullion export were removed in the seventeenth and eighteenth centuries as one "in which the flow of precious metals is determined by the perfectly natural and automatic action of international trade."[124]

In the case of banking, we have already encountered on a number of occasions the indissolubility of trade from early internationalist merchant banking in particular. While there were many merchants who were not bankers, there were, prior to the Rothschilds, no important merchant bankers who were not also merchants. "International trade and international banking," confirms Charles Kindleberger, "were widely overlapping activities until the middle of the nineteenth century."[125] And even as they began operationally to diverge from one another around that time, they remained causally connected in a number of important ways. Most obviously, as Stefano Battilossi notes, European banks that opened overseas branches in the late nineteenth and early-twentieth centuries were very often "responding to the 'gravitational pull effect' exercised by national trade."[126] This was demonstrably the case, for example, with German banks' internationalization.[127] More broadly, we can say that throughout history, international trade has been a primary wellspring of internationalized banking as well as of internationalized monetary networks.

War

No less fundamental to the emergence of cross-border finance and banking has been the only somewhat less unceasing human disposition towards warfare. One of the many seeming oddities of the history of money in medieval Europe, for instance, is the fact that English pennies somehow came to constitute a substantial portion of the medium of exchange in parts of continental Europe in the late thirteenth century; the explanation for this puzzle lies in the fact that Edward I had shipped enormous quantities of these coins to the Low Countries to pay his troops and to subsidize local military allies.[128] History is littered with comparable episodes attesting to the role of war in stimulating monetary circulation.

War has also, we have seen, been the foundation upon which international investment portfolios and international banking dynasties have been erected. European monetary systems had not matured particularly far when already individual states' war financing requirements began to outrun the ability to meet those requirements from local sources alone. The upshot was a mushrooming of cross-border financing, increasingly managed and often underwritten by multi-territorial merchant banks, which ultimately led to proliferating defaults on government bonds from the Early Modern era onwards.[129] J. F. Wright points, in the case of Britain, to just how financially-material warfare could be: "Expensive wars occupied more than half the 65 years after 1750 and increased the nominal British national debt 10-fold, so that by 1815 the debt was about twice the level of national income."[130] And among the various banks whose internationally-derived fortunes were inextricably bound up with international warfare, none stands as prominently as the Rothschilds, who essentially secured their dominance in and through the Napoleonic Wars.[131]

Empire

The third overarching explanation for the long history of international financial integration charted above is very much intertwined with trade and warfare; in fact it was often a means to lubricate the former and typically required the latter for its implementation or maintenance. This was empire, broadly conceived – whether such imperialism comprised (colonial) settlement or not. Here, arguably, given that empire entailed geographical capture and incorporation by its very nature, the stimulus to territorial connectedness in finance was most direct of all: the financial world was integrated, in short, because the *political-economic* world was integrated.

Examples abound of empire providing the immediate structural context for international specie flows, international investment, and international banks. Think, for example, of the Spanish colonies in sixteenth-century Latin America, and of how economic and social life there came to be dominated by European demand for gold and silver.[132] And in a later era, consider the case of the British Empire. As we have already seen, a substantial share of exported British capital was directed to imperial possessions. Indeed, for critics such as Lenin and J. A. Hobson, lending was "considered to be part of the process of founding and maintaining the British Empire."[133] The same Empire was also the backbone of the overseas branch networks of the nineteenth-century British multinational banks, the "size and power" of this empire being identified by Geoffrey Jones as "perhaps the single most important country-specific source of competitive advantage for [those] banks."[134] Throughout history, empire and international finance have gone hand-in-hand.

Modernization

While financial investment across borders clearly has a long history extending back well into the Early Modern era, historians have shown that the scale of international investment flows remained relatively modest until midway through the nineteenth century, from which point such flows transformed into a veritable cascade. This growth was a function in no small part, of course, of it being the age of high imperialism. But such growth was also a function of the other striking feature of nineteenth-century global history, one itself intimately bound up with the development of empire: modernization.

In its twinned industrialization and urbanization dynamics, modernization involved a demand for capital previously only paralleled by warfare, although in this case the demand came from both the public sector and from private companies. With domestic savings rarely sufficient to finance large-scale modernization, and often representing a more expensive option in any event (see below), investment was typically secured overseas – facilitated once again by bankers only too willing to oblige.[135] The period from the 1870s through to the end of the nineteenth century, in particular, saw: a step change in growth in the American economy; the spread of the industrial revolution to new European territories, including Russia and Sweden; and massive (if partial) exercises in the "modernization" of European settler colonies around the world. In all cases, the developments in question would arguably have been impossible in the absence of the internationally-derived investment that largely funded them.

Economics

The fifth and final set of factors that serves to explain the internationalized nature of money, finance and banking through to the 1920s I have elected to group together under the header "economics." This may strike readers as strange, given that I emphasized above that internationalization during the periods in question was explicitly *not* driven by economic doctrine and its active propagation. If not economic "theory," then, what aspects of economics are we concerned with here?

Over the course of the long history narrated above, the open and integrated nature of international finance was increasingly a function not of economic theory but of *economically-driven human practice*. More specifically, various fundamentally *economic* conditions or motivations can be seen to have consistently encouraged the evolution of internationalized rather than nationally-restricted financial constellations. Once again, we have seen this to some extent already, in the shape of simple relations of supply and demand: demand for funds, driven by the costs of war or of social modernization, finding ready supply in some instances only overseas. Some historians, meanwhile, suggest there have been occasions when the reciprocal relation obtains: capital export arising from the lack of domestic outlets for locally-generated surpluses.[136] But beyond basic equations of supply and demand, a host of other economic principles have also variously been in play.

Such principles are ultimately little different from those enshrined in modern asset management: maximizing yields, diversifying portfolio risk, minimizing transaction costs, and so on. The key insight here, however, is that such principles historically found expression in *geographical* strategies as much as anything else. As a host of studies have shown, cross-border investment has long provided plentiful opportunities for creative – although also sometimes massively destructive – portfolio adjustments. Early nineteenth-century European investors, for example, commonly regarded ownership of US securities as an effective means of diversifying their portfolio against country risk, and at little cost in terms of liquidity.[137] Similarly, eighteenth-century Dutch investors had been famously adept at switching funds between geographical markets as real rates of return fluctuated in response to changing tax laws, bond coupons and inflation trends in different territories.[138] In these and other instances, the practical economics of investment predictably favored open international financial markets – and the greater range of options they afforded – over more constrained, nationally-delimited alternatives; and so, of course, it remains the case today.

Thinking About Financial Geography

In this final section of the chapter, my argument will be that financial "globalization" before the Great Depression and the accompanying lurch to financial protectionism in the 1930s can be distinguished from financial "globalization" in the post-1950s era in part through what it lacked: a conspicuous, calculated appeal to economics to validate open markets in money and banking. (As we shall see in Chapters 4 and 5, economic arguments, particularly those relating to questions of productiveness, became an increasingly critical and powerful component of the rhetorical toolkit as Western banks and their government sponsors went about dismantling protectionist foreign borders in the second half of the twentieth century.)

I develop this argument in three stages. First, I suggest that for a number of important reasons, we should not be unduly surprised that there was no such appeal to economic theory or principles in the "first" era of global finance. Second, I specifically consider two conceptual economic models that sometimes *are* assumed to have been put to work discursively in the service of financial internationalism (or, at the very least, to have been *available* for such active mobilization). I show that neither of these two – the "price-specie flow" model and a more generic model of free capital mobility – was actively exploited in such a way, and that the latter did not actually crystallize *as* a formal theory until a much later date. Finally, I demonstrate that to the extent that economic concepts *were* marshaled specifically in relation to the practical political-economy of cross-border capital movements, they were, in fact, all directed *against* open borders; they championed, to one degree or another, financial protectionism as opposed to free capital movements.

Pushing at open doors

That the generally open and integrated nature of international finance and banking up to and including the 1920s was not actively buttressed by the mobilization of supportive economic concepts in the way it came to be in the second half of the twentieth century is, in two important respects, not in the least surprising. For one thing, there was, for much of the long period we have covered here, no such thing as "economics" or "political economy." As we saw in Chapter 1, classical political economy only began to crystallize as a discrete and identifiable discourse in the late eighteenth century. Granted, its primary conceptual forebears, mercantilism and physiocracy, were older, the roots of the former usually being pegged as far back as the early sixteenth century. But that still leaves the entire Middle Ages as an era lacking recognizable economic theory – the selective theorems of isolated voices, such as Aquinas, aside – but characterized, as we have seen, by financial practices, artifacts, and institutions that extended widely and relatively freely across geopolitical boundaries.

Second, and more materially, it is patently the case that for a variety of reasons, supportive economic concepts were not *required* to open up cross-border monetary and financial relations. Often this was a question merely of highly favorable socio-political conditions. In the context, for example, of the colossal and long-standing empires created by the British, Spanish, and other European nations, it was more-or-less axiomatic that unless it was deemed explicitly inadvisable by the relevant authorities, national monies, financial markets and banking institutions could and should also be international ones.

Yet the lack of a need for usable and affirmatory economic concepts was actually a far more generalized condition. Perhaps the single most important conclusion to be gleaned from the long history summarized in the first section of this chapter is that until the dawn of generalized financial protectionism in the twentieth century, money and banks moved freely across borders *unless they were specifically prevented from doing so.* In other words, openness was typically the default state of affairs, not something that had to be actively petitioned for and implemented; the financial world was open because, essentially, it was *not closed*.[139] If we focus here on banks, there is plenty of evidence as to this intrinsic openness, especially for the nineteenth century. Stefano Battilossi reports that foreign bank entry into new markets was "generally unhindered."[140] Geoffrey Jones comes to a similar conclusion. "Receptivity towards foreign banks was high in most areas of the world," he observes, this reflecting the fact that there were "few prudential regulations and no exchange controls in the world economy" and that "home and host country regulatory controls over multinational banks were very limited."[141] Arguments for openness were not needed because the world *was*, for the most part, open.

Needless to say, numerous individual exceptions to this open norm can be pinpointed in various places and at various junctures, from the Early Middle Ages all the way up to the first two decades of the twentieth century. We have encountered some of these exceptions above. But even in these instances, it should be emphasized, there was seemingly still no material need for economic arguments geared to disabling the border obstacles that were confronted. To understand why this was so, we need to recognize three important factors.

First, where there actually existed a will to put in place capital controls of one variety or another, the policing of such controls was another matter entirely. Certainly, until well into the nineteenth century, it tended to be the case that restrictions on the cross-border movement of money, in particular, were readily circumvented. The result was that most attempts rigorously to enforce border restrictions were essentially failures. "A local authority that might have wished to make money dear or plentiful," R. B. Zevin observes, "was thwarted by direct and effective financial openness."[142] In the absence of a critical mass of successful, enduring exercises in cross-border capital control, a pressing requirement to argue conceptually against such controls simply did not materialize.

Second, the obstacles periodically encountered at national borders, while perhaps militating against an open and integrated market in money or banking, were often not in fact the work of the authorities who presided over those political borders. When, for example, American banks first sought to break into the market for Chinese railroad financing in the first decade of the twentieth century, the difficulties they faced comprised not so much Chinese resistance to foreign capital, but what Jeffry Frieden refers to as "the European monopoly of Chinese finances."[143] It was a question of incumbent external-banker power rather than formal, domestically-created barriers to entry. Such idiosyncratic political obstacles were not susceptible to, and thus did not call for, a generalist, economically-oriented argument in favor of open borders.

Lastly, and most significantly, where those financial sector participants favoring open and integrated international monetary and banking markets encountered national spaces displaying some degree of closure, *other* methods of prising open those spaces tended to be sufficient. Here, the same example – that of US banks seeking entry to the early twentieth-century Chinese market – is again illuminating. When, in 1911, the first Chinese loan with US bank participation (alongside British, French, German, Russian, and Japanese banks) was signed, it was avowedly the result of what was at this time coming to be called "dollar diplomacy" – that is, "the simultaneous foreign expansion," in Frieden's words, "of American financial and political power"; or, in Karl Polanyi's rather more vivid phraseology, "the steel lining to the velvet glove of finance."[144] It was US government-backed negotiations with European banking rivals, together with a "threatening telegram" from President Taft to the Chinese regent, that ultimately did the trick. British, French, and German overseas banks also worked closely with their own respective foreign ministries, in similar political-financial market-entry initiatives, between 1890 and 1914.[145] With such initiatives bearing fruit, there was little practical need at the time for a "neutral" economic rationalization for open borders.

This, of course, is not to suggest that such overt "dollar diplomacy" exercises were *absent* from the portfolio of methods employed to open up international banking markets from the 1960s onwards, which are addressed later in the book. They were not. The difference, however, is that such exercises later came to be actively and explicitly layered, uniquely, with what was marketed as the objective economic "sense" of open markets.

Absent ideas and ideas absent application

The propagation of such "sense" did not figure, I maintain, in the formal scaffolding of globalized finance prior to the Great Depression. And yet: it has elsewhere been argued, or at least implied, that two closely-related conceptual economic models *were* material in fostering financial internationalism in the nineteenth century in particular. It is important therefore briefly to consider each of these "models," if only to understand how and why this (mis)conception might have arisen, and to demonstrate that it is indeed a misconception.

The first such model is the so-called "price-specie flow" model of international trade. The early elaboration of this model is generally attributed to two eighteenth-century writers: Isaac Gervaise, who published *The System or Theory of the Trade of the World* in 1720; and, more famously, David Hume, in his paper "Of the balance of trade" first published in 1752.[146] The basic premise of this model, in these early forms, was that in a theoretical scenario featuring gold as means of international payments and either gold itself, or tokens fully convertible into gold, as each nation's currency, the free flow of gold across borders would allow for a self-correcting system whereby trade imbalances "automatically" balanced out, hence helping to maintain stable exchange rates. To simplify, trade imbalances would stimulate specie flows to fund those imbalances; these flows, by impacting national money supplies, would cause inflation or deflation; and these price effects would, in turn, correct the trade imbalances that provoked the initial specie shipments. It was an elegant model, and at its core sat the assumption of the gold standard; it was a "gold standard model."

The elaboration of this model in the eighteenth century has led to the suggestion that such a gold standard *theory* ultimately contributed directly to the spread and maintenance of the gold standard in *practice*. Such a proposition is arguably most closely associated with Karl Polanyi. Polanyi's *The Great Transformation* placed the gold standard at the very center of the nineteenth-century "utopian endeavour of economic liberalism to set up a self-regulating market system."[147] But more pointedly, as Fred Block has noted, Polanyi regarded the gold standard as "an extraordinary *intellectual* achievement" based on "the *theory* of self-regulating markets."[148] He writes extensively and forcefully about an "unshakeable belief," particularly in England, "in the automatic steering mechanism of the gold standard." He believed, in other words, that the gold standard monetary framework that ultimately came to envelop most of the world by the end of the nineteenth century was intellectually-driven and theoretically-derived. And he was also in no doubt that such derivation was actively and deliberately managed. He was definitively opposed to the notion that any aspect of laissez-faire political economy reflected some sort of "natural" development; it always represented, rather, "purposeful action."[149]

Polanyi was clearly right to posit the gold standard as a central pillar of late nineteenth-century free-marketism. He is, moreover, brilliant when eviscerating the rampant contradictions of the gold standard in operation (not least "the ruinous effects of abrupt changes in the price level necessitated by the maintenance of stable exchanges") or when detailing the reasons for and course of the gold standard's ultimate dissolution.[150] But on the question of how the gold standard actually came to be adopted as a real, material constellation of political-economic regulations and practices, he is notably weak. "Purposeful action" is, on this particular count, implied but nowhere illuminated, either for England – the first country, as we saw above, to move onto gold – or for other countries. Polanyi envisioned the gold standard as an intellectual achievement, but did not once refer to the price-specie flow model or to the work of Gervaise or Hume on such matters. And, by the time that, on Polanyi's telling, the gold standard first emerged as a key tenet of economic liberalism in England (the mid-1820s), England had in fact already been on a de facto gold standard for over a century.[151]

More important than these quibbles, however, is the fact that an extensive body of scholarship on the gold standard, researched and written since Polanyi's day, has shown that the staggered adoption of the gold standard was not driven by and based upon the economic theory of Gervaise, Hume or anybody else; and nor, indeed, does it seem to have resulted in many instances from "purposeful action" (of the kind that Polanyi depicts) on the part of those nations already on gold. In England, its adoption has been characterized as essentially "accidental," effectively occurring in 1717 "when Sir Isaac Newton, as master of the mint, set too low a gold price for silver, inadvertently causing all but very worn and clipped silver coin to disappear from circulation."[152] Elsewhere, the introduction of the gold standard is perhaps best conceptualized as an increasingly practical expedient of the international commercial environment, though certainly wars and colonial rule provided enhanced *opportunities* to move to gold in some important cases.[153] Given England's increasing dominance of both trade and finance during the nineteenth century, the rationale for *not* switching to gold became progressively weaker and weaker, and as other individually important commercial nations took the decision to switch – first Portugal, then Germany – the network externalities of the gold standard became stronger and stronger.[154] There being little or no evidence of, for instance, English lobbying of major European nations, the consensus thus seems to be that the international gold standard cohered largely as the result of the "unilateral," albeit not independent, "actions of individual governments."[155] It was not purposefully driven, and *certainly* not by economic wisdom.

The price-specie flow model was, at its core, an argument about mechanisms of adjustment in international trade balances. In the sense that capital mobility was a key assumption of the model, it (the model) was based *on* capital mobility; but it was not a model *of* capital mobility. It is often suggested, however, that such a model did later emerge in a more generic form: a model of free trade in money and finance, to complement the model of free trade in goods that is most closely associated with Adam Smith and David Ricardo. Today, quite clearly, the two do very frequently go hand-in-hand, or at least are positioned that way. And it is often presumed that they did likewise in the late eighteenth and the nineteenth centuries – that liberal economics as developed by Smith and Ricardo advocated the free movement of capital across borders.[156] But did it? And, if so, was such a model part of a conceptual undergirding of nineteenth-century internationalized finance and banking?

The answers to these questions are, respectively, no and no. Let us consider Smith first. Smith actually wrote nothing to suggest he actively supported open trade in money across international borders. Indeed, the Humean price-specie flow model that assumed such freedom of movement was itself entirely absent from *The Wealth of Nations*, a fact once labeled one of "the mysteries of the history of economic thought."[157] More broadly, it is extremely telling that modern free trade proponents, who of course frequently invoke Smithian arguments, "despair," in the words of the American libertarian Murray Rothbard, "of [Smith's] confused and scattered, as well as hopelessly inadequate, theory of money and theory of international monetary relations."[158] This was, quite simply, not one of Smith's main areas of focus.

Also, and of critical importance in the context of this book, Smith's arguments on free trade in goods – which *were* of course brought to bear in the domain of nineteenth-century national and international political-economic relations – were very much arguments *about goods.*[159] This can hardly be emphasized enough. As we shall see in Chapter 5, Smithian and Ricardian free trade theory would come to be actively appropriated and reworked in the late twentieth century by Western advocates of transnational banking and of unrestricted international trade in financial *services.* But for Smith, "positive" free trade was clearly about goods, *not* (also) services. If one reads closely his most impassioned championing of free trade, in the first chapter of Book IV of *Wealth*, it is strikingly evident that his arguments concerned the outputs of what he saw as economically *productive* activities. He talks at length about the relationship between free trade and improvements in the "productive powers of labour." Given Smith's famous views on what types of labor and economic activity were productive (Chapter 1), that those activities whose outputs should be freely tradable across borders did not include banking scarcely required spelling out.

Ricardo, as we know, subscribed to the exact same position on productive and unproductive labor and the question of where the boundary between them should be drawn. Yet what about money, and specifically the question of its cross-border mobility? Here, we encounter an even more fascinating set of issues than with Smith. For, not only did Ricardo not support the free movement of capital. But his celebrated theory of comparative advantage, which provided the conceptual basis for his own – and so much later – international free trade advocacy, actually *depended upon* the presumption of a certain degree of cross-border capital *immobility*. As he explained in his *Principles*, precisely "the difficulty with which capital moves from one country to another" explains why the mechanism of comparative advantage – the mutually-beneficial exchange of exports of different products according to the differential levels of productivity with which they are produced in different places – "*could not take place between the individuals of the same country,*" where capital moves so much more freely.[160] Free trade in capital would, by implication, undermine the very conditions necessary for mutually-beneficial free trade in commodities.[161] And for what it is worth, Ricardo rejected Hume's price-specie flow model as well.[162]

Hence, in sum, we can conclude firstly that neither Smith nor Ricardo argued in favor of free capital movements. It is not unimaginable, of course, that their contemporaries could have adulterated their ideas on free commodity trade, and mobilized them in the service of open international monetary systems – just as, I suggested above, those ideas would later be put to work, in tainted form, by twentieth-century protagonists of open international banking markets. But there is no evidence that this was the case, in respect either of the gold standard or any other aspect of financial internationalism.[163] As I have already emphasized, money, finance, and banking, prior to the twentieth century, were open and integrated largely by default; they did not need to be *made* that way. The second half of the twentieth century, as we will see later on, would present an entirely different set of circumstances. And it was only then, as Jagdish Bhagwati has argued, that "the idea and the ideology of free trade and its benefits" *would* come to be "hijacked" not only by the champions of open international markets in financial services but also, to the degree that their identity differed, "by the proponents of capital mobility."[164]

Minded to protect

To conclude this chapter, I will demonstrate relatively briefly that where economists developed prescriptive arguments concerning money, finance, and geopolitical boundaries in the centuries preceding World War I, such arguments were much more commonly geared to opposing, rather than supporting, open borders. I will also show that this bias was especially pronounced when it comes to the more specific matter of such "theory" being actively mobilized in the policy sphere: only economic thinking that was anti-deregulation, or *for* capital controls, was materially applied to real-world questions of actual financial coordination. My objective here is not to provide a comprehensive overview of such protectionist thought, but simply to indicate some of its most common forms.

We can begin with the eighteenth century, for immediately we encounter some of the same figures discussed just above, including most notably David Hume and Adam Smith. If Smith neglected Hume's price-specie flow model, the two were united – despite Hume's belief in the positive balance-of-payments effects of free money movement – on another aspect of cross-border finance that exercised many eighteenth-century economic thinkers. This was the question of the existence, as discussed in the first section of this chapter, of significant foreign holdings of British national debt, particularly (though not exclusively) among Dutch nationals. Smith discussed this issue in *The Wealth of Nations*, and Hume did so in his famous 1752 essay "Of public credit." "As foreigners possess a great share of our national funds," Hume worried, along similar lines as Smith did later, "they render the [English] public, in a manner, tributary to them."[165] Even more vociferous in his concerns, meanwhile, was James Steuart.[166]

The concerns voiced by such critics were essentially of two kinds, and it is important and productive, for reasons that will shortly become apparent, to treat these separately. One worry was that foreign holders of the national debt were somehow more capricious than their domestic equivalents, and that they were therefore likely to be less committed to their investment; they were, put bluntly, deemed less reliable. This, as Jeremy Bentham remarked, fueled concern – not shared by Bentham himself, it must be said – that "money borrowed of foreigners will be perpetually liable to be recalled," with destabilizing implications.[167]

The second, very different worry, again noted by Bentham (and again critically), was simply that interest paid to foreign debt holders was "so much money sent out of the country."[168] It was money "lost." The reason for highlighting this concern separately is twofold. First, while this was part of Steuart's critique, it was definitively *not* part of Smith's. Second, it expressed quite precisely a much wider and much more longstanding concern regarding open financial borders and integrated financial markets in general. This was the belief, widely regarded by economic historians as a hallmark of mercantilist economic thought, that any net loss of money from a country represented a destruction of national wealth.

We have already come across mercantilism in Chapter 1, where we saw that mercantilist economists – who included James Steuart, but not Hume or Smith – believed that wealth consisted primarily of precious metals and that running a positive balance of trade thus increased wealth since it implied greater inflows than outflows of bullion- or coin-based payments. What we did not see in Chapter 1, however, was the fact that mercantilism existed historically as *a set of policies* as well as being a set of theoretical economic doctrines. It is this fusing of theory and practice that is of utmost relevance here – for mercantilism was *the* primary example, in pre-twentieth century history, of international monetary relations being materially shaped by *ideas* about money and its geographical economics.

Mercantilism dominated European economic thinking from the early sixteenth century essentially up until the time of Adam Smith. Its most direct and substantive physical expression was protectionist trade and monetary policies, which were pursued in a number of different countries, but perhaps most famously in England and in France. In view of the preoccupation with levels of precious metal reserves, exports of gold and silver were, for varying periods of time, prohibited, albeit (as discussed above) with varying levels of success. And because it was believed that consistent wealth creation required a surplus of commodity exports over imports, the latter were discouraged in various ways, the imposition of tariffs being the most common. Where imports were deemed absolutely necessary, merchants were encouraged as far as possible to exchange domestic goods for them instead of paying with money.

When the principles of mercantilism were steadily picked apart in the late eighteenth century by, in particular, Smith, the shift in economic thought associated with this dismantling represented, William Shaw would later argue, "a revolution of theory." Shaw noted that alongside this "revolution," meanwhile, there took place (merely) "a *change* of fact and practice" in the sphere of actual economic structures and flows.[169] It is, I think, worth reflecting briefly on the particular terms Shaw used here, for in the realm specifically of *monetary* theory and reality one is appropriate but the other, it seems to me, is not.

"Fact and practice" indeed did not revolutionize; they *did* merely change, and then not particularly profoundly. National monetary protectionism, as we saw early in this chapter, had never been as widespread, effective or durable as mercantilist thinkers would have liked. When Smith published *The Wealth of Nations*, moreover, it had been more than 20 years since the French had abolished restrictions on commerce in money (and more than a century since England had done so). The monetary and financial world was, and had long been, broadly open and integrated; no "revolution" was required to free it from a suppositional mercantilist vice.

But, *contra* Shaw, the "theory" of money and finance did not really revolutionize either. If it had, we would find in Smith the kind of ardent advocacy of free capital movement that is sometimes now imputed to him, but which in reality *Wealth* conspicuously lacks. To be sure, Smith refuted mercantilist monetary theory, and stridently; but he did not install an oppositional monetary model in its place; he remained much more ambiguous than that. And this, surely, is not altogether surprising, at least not if one thinks about the nature of the world in which Smith was thinking and writing. (Economic theorization does not occur in a social vacuum; the theories that economists bequeath to us, like economists themselves, are creatures of their times.) Protectionism in commodity trade was alive-and-well, so here was something real and tangible to think about and argue against, as Smith clearly did. By contrast, protectionism in monetary policy was effectively history, and had never been extensive or debilitating; there was, therefore, no existing, live "problem" – no systematic capital controls – in relation to which a theory of the imperative of open money and banking markets could gain traction and hence cohere. In this respect, we shall see in Part II, the mid-twentieth century would present a wholly different set of circumstances.

Notes

1   A. Ferguson, *An Essay on the History of Civil Society*, 8th edition, A. Finley, Philadelphia, 1819 [1767], pp.221–222.
2   S. Battilossi, "Financial innovation and the golden ages of international banking: 1890–1931 and 1958–81," *Financial History Review*, 7, 2000, pp.141–175.
3   The key texts include E. Helleiner, *States and the Reemergence of Global Finance: From Bretton Woods to the 1990s*, Cornell University Press, Ithaca, 1994; B. Eichengreen, *Globalizing Capital: A History of the International Monetary System*, 2nd edition, Princeton University Press, Princeton, 2008; and R. Abdelal, *Capital Rules: The Construction of Global Finance*, Harvard University Press, Cambridge MA, 2007.
4   R. Lopez, "The dollar of the Middle Ages," *The Journal of Economic History*, 11, 1951, pp.209–234. On this sub-period see also C. Cipolla, *Money, Prices and Civilization in the Mediterranean World: Fifth to Seventeenth Century*, Princeton University Press, Princeton, 1956, and J. Porteous, *Coins in History*, Weidenfeld & Nicolson, London, 1969, pp.14–33.
5   P. Spufford, *Money and Its Use in Medieval Europe*, Cambridge University Press, Cambridge, 1989; the quotations are from pp.27,33. "Frankia" refers to the Frankish Empire that, at its peak in the ninth century, covered the bulk of what is now Western Europe – the British Isles, Iberia, southern Italy and Scandinavia excluded.
6   B. Cohen, *The Geography of Money*, Cornell University Press, Ithaca, 1998, p.28.
7   Spufford, *Money and Its Use*, p.87.
8   D. Graeber, *Debt: The First 5,000 Years*, Melville House Publishing, Brooklyn, 2011. The quotation is from p.74.
9   Ibid, p.338.
10 G. Arrighi, *The Long Twentieth Century: Money, Power, and the Origins of Our Times*, Verso, London, 2010, pp.97,115.
11 Spufford, *Money and Its Use*, p.101.
12 J. Day, *Money and Finance in the Age of Merchant Capitalism*, Blackwell, Oxford, 1999, p.17.
13 N. Mayhew, *Coinage in France from the Dark Ages to Napoleon*, B. A. Seaby, London, 1988, p.61.
14 H. Miskimin, *The Economy of Early Renaissance Europe 1300–1460*, Prentice-Hall, Englewood Cliffs, 1969, p.139.
15 Spufford, *Money and Its Use*, p.373.
16 R. de Roover, *Money, Banking and Credit in Mediaeval Bruges*, The Mediaeval Academy of America, Cambridge MA, 1948, pp.185, 237.
17 F. Lane, "Exportations vénitiennes d'or et d'argent de 1200 à 1450," in J. Day (ed), *Études d'histoire monétaires* (PUL, Lille, 29–48).
18 While this was a financial innovation for the *European* world, comparable debt instruments are believed to have circulated earlier in China (by around the year 800) and *much* earlier in Mesopotamia (in the Bronze Age). See Graeber, *Debt*, pp.214, 269 respectively.
19 De Roover, *Money, Banking and Credit*, p.49. Over time, such bills also became vehicles of speculation, particularly with the rise of "negotiability" – a concept explained in the following paragraph of the main text. For an excellent discussion, see A. Kessler, *A Revolution in Commerce: The Parisian Merchant Court and the Rise of Commercial Society in Eighteenth-century France*, Yale University Press, New Haven, 2007, chapter 5.

20 R. de Roover, *The Rise and Decline Of The Medici Bank, 1397–1494*, Harvard University Press, Cambridge MA, 1963; Day, *Money and Finance*.

21 O. Cox, *Foundations of Capitalism*, Philosophical Library, New York, 1959, p.164.

22 Day, *Money and Finance*, p.11.

23 Arrighi, *Long Twentieth Century*, p.106.

24 De Roover, *Rise and Decline*, pp.279–357.

25 M. Veseth, *Mountains of Debt: Crisis and Change in Renaissance Florence, Postwar Britain, and Postwar America*, Oxford University Press, New York, 1991, p.7. See also J-C Hocquet, "City-state and market economy," in R. Bonney (ed), *Economic Systems and State Finance* (Clarendon Press, Oxford, 1995, 81–100).

26 N. Ferguson, *The Ascent of Money: A Financial History of the World*, Penguin, London, 2008, p.73.

27 M-T. Boyer-Xambeu, G. Deleplace and L. Gillard, *Private Money and Public Currencies: The Sixteenth Century Challenge*, M. E. Sharpe, Armonk NY, 1994, p.105.

28 W. Shaw, *The History of Currency, 1252 to 1894*, Wilsons & Milne, London, 1896, p.162.

29 C. Boix, *Democracy and Redistribution*, Cambridge University Press, Cambridge, 2003, p.227.

30 E. Coppieters, *English Bank Note Circulation, 1694–1954*, Louvain Institute of Economic and Social Research, Hague, 1955.

31 The best synthesis on contemporary trends in government debt origination across Western Europe is provided by M. Körner, "Public credit," in Bonney (ed), *Economic Systems and State Finance* (507–538), at pp.515–532.

32 R. Bonney, "Introduction," in his (ed), *The Rise of the Fiscal State in Europe c.1200–1815* (Clarendon Press, Oxford, 1999, 1–18), p.12. Cf. M. t'Hart, "The emergence and consolidation of the tax state," in Bonney (ed), *Economic Systems and State Finance* (261–294), who writes (p.286): "In the sixteenth century, few states contracted long-term debts, though certain of the city-states, and Spain, were the earliest and most notable exceptions. Yet by the end of the seventeenth century, almost all states were permanently in debt."

33 J. de Vries and A. van der Woude, *The First Modern Economy: Success, Failure, and Perseverance of the Dutch Economy, 1500–1815*, Cambridge University Press, Cambridge, 1997, pp.113–129. In fact L. Neal, "How it all began: the monetary and financial architecture of Europe during the first global capital markets, 1648–1815," *Financial History Review*, 7, 2000, pp.117–140, at pp.122–123, argues that there was in reality no such thing in the Netherlands during this era as "a truly national debt backed by a national taxing authority," since public debt instruments were invariably issued by particular provinces.

34 J. Conklin, "The theory of sovereign debt and Spain under Philip II," *Journal of Political Economy*, 106, 1998, pp.483–513; J. Gelabert, "Castile, 1504–1808," in Bonney (ed), *The Rise of the Fiscal State* (201–242).

35 E. Hamilton, "Origin and growth of the national debt in Western Europe," *American Economic Review*, 37, 1947, pp.118–130; D. Stasavage, *Public Debt and the Birth of the Democratic State: France and Great Britain 1688–1789*, Cambridge University Press, Cambridge, 2008.

36 Neal, "How it all began"; the quotation is from p.133. See also E. Schubert, "The ties that bound: market behavior in foreign exchange in Western Europe during the eighteenth century," Unpublished PhD thesis, University of Illinois at Urbana-Champaign, 1986.

37 S. Chapman, *The Rise of Merchant Banking*, Routledge, London, 2005, pp.2–3; de Vries and van der Woude, *The First Modern Economy*, pp.141–144.

38 Stasavage, *Public Debt*, chapter 3.

39 E. Kerridge, *Trade and Banking in Early Modern England*, Manchester University Press, Manchester, 1991, p.3.

40 P. Dickson, *The Financial Revolution in England: A Study in the Development of Public Credit, 1688–1756*, Macmillan, London, 1967, remains the landmark account. See also, among countless others: P. O'Brien and P. Hunt, "England, 1485–1815," in Bonney (ed), *The Rise of the Fiscal State* (53–100); J. Brewer, *The Sinews of Power: War, Money and the English State, 1688–1783*, Harvard University Press, Cambridge MA, 1990, chapter 4; and Stasavage, *Public Debt*.

41 The government's long-term debt took two main forms in this period (the first half of the eighteenth century). One was loans from joint-stock companies, of which the Bank of England was one (see the following paragraph in the main text). The other was general public loans, including annuities and lottery tickets.

42 J. Wright, "The contribution of overseas savings to the funded national debt of Great Britain, 1750–1815," *The Economic History Review*, 50, 1997, pp.657–671.

43 http://www.bankofengland.co.uk/about/legislation/1694charter.pdf (retrieved December 2010).

44 J. Sinclair, *The History of the Public Revenue of the British Empire, Volume 3*, Cadell and Davies, London, 1804, appendix V.

45 L. Neal, "Efficient markets in the eighteenth century? The Amsterdam and London Stock Exchanges," *Business and Economic History*, 11, 1982, pp.81–100, at p.82.

46 G. Dempster, J. Wells and D. Wills, "A common-features analysis of Amsterdam and London financial markets during the eighteenth century," *Economic Inquiry*, 38, 2000, pp.19–33, at p.20.

47 See A. Carter, *Getting, Spending and Investing in Early Modern Times: Essays on Dutch, English and Huguenot Economic History*, Van Gorcum, Assem, 1975; Neal, "Efficient markets"; and Schubert, "The ties that bound."

48 W. Scott, *The Constitution and Finance Of English, Scottish and Irish Joint-Stock Companies to 1720, vol. 3*, Cambridge University Press, Cambridge, 1912, p.327.

49 P. Mirowski, "The rise (and retreat) of a market," *Journal of Economic History*, 41, 1981, pp.559–577, at p.562.

50 D. Landes, *The Unbound Prometheus: Technical Change and Industrial Development in Western Europe from 1750 to Present*, Cambridge University Press, Cambridge, 1969, p.168.

51 See especially, on this relationship, two insightful, though unpublished papers by Meir Kohn: "Early deposit banking," Working Paper 99–03, 1999, Department of Economics, Dartmouth College, and "Payments and the development of finance," Working Paper 01–15, 2001, Department of Economics, Dartmouth College.

52 M. Körner, "Protestant banking," in Y. Cassis and P. Cottrell (eds), *The World of Private Banking* (Ashgate, Farnham, 2009, 231–246), p.231.

53 J. Strieder, *Jacob Fugger the Rich: Merchant and Banker of Augsburg, 1459–1525*, Adelphi, New York, 1931, p.104.

54 See especially Körner, "Protestant banking."

55 Ibid, p.246.

56 H. Bauer and W. Blackman, *Swiss Banking: An Analytical History*, Palgrave Macmillan, Basingstoke, 1998, p.51.

57 Chapman, *The Rise of Merchant Banking*, p.3. Cf. Körner, "Public credit," p.534: "Whether it be the French *Banque protestante* in association with the *international huguenote* centred in French-speaking Switzerland, Frankfurt, Hamburg, Amsterdam and London, or the network of Portuguese Jews active in Bordeaux, London and Hamburg, or again the spider's web of the *Banque catholique* dominated by Italians, the world of international finance was controlled by groups of banking houses connected to each other by the affinities peculiar to social, economic, professional and confessional minorities, which developed exceptional strength thanks to their cohesion, their internationalism, and their personal and family ties."

58 Kohn, "Early deposit banking," p.4.

59 Kerridge, *Trade and Banking*, p.4.

60 Arrighi, *Long Twentieth Century*, p.135.

61 There are many excellent discussions of this bank, its history, and its role, not least Adam Smith's famous "digression" in Book IV of *The Wealth of Nations*. I found the brief but careful analysis by P. Dehing and M. t'Hart, "Linking the fortunes: currency and banking, 1550–1800", in M. t'Hart, J. Jonker and J. van Zanden (eds), *A Financial History of the Netherlands* (Cambridge University Press, Cambridge, 1997, 37–63), at pp.45–51, especially helpful, and this is my main source here, together with S. Quinn and W. Roberds, "An economic explanation of the early Bank of Amsterdam, debasement, bills of exchange, and the emergence of the first central bank," Working Paper 2006–13, Federal Reserve Bank of Atlanta, September 2006.

62 On the Bank of Amsterdam's "perfection" of the negotiability of bills of exchange, see the illuminating discussion in L. Neal, *The Rise of Financial Capitalism: International Capital Markets in the Age of Reason*, Cambridge University Press, Cambridge, 1990, pp.4–8.

63 M. Flandreau, C. Galimard, C. Jobst and P. Nogués-Marco, "The bell-jar: commercial interest rates between two revolutions," in J. Atack and L. Neal (eds), *The Origins and Development of Financial Markets and Institutions: From the Seventeenth Century to the Present* (Cambridge University Press, Cambridge, 2009, 161–208), make a similar argument for bills of exchange more generically in this era, suggesting that the market for such bills "had a global scope because it was collateralized by commodities with an international circulation" (p.162).

64 The key text here is Neal, *The Rise of Financial Capitalism*. See also, more recently, Atack and Neal (eds), *Origins and Development*.

65 Dehing and 't Hart, "Linking the fortunes," pp.51–61.

66 On the latter, see O. Gelderblom and J. Jonker, "With a view to hold: the emergence of institutional investors on the Amsterdam securities market during the 17th and 18th centuries," in Atack and Neal (eds), *Origins and Development* (71–98).

67 See especially A. Murphy, *The Origins of English Financial Markets: Investment and Speculation before the South Sea Bubble*, Cambridge University Press, Cambridge, 2009.

68 Dempster et al., "Common-features"; Neal, "Efficient markets"; Schubert, "The ties that bound."

69 This paragraph draws mainly on Schubert, "The ties that bound," and Neal, "How it all began."

70 See also R. Bonney, "The eighteenth century II: the struggle for great power status and the end of the old fiscal regime," in his (ed), *Economic Systems and State Finance* (315–390).

71 E. Helleiner, *The Making of National Money: Territorial Currencies in Historical Perspective*, Cornell University Press, Ithaca, 2002.

72 See Cohen, *Geography*, pp.33–34.

73 M. Flandreau and C. Jobst, "The ties that divide: a network analysis of the international monetary system, 1890–1910," *The Journal of Economic History*, 65, 2005, pp.977–1007.

74 The quotation is from Cohen, *Geography*, p.31; the statistic from Eichengreen, *Globalizing Capital*, pp.22–23.

75 "Nothing was more crucial to British financial superiority. The pound in those years was as good as gold." P. Cottrell, "Great Britain: the international markets, 1918–1939," in G. Feldman, U. Olssen, M. Bordo and Y. Cassis (eds), *The Evolution of Modern Financial Institutions in the Twentieth Century* (Università Bocconi, Milan, 1994), p.27. Indeed such was the close connection between the gold standard and sterling's superiority that historians have sometimes referred to the former as the "sterling standard."

76 K. Polanyi, *The Great Transformation: The Political and Economic Origins of Our Time*, Beacon Press, Boston, 2001 [1944].

77 Eichengreen, *Globalizing Capital*, p.11.

78 Ibid., pp.6–42.

79 M. Bordo and H. Rockoff, "The gold standard as a 'Good Housekeeping seal of approval'," *Journal of Economic History*, 56, 1996, pp.389–428.

80 G. Gallarotti, *The Anatomy of an International Monetary Regime: The Classical Gold Standard 1880–1914*, Oxford University Press, New York, 1995. Though *not*, I hasten to add, without the need for nation-state intervention in international economic flows more widely: as Polanyi showed, one of the many ironies of the gold standard's broad adoption was that it led to an *increase* in the national use of protective tariffs for manufactured and agricultural goods. On the myriad wider disjunctures between the "theory" of the gold standard (as an automatically self-regulating monetary system) and its actual political-economic reality, see the excellent B. Eichengreen and M. Flandreau (eds), *The Gold Standard in Theory and History*, Routledge, New York, 1985.

81 See, in particular, R. Goldsmith, *Comparative National Balance Sheets: A Study of Twenty Countries, 1688–1978*, University of Chicago Press, Chicago, 1985; R. Zevin, "Are world financial markets more open? If so, why and with what effects?," in T. Banuri and J. Shor (eds), *Financial Openness and National Autonomy* (Oxford University Press, Oxford, 1992, 43–84); J. Lothian, "Financial integration over the past three centuries," *Bancaria*, 9, 2001, pp.82–88; R. Baldwin and P. Martin, "Two waves of globalization: superficial similarities, fundamental differences," NBER Working Paper no.6904, 1999; M. Schularick, "A tale of two 'globalizations': capital flows from rich to poor in two eras of global finance," *International Journal of Finance and Economics*, 11, 2006, pp.339–354; M. Bordo, B. Eichengreen and J. Kim, "Was there really an earlier period of international financial integration comparable to today?," in S. Lee (ed), *The Implications of Globalization of World Financial Markets* (Bank of Korea, Seoul, 1998, 27–82).

82 Körner, "Public credit," p.533.

83 Ferguson, *Ascent*, p.81.

84 Data extracted from M. Wilkins, *The History of Foreign Investment in the United States, 1914–1945*, Harvard University Press, Cambridge MA, 2004; R. Sylla, J. Wilson and R. Wright, "Integration of trans-Atlantic capital markets, 1790–1845," *Review of Finance*, 10, 2006, pp.613–644; and J. Frieden, *Banking on the World: The Politics of American International Finance*, Harper & Row, New York, 1987.

85 Schularick, "A tale," pp.342–343. See also M. Obstfeld and A. Taylor, "Globalization and capital markets," in M. Bordo, A. Taylor and J. Williamson (eds), *Globalization*

in Historical Perspective (University of Chicago Press, Chicago, 2003, 121–183), and I. Stone, *The Global Export of Capital from Great Britain, 1865–1914: A Statistical Survey*, St. Martin's Press, New York, 1999.

86   Carter, *Getting, Spending and Investing*, p.43.

87   A. Cairncross, *Home and Foreign Investment, 1870–1913: Studies in Capital Accumulation*, Cambridge University Press, Cambridge, 1953, p.2.

88   L. Davis and R. Gallman, *Evolving Financial Markets and International Capital Flows: Britain, the Americas, and Australia, 1865–1914*, Cambridge University Press, Cambridge, 2011, p.5; L. Davis and R. Huttenback, *Mammon and the Pursuit of Empire: The Political Economy of British Imperialism, 1860–1912*, Cambridge University Press, Cambridge, 2009, p.46.

89   Davis and Gallman, *Evolving Financial Markets*, p.5.

90   J. Keynes, *The Economic Consequences of the Peace* (Macmillan, London, 1919), as reprinted with an introduction by R. Lekachman, Penguin, Harmondsworth, 1988, p.10.

91   R. Tilly, "International aspects of the development of German banking," in R. Cameron and V. Bovykin (eds), *International Banking, 1870–1914* (Oxford University Press, Oxford, 1991, 90–112), p.90.

92   A. Fishlow, "Lessons from the past: capital markets during the 19th century and the interwar period," *International Organization*, 39, 1985, pp.383–439.

93   B. Stallings, *Banker to the Third World: U.S. Portfolio Investment in Latin America, 1900–1986*, University of California Press, Berkeley, 1992, pp.58–59.

94   Ibid; Frieden, *Banking*, pp.16–19. On the nature, extent and geography of British investment in Latin America before 1914, see I. Stone, "British direct and portfolio investment in Latin America before 1914," *Journal of Economic History*, 37, 1977, pp.690–722.

95   Frieden, *Banking*, pp.25–40.

96   Y. Park and J. Zwick, *International Banking in Theory and Practice*, Addison-Wesley, Reading MA, 1985, p.4.

97   The literature on these two banks is large, but Chapman, *The Rise of Merchant Banking*, pp.16–38, provides a good introductory overview. On the Rothschilds, see N. Ferguson, *The World's Banker: The History of the House of Rothschild*, Weidenfeld & Nicolson, London, 1998; on Barings, P. Austin, *Baring Brothers and the Birth of Modern Finance*, Pickering & Chatto, London, 2007.

98   R. Cameron, "Introduction," in Cameron and Bovykin (eds), *International Banking* (3–21).

99   M. Flandreau and J. Flores, "Bonds and brands: foundations of sovereign debt markets, 1820–1830," *Journal of Economic History*, 69, 2009, pp.646–684.

100   G. Jones, "Introduction," in his (ed), *Multinational and International Banking* (Edward Elgar, Cheltenham, 1992).

101   Ferguson, *Ascent*, p.83.

102   V. Carosso and R. Sylla, "US banks in international finance," in Cameron and Bovykin (eds), *International Banking* (48–71); M. Wilkins, "Foreign banks and foreign investment in the United States," in Cameron and Bovykin (eds), *International Banking* (232–253), and "Banks over borders: some evidence from their pre-1914 history," in G. Jones (ed), *Banks as Multinationals* (Routledge, London, 1990, 217–247).

103   Polanyi, *Great Transformation*, p.10, original emphasis.

104   A. Baster, *The Imperial Banks*, P. S. King, London, 1929, and *The International Banks*, P. S. King, London, 1935. Note that the other main category of British bank in this era – the clearing bank – did not attempt to develop any sort of

international activity or presence in this period, only doing so later, in between the two world wars.

105 Jones, "Introduction," p.xiii.

106 Cottrell, "Great Britain." For more detailed discussions see, among other examples, D. Merrett, "Paradise lost? British banks in Australia," in Jones (ed), *Banks as Multinationals* (62–84), I. Drummond, "Banks and banking in Canada and Australia," in Cameron and Bovykin (eds), *International Banking* (189–213), and J. McGuire, "The imperial impact on the globalization of Indian finance prior to the First World War: the role of the British colonial exchange banks," in A. Bagchi and G. Dymski (eds), *Capture and Exclude: Developing Economies and the Poor in Global Finance* (Tulika Books, New Delhi, 2007, 85–114).

107 G. Jones, *British Multinational Banking, 1830–1990*, Clarendon Press, Oxford, 1995, p.61.

108 Tilly, "International aspects," pp.108–109.

109 Carosso and Sylla, "US banks."

110 E. Perkins, "Managing a dollar-sterling exchange account: Brown, Shipley and Co. in the 1850s," *Business History*, 16, 1974, pp.48–64.

111 G. Jones, "Banks as multinationals," in his (ed), *Banks as Multinationals* (1–13).

112 Tilly, "International aspects," p.109; see also P. Hertner, "German banks abroad before 1914," in Jones (ed), *Banks as Multinationals* (99–119).

113 Carosso and Sylla, "US banks"; C. Kobrak, *Banking on Global Markets: Deutsche Bank and the United States, 1870 to the Present*, Cambridge University Press, Cambridge, 2007.

114 F. Bonin, "The case of French banks," in Cameron and Bovykin (eds), *International Banking* (72–89).

115 Respectively: R. Aliber, "International banking: a survey," *Journal of Money, Credit and Banking*, 16, 1984, pp.661–712; Jones, *British Multinational Banking*, p.102.

116 H. Cleveland and T. Huertas, *Citibank 1812–1970*, Harvard University Press, Cambridge MA, 1985.

117 Park and Zwick, *International Banking*, p.5. One other country to begin developing a more substantial overseas banking presence in the same period as US firms – that is, from 1900–1930 – was Italy. See R. Di Quirico, "The initial phases of Italian banks' expansion abroad, 1900–31," *Financial History Review*, 6, 1999, pp.7–24.

118 Jones, "Banks as multinationals," p.3. For similar observations, see also Battilossi, "Financial innovation."

119 E.g. Spufford, *Money and Its Use*; De Roover, *Money, Banking and Credit*.

120 See especially Cairncross, *Home and Foreign Investment*, pp.209–221.

121 E.g. C. Kindleberger, "International banks as leaders or followers of international business: An historical perspective," *Journal of Banking and Finance*, 7, 1983, pp.583–595, at pp.585–586; though Zevin, "Are world financial markets more open?," among others, disputes the importance of technology.

122 G. Dwyer and J. Lothian, "The economics of international monies," FRB of Atlanta Working Paper No. 2003–37, December 2003, p.19.

123 Spufford, *Money and Its Use*, p.157.

124 Shaw, *History*, p.161.

125 Kindleberger, "International banks," p.583.

126 Battilossi, "Financial innovation," pp.147–148.

127 Tilly, "International aspects."

128 Spufford, *Money and Its Use*, pp.162, 390.

129　Perhaps the most comprehensive study of such defaults is Christian Suter's work on the external public debt of "peripheral" states from 1820 onwards, *Debt Cycles in the World-economy: Foreign Loans, Financial Crises, and Debt Settlements, 1820–1990*, Westview Press, Boulder, 1992.

130　Wright, "Contribution," p.657.

131　Ferguson, *World's Banker*. While bankers thus often had a vested interest in war, one of the great insights of Polanyi's *Great Transformation* is that they also – paradoxically – gained substantially, over the long term, from peace. The following sentence (p.16) distils this paradox perfectly: "Every war, almost, was organized by financiers; but peace also was organized by them."

132　A. MacEwan, *Debt and Disorder: International Economic Instability and U.S. Imperial Decline*, Monthly Review Press, New York, 1990, chapter 3.

133　Stallings, *Banker*, p.37.

134　Jones, *British Multinational Banking*, p.103.

135　Kindleberger, "International banks," pp.586–587.

136　On this argument, see the helpful discussion in Stallings, *Banker*, pp.20–27.

137　Sylla et al., "Integration," p.7.

138　Dempster et al., "Common-features," p.21; Dehing and 't Hart, "Linking the fortunes," pp.56–58.

139　"At the time these arrangements," Rawi Abdelal concurs, simply "seemed natural." *Capital Rules*, p.5.

140　Battilossi, "Financial innovation," p.147.

141　Jones, *British Multinational Banking*, p.103.

142　Zevin, "Are world financial markets more open?," p.46.

143　Frieden, *Banking*, p.23.

144　Ibid, p.22; Polanyi, *Great Transformation*, p.14.

145　E.g. Jones, *British Multinational Banking*, pp.130–134. Polanyi puts it like this: "There was intimate contact between finance and diplomacy; neither would con- sider any long-range plan, whether peaceful or warlike, without making sure of the other's goodwill." *Great Transformation*, p.10.

146　I. Gervaise, *The System or Theory of the Trade of the World*, Woodfall, London, 1720; D. Hume, "Of the balance of trade," in his *Political Discourses* (Kincaid and Donaldson, Edinburgh, 1752, 79–100). Among the many economic historians who pinpoint these two as the key model developers, see especially J. Letiche, "Isaac Gervaise on the international mechanism of adjustment," *Journal of Political Econ- omy*, 60, 1952, pp.34–43, and D. Fausten, "The Humean origin of the contemporary approach to the balance of payments," *Quarterly Journal of Economics*, 93, 1979, pp.655–673.

147　Polanyi, *Great Transformation*, p.31.

148　F. Block, "Introduction," in K. Polanyi, *The Great Transformation: The Political and Economic Origins of Our Time* (Beacon Press, Boston, 2001 [1944], xviii-xxxviii), p.xxx, emphasis added.

149　Polanyi, *Great Transformation*, pp.144, 148.

150　Ibid, p.208.

151　Eichengreen, *Globalizing Capital*, p.6.

152　Ibid, p.6.

153　See, for instance A. Bagchi, "Global financial integration – I: The overlooked historical context of the current period," in Bagchi and Dymski (eds), *Capture and Exclude* (3–20), at pp.6–8.

154 The clearest and most influential articulation of this argument is in Eichengreen, *Globalizing Capital*, pp.6–42.

155 B. Eichengreen and M. Flandreau, "Editors' introduction," in their (eds), *Gold Standard* (1–30), p.6.

156 E.g. K. Vandevelde, "The political economy of a bilateral investment treaty," *American Journal of International Law*, 92, 1998, pp.621–641, at p.624. This belief is a longstanding one. In the aftermath of World War II, when capital controls were being formally integrated into the governance architecture of international finance, it was frequently asserted that the *new* economic wisdom underpinning such an approach – on which see Chapter 3, below – contrasted explicitly with the wisdom of the leading nineteenth-century political economists. The US economist Arthur Bloomfield, "Postwar control of international capital movements," *American Economic Review*, 36, 1946, pp.687–709, at p.687, put it this way in 1946: "Unfettered freedom of individuals to transfer funds across national boundaries ... has long been a hallowed dogma of traditional economic thought, and in this respect the present-day enthusiasm among economists for exchange control over capital movements represents a sharp break with past orthodoxy." As I proceed to explain now, I disagree with this reading.

157 J. Viner, *Studies in the Theory of International Trade*, Allen and Unwin, London, 1937, p.87.

158 M. Rothbard, *Economic Thought Before Adam Smith*, Edward Elgar, Cheltenham, 1995, p.461.

159 The mobilization of Smith's work in this area is most often discussed in relation to opposition to the English Corn Laws, which, between 1815 and 1846, imposed tariffs on imported grain. But as Bernard Semmel, *The Rise of Free Trade Imperialism: Classical Political Economy, the Empire of Free Trade and Imperialism 1750–1850*, Cambridge University Press, Cambridge, 2004, has demonstrated, Smith's arguments in favor of free trade were also put to work by proponents of British imperial expansion.

160 D. Ricardo, *On the Principles of Political Economy, and Taxation*, 3rd edition, John Murray, London, 1821, p.141, original emphasis.

161 This aspect of Ricardo's formulation is scandalously under-recognized. R. Went, "Globalization in the perspective of imperialism," *Science & Society*, 66, 2002–3, pp.473–497, at p.485n10, is one of very few to note it. Another, more obliquely, is Jerry Mander, "Intrinsic negative effects of economic globalization on the environment," in J. Speth (ed), *Worlds Apart: Globalization and the Environment* (Island Press, Washington, 2003, 109–130), p.113, who observes that "free trade in money ... defies traditional free trade ideology as espoused by the late economic gurus Adam Smith and David Ricardo." And cf. R. Unger, *Free Trade Reimagined: The World Division of Labor and the Method of Economics*, Princeton University Press, Princeton, 2007, p.66.

162 H. Grubel, "Ricardo and Thornton on the transfer mechanism," *Quarterly Journal of Economics*, 75, 1961, pp.292–301, at p.296.

163 Indeed as late as the 1930s, as E. Helleiner, "When finance was servant: International capital movements in the Bretton Woods order," in P. Cerny (ed), *Finance and World Politics: Markets, Regimes, and States in the Post-Hegemonic Era* (Edward Elgar, Aldershot, 1993, 20–48), p.29, has argued, the idea of "free finance" had still not achieved "the same sacred status" as that of "free trade," and even among those who believed in the "absolute benefits" of free capital mobility – not least the American

Harry White, a key figure in Chapter 3 – "there was a widespread feeling that the classical case in favor of free trade was less relevant to the financial sector."

164   J. Bhagwati, "The capital myth: the difference between trade in widgets and dollars," *Foreign Affairs*, 77(3), 1998, pp.7–12, at p.11.

165   D. Hume, "Of public credit," in his *Writings on Economics* (ed. E. Rotwein, Transaction Publishers, New Brunswick, 2007, 90–107), p.96. Smith's arguments are in "Of public debts," in Chapter 3 of Book V of *The Wealth of Nations*.

166   Steuart, "Of public credit," part 4 of Book IV of *An Inquiry Into the Principles of Political Economy*.

167   J. Bentham, "Defence of usury," in *Jeremy Bentham's Economic Writings*, vol. 1 (ed. W. Stark, Allen and Unwin, London, 1952), p.200.

168   Ibid, p.199.

169   Shaw, *History*, p.161; emphasis added.

Part II

Worlds Aligned

From the Great Depression to the Eve of the Big Bang

3

Enclosing the Unproductive

> Bertrand Russell is credited with having said that mathematics is the science in which you do not know what you are talking about nor whether what you say is true. Does this not apply to national accounts too?
>
> Georges Als (1988)[1]

In the 1920s, and then with an even greater intensity of force and effect in the 1930s, the world of international money and banking shrunk back from its previously open and integrated configuration to become, in short order, a collection of largely self-contained financial islands. It would remain thus through to at least the end of the 1950s. Only from the beginning of the 1960s did the accordion begin to de-compress, and global finance and banking begin the long and uneven process of disassembling the territorial borders that had been erected during the preceding 30 to 40 years.

The period of assembly and defense of these financial borders provides the immediate historical backdrop to this chapter. Its objective, however, is not simply to offer a narrative of key events, or, more ambitiously, to offer explanations as to why things happened the way they did. Plenty of fine existing studies cover both of these bases, and I draw on them extensively here. My task, rather, is to trace the evolving relationship between developments in financial boundary construction and developments in economic ideas *about* such boundaries – particularly insofar as those ideas also pertained to another type of boundary, namely that which separated economic "productiveness" from unproductiveness. This relationship, I argue, became increasingly close and increasingly material during the period in question; and it is a relationship to which the existing literature on historical geographies of finance and banking does not do justice.

Banking Across Boundaries: Placing Finance in Capitalism, First Edition. Brett Christophers.
© 2013 John Wiley & Sons, Ltd. Published 2013 by John Wiley & Sons, Ltd.

The essential thrust of the argument can be summarized as follows. When the financial world fractured spatially beginning in World War I, it did so reactively and pragmatically; this was a retrenchment driven by immediate, pressing political-economic exigencies, not one occurring in response to the formulation, mobilization, and application of economic ideas. Yet, critically, in the 1930s and 1940s, various socio-technical apparatuses of economic representation came to suggest that this protectionism in finance and banking, if not originally based *on* economic theory, was nonetheless economically right and proper; and they did so specifically through recuperation of nineteenth-century political economy's productive/unproductive dichotomy, albeit with the "labour" epithet now conspicuously dropped. This recuperation took two forms. First, and as previously noted by a handful of economic historians, there arose a conceptual distinction between productive and unproductive flows of capital. This distinction, moreover, was invoked not only to justify a posteriori the inter-state capital controls that already existed in the inter-war period, but also – and arguably more importantly – to rationalize a priori the selective maintenance of such controls in the post-war period. The second form of recuperation of the productive-unproductive distinction, meanwhile, occurred in relation to economically-active institutions and the products or services they offered. The primary setting for this recuperation was the new calculative practice of national accounting, which was predicated upon the envisioning of a "production boundary" dividing productive activities from unproductive ones. The common determination, in the early days of national accounts, that banking was economically unproductive, fitted with the prevailing protectionist world even if it did not actively underwrite it. And in all of this, I show, the figure of John Maynard Keynes loomed especially large. For it was in his writing, his policy interventions, and his shaping of emergent systems of statistical representation that a melding of the twin arguments about productiveness – of capital flows and of banks – both with one another, and in turn with arguments about financial internationalization, began to achieve their clearest expression.

Given the various interconnected dimensions of this argument, I lay it out here in a series of stages. The first part of the chapter looks, in overview, at the raw facts of what happened in international finance and banking from the 1920s through to the 1950s. The basic story, as indicated, is one of national banking and monetary systems turning in on themselves. There was, however, a stuttering nature to this process of enclosure – assorted capital controls imposed during or immediately after World War I were in many cases lifted in the mid- to late 1920s, before being reinstalled in the following decade – and the types of boundaries implanted varied considerably across both time and space. Relying on the extensive secondary literature on such matters, I draw out the main developments and the explanations that have been posited for these.

The second section examines the first of the ways in which a distinction between economic productiveness and unproductiveness was pictured and, more pointedly, was yoked to the question of financial protectionism. Here the narrative turns to the middle part of the period in question, and specifically to the Bretton Woods conference of 1944, where the key decisions were made which would lead to the creation of a post-war monetary and financial architecture with capital controls still woven into its fabric. Keynes was one protagonist. Others, of equal or perhaps even more importance in the context of the Bretton Woods negotiations and decisions themselves, were the Americans Henry Morgenthau and Harry White. Again, with this part of the story having already been rehearsed, at least in part, elsewhere, my analysis is a relatively summary one.

A fuller analysis follows in the third part of the chapter, whose subject is the birth, in the US and various parts of Europe in the 1930s and 1940s, of systematic, government-sponsored attempts to create economic accounts for nation-states. I show that a division between productive and unproductive economic activities, which had been central to classical political economy but theoretically dismissed by the ascendant neoclassicism of the early twentieth century, was fundamental to the generation of these accounts – and especially to the one method of calculating national economic output (the "output" or "product" method) that allowed the relative contributions of different industry sectors to this output to be confidently measured. I discuss the political, economic, and intellectual contexts in which the birth of national accounting occurred, for these were not immaterial. And I explain why, with national accounts having since become, over time, a crucial tool for the demonstration of economic and social worth, a critical understanding of the "production boundary" that traverses such accounts is so important.

The last two sections of the chapter address the more specific question of the place of financial services in general, and banking in particular, in the differentiations effected and the representations generated by national accounts. To distill this question to its pure essence, which side of the production boundary did banks sit on? The answer to this question, we shall see, has been multi-dimensional and manifestly problematic ever since the time of its initial posing in the national accounting context in the 1930s. Section four closely considers the nature of the question and the nature of the problems it elicited. These problems are reducible, in large part, to the fact that if banking services and revenues were treated in the national accounts in the same way as other companies' services and revenues, the accounts would show banks as being only negligibly positive contributors to national economic output or, more likely, as negative contributors – or unproductive "leeches" on the income stream, as one national income statistician would later, famously, put it. My discussion focuses on how and why this "problem" arose and on why – for it is not necessarily self-evident – this *was* generally (though certainly not always) regarded as a problem.

The final section of the chapter analyzes the different responses to this "problem" in selected countries, by those countries' national income statisticians. For, in the early days of national accounting, international harmonization of accounting standards was limited and many different methods were employed, *particularly* vis-à-vis the thorny question of accounting for banks. I focus on the response in what were arguably Europe's three major economic powers in the early- to mid-twentieth century, and certainly the three, crucially, with the most developed national and international banking industries prior to the onset of World War I: France, Germany, and the UK. The response, as we shall see, was subtly but substantively different in each place, yet in none, at least initially, did the national accounts envision banks as economically productive (and nor would they in France or the UK for several decades). The importance of this withholding of productiveness, in the prevailing context of protectionist national banking and finance systems, is the main subject of concern in this section. I then conclude the chapter with a brief segueway to Chapter 4, since the latter will shift our focus to the single major economic power of the day whose national accounts *did* show banking as a productive economic sector, and it will argue that the identity of this country should come as no surprise: it being the country which had the greatest immediate capacity to re-internationalize its banking sector, which had financial institutions agitating already for open international financial markets in the 1940s, which was the lightest user of capital controls internationally in the late 1940s and the 1950s, and whose banks would indeed become in the 1960s the first actually to re-colonize foreign markets. This, of course, was the United States.

The Retreat to the Nation

How and why did the first "golden age" of international banking and finance come to such a comprehensive end in the 20 years following the outbreak of World War I? That the formerly open and integrated world financial system – and, with it, the highly internationalized banking sectors of countries such as the UK – did splinter dramatically in those two decades, and then remain largely fragmented through to the end of the 1950s, is a matter of historical record. After around 15 years of inter-territorial monetary boundaries being laid down sporadically, unevenly, sometimes only temporarily, but ultimately generically and durably, international financial markets were, as Eric Helleiner writes, "almost completely absent from the international economy during the three decades that followed the financial crisis of 1931."[2] Much the same can be said of the financial institutions that populated and coordinated those international monetary and financial markets. "For more than 30 years, from the Great Depression until the late 1950s," write Yoon Park and Jack Zwick, "international banking was in a state of hibernation."[3]

Before examining the various key stages of the process of enclosure, we can usefully offer an overall answer to the question of how and why such enclosure occurred. Here, as in the narration of the discrete episodes and events which follow, I am indebted primarily to the clear analysis provided by Barry Eichengreen.[4] His account shows that the period in question saw a profound process of inter-penetration of economics and socio-politics, whereby major national governments increasingly came to recalibrate economic and monetary policy in response to shifting social and political objectives. This marked an important change from the pre-war gold-standard era, in which central banks and treasuries were typically more able to focus on the "technical" demands of currency stability and gold convertibility. Following World War I, however, specifically domestic policy objectives, relating to issues such as growth and employment, became considerably more important, and these could often be pursued through a re-targeted monetary policy. Crucially,

Eichengreen argues, the free international capital mobility that had tended to support central banks' agendas before the war (for example, relieving the pressure to defend weak exchange rates) tended to militate *against* the agendas which those banks adopted in the war's wake.

Three main stages can be isolated in the shift from the integrated international financial architecture of the pre-war era to the fragmented and boundary-riven architecture of the 1930s through 1950s. The first began with the outbreak of war in 1914, and ran through to the mid-1920s. War itself was the critical catalyst. With stocks of gold needed to fund war efforts, controls on its export were soon imposed. Next, although certainly not everywhere, came controls on transactions in foreign currency, and then a rolling back of the gold-standard statutes requiring governments to back currency with the metal (the governments in question now issuing fiat money instead). "Fixed exchange rates, international commerce, and cross-border investment," Rawi Abdelal summarizes, all "collapsed."[5] The early 1920s was thus a period of floating exchange rates. As Eichengreen observes, these would, in time, come to be highlighted as the reason for a sudden increase in the middle years of the decade in seemingly speculative international "hot money" flows – or flows of what would later be labeled "unproductive" capital – pursuant to governments lifting the war-time restrictions on international gold and capital transactions.

The second phase that can be extracted from Eichengreen's narrative comprises the few short years to the end of the decade. This saw the resurrection of the gold standard, allied, in some countries, with currency reform. Yet, with the domestic growth and employment objectives mentioned earlier now to the fore, the inter-war gold standard system was much more fragile than its storied forebear, and when it was disturbed "financial capital that had once flowed in stabilizing directions took flight": mainly, until 1928, to the US, despite the latter's increasingly positive balance of payments.[6]

It was, of course, worldwide depression in the 1930s that initiated the third and last stage of financial fragmentation, decisively hammering a final nail in the coffin of the "golden age" international financial system which the inter-war gold standard had tried with limited success to reproduce. The dominoes fell rapidly and dramatically. First, gold convertibility was suspended in primary-producing countries such as Argentina and Uruguay. Second, the crisis spread to Europe – declining demand, falling prices, and rising real levels of debt triggering banking crises, the suspension of convertibility and the imposition of exchange controls in Austria and Germany in 1931. Third, and in the act which for Eichengreen "symbolized the interwar gold standard's disintegration," Britain, too, was forced to suspend convertibility, after interest rate rises failed to halt capital outflows.[7] Fourth, and finally, the US followed suit in 1933, amidst deep depression and widespread bank failure. By the middle of the decade, what had two decades earlier been a world of massive, cheap and unhindered cross-border capital movements had become a world of financial protectionism in which money was essentially confined to national circulation except insofar as it explicitly funded commodity trade. Even the latter, however, was limited in scale, since goods tariffs and import quotas were widely mobilized to battle the effects of competitive currency depreciations.

The implications of these changes for cross-border banking are not hard to fathom. As boundaries were drawn and policed between countries' money and capital markets, and increasingly also their commodities markets, so international banks' raison d'être was essentially suppressed; such banks had originally developed, we can recall from Chapter 2, to manage and profit precisely from the growing economic connections between those markets. Granted, banks could still, in theory, profit from operating abroad on an effectively independent basis. But the lack of credible synergies with domestic banking businesses was the least of the factors disfavoring such stand-alone foreign operations. With control of national monies and finances regarded as paramount by politicians, and with the events of the early 1930s having ravaged the banking systems of so many countries, the domestic political and social climate was nowhere especially conducive to foreign bank maintenance or, still less, incursion. Equally, just as there was little in the way of actual cross-border capital flow for banks profitably to lubricate, so it was apparent to such banks that there was little if any international appetite for such flows to recommence. There was, therefore, no compelling reason to establish or in some cases even maintain foreign "placeholder" operations, ready for the time when free capital mobility again prevailed. As a result, the international banking business was rapidly rendered "practically dormant."[8] It would remain thus until the very end of the 1950s.

The principal insight we need to digest from this capsule history of the quarter-century beginning in 1914 is, in the present context, as follows. International finance and banking were transformed, in general, into national finance and banking. The global financial world became much less open, and significantly more fragmented. The drivers of these developments were the enormous disruptions in national *and* international politics *and* economics represented by war and depression. Governments – and in turn, financial institutions – responded to these disruptions by taking the actions outlined here. These were deliberate and thoughtful but not thought-*driven* actions; the actions were, quite clearly, event-driven. Capital mobility had to be restrained because it *manifestly* undermined firstly war financing, and later the domestic growth and employment agendas which materialized in the shadow of war. Yet if financial enclosure in this period did not emerge out of economic ideas about capital mobility or immobility, such ideas did now begin to coalesce, particularly around the perceived undesirability of the aforementioned flows of "hot money"; and these new ideas *would* contribute materially, we shall now see, to the reproduction of financial enclosure in the aftermath of the next Great War.

Bretton Woods and the Properties of Mobile Capital

The capital controls put in place in the early 1930s remained firmly in place as the 1930s came to a close and World War II drew near. The war, unsurprisingly, served merely to reinforce them. But long before this war ended, the major Allied powers, and the US and UK in particular, began contemplating and actively discussing prospects for a post-war monetary and financial order. Two common concerns characterized these contemplations and discussions. First, there was a consensus that whatever policies were to be implemented in regard to cross-border capital mobility, cross-border commodity mobility – in other words, trade in goods – needed somehow to be boosted. Second, with the disruptive impacts of floating exchange rates in both the 1930s and the early 1920s still fresh in the mind, a regime of fixed exchange rates was deemed highly preferable. These discussions culminated in the famous United Nations monetary and financial conference held in Bretton Woods, New Hampshire in July 1944, where the 44 attending nations mapped out the primary contours of the post-war order.

In this section, a single key feature of the Bretton Woods deliberations and decisions will be emphasized.[9] This is the fact that not only were economic ideas about cross-border capital mobility actively mobilized, but these ideas explicitly recuperated the productive/unproductive dualism which we discussed at length in Chapter 1. On this occasion, it was specifically flows of capital across borders that were deemed to be productive or not, and which therefore merited encouragement or circumscription accordingly. The argument that there existed such things as unproductive capital movements ultimately came to underpin and legitimate the post-war use of capital controls; such controls were to be used to thwart those unproductive movements, *and unproductive movements alone*. While various authors have remarked upon this appeal to the language of economic productiveness, the conceptualization itself has not received close attention, nor therefore been considered in its relation either to historical conceptual antecedents or to contemporary conceptual parallels.[10] Both, in my view, are important tasks.

But if ideas around productive and non-productive capital movements were brought to bear (and we shall shortly see exactly how they were), whose ideas were these? Most accounts of Bretton Woods, and of the capital controls which it legitimated, rightly cite John Maynard Keynes as one of the main intellectual inspirations. He was, after all, Britain's chief spokesman at the conference. He also, quite clearly, favored capital controls and actively lobbied for a post-war order featuring their use.

Moreover, Keynes had, in 1933, written a famous article in *The Yale Review*, quoted as if not more frequently today as in Keynes's own era, in which he explicitly excluded finance from the list of things – "ideas, knowledge, science, hospitality, travel" – "which should of their nature be international." Indeed, he even suggested, in heresy of heresies, that *manufactured goods* should be "homespun" where "reasonably and conveniently possible." But this latter was almost an aside; his central thrust was self-evident in his insistence that, "above all, let finance be primarily national." National circumscription of finance was not "an ideal in itself" but rather would, Keynes averred, provide two potential benefits. First, and most directly, it would assist in "the creation of an environment in which other ideals" – such as, perhaps most notably, full employment – "can be safely and conveniently pursued." ("Available domestic policies," he wrote earlier in the same piece, and in a reference to the "hot money" flows of the 1920s mentioned above, "might often be easier to compass, if the phenomenon known as 'the flight of capital' could be ruled out.") Second, Keynes thought, financial protectionism might better help deliver the international peace that "the age of economic internationalism" had so palpably and painfully failed to sustain.[11]

Was the Keynes of this 1933 article, then, the intellectual bedrock of Bretton Woods and of the distinction between productive and unproductive capital flows which molded the resulting guidance on use of capital controls? Indeed, was this article representative of Keynes's writings and statements more broadly, and over an extended period – of a Keynes consistently opposed both to those so-called "flights of capital" and, à la Ricardo, to the famous price-specie flow model of the eighteenth century?

A wider reading of Keynes shows that it actually was not, and for this and other reasons we need to caveat somewhat the importance of Keynes's thinking – if not his on-the ground negotiating work – specifically for the Bretton Woods capital controls policies. First of all, by the time that Bretton Woods came around a decade later Keynes had, Louis Pauly suggests, moved away from his earlier (i.e. 1933) view that internationalism of finance was *not* necessary "of its nature."[12] Also, and looking backwards in time as opposed to forwards, the 1933 position contrasted markedly with what Keynes had said even in the relatively recent past in regards to "hot money" flows of "speculative" foreign exchange transactions. His *Tract on Monetary Reform* (1923) had, as Michael Lawlor relates, "denigrated naïve attacks on foreign exchange speculation as demagoguery and superstition." In fact as late as 1930, with the full experiences of the 1920s to read from, Keynes still saw such speculation as a predominantly stabilizing force.[13]

This vacillation in Keynes's thinking is certainly one reason to be careful of overstating his intellectual influence at Bretton Woods with regards to the specific issue of capital mobility. There is, however, another one, which is arguably just as if not more important. What I want to suggest here is that if we conceive of Keynes as a critic of "finance" in terms of its commoditized materialities – as a *thing*, that is to say, and one with characteristic movements and mobilities – we risk making a categorical mistake. For, if we read him closely, including in the 1933 piece on financial protectionism, it is clear that financial instruments and motions are not really his targets. His primary objects of concern, as they had been for the classical political economists, tended rather to be *institutions* – the institutions of capitalism, which in the case of finance meant the institutions of financial capitalism, or banks. The two phenomena are, to be sure, connected: one cannot have financial institutions without money and financial instruments; and a critique of the former is hard to imagine without a critique, at some level, of the latter. But it is also the case that the two are not coterminous. Keynes oriented his critique more towards financiers than finance, and for this reason, among others, we will deal with him in more detail later in the chapter when our analysis shifts from the question of capital flows to that of capitalist companies.

None of the above, I hasten to add, is intended to diminish Keynes's broad intellectual influence on many of the participants at Bretton Woods, nor his tangible contributions there as a negotiator, nor indeed his in situ support for post-war capital controls. But his support for such controls does not appear to have been theoretically-based. It was more ad hoc, and pragmatic; he thought the state should be able to impose controls, as Pauly states, "as and when it perceived the need to arise," which in practice of course meant when more important political-economic objectives galvanized such a need.[14] The need was *not* conceptually-ordained, and certainly not the product of a perceived meaningful distinction between "unproductive" and "productive" capital flows.[15]

If not the Englishman Keynes, therefore, who was responsible for the marshaling of a discourse of "productiveness" in relation to capital flows, which came then to shape the decisions taken at Bretton Woods? To answer this question, we need to look across the Atlantic, specifically to the persona of Harry Dexter White. An economist with degrees from Stanford and Harvard, White worked at the US Treasury Department from 1934, eventually taking charge of all of its international affairs. White was the Treasury's most important figure in terms of both its preparatory groundwork for Bretton Woods and its on-the-ground negotiating team at the conference itself.

White essentially believed, contra Keynes circa 1933, that finance *should* "of its nature" be international – but that there were, potentially, limited exceptions to this general economic rule. According to this way of thinking, the use of inter-state capital controls should only ever be contemplated in exceptional circumstances. Such controls should definitely not be the generalized feature they had been in the 1930s. Yet on what conceptual grounds did White base this argument? It was here that the question of productiveness entered the equation: the boundary between the productive and the unproductive was the means of distinguishing the norm from the exception. Capital in motion, including across borders, was in White's view characteristically and normally "productive," and it was this productiveness that therefore warranted free trade in money. For capital movements to be unproductive was to *be* exceptional.

So it was, then, that in drafting the US Treasury's proposal in 1943 for what would become, post-Bretton Woods, the International Monetary Fund, White included the following undertakings among those which member countries would be required to commit to: "Not to enter upon any new bilateral clearing arrangements, nor engage in multiple currency practices, which in the judgment of the Fund would retard the growth of world trade or the international flow of productive capital." The Fund itself, meanwhile, was expected to "create conditions under which the smooth flow of foreign trade and of productive capital among the member countries will be fostered."[16] The word "productive" was, Pauly argues, "carefully chosen," and was "generally understood" to distinguish normal capital flows specifically from "speculative" and thus unproductive ones.[17]

The productive/unproductive categorization of capital flows introduced by White powerfully guided the discussions which took place in the months leading up to the Bretton Woods conference, the negotiations at the conference itself, and the decisions made during the latter – especially the eventual agreement that states *should* have capital controls at their unilateral disposal to choke off unproductive capital movements, but that controls were indeed not to be a universal and standardized component of the post-war order and specifically should not serve to inhibit capital flows tied to trade in goods. In his foreword to the "Joint statement by [international] experts" issued just two-and-a-half months prior to Bretton Woods, Henry Morgenthau, Secretary of the US Treasury and president of the July conference, had identified "the revival of international investment for productive purposes" as one of the principal objectives of the would-be Fund, thus reaffirming the proposal authored by White and signaling – unambiguously – that from America's perspective, at least, a basic commitment to "productive" capital mobility was a sine qua non of any future consensual international financial architecture.[18] Furthermore, as Abdelal in particular has demonstrated, *ongoing* debate about capital mobility in the years following Bretton Woods, within not only the IMF but also the EC and the OECD, would remain animated by the productive/unproductive dualism, with the continued availability of capital controls relying on a continued belief in the undesirability of speculative "hot money" – as opposed to "productive" – capital flows.[19]

Yet we should be cautious about pushing this argument too far. Conceptual economic ideas *were* mobilized to inform and shape capital account-related economic policy at Bretton Woods and in its aftermath, but such policy remained highly pragmatic. It was certainly *more* considered, measured and conceptually-grounded than the instinctual and reactive international monetary policymaking which characterized the period from 1915 to the early 1940s. This was not, however, theory-led policy; the theory was invoked, rather, to lend conceptual credibility to policies ultimately mandated by politics – in this case, the politics of interventionist welfare states, especially those in Western Europe, demanding policy autonomy and stable exchange rates.[20] As Matthew Watson has argued, therefore, "it would be a mistake to over-intellectualise the issue and to claim that the mood of the times was simply due to the power of ideas."[21]

We should also take especially careful note of the way in which the US, through White, framed the issue. Yes, the theoretical existence of unproductive capital flows was posited as justifying the selective use of capital controls. But the argument was always "productive" (normal, essential, irremissible) first, "unproductive" (exceptional) second – and almost a token allowance. A line, in a sense, was being drawn in the sand, and in more ways than one. Whilst the central argument from out of America was that capital mobility was *normally* productive, Keynes, notwithstanding his vacillation on such matters, never presented a case for "productive" capital flows as such. Indeed, as Helleiner notes, Keynes, and the Bank of England alongside him, had "strongly opposed" White's use specifically of the words "productive capital."[22] This is significant because, as we shall see in the following chapter and in later sections of this one, a similar bifurcation of perspectives between the US and the UK was also occurring at around the same time in regard to the envisioning of the productiveness – or otherwise – not of financial flows but of financial institutions.

For now, the important point is simply to recognize the materiality, before, at and after Bretton Woods, of White's ideas and wording, the notion of the "unproductive" validating protectionism where states chose to enforce it. But as well as being material and, as Pauly suggests, "carefully chosen," I want to suggest in concluding this section that White's words were also deeply ironic. White, along with his colleagues in the US Treasury, was a neoclassical economist by training. Yet neoclassicism, we saw at the end of Chapter 1, had supposedly banished the language of productiveness and unproductiveness, at least insofar as such language pertained to economics. So what was going on here? White's appeal to this language is indicative of what I will go on to argue, in greater depth, had *actually* happened – which is that neoclassicism had in reality simply shifted the locus of the productive/unproductive dichotomy, while making it implicit rather than explicit. Precisely because neoclassicism had failed truly to eradicate this dichotomy, but had instead merely buried it just beneath the surface of its market diagrammatics, the dichotomy in question was always liable to bubble up in different places in the shape of exactly the kind of irony apparent here. And such ironic emergence would turn out to be even more palpable, important and enduring in the domain of economic representation to which we turn now.

The Birth of National Accounting and the Rebirth of Economic Productiveness

At the same time as White was formulating his proposals for the IMF, other economists and statisticians were working on a set of entirely different questions, but where the "solutions" provided would also come to depend squarely on a productive/unproductive differentiation. These questions concerned the creation of economic accounts for nation-states. If White's categorization shaped ongoing debate in one important area of international economic policy, the differentiation between productiveness and unproductiveness introduced in the national accounting context would ultimately have a much more broadly-based pertinence to the evolution of post-war capitalism at large – and in particular to how such evolution would come to be analyzed, envisioned, and managed.

The practices and products of national accounting feature centrally throughout the remainder of this book. National accounts are the calculative and representative apparatus dedicated to the formulation and publication of statistics designed to capture the overall level and composition of the economic activity of a nation-state. Foremost among these statistical measures are the headline numbers for national income and output, including most recognizably gross domestic product (GDP) and gross national product (GNP). As Helen Boss, among many others, has pointed out, the question of what constitutes wealth *production* sits at the very core of the national accounting framework, since the aim of these accounts is to measure output, and output is, quite simply, "what designated producers produce."[23]

But this "definition" of output begs, of course, a very obvious and immediate question: who is a "producer" and who is not, and how may we distinguish between them? If this question sounds familiar, then so it should, for this of course was precisely the question that Thomas Malthus had argued sat at the very core of political economy, and to which, as we saw in Chapter 1, so many different answers were provided by the likes of the Mercantilists, the Physiocrats, and later Adam Smith and his successors. National accounting rediscovered this question. Where eighteenth- and nineteenth-century political economists chose to differentiate productive from unproductive *labor*, however, and where Harry White latterly conceptualized productive and unproductive capital *flows*, twentieth-century national accounting would refer instead to productive and unproductive activities and "outputs," and thus to the productiveness or unproductiveness of the industries or sectors which offered these.[24]

In order to enable differentiation *between* productiveness and unproductiveness, national accounting introduced the pivotal notion of a "production boundary." Any activity or institution deemed to sit on the "right" side of this boundary was considered economically productive; anything placed on the other side was not. As such, and as we shall see in practice in what follows, economic "productiveness," as represented in national accounts, can be made and remade in two different ways: either by moving an activity across the production boundary, or by changing the terms of placement of the production boundary itself.

This brief introduction to national accounting and its reliance on the concept of a production boundary begins to hint at why much of the rest of this book is taken up with its metrics and machinations. But let us make its materiality as clear as possible as quickly as possible. The Western world has become increasingly preoccupied over the past half-century with questions of worth, or value, and in particular with questions of *economic* worth or value; indeed, what Michel Callon and Koray Çalışkan have called the "economization" of society has advanced to such an extent that the former (value per se) is very often reduced to the latter (economic value).[25] Moreover, our preoccupation with economic worth has become almost an obsession where the more specific matter of *measuring* such worth quantitatively is concerned. And this, of course, is where national accounting and measures such as GDP come into their own. Because they provide measures of economic output, and *especially* because they enable different industries' or sectors' relative contributions to output to be quantified – "this sector represents half of our national economy, that sector only a quarter," and so forth – the national accounts have come to represent a perfect vehicle for the ongoing enactment of our obsession. As I demonstrated in the introduction, we draw upon GDP data repeatedly and religiously to prove an activity's economic and, thus, broader social worth. Indeed, the authority that such mobilization accords to GDP data explains precisely why the former French President Nikolas Sarkozy focused explicitly on this metric in his underappreciated critique of both our "cult of figures" and the "cult of the market" that infuses it.[26]

Before moving on to consider the particular circumstances of national accounting's origins, and the question of how measures such as GDP are generated by national accountants, one more key point needs emphasizing. This is that the national accounts are not *only* a principal vehicle for the performance of our obsession with economic worth. They also, to some degree, created this obsession in the first place – or at least allowed it to materialize and to take the form it ultimately did. It may seem strange to the contemporary reader, but in the first half of the twentieth century questions of absolute and relative economic contribution and worth were not important components of Western social and political discourse. Unlike today, there was, as Jim Tomlinson has shown in an important essay, next to no concern about whether this or that activity was economically productive; "concern with productivity was episodic, underdeveloped and ill-focused." The apparent disappearance of questions of productiveness from mainstream economics had possibly played a role in this. In any event, it was only from the 1940s onwards that concerns about productiveness began to rise "to a wholly new prominence in [social and political] discourse about the economy." And this rise, as Tomlinson demonstrates, was indelibly linked to "the rise of measurement of the national economy."[27] The growth of national accounting and its measures of output not only provided a forum for the quantification of productiveness, but *made* productiveness something that appeared worthy of social and political consideration.

Yet for such a powerful statistical metric that is so frequently and materially invoked, there is a remarkable lack of knowledge, in political, academic, and popular circles, about what GDP actually is and how, where and when it came into being. The late Hungarian statistician Zoltan Kenessey articulated this incongruence thus: "Data pertaining to concepts such as GDP (or GNP) are quoted daily by the media. Yet the genesis of these concepts is not well known, *not even among professional economists or statisticians*."[28] If we want critically to discuss national accounting data and their uses, however, it is vital to illuminate something of this etiology. After all, given the visibility and taken-for-grantedness of measures such as GDP, one could be forgiven for thinking not only that these measures have a long legacy, but that there was some sort of inevitability or naturalness to their original materialization. Neither assumption, though, is correct: national accounts are a relatively recent invention, emerging out of a very particular configuration of socio-economic, political, and intellectual circumstances.

To be sure, estimates of levels of national economic activity had been produced since at least the mid-seventeenth century. But until well into the twentieth century these estimates, the bulk of which emanated from France and the UK, were intermittent and were exclusively the products of individual enterprise rather than any sort of systematic, state-sponsored initiative. Such initiatives only began to come together after 1930, with Canada, the US, the UK and a handful of continental European nations – Sweden and the Netherlands among them – leading the way. Yet progress was slow, and it took 20 years for the production of comprehensive national accounts on a continuing basis to become firmly established in a critical mass of Western territories. (Only nine countries had implemented continuing government estimates by 1939.[29]) Certainly any moves towards international harmonization only gathered pace right towards the end of that period, for although the Committee of Statistical Experts of the League of Nations had agreed in 1939 to work in such a direction, collective endeavor was then stymied by war, and it was not until 1953 that the United Nations Statistical Commission published its first international standard, the System of National Accounts (SNA).[30]

What was it about the period from 1930 to 1950, then, that stimulated for the first time the political will and drive, in the US and parts of Europe, to seek to capture systematically "the national economy" in statistical form? Most historians point to the same constellation of developments.[31] The Great Depression was one major catalyst, leading the US Senate to call in June 1932 for estimates of US national income, by industrial source, for the period 1929–31. The other, not surprisingly, was World War II – at which point the focus of major developments in national accounting shifted to Europe, and especially to the UK.

We will have cause later in this chapter and in Chapter 4 to consider in more detail some of the key developments that occurred in these different places (particularly the US and the UK), and the vital intellectual roles played by individual economists and statisticians – Keynes among them. Here, in highlighting the importance of the Great Depression and World War II as spurs to the production of national accounts, we can usefully connect back to a discussion from earlier in this chapter, namely around the growing national protectionism in finance and trade in the same period. For the two, of course, were closely connected, in a number of critical ways. Protectionism increased as national governments became increasingly concerned to manage their domestic economies towards the realization of new domestic social objectives; managing these economies required, or at least was perceived to require, *knowing* those economies quantitatively; and in the 1930s and 1940s, protectionism made the "national economy" now being measured more of an empirical and measurable reality, with fewer external connections disrupting such a reality, than it had been for many centuries or has been since.

If most users of GDP data know little or nothing of these historic-geographic origins, the methodological basis by which GDP measures are calculated is perhaps only marginally better appreciated. Understanding the crux of this methodology is, however, critical, not least in terms of grounding the arguments which follow in this and later chapters. There are in fact three different principal methods for calculating the total value of national economic output (GDP), and in reality published GDP figures are usually based on the reconciliation of estimates obtained from each – which, for various reasons, rarely match up.[32] The first method is the income method, where GDP is calculated as the sum, across all economic "producers," of the different primary sources of income: wages, corporate trading profits, rent, interest and dividends. The second approach is the expenditure method. Here, GDP represents monies *spent* on so-called "final" goods and services, summed across the three key categories of economic "actor" – government, business, and consumers – and then adjusted for net trade flows. The third and final method is the output or product method. Since this last is the most important method in the present context, we need to discuss it in more depth.

The output or product method arrives at an aggregate GDP figure by summing output on an industry-by-industry basis. It generates, in doing so, the "production account." The critical factor, however, is that since the output of one industry is often the input of another, double-counting concerns loom large: were the value of the output of an automotive components manufacturer to be simply added to the output of a car manufacturer which uses those components, cumulative output value would inevitably be overstated. National accountants have two different ways of getting around this problem. One is to sum, for each industry, only "final" goods and services outputs, which is to say those acquired by consumers or exported. The other, more common approach is to sum not outputs but "gross value-added" (GVA), which essentially equates to outputs *minus inputs* for each industry. Total GVA, summed across all industries, is effectively – although not exactly – total GDP.[33] Meanwhile, the reason why this third method for calculating GDP is the most material for our purposes should, by now, be evident: for it is *only* with the product method that national economic output can be readily broken down into the estimated relative productive contributions of different industrial sectors, banking among them.

This still leaves one final, crucial question to be addressed, however. *Which* industries – or, more broadly, which sets of social agents – are considered to be economically productive, and thus to merit an output or GVA calculation in the national accounts? How, in effect, does a set of social agents *become*, for national accounting purposes, a thing called a productive "industry"? Or, giving the same question a different inflection, where exactly is the production boundary placed, and which activities does this placement render productive (and calculable) and unproductive (and valueless) respectively?

I do not intend at this point to try to offer a full answer to this question. For one thing, innumerable different answers have been postulated at different times and in different places. For another, and more pointedly, the variation in these answers – specifically insofar as they pertain to banking and financial services – is precisely my object of extended critical analysis. Nevertheless it is helpful, I think, to indicate at this juncture the generic shape of the answer which has essentially informed and animated Western national accounting from its origins through to the present day. Thus, *in general*, activities are considered productive if they are deemed to produce a "useful output" and if a value can be assigned to this output through either imputation (a concept and practice we will have occasion to consider in some detail later) or payment actually made. The "production boundary" separates those activities which fulfill both of these criteria from those which do not.

In my discussion below of the treatment of banking services in national accounts, I will be focusing closely on this question of where the production boundary is placed, and on how different placements necessarily entail different framings of particular economic activities. I do so, and indeed insist on the importance of doing so, because as Anwar Shaikh and Ahmet Tonak observe in their critique of Western national accounting, what counts as "productive" and what does not clearly "changes the very nature of the accounts, the picture that we see, and the conclusions that we draw."[34] What is especially interesting to note, however, is that while there is a longstanding tradition of questioning *exclusions* from the productive domain, and the effects of such exclusions on the social valuation of the activities in question – the classic example being household labor – much less critical attention has been paid to what gets *included*.[35] How and why do certain activities come to be considered "productive," and what are the effects of *these* (mis)representations?

Shaikh and Tonak's critique is actually an important exception in this regard. They consider unproductive a range of activities which Western national accounts, today, typically treat as productive. One such activity, notably, is financial services provision. Such services, the authors claim, "derive their revenues from the recirculation of the money flows generated by the [economy's] primary sectors" and hence merely "preserve or circulate [social] wealth, or help maintain and administer the social structure in which it is embedded."[36] This argument is directly inspired by the Marxian distinction, discussed in Chapter 1, between production and circulation, and by Marx's own placement of finance in the latter sphere. If we follow Marx, Shaikh and Tonak argue, finance is unproductive, and thus should be excluded from our estimations of economic output. They go on to show that this – excluding finance – was precisely the approach of the Material Product national accounting system used in the former Soviet Union, Eastern Bloc countries and, until 1993, China. They rightly point out, furthermore, that there remains considerable confusion around this system, particularly the widely-held view that its restriction of "productiveness" to physical goods was derived from Marx. While disabusing readers of this particular misconception (about the Material Product system, and about Marx), however, they effectively reproduce another: which is that we need to look to the former Communist states for real-world examples of national accounts that treat financial services as unproductive. This, as we shall shortly see, is simply, and critically, not the case.

The Banking Problem

Reviewing in the mid-1980s the various approaches taken internationally, over the previous four decades, to the treatment of financial services in national accounts, Bryan Haig reflected that all had made attempts to one extent or another "to solve the banking problem."[37] This so-called "banking problem" is the primary focus of the rest of this chapter. The present section discusses, first, how and why this problem arises and what form it takes. As we shall see, it centers on the question of how the productiveness (or otherwise) of banking is to be measured. More particularly, it concerns the placement of a specific subset of financial services – banks' *intermediation services* – vis-à-vis the production boundary: which side of this boundary do such services properly sit on? The "problem," in short, is that the generic national accounting treatment of interest flows necessitates a placement of intermediation services on the "wrong" side of the fence, thus (usually) also rendering the banking sector in toto unproductive in terms of its reported contribution to national economic output. The question of why such an outcome should be considered a "problem," and by whom, is the second issue addressed in this section.

Two pieces of scene-setting are required before we can delve into the question of why and where the banking problem materializes. First, it is necessary to highlight the way in which national accounts distinguish between "income" and "transfer" items. As we saw above, for an activity to be considered "productive" in the national accounts it must generate a "useful output" to which it is possible to assign a value. Usually, this value is based on payment rendered for the output in question. But there are certain economic situations in which payments are made but production is *not* considered to have taken place – namely, where there is deemed to be no "output," or where any output is not regarded as "useful" – and it is in these situations that the income/transfer distinction arises. The payments in question, which include things like unemployment benefit and state pensions, are treated as transfer items rather than income. The conceptual reasoning for this treatment is that such payments represent "a redistribution of existing incomes" rather than "any addition to current economic activity."[38] They are not, in other words, remuneration for *productive* work.

The second form of scene-setting concerns the various different activities carried out by banks, and the importance of categorizing these in a meaningful fashion. Because banks engage in a wide range of operations, because these are typically treated in different ways in national accounts, and because, most especially, the "banking problem" crystallizes in relation to only one subset of such operations (albeit an extremely important subset), it is vital to try to impart some order to the picture at the outset. Banking activities can, of course, be segmented in many different ways. The approach taken here, I should therefore emphasize, has been chosen purely to illuminate as clearly as possible the particular issue in hand.

The first thing to note is that we are not concerned with insurance activities; our field of interest, rather, is banking, of all types. Broadly-speaking, banks engage in three types of activities and make money in different ways from each. First, they provide services for which they are explicitly paid fees: capital raising; mergers and acquisitions advice; fund management; currency transfer; and so on. Second, they provide so-called intermediation services, where their role is to facilitate exchange between buyers and sellers of financial assets. The most obvious example of such market-making is the taking of plain-old cash deposits and the making of cash loans – where depositors are the sellers of cash (or, more accurately, of the right to use that cash until such time as it is reclaimed), and borrowers are its buyers. Much of the difference between "high street banks" and "investment banks" is located in the fact that they simply make markets in different types of assets: the former in cash, the latter in, inter alia, debt and equity securities and derivatives thereof. The key point here, however, is that with all such cases of financial intermediation, banks generate positive net revenues only through setting a margin between the prices at which assets, or the use of such assets, can be bought and sold: either a "buy/sell margin" (different cash prices, for instance, for the purchase or disposal of company shares) or an interest margin (different interest rates, most recognizably, on cash deposits or loans). Third, and last, banks strategically buy and sell assets themselves, using their own funds. Sometimes this is called trading (particularly over short time horizons), at other times investing (and at still others, of course, speculating); but in all cases, the aim is to profit from any ongoing income generated by holding such an asset, and/or from selling the asset at a higher effective price than that at which it was purchased.

With this tripartite classification of banking activities in hand, we can proceed directly to the aforementioned banking problem in national accounting. For, of these three categories of activity, two have historically posed no substantive problems for estimating GDP. Services where an explicit, direct fee is charged are deemed to sit comfortably on the productive side of the production boundary, and assigning a value to such services in the production account is usually a straightforward affair. It is clear what service has been provided, who has provided it, and, ordinarily, how much they have been paid for it.

All monies generated through the buying and selling of assets with proprietary bank funds, meanwhile, whether such monies take the form of interest, dividends or capital gains, have historically been excluded from this account – just as they would be if it were an individual doing the buying or selling. No service or product has been tendered, and hence no value, the argument goes, has been added. Interestingly, the late 1990s and early to mid-2000s saw something of a push, in certain quarters of the international national accounting community, to reconsider this stance. Perhaps, it was suggested, this traditional approach was wrong, and earnings from so-called "own funds" and/or from holding gains *should* be included as part of banks' "productive output"?[39] Doing so would, of course, tend to inflate the estimated contribution of the banking sector to national GDP. Not surprisingly, the financial crisis which began in 2007 abruptly killed off such notions: the idea that national accounting might have been *under*estimating banks' productiveness rapidly became sacrilegious.

If banks' fee-based services and proprietary investment activities are treated as productive and unproductive respectively, what, then, of their final category of activity – intermediation services? These, it turns out, are where full responsibility for the "banking problem" lies. Part of this problem is essentially conceptual. What useful "service," if any, is actually being provided by the banks here? Or, to turn this question around: if the holding of deposits or the making of loans really were a commercial "service" of some kind, would companies and individuals not be prepared to make explicit payments to banks in kind, aside from nominal regular maintenance charges on some accounts and occasional ancillary fees such as for early loan repayment? Where, as is ordinarily the case, banking is provided "free," how can it be a productive, valued service?

The numerous historical attempts to solve the "banking problem" have therefore been partly about tackling this conceptual conundrum. Practitioners have offered various different answers as to the essential nature of the supposed intermediation "service." "Some explanations," observed Carol Carson and Jeanette Honsa in an article published in 1990, "refer to the services of liquidity provided by the financial institution. Others stress checking and bookkeeping services or safety." But the very fact that different protagonists were seen to identify *different* service forms underlines the essential problem. There was, at this stage at least, no agreement on what the core, useful intermediation "service" actually *is*, Carson and Honsa acknowledging that the "precise nature of the services" provided by banks, and which national accountants still struggled to define, "is not clear."[40]

Yet such conceptual issues have never been the primary concern for the national accountants who have grappled with the "banking problem." Their main concern, rather, has been with how the output value of banks' intermediation activities might be quantified *if* such activities are treated as providing a service with a useful output. Once more, it bears reiterating: only activities with useful outputs *to which a value can be assigned* successfully cross the production boundary. What is this value?

We begin to grasp the crux of the banking problem when we recognize that one cannot simply use actual service payments as the basis for such value, since, as we have seen, explicit fees paid by discrete, identifiable customers are not ordinarily levied in respect of intermediation (the "service" is provided "free," such provision being funded through a margin as opposed to a transparent charge). This, therefore, leaves only one possible means by which banks' intermediation activities can be enabled to successfully negotiate the production boundary: an *imputation* of the value of the "output" of such services. As we shall see in Chapters 4 and 5, this solution has gained increasingly widespread traction over the course of the history of national accounting and has taken many different individual forms in different times and places.

While the exact methodologies of imputation are not relevant at this juncture, one comment on a shared characteristic of such methodologies is extremely pertinent. This is that, directly or indirectly, they all include the net interest revenues generated through intermediation within what is deemed to be the "productive" revenue of the banking sector. And in so doing, national income statisticians make a key exception from the generic conventions of the national accounting calculus. For, as Haig explains, using the transfer/income distinction introduced above, interest is as a rule *excluded* from the productive domain:

> It has long been accepted by national income statisticians that receipts and payments of interest are transfer items which do not result in current productive activity. Accordingly, net receipts of interest are not counted in national income and expenditure, nor in the contribution of industries or sectors to total national product.[41]

In other words, net interest earned by retailers, automobile manufacturers, pharmaceuticals companies and so forth is excluded from "productive" proceeds; it is a transfer item, not income, representing economic redistribution rather than additive economic output. Where an imputation is made for intermediation, banks are therefore made an exception. Granted, this exception has a putative rationale (banks' net interest earnings being uniquely derived from the provision of a *service*). Yet it is an exception nonetheless.[42] And it is an exception, as we shall see, which not all Western national accounting communities have always considered necessary or desirable.

In the absence of an imputation, meantime, banks' intermediation activities necessarily sit on the unproductive side of the production boundary, and the *only* banking activity to register a positive output entry in the national production account is the first of our three categories: services for which banks *are* explicitly paid fees. Which brings us, finally, to the ultimate crystallization of the "banking problem." If banks' GVA is calculated on the basis of only limited revenues (including no proprietary investment or intermediation-based earnings) but a full set of inputs (i.e. all costs, excluding interest payments on intermediated funds), the accounts' picture of the sector's contribution to national output will inevitably be a distinctly unflattering one.

How unflattering is obviously one important question. In the 1940s and 1950s, when national accountants were first tussling with these quandaries, the picture *sans* imputation was *extremely* unflattering, which explains in part the broad and rapid consensus that there *was* a problem with how banks were to be represented. In that era, banks were still, in very large part, intermediation-focused businesses; fee-earning activities and trading with own funds were much less significant than today. As such, if net interest earnings were simply excluded from the calculation of GVA, there was very little left on the positive side of the ledger, and more often than not a *negative* GVA – that is to say, larger sector inputs than outputs – would be the result. This was precisely the outcome, for instance, in the official Australian national accounts of 1946 and 1947.[43] Thus, the influential UK national income statistician Richard Stone confirmed for a wider audience in as early as 1947 that with no imputation for intermediation services a banking sector "deficit rather than a surplus would appear."[44] Writing a decade later, Paul Studenski put the matter more starkly, noting that in the many instances where banking sector operating costs were indeed greater than the sum of explicit charges to customers, such an accounting approach would entail the representation of banking as "a drain on national income rather than a contribution."[45] Perhaps most stark of all, however, were the words of the US statistician John Gorman another decade on. "In effect," he wrote in 1969, "our simple commercial bank would be portrayed as a leech on the income stream."[46]

The Western banking sector has, of course, changed enormously since Stone, Studenski and even Gorman articulated the concerns which Haig later captured with the "banking problem" epithet. As fee-earning businesses and the investment of proprietary funds have become increasingly material, the relative contribution to sector revenues of intermediation-derived net interest income has gradually fallen.[47] Such income remains, however, highly material. Ewald Engelen and co-authors have recently shown that across six major Western markets, the average contribution of interest income to bank profits fell by more than 20 percent between 1984 and 2007 alone – but that even subsequent to this decline, the average contribution was still above 50 percent.[48] Not all such income is generated through intermediation, of course, but much of it is, and it is thus clearly the case that placing intermediation services outside the production boundary would still, today, result in a serious dent in estimated sector value-added. The economic *basis* of national accounting's banking "problem" has not disappeared, therefore; even in the context of a sector less reliant on intermediation, what two UK national income statisticians recently referred to as the "threat" of showing a negative or marginal banking GVA remains, theoretically, live.[49] The implied GVA number would not, in most countries, be quite as unflattering today as it would have been 50 or 60 years ago; but it would be considerably *less* flattering than a number allowing for the incorporation of contemporary net interest earnings via imputation.

All of this leaves open, however, the question that is perhaps most important of all – namely, why it was that many early national accountants saw an envisioning of the banking sector as a "drain" or "leech" on national income *as a problem*, and why most of their successors have continued to do so. (In his 2005 history of national accounting, André Vanoli, articulating the broad consensus amongst his contemporary peers, dismissed such an envisioning as "totally unrealistic."[50]) What exactly is the nature of the "threat"?

It would not be altogether unexpected if some readers were to suspect that a "negative" representation of banking productiveness was and is considered problematic in a political sense. After all, as we saw in the introduction to this book, the financial services sector takes considerable interest in how it is represented in the political and public eye, not least in terms of the nature and scale of its contribution to the economy; and the sector has never been slow to contest directly and forcefully representations that it considers unduly or unfairly negative. It is also demonstrably the case that banks and other financial services companies, in many countries, have considerable resources at their disposal to conduct just such representational battles. It is certainly not inconceivable, therefore, that national income statisticians might have deemed the envisioning of an unproductive banking sector as a *political* problem – as a representation that was and is unlikely to curry favor amongst powerful industry executives (and perhaps, by extension, among their supporters in government), and which was and is unworkable accordingly.

The research conducted for this book suggests, however, that politics has never been the source of national accountants' enduring "problem" with the banking sector and how to account for its output. This research incorporated discussions with national accountants who have worked at the coalface of the "business" over the past 30 years, both within national statistical offices (among them the Dutch, French, UK, US, and Swiss offices) and within the statistical teams of key multilateral institutions such as the UN. Many such individuals have played seminal roles in shaping the evolution of national and international accounting standards over the past three decades, including in relation specifically to the treatment of financial services. When discussion turned to the matter of the "leech" image arising from a decision not to impute for intermediation, however, it became clear that the problems such an image posed for these individuals – theoretically, or practically – were not political ones. None admitted to having had concerns over how their representations of the banking sector might be received, and none admitted to having felt pressured, implicitly or explicitly, towards methodologies producing more (or even less) positive pictures of the sector in question.

In fact the discussions threw up findings that were, to this author at least, somewhat surprising. Until perhaps the late 1980s at the earliest, bankers appear to have shown little or no specific concern with the *mechanics* of national accounting and of the treatment of the banking sector it offered, even in countries where the resulting picture of the sector's output contribution was indeed unsympathetic. The interminable debates over treatment of financial intermediation services in the accounts, which we will trace something of through the rest of the book, were always, says André Vanoli, a "technical debate among national accountants that did not interest bankers."[51] There was scarcely any direct interaction between the practitioner and banker communities during this period, and certainly, to the best of this author's knowledge, no substantive attempts by the latter to influence discussions amongst the former.

This is not to say, of course, that bankers did not use national accounting statistics where and when it suited them to do so. Much of Chapter 4 and Chapter 5 is taken up with such deployment, both by bankers and by the political institutions that have championed their cause. Prior to 1990, and *especially* since, the calculus of national accounting has been mobilized at the very heart of the self-aggrandizing discourse of bank "productiveness." Yet the point to be emphasized here is that this has more often than not been – and I use the word advisedly – an ignorant mobilization. As the Swiss national income statistician Philippe Stauffer writes: "Bankers use national accounting figures, but often do not really know what they are using."[52]

The last two decades have seen rather more direct contact between bankers and national accounting practitioners, although such contact typically remains sporadic and small-scale. In the UK, such contact has been occasioned, inter alia, by the convening of meetings of the Financial Statistics Users' Group (FSUG) since the mid-1990s. Representing "the interests of users of financial and macroeconomic statistics," and affiliated to the Royal Statistical Society, the FSUG "improves members' understanding of compilation methodologies, obtains practitioner views on existing statistics or potential improvements, provides a topical discussion forum for compilers and users, and promotes expertise amongst users."[53] The treatment of financial services in the national accounts has often featured on the group's agenda over the years. An April 2001 meeting, for instance, covered this topic in detail, and saw two representatives of the body which produces the UK's national accounts – the Office of National Statistics (ONS) – tell the assembled audience "how the ONS collected financial services data, how the sector was incorporated into the UK's National Accounts and the ways that the National Accounts could be used to measure the contribution of financial services."[54] In other countries, contact between bankers and national accountants has taken alternative forms. Switzerland, for example, "sponsored" in 2002 an OECD task force to rethink the treatment of banks in national accounts, and the Swiss accountancy practitioners leading this team met with bankers to do much the same things as the ONS representatives at the UK FSUG meeting: to present "the 'theory' behind the national accounting figures."[55]

By the stage in the late 1990s and the 2000s that such meetings were occurring internationally on a more regular basis, the banking "problem" – the risk of representing banks as parasites – had, as we shall see later on, effectively been resolved in most Western countries. The most notable of those countries which *had* represented banks as such in their national accounts, no longer continued to do so. The theoretical "threat" to banks had therefore diminished. It is therefore somewhat ironic, though I do not wish to dwell on the irony, that only now – having only recently begun to take an active interest in the methodology of accounts generation – did bankers pause to question whether the picture of their economic contribution was a sufficiently positive one. Once they did so, moreover, they frequently found themselves to be dissatisfied. Stauffer notes that before the recent financial crisis, bankers were "convinced that the national accounts measures were biased, and underestimated the contribution of bank output to GDP" (though he goes on to say that "the crisis ended this feeling").[56] Yet even then, Stauffer confirms, "there was no attempt to lobby national accountants" for a "better" picture.[57]

In general, over the course of the seven-decade history of systematized national accounting in the West, it would be fair to say that any influence wielded by bankers in regard to the conventions of national accounting has been more *indirect* than direct. To the extent that there has been any such influence, it has been channelled primarily through two main state institutional filters: national central banks and national treasury departments. Both types of institution, the former in particular, are inevitably inhabited in large part by bankers, many of whom have been employed at some stage in the private sector. And both central banks and treasuries have usually worked closely with national statistical offices in formulating accounting treatments and collating the necessary statistics to effect such treatments. As the UK ex-national income statistician Geoff Tily, now with the Treasury, recounts, his time at the ONS saw "a lot of discussion with the Bank [of England] and the Treasury around conceptual issues."[58] It is extremely hard to gauge the materiality of any such state-institution-mediated "banker influence" on the evolution of the national accounting calculus and its conventions for quantifying bank output. What remains clear, however, to this author at least, is that national accountants have never seen the "problem" of potentially envisioning the banking sector as a "leech" as a political problem – they have never *felt* politically compromised, directly or indirectly.

I will argue here, instead, that the problem has always been principally an intellectual one – but that it is no less significant or interesting for that. To understand why the prospect of banks appearing in the national accounts as a "drain" on the national income has usually been seen as problematic by national accountants, we need to understand not the latter's socio-political environment so much as the intellectual worldview they bring to bear in their work: the conceptual discourses in which they are schooled and steeped. We need to think closely, that is to say, about the relationship between accounting *for* wealth and theorizing *about* wealth.[59] For, ultimately, the reason why the banking "problem" *has* typically been a problem is that according to the conceptual framework inhabited by most national income practitioners, the notion of banks being economically unproductive simply does not make sense. In the rest of this section I explain why.

A creature of the twentieth century, national accounting developed as a calculative economic technology at a time when, as we have seen, the political-economic approaches of the nineteenth century had been thoroughly usurped by neoclassicism as the dominant intellectual toolkit for understanding economic dynamics. This was a transition of enormous relevance for the story of representational developments we are seeking to understand here. The national accounting offices which sprung up around the world from the 1940s onwards were populated with economists trained at university not in political economy but in the marginalist theories of neoclassicism. (Where developing countries lacked the resources to adequately staff their own nascent offices, meanwhile, the IMF was on hand to train up aspirant indigenous statisticians in its own neoclassical image.[60]) Moreover, neoclassicism's favorite representational technique – econometric model-building – was itself a pivotal driver of the rapid international development of national accounting during this period.[61] In the half-century since, during which time national accounting has infiltrated the governmental calculus of even the smallest national polity, its progenitors have continued to be cut exclusively from the neoclassical cloth – even if, for reasons we shall touch upon shortly, the level of ongoing operational interaction *between* academic economics and national accounting practice has gradually but definitively declined.[62]

Here we need to remind ourselves, from Chapter 1, of what neoclassical economics has to say about economic productiveness and unproductiveness. What we learned there was that neoclassicism scotches the very idea, so central to classical and Marxian political economy, that some activities and labors are inherently productive while others are inherently unproductive. Never mind what sort of work goes into producing a product or service, we are told: if something generates market demand, it clearly has utility, and is thus productive. There are no *innate qualities* of productiveness; hard-and-fast distinctions cannot be drawn. Considering the broad constellation of activities that we think of as "the banking sector," therefore, what matters is ultimately this: banks are highly revenue-generative and usually relatively profitable, have become more so over time, and thus, ipso facto, *must* be productive. The "banking problem" for neoclassically-trained economic statisticians faced with reporting banks as unproductive parasites was thus, more accurately, an unpalatable paradox: the "paradox of a prosperous industry," in the words of an influential 1952 Organization for European Economic Cooperation document on precisely this subject, "showing a negligibly positive, or even negative, contribution to the national product."[63] For a prosperous sector to be envisioned as unproductive was, in short, counter-intuitive.

It is worth pausing at this point to historicize this paradox. It was, we need to recognize, a product very much *of* its neoclassical age. The concept of banks being profitable but not productive would not have struck earlier generations of (political) economists as the least bit paradoxical. In his famous discussion of the Bank of Amsterdam, Adam Smith noted that its various intermediation services – such as "selling bank money at five per cent agio, and buying it in at four" – allowed the Bank to earn "a good deal more than what is necessary for paying the salaries of officers, and defraying the expense of management," and thus to generate a profit. Yet this was not because there was anything inherently productive about what the Bank was doing. On the contrary: "Public utility, however, and not revenue, was the original object of this institution... The revenue which has arisen from it was unforeseen, and may be considered as accidental."[64] A century later, of course, Marx was also moved to comment on banking profitability, and was equally scathing of the idea that such profits derived from productiveness. Where Smith saw a benign accidentality, Marx saw power – the power of finance capital. What Smith and Marx *shared*, however, was the belief that it was entirely possible for an activity to be revenue and profit-generative without contributing to the creation of value. There was no paradox. (Or rather, for Marx at any rate, the paradox was not that banks made profits without producing value, but that industrial capitalists allowed them to do so.) This configuration of possibilities only came to *appear* paradoxical to economists during the twentieth century.

Had the national accountants of the 1940s, 1950s and later decades been schooled mainly in the political economy tradition of Marx or even of Smith rather than that of neoclassicism, there *would have been* no "banking problem" – banks *were*, in this tradition, unproductive, hence representing them as such would have been entirely logical, whatever the level of revenues and profits that such institutions generated. In support of this proposition, we shall see in the next section that in Western countries where national income statisticians, in the early days of national accounting, retained vestiges of political-economic thinking or at least remained more favorably inclined towards the Smithian or Marxian way of conceiving the world, a picturing of banks as unproductive was indeed considered less problematic, and in some instances as not problematic at all.

To conclude the current section, however, I will explore a little further this notion of a "problem." To be sure, there was a problem, or a paradox, of a sort, that national accountants wrestled with in seeking to account for banks' intermediation services. I want to suggest, however, that we can usefully consider the possibility that the real problem was less with banking and its placement in the accounts, and more with the relationship between national accounting practice and neoclassical theory – and arguably even with neoclassicism, and its core conceptual claims, itself.

We already know that in advancing a utility or "subjective preference" theory of value and rejecting labor theories of value, neoclassicism had – or at least, claimed to have – consigned the notion of a rigid divide between productiveness and unproductiveness to the scrapheap of economic history. It is important to ask, however, whether this was really what had happened. An alternative interpretation is that the neoclassical reconfiguration of value theory actually retained a central place for the divide in question, yet veiled its continuing materiality specifically by shifting its locus of application. For the great political economists of the eighteenth and nineteenth centuries, the productiveness or otherwise of an activity was determined already at the moment of the input of labor, and depended on whether such labor, for instance, created material goods (Smith) or was exploited in capitalist production as opposed to circulation (Marx). Rather than discarding this judgment on productiveness, neoclassicism, on my reading, *delayed* it; what had been determined at the moment of labor input was now assessed at the final moment of market output, with everything that came before (the amount of labor, the nature and location of its purchase, and so on) judged immaterial. Monetary sale implied "productiveness." It was still, and remains, a productive/ unproductive divide, only one not articulated as such.

One of national accounting's great fascinations, it seems to me, is the fact that it makes this particular productive/unproductive divide inescapable, and thus renders the neoclassical veiling transparent. This is the lesson of the banking problem. Even if it was conceived and administered by neoclassicists, and even if it

neglected many of the *other* key concerns of political economy such as "the nature
of the ownership of resources, the control of productive assets, and the location
and concentration of economic power," national accounting did not and could
not relinquish the productive/unproductive divide that neoclassicism had theoretically (but *only* theoretically) disavowed.[65] Monetizable market demand was
not just the preferred measure but the essential definition of productiveness in this
calculus.[66] The solid production boundary thus conceived sat at its very heart and
structured all of its assignations and representations. To appreciate this is to
understand, I think, a considerable part of what Utz-Peter Reich identifies as the
"disappointment of national accountants and statistical practitioners with the
microeconomic theory of value."[67] The theory putatively refutes one of national
accounting foundational tenets; and a schooling in such theory therefore has the
potential to throw up just the kind of irritating practical paradox that the banking
"problem" epitomizes.

To flesh out these various frictions is also, more importantly, to begin to discern
and understand the tensions, if not outright contradictions, in the work of someone like Alfred Marshall. Widely regarded as one of the fathers of neoclassical
economics, Marshall, like William Jevons, poured scorn on the political economists' invocation of a productive/unproductive divide. "There is not in real life,"
he argued in his *Principles of Economics*, "a clear line of division between things
that are and are not capital, or that are and are not necessaries, or again between
labour that is and is not productive." As such, he went on, all distinctions "in
which the word productive are used are very thin and have a certain air of unreal-
ity." The saving grace, from Marshall's perspective, was that the occasions on
which such lines need to be drawn "seldom or never occur."[68] And yet: this was
the same Marshall who *defined* a production boundary (perhaps the most famous
of all such lines) and, through this and other conceptual innovations, stimulated
much of the early development of national accounting in the UK by the likes of
Arthur Bowley, Alfred Flux, and Josiah Stamp, two of whom were his students![69]
National accounting's problematic relationship with neoclassicism was also
apparent, we shall see below, with Keynes, who, while of course better known for
his work in macroeconomics than in neoclassical microeconomics, essentially
"accepted the neoclassical reformulation of value theory."[70]

If Marshall exhibited some of these tensions in a generic sense, his fellow neoclassicist Joseph Schumpeter, with whom we shall conclude this section, did so in
relation, inter alia, specifically to the financial intermediation services we have been
considering. If anything, Schumpeter was even more scathing than Marshall in his
dismissal, in the *History of Economic Analysis*, of the "dusty museum piece" that
was political economy's productive/unproductive distinction.[71] And yet: his work
on business cycles explicitly invokes the qualitatively and quantitatively different
roles of "productive" and "unproductive" activities during the upwards component
of the cycle; and his work on profit and interest, even more pertinently, distinguishes between "productive" and "unproductive" interest, the latter arising where
"interest is only demanded and paid because it is possible to demand and pay it."[72]
Indeed, Schumpeter, in the latter work, comes dangerously close to sounding like

Marx, identifying interest in general as "a tax upon profit" – with all that that definition implies about the "productiveness" of banking intermediaries.[73] In other words, we can detect in Marshall and Schumpeter a tendency that, by my argument, betrays neoclassical economics more generally, which is to fall back upon a dualism that had notionally been eradicated. The productive/unproductive dichotomy is, in a sense, the elephant in neoclassicism's room; and for conspicuously giving that elephant its head, national accounting was guaranteed a problematic long-term relationship with its theoretical counterpart.

Banking Problem? What Banking Problem?

If one reads through the archives of the early years of systematic national accounting in the West, it rapidly becomes apparent that, as I indicated earlier, the majority of those "thinkers" in this tradition who explicitly reflected on the "banking problem" in writing regarded it as exactly that – as something problematic, and in need of fixing. Richard Stone, the UK economist who led the post-war formulation of the UN's first (1953) SNA, argued that showing the banking sector with negative value-added would be "clearly unsatisfactory."[74] Paul Studenski, New York University professor and consultant to the US government, used the words "wholly misleading" in his opus *The Income of Nations*, flagging the problem as an "incongruity" that "would obviously make no sense."[75] Richard Speagle and Leo Silverman, albeit writing from the decidedly partisan perspective of an association with the New York State Banking Department, concluded simply that showing "a large negative [sector] income, implying that banking was feeding on the rest of the economy," was an "absurdity."[76] And the list goes on.

What, however, about the practical *reality* of national accounts? Did the practitioners who actually produced national accounts, on the ground, always and everywhere agree with this broad consensus, or were there substantive dissensions, reflected perhaps in contrary treatments – treatments that did *not* impute a positive value for intermediation services, and hence which did not staticize away the conceptual problem in question? Even where those with the responsibility for crafting accounting methodologies did agree that a negative representation of the banking sector would be problematic, was it always and everywhere expedient for them to find a satisfactory and workable solution to the problem? These are the broad questions addressed in this final section. Where Chapter 4, which follows, focuses on one country where practising statisticians immediately took the bull by the horns, so to speak, and implemented a working solution to the banking problem (the US), our focus here is on three countries displaying a very different statistical history. Each treated intermediation services, and thus the banking sector more generally, in a different way; but in *none* did the initial accounts framework allow for a directly positive envisioning of bank productiveness.

The three countries in question are France, Germany, and the UK. While I will make reference, both here and later in the book, to the treatment of banking services in the national accounts of other countries – and of course in the

methodological standards drafted by international statistical authorities such as
Eurostat and the UN's Statistical Office, to which the various national treatments
have by no means always and everywhere conformed – the spotlight throughout
will be trained largely on these three and the US. Why? The question has a simple
answer. My overarching interest in the book is in the relationship *between* boundary crossings: between banks' crossing of conceptual (productive/unproductive)
boundaries and their crossing of geopolitical boundaries. We have already seen
that the most internationalized financial systems prior to geo-financial retrenchment in the decades following World War I were those of the four countries in
question. This fact makes their representations of banks' productiveness during
those protectionist decades especially pertinent. What is also pertinent is the fact
that once the international financial world began to be opened up once more from
the 1960s, it was US banks, followed later by banks from the UK, France, and
Germany (plus those of a small number of other countries, most notably Japan),
that again took the lead.

How, therefore, did the first sets of national accounts of France, Germany, and
the UK envision banks in general, and their services of intermediation more specifically? We can take Germany first, since it is the simplest to deal with. Due to
the occlusion of official government statistics from the mid-1930s to the end of
World War II on account of their subsumption into the closely-held regime of
power-knowledge that constituted the Third Reich, Germany's role in the early
history of national accounting has often been underplayed. The fact of the matter,
however, is that Germany was already producing such accounts from 1926: "the
first regular series," as Adam Tooze observes in his brilliant book on statistics and
statecraft in early-twentieth century Germany, "to be produced by any major capitalist state."[77]

The critical features of these pioneering accounts from our particular
perspective here were how they were constructed and, accordingly, what they
were and were not able to illuminate about the constitution of the national
economy. Up until 1941, Paul Jostock has noted, the accounts were based
exclusively on income tax data. What this meant was that of the three available methods for estimating the size of the national economy (the income,
expenditure, and product methods), only the first was viable. As such, the
early official German estimates, in the 1920s and 1930s, are estimates exclusively of national *income*, broken down by type of income. Such estimates
therefore "do not permit," Jostock crucially observes, "a distribution of
national product by industrial origin."[78]

Because of this particularity, the "banking problem" simply did not arise in
national accountancy practice in Germany at this time. (And it would not arise
there until 1949, from which year the Federal Republic, now using the product
method, began producing its own national accounts – a development we shall
touch upon briefly below.) Was this merely a fate of circumstance, the "innocent"
upshot of a purely pragmatic decision on generic accounting methodology? Most
likely it was; although there are hints, if nothing more, of a more deliberate eva-
sion, in Studenski's later observation that "by computing national income by the

income-distributed method alone, without showing its distribution by industrial divisions or by final products," the "problem of how to treat banking services was avoided" by German statisticians.[79]

Whether such a problem was conceived and (actively) avoided or never arose in the first place, the German approach differed markedly from the approaches taken in France and the UK, in both of which the product method – and thus an estimated breakdown of output by industry – was part of the national accounting system from early on. In France, such a system emerged slightly later than in Germany, the UK or the US, with formal accounts not appearing for the first time until the early 1950s. They did so under the auspices of the statistical service of the Ministry of Finance, the *Service des Etudes économiques et financières* (SEEF). The accounts' production and use both reflected and underpinned the wider post-war project of social and economic modernization.[80]

How were banks envisioned in these accounts? The first important observation we can make is that they – or "financial institutions" more generally – were deemed sufficiently distinctive to warrant isolating as one of the five main categories of economic agent in the accounts, alongside households, other commercial enterprises, government, and the rest of the world. The second, more critical observation is that such institutions were assumed to have zero output – to be, that is to say, wholly *un*productive economic agents. This zero rating, moreover, was extended across the full gamut of financial sector activities: to own-fund investment, *and* to intermediation services, *and even* to services for which financial institutions did explicitly levy fees and receive direct monetary payment. This represented, in other words, a wholesale and categorical denial of financial sector productiveness; not so much a question of the banking "problem" being recognized but being deemed not to require a solution, rather an explicit denial of there *being* a banking problem at all. Envisioning banking as unproductive was not problematic; it was an accurate representation of economic reality as French national income statisticians appeared to see it.

We will attempt below to try to explain this particular treatment. But it is worth appreciating here that it was no fleeting ephemera, a temporary aberration that was quickly perceived as such and rapidly corrected. The French national accounts continued to show banks as entirely without productive economic output until 1975. Certainly, there have been other examples of "Western" countries totally omitting income generated through banking from the national product; Australia, for example, did so through to 1937/38.[81] Then, of course, there are the countries of the Eastern Bloc, which, including *East* Germany after World War II, also rendered banks unproductive in the accounting tableau in their use of the Material Product System.[82] To the best knowledge of this author, however, the national accounts of France presented such an image of banks for a longer period than any other Western nation in the post-war era.

The UK, meanwhile, pursued yet another alternative course. The first official GDP estimates, for 1938 and 1940, were published in 1941, but these used "only" the income and expenditure methods of sizing the national economy. The question of how to deal with the banking sector, and in particular its services of intermediation, thus did not surface until the product/output method – and hence the production account – was added to the mix in 1946.[83]

The UK's national income statisticians clearly agreed with Stone that banks' intermediation services, in not being explicitly paid for, presented a dilemma. They also, equally clearly, disagreed with their French counterparts, in the sense that they did not think that showing banks as unproductive actors was unproblematic. It *was*, or would be, a problem, conceptually if not politically. But the key feature of this particular story is that these statisticians were not ready to take the step that, as we shall see in the next chapter, their US counterparts took, which was to "solve" the problem in such a way that the troublesome representation in question was avoided. Instead, they offered a treatment whereby only the few financial services for which UK banks explicitly charged their customers were deemed ultimately to make a net positive contribution to output, and hence under which banks' overall proportional contribution to GDP would indeed register as negative or only very marginally positive. Before considering how the statisticians in question rationalized this choice, we need to examine the exact nature of their treatment of intermediation.

Rather than excluding the revenue flows associated with financial intermediation services from the production account entirely, the UK's statisticians adopted a seemingly even more perverse and tortuous approach. They *did* impute an output value to such services, namely by deducting banks' interest payments on liabilities acquired through intermediation (mainly cash deposits) from the interest income they generated on assets acquired in the same capacity (mainly cash loans). However, instead of treating this net interest revenue as the input – or, in the lexicon of national accounting, "intermediate consumption" – of one or more other sectors of the economy (as in the US methodology we will look at later, for example), they treated it as the input of … the banking sector itself! It was, in other words, output *and* input, and hence always netted out to zero. The result, of course, was that the banking sector's reported value-added was precisely the same as if those interest flows had been treated as transfer items rather than income (as in Australia in 1946–47), and simply excluded from the production account accordingly.

Was this an ideal solution? Patently, not. But it was a better solution, the statistical office believed, than any others on the table. Treating the "output" of banks' intermediation services as a charge not on the banks themselves but on other economic agents was something that was actively considered, but ultimately resisted. Why? Because any such distribution of these "imputed charges" to third parties would be "purely hypothetical" and, as such, "*would be more misleading than the paradox of financial concerns appearing to make a steady annual loss.*"[84] In other words, while the envisioning of banks as unproductive, or as "leeches" on the national income stream, was indeed considered problematic, "paradoxical" and "misleading," it was not seen as problematic *enough* to warrant an accounting solution which was considered technically unsound; it was problematic, but not *that* problematic.

I will spend the final few pages of this chapter mainly in lending some wider explicatory context to what, on first blush, may seem like odd representations of banking productiveness for the official statistical mouthpieces of – in particular – the French and UK governments to have been propagating in their benchmark renderings of the national economy. First, however, I want to pause to emphasize the contemporary *materiality* of these renderings. In all the countries where systematic national accounts first developed, they did so ultimately because the government believed they were needed. Independent scholars, of various sorts, had of course been making estimates of national income for a very long time; the singular reason why such estimates did not develop into systematized, government-supported initiatives *before* the early- to mid-twentieth century is that the powers-that-were, to the extent they were even aware of such estimates, saw them as vain academic exercises rather than something useful and worth investing in.

In the West, all of that changed in the 1930s and 1940s. It typically did so, furthermore, in such a way that governments' new-found interest in national economic statistics centered explicitly on the question of the extent to which different industries contributed to economic output. The demand for numbers, in other words, reflected a demand for knowledge about economic productiveness and its constituent parts. And this was nowhere more true, crucially, than in the UK and France. In the former, historians point to the outbreak of World War II, and the summer of 1940, as the pivotal moment of stimulus to the formal national accounting project. Mark Perlman and Morgan Marietta relate the relevant part of the story as follows: "At that point John Maynard Keynes was the economic advisor to the War Cabinet and proposed that a British national accounts system be created *in order to identify production capacities throughout all industries.*" The accounts were necessary, in other words, because "maximizing war production" was suddenly a political priority, and thus knowing the contribution of different industries to this production was essential. [85] The more profound question underlying such demand was captured, of course, in the title of the book Keynes published the same year: *How to Pay for the War.*[86]

In France, the perceived need for national accounts reflected a similar political imperative of maximizing national economic output, but there the latter crystallized, not surprisingly, immediately after the war rather than during it. Reeling from the ravages of war, rebuilding the economy and society through a prioritization of productive activities became *the* state mission. "Maximising the productive power of the [French] nation," Peter Miller observes, simply but vitally, "was the political goal of post-war modernisation." It was as basic as that; basic or not, however, it would be wrong to underestimate quite how significant this objective was for the form and content of the national accounts that would serve to inform and shape the intended economic transformation. "For what were the French national accounts to be," Miller asks rhetorically, "if not accounts of *productive* activities?"[87]

Given these two national contexts, the fact that the early national accounts of each country denied the decisive stamp of productiveness to the banking sector is of the greatest historical import. This import extended, moreover, to the philosophy, politics, and practice of banking across national boundaries, as well as within them – or so I shall argue shortly. But to get to that argument we need to consider the key question of why the French national income statisticians decided that picturing an unproductive banking sector was unproblematic, and why the UK's statisticians decided it was not problematic enough to justify a compromised methodological solution.

It is undoubtedly the case that specifically technical concerns were relevant in both places. Thus, just as the UK statistical team was discomfited by the idea of implementing a treatment relying on a "purely hypothetical" distribution of imputed charges, so there was a "mechanical" factor in play in France: the fact, as André Vanoli has argued, that the national accounts were practically used predominantly for short-term forecasting, thus placing the emphasis of measurement squarely on market-priced transactions.[88] On my reading, however, we simply cannot understand the UK and French approaches unless we understand the immediate, and indeed wider, intellectual contexts in which they were decided upon.

The present-day Swiss national accountant Philippe Stauffer alludes to these contexts in noting that in the early years of Western national accounting more generically, "there was strong feeling, especially among 'left-oriented thinkers', that banks did not have production per se."[89] This is absolutely the frame within which we need to understand the French national accounting treatment of banks. François Fourquet's seminal text on the relationship between national accounting and planning in post-war France makes it clear that the SEEF was populated with figures who, even if influenced by the neoclassical economics of Léon Walras, retained strong vestiges of nineteenth-century political-economic thinking. And it *was* thinking of a leftist strain, and hence more Marx than Malthus. The SEEF was widely acknowledged as being on the left politically; it operated according to an avowedly collective work ethic; and it even accepted into its ranks those suspected of being communists.[90] The decision to exclude financial institutions from the all-important production account was not, in this environment, an incongruous one.

The situation was altogether different in the UK. The Central Statistical Office was no communist stronghold. Yet it is very much the case that the experiences of the 1920s and 1930s had hardened attitudes towards the banking sector among leading British economists, including those who played important roles on the early national accounting scene. One of these was Josiah Stamp. President of the Royal Statistical Society in the early- and mid-1930s, Stamp had by that point worked on national income estimates on-and-off, both individually and in collaboration with Arthur Bowley, for the best part of two decades, and this work has been widely credited with shaping the more systematic work by others which soon followed.[91] Stamp was also a director of the Bank of England in the 1930s, but this did not stop him from expressing concern and skepticism over the role of the contemporary commercial banking system. One does not need to invoke the most infamous quotation with which he is often now credited – the one which starts "Banking was conceived in iniquity..." – to appreciate his increasingly critical perspective.[92] In a 1930 speech at a luncheon held, significantly, at the highly symbolic location of the Bond Club of New York, Stamp clarified his critique in sober, but no less critical terms.[93]

For all the importance of Stamp and others, however, it is Keynes that stands above the crowd as the key figure in the materialization of the UK national accounts, *and* as UK-based professional economics' most strident critic of the banking sector in that era. Keynes's role in relation to the national accounts was, as Geoff Tily has recently emphasized, "multifaceted: he was a user, supporter and producer." We have already touched upon the importance of his *How to Pay for the War* (1940), at which point Keynes "became directly involved in the construction of national accounts."[94] Yet equally important, in many respects, was his earlier, more explicitly theoretical, and of course more famous, *General Theory* (1936). This was not just because the analysis therein was framed at the scale of the nation, which meant that, as Kendrick has observed, "attempts to test and apply his theory gave an impetus to estimation of [national economic] aggregates."[95] It was also, Vanoli notes, because the *Theory* posited equations describing the relationships between the national accounts' key concepts – "concepts such as income, consumption, investment and saving" – and in doing so gave the development of such accounts a genuine scholarly imprimatur.[96] One could justifiably argue, as a result, that Keynes is *the* key historical figure in the initiation of the complex, multi-directional and ongoing interplay between economic theory, national accounting metrics, economic policy, and economic reality.[97]

As we saw earlier, economists' active involvement in national accounting – or even simply the emergence of the modern calculus of national accounting *alongside* the theoretical work of such economists – often served to sharpen, or sharpens for us in retrospect, important tensions in their economic vistas, particularly in relation to value theory and the putative neoclassical dismissal of political economy's binaries. This was no less true of Keynes than of figures like Alfred Marshall. For all his emphasis on macroeconomic aggregates, Keynes was a neoclassicist on fundamental questions of value. He too, however, like Marshall and Schumpeter, though in a different way again, fell back on the conceptual dualism of productiveness and unproductiveness which pure neoclassicism sought to eschew but which national accounting formally institutionalized. In Keynes's case, echoing the work of John Stuart Mill perhaps more clearly than any other predecessor, the productive/unproductive division in question applied nominally only to *consumption*. Yet Keynes's definition of "unproductive consumption," in drawing upon its role in the productive sphere – it was that consumption which could be "foregone by the consumer without reacting on the amount of his productive effort" – arguably remained haunted still by the classical conception of productive *labor*.[98]

Given Keynes's pivotal role in the history of the UK national accounts both up to 1940 and in the early 1940s (he wrote the text for the first official estimates in 1941, for instance), the accounting system he helped shape can be read as, to one extent or another, a manifestation *of* his economic worldview. Specifically bearing in mind its allowance for productive/unproductive distinctions, where, in that worldview, did banks "fit"? This is no straightforward matter. Conventional wisdom of the early twenty-first century has Keynes as a persistent critic of finance, and especially of what we usually think of as "speculative" finance – the quote from the *General Theory* about things becoming problematic "when enterprise becomes the bubble on a whirlpool of speculation" is a particular favorite – but inevitably things are rather more complicated than that.

If we wind back two decades from the General Theory, to when Keynes was in his early thirties and his economics in its relative infancy, we find a scholar whose views on banks could not be farther removed from those imputed to today's stereotype. A pair of articles from The Economic Journal in 1914 is especially insightful. In the first, Keynes offered a very gentle critique of the recent activities of certain UK clearing banks, his criticism extending no further than accusing them of "a lack of courage."[99] Three months later a follow-up, of sorts, appeared, in which Keynes seems rather taken aback by complaints from bankers about what he had had to say in the first piece. Defensive, and almost painfully eager to placate his critics, Keynes offered a highly revealing mea culpa, admitting that he had been less than fair, and insisting that his disappointment in the banks' timidity

> was that of an admirer, my complaints those of a true lover. I believe our banking system, and indeed the whole intricate organism of the City, to be one of the best and most characteristic creations of that part of the genius and virtue of our nation which has found its outlet in "business"...[100]

Over the course of the next 20 years, however, Keynes's views on banking gradually, but ineluctably, changed. The change was first clearly evidenced in his Treatise on Money, published in 1930. Here Keynes took the banks to task for acting against the interests of productive investment, and indeed did so with such verve that one contemporary reviewer of the book summoned the powerful, Biblical image of Keynes "scourging the money-changers."[101] This scourging was renewed in the General Theory six years later, and was now distilled into his famous critique of the rentier.[102] Keynes advocated the "euthanasia" of the latter on the grounds that "he" had hobbled the economy of the Western world in the early 1930s by exploiting the scarcity value of capital to keep interest rates high, thus choking off productive investment.

The rentier and the banker, of course, are not necessarily the selfsame. Keynes, however, did tend typically to equate the two, or at the very least to argue that their interests were aligned and that the culpability of the rentier was also that of the banking community. Indeed, as writers such as Dudley Dillard and Keynes's biographer Robert Skidelsky have intimated, it was in conflating these two and in simultaneously theorizing an adversarial relationship between the banker-rentier and an alliance of laborers and industrial capitalists that Keynes departed perhaps most materially from Marx.[103] As Skidelsky observes, in his biography not of Keynes but of the fascist politician Oswald Mosley: "He [Keynes] tended to assume an identity of interest between workers and manufacturers against their common enemy – the rentier and banker."[104] In this way, Keynes played no small part in cementing the (to my mind, unhelpful) popular notion of a distinction between a "financial economy" on the one hand and a "real economy" of workers and industrialists on the other. It was, most critically of all, in making this particular distinction that Keynes formulated the critique of "finance" which post-Keynesians still find so appealing today. Will Hutton makes the argument as powerfully as anyone else:

> For Keynes, the interaction of the financial system with the real economy is capitalism's existential problem. Banks are where our savings reside without any promissory note about when we intend to spend them, so that the spectre permanently hovers over the economy of there either being too little spending or too much. The job of finance is to recycle those savings back into investment and so sustain overall levels of demand, production and employment at a balanced rate. Free-market economists maintain that free decisions in free financial markets will propel the rate of interest to take the entire weight of this existential task. Keynes disputed this to the depths of his being.[105]

It is precisely in the context of Keynes's critique of financial capitalists that we need, I would argue, to understand two things. The first, and the more straightforward to foreground, is the representation of banking as unproductive or only marginally productive in the early UK national accounts. That the producers of those accounts were relatively comfortable with such an image seems entirely reasonable when one appreciates what Keynes and other economists who helped catalyze and shape the accounts thought about banks' role in the economy.

The second, meanwhile, is Keynes's views on international finance and, as discussed near the beginning of this chapter, his growing belief in the early 1930s that finance should be "primarily national." As I suggested in my brief discussion of the intellectual backdrop to Bretton Woods, *this* – Keynes's views on banks and banking – much more than his views on capital flows (à la Harry White), underwrote his support for financial protectionism. So much is clear if we return to the "self-sufficiency" article armed now with this knowledge of the particular lineaments of Keynes's critique. In championing protectionism, his strongest concerns were with not monetary movements but corporate capitalist characteristics. "The decadent international but individualistic capitalism, in the hands of which we found ourselves after the war, is not a success," Keynes maintained. "It is not intelligent, it is not beautiful, it is not just, it is not virtuous – and it doesn't deliver the goods." Even more pointedly, and stripping away any lingering ambiguity, Keynes styled himself as one "who in the last resort prefers anything on earth to what the financial reports are wont to call 'the best opinion in Wall Street'."[106] Keynes, in other words, passionately opposed this so-called "best" of Wall Street.

I would also argue, further, that these two things – the economic envisionings of national accounting, and protectionism in global finance – were not unrelated. More specifically: perspectives on the desirability or otherwise of financial internationalization now inhabited the same conceptual space as perspectives on the productiveness of banking, as articulated most materially in the national accounts. The latter perspectives perhaps did not (yet) directly and tangibly underwrite policy *practice* regarding financial boundaries. They were, however, closely aligned with the theoretical rationality thereof, which, as posited by Keynes and the other European negotiators at Bretton Woods, largely supported the enclosure which had come to dominate international financial relations between the two World Wars.[107]

How might we seek to capture the nature of this particular conceptual relationship at this particular historical juncture? Think of it, I would suggest, this way. In their politically-potent national accounts, France and the UK, two of the world's major forces in international banking prior to World War I, now showed banks as having no productive output or, in the case of the UK in most years, *negative* output: as a leech upon – in the context of international banking – *other countries*' national income streams. Such a representational milieu was hardly propitious, I would submit, for the re-emergence of UK- or French-led cross-border banking, especially if one considers that these were precisely the years during which the colonial architecture which buttressed much of the legacy British and French international banking networks was being dismantled. And when, as we will see in the following chapter, international banking did begin to re-emerge from its 30-year period of hibernation in the early 1960s, it would indeed not be British or French banks leading the way. It took more than another decade for such banks to begin again to compete aggressively overseas – *and*, in parallel, for the national accounts in those countries to re-classify banks as productive rather than unproductive actors.

On my reading, Keynes's singular importance with regard to the particular historical-geographical conjuncture I have discussed in the present chapter is that it was in and through him and his various interconnected contributory roles – professional economist, public intellectual, government advisor and negotiator and, not least, protagonist and producer of national accounts – that, as they used to say of the city of Los Angeles, "it all comes together." By means, in particular, of his critique of the rentier-banker, Keynes effected a pivotal rapprochement between ideas about banks' positioning vis-à-vis economic and geopolitical boundaries respectively. In doing so, he brought those two sets of ideas closer together than they had ever been before.

If Keynes epitomized in many respects this particular constellation of policies, ideas, and representations of banks' various boundary negotiations, specifically as it came to cohere in the UK and – similarly, but by no means identically – France in the years prior to and immediately after World War II, what of the third European country whose national accounting treatment of financial services we considered above? In Germany, as we saw, the national accounts of the early 1930s had simply avoided the question of banks' productiveness altogether. When, subsequent to its shrouding in the Nazi era, German national accounting re-emerged to the international eye after the war, it had of course been bifurcated. In the process, the new national accounting systems came to reflect very closely the political-economic orthodoxies of the dominant external influences on either side of the border.

On one side, in the German Democratic Republic, under direct Soviet influence, the explicitly communist Material Product System of accounting was implemented and, as we saw above, it judged that banks had no production. On the other side, in the new Federal Republic, the accounts, like the broader political economy of the nation, headed in another direction entirely, *including* in their statistical treatment of banks. The predominant influence now, of course, came from the West, in the shape of new integrative transatlantic institutions and, perhaps above all else, the US. As Utz-Peter Reich has noted, we cannot understand the evolution and form of national accounts in post-war West Germany except in relation to "the so-called Marshall plan introduced by the United States in order to contain communism in Europe. The aid granted on the basis of the program," Reich continues, "was coupled with a demand for macroeconomic figures, and the newly founded OEEC promoted the setting up of national accounts for that purpose."[108] The American influence on West German national accounting practices would be, in short, writ large; and the appraisal of banks' productiveness in the national accounts of the US itself, together with the relationship between this appraisal and the place of US banks in the international financial system, is the subject of the next chapter.

Notes

1   G. Als, "The nightmare of economic accounts in a small country with a large international banking sector," *Review of Income and Wealth*, 34, 1988, pp.101–110, at p.110.

2   E. Helleiner, *States and the Reemergence of Global Finance: From Bretton Woods to the 1990s*, Cornell University Press, Ithaca, 1994, p.1.

3   Y. Park and J. Zwick, *International Banking in Theory and Practice*, Addison-Wesley, Reading MA, 1985, p.7. Cf. M. Moffitt, *World's Money: International Banking from Bretton Woods to the Brink of Insolvency*, Simon & Schuster, New York, 1983, p.42: "Banking across national borders ground to a halt in the early 1930s and really did not resume until after the Second World War."

4   B. Eichengreen, *Globalizing Capital: A History of the International Monetary System*, 2nd edition, Princeton University Press, Princeton, 2008. Another good summary account is found in E. Helleiner, "When finance was servant: International capital movements in the Bretton Woods order," in P. Cerny (ed), *Finance and World Politics: Markets, Regimes, and States in the Post-Hegemonic Era* (Edward Elgar, Aldershot, 1993, 20–48), at pp.21–26.

5   R. Abdelal, *Capital Rules: The Construction of Global Finance*, Harvard University Press, Cambridge MA, 2007, p.5.

6   Eichengreen, *Globalizing Capital*, p.44.

7   Ibid, p.82.

8   J. Frieden, *Banking on the World: The Politics of American International Finance*, Harper & Row, New York, 1987, p.51.

9   Which is to say that readers interested in more holistic accounts of Bretton Woods, and of the institutions and practices it gave rise to, should look elsewhere – in the first place to, I would suggest, the discussions in Helleiner, *States*, chapter 2, and Eichengreen, *Globalizing Capital*, chapter 4.

10 Those who refer to this discourse include L. Pauly, "Capital mobility, state autonomy and political legitimacy," *Journal of International Affairs*, 48, 1995, pp.369–388, at p.375; Helleiner, *States*, pp.36–37, 44–46, 95–96; Abdelal, *Capital Rules*, pp.46, 51–54; and L. Panitch and S. Gindin, "Finance and American Empire," in L. Panitch and M. Konings (eds), *American Empire and the Political Economy of Global Finance* (Palgrave Macmillan, New York, 2008, 17–47), p.25.

11 J. Keynes, "National self-sufficiency," *The Yale Review,* New Series 22, 1933, pp.755–769; the quotations are from pp.757, 758, 762.

12 Pauly, "Capital mobility," pp.374–375.

13 M. Lawlor, "Keynes and the financial market processes in historical context: from the *Treatise* to *The General Theory*," in P. Arestis, G. Palma and M. Sawyer (eds), *Capital Controversy, Post-Keynesian Economics and the History of Economic Thought: Essays in Honour of Geoff Harcourt, Volume One* (Routledge, New York, 1997, 217–228); the quotation is from p.219.

14 Pauly, "Capital mobility," p.375.

15 In fact Keynes believed that all international financial flows, not just those associated with speculation, had the *potential* to disrupt national macroeconomic planning (Helleiner, "When finance was the servant," p.26), making the idea of a categorical differentiation among them intrinsically problematic.

16 US Treasury, *Preliminary draft outline of a proposal for an international stabilization fund of the united and associated nations,* US Department of the Treasury, Washington, 1943, pp.20, 3.

17 Pauly, "Capital mobility," p.375.

18 Department of State, *Proceedings and documents of United Nations monetary and financial conference. Bretton Woods, New Hampshire. July 1–22, 1944, vols I and II,* GPO, Washington, 1948, p.1630. Helleiner, *States,* pp.44–49 is especially helpful on some of the international disagreements – especially between the US and the UK – on these issues, and on the compromises in policy and agreement wording which resulted.

19 Abdelal, *Capital Rules,* pp.51–54.

20 See especially Helleiner, *States.*

21 M. Watson, *The Political Economy of International Capital Mobility,* Palgrave Macmillan, Basingstoke, 2007, pp.100–101. Cf A. Leyshon and A. Tickell, "Money order? The discursive construction of Bretton Woods and the making and breaking of regulatory space," *Environment and Planning A,* 26, 1994, pp.1861–1890, at p.1862, for whom "the regulatory order which the [Bretton Woods] system sought to impose upon capitalism was *profoundly influenced* by a shift in the prevailing intellectual climate, associated with the rise of a new practical economic discourse" (emphasis added).

22 Helleiner, *States,* p.45.

23 H. Boss, *Theories of Surplus and Transfer: Parasites and Producers in Economic Thought,* Unwin Hyman, Boston, 1989, p.227.

24 Cf. P. Miller, "Accounting for progress — National accounting and planning in France: A review essay," *Accounting, Organizations and Society,* 11, 1986, pp.83–104, at p.88: "The distinction between the productive and the unproductive underlies much of the debates over the categories to be adopted within a national accounting system"; also W. Beckerman, *An Introduction to National Income Analysis,* Weidenfeld & Nicholson, London, 1968, p.92: "This distinction between productive activities and all other transactions is absolutely central to the basic concepts of national accounting."

25 M. Callon and K. Çalışkan, "Economization, part 1: shifting attention from the economy towards processes of economization," *Economy and Society,* 38, 2009, pp. 369–398.

26 J. Lichfield, "Sarkozy proposes the *joie de vivre* index," *The Independent,* 14 Sep 2009. There is, of course, an enormous critical literature now on the power more generally of accounting and accountants within modern society. See, for instance, the excellent collection of essays edited by Anthony Hopwood and Peter Miller,

Accounting as Social and Institutional Practice, Cambridge University Press, Cambridge, 1994; also important papers by R. Hines, "Financial accounting: in communicating reality, we construct reality," *Accounting, Organizations and Society*, 13, 1988, 251–261 and G. Morgan, "Accounting as reality construction: Towards a new epistemology for accounting practice," *Accounting, Organizations and Society*, 13, 1988, 477–485. On the socially material role of national accounting (as opposed to company accounting) more specifically, see especially N. Ruggles and R. Ruggles, *National Accounting and Economic Policy: The United States and the UN Systems*, Edward Elgar, Cheltenham, 1999, and M. Ward, *Quantifying the World: UN Ideas and Statistics*, Indiana University Press, Bloomington, 2004.

27   J. Tomlinson, "The politics of economic measurement: the rise of the 'productivity problem' in the 1940s," in Hopwood and Miller (eds), *Accounting* (168–189), pp.168–169.

28   Z. Kenessey, "Preface," in Z. Kenessey (ed), *The Accounts of Nations* (IOS Press, Amsterdam, 1994), p. v; my emphasis.

29   J. Kendrick, "The historical development of national accounts," *History of Political Economy*, 2, 1970, pp.284–315, at p.306.

30   On the history of the UN's role in developing international national accounting standards, see Ward, *Quantifying*.

31   Paul Studenski's magisterial *Income of Nations*, New York University Press, New York, 1958, remains the authoritative account of the period up to 1950. Kendrick, "Historical development," is shorter and more accessible, but, likewise, dated. André Vanoli's *A History of National Accounting*, IOS Press, Amsterdam, 2005, is the fullest attempt to trace developments up to the present day.

32   The reader will notice here that my focus is on GDP rather than GNP. The reason for this emphasis (in this section of the book, at any rate) is simply that of the two, GDP is the more frequently invoked in social and political discourse. The difference between them is that GDP is based on location (output produced within a country's borders), while GNP is based on ownership (the output of enterprises owned by a country's citizens).

33   Like GDP and GNP, GDP and GVA are very close relations, but are not identical. To derive GDP from cumulative all-sector GVA, it is necessary to add total product-based taxes and deduct total product-based subsidies. A. Hopwood, S. Burchell and C. Chubb, "Value-added accounting and national economic policy," in Hopwood and Miller (eds), *Accounting* (211–236), offer a useful account of the political-economic history of the concept of "value added" in accounting practices.

34   A. Shaikh and E. Tonak, *Measuring the Wealth of Nations: The Political Economy of National Accounts*, Cambridge University Press, Cambridge, 1994, p.229.

35   On household labour and national accounting, the classic feminist critique is M. Waring, *If Women Counted: A New Feminist Economics*, Macmillan, London, 1989.

36   Shaikh and Tonak, *Measuring*, pp.52, 2.

37   B. Haig, "The treatment of interest and financial intermediaries in the national accounts of Australia," *Review of Income and Wealth*, 32, 1986, pp.409–424, at p.415.

38   Office for National Statistics, *United Kingdom National Accounts: The Blue Book 2006*, Palgrave Macmillan, Basingstoke, 2006, p.21; original emphasis.

39   E.g. M. Jayasinghe, "On the mechanics of measuring the production of financial institutions," MPRA Paper 7694, 2005 (available at http://mpra.ub.uni-muenchen. de/7694/1/MPRA_paper_7694.pdf); and see also the papers collected together in section STCPM28 (pp.315–366) of the Irving Fisher Committee on Central Bank

Statistics, "IFC's contribution to the 57th ISI Session, Durban, 2009," IFC Bulletin No. 33, July 2010, available at http://www.bis.org/ifc/publ/ifcb33.pdf.

40   C. Carson and J. Honsa, "The United Nations system of national accounts: an introduction," *Survey of Current Business*, 70(6), 1990, pp.20–30, at p.23.

41   B. Haig, "The treatment of banks in the social accounts," *Economic Record*, 49, 1973, pp.624–628, at p.624.

42   As Frits Bos, "The national accounts as a tool for analysis and policy; past, present and future," Unpublished PhD thesis, Universiteit Twente, 2003, p.194, notes starkly of the conceptual implications of this exception: "lending money by a bank is production" whilst "lending money by non-financial producers or households is no production." Cf. R. Speagle and L. Silverman, "The banking income dilemma," *Review of Economics and Statistics*, 35, 1953, pp.128–139, at p.129: "the lending institution is 'productive,' but the wealthy relation financing his nephew's college education is not."

43   Haig, "Treatment of interest," p.409.

44   R. Stone, "Definition and measurement of the national income and related totals," in Sub-Committee on National Income Statistics of the League of Nations Committee of Statistical Experts, *Measurement of National Income and the Construction of Social Accounts* (United Nations, Geneva, 1947, 23–116), p.40.

45   Studenski, *Income*, p.192.

46   J. Gorman, "Alternative measures of the real output and productivity of commercial banks," in V. Fuchs (ed), *Production and Productivity in the Service Industries* (Columbia University Press, New York, 1969, 155–199), p.156.

47   See, for instance, P. dos Santos, "On the content of banking in contemporary capitalism," *Historical Materialism*, 17, 2009 , pp.180–213.

48   E. Engelen et al., *After the Great Complacence: Financial Crisis and the Politics of Reform*, Oxford University Press, Oxford, 2011, pp.115–116.

49   G. Tily and G. Jenkinson, "Recording payments for banking services in the UK National Accounts: A progress report," Office for National Statistics, available at http://www.statistics.gov.uk/articles/nojournal/FISIM_progress_report.pdf (retrieved October 2009), p.2.

50   Vanoli, *History*, p.156.

51   Interview with author, 12 August 2010.

52   Email to author, 19 August 2010.

53   http://www.statistics.gov.uk/about/statisticsusers/fsug.asp (retrieved April 2011).

54   D. Wallace, "Measuring the contribution of financial services to the economy: a report on a meeting of the Financial statistics Users' Group," Bank of England, available at http://www.bankofengland.co.uk/statistics/Documents/ms/articles/artmay01.pdf (retrieved February 2009), p.2.

55   Philippe Stauffer, email to author, 19 August 2010.

56   Ibid. See also P. Stauffer, "A tale of two worlds: how bankers and national accountants view banking," Paper prepared for the 28th General Conference of the International Association for Research in Income and Wealth, 2004, available at http://www.iariw.org/papers/2004/stauffer.pdf (retrieved Jan 2010), p.3: "bankers are often critical and tend to question the conventions for measuring banking output in [national accounts]."

57   Email to author, 19 August 2010. In contrast, lobbying by bankers on *company* accounting standards has been widely reported. See, for instance, S. Zeff, "'Political' lobbying on proposed standards: a challenge to the IASB," *Accounting Horizons*, 16, 2002, pp.43–54, especially at pp.49–50.

58   Interview with author, 18 August 2010.

59 This relationship in itself is the subject of an important and growing literature. A good place to start is with Mary Poovey's discussion of the very early days of this relationship, before the 1750s, in her *A History of the Modern Fact: Problems of Knowledge in the Sciences of Wealth and Society*, University of Chicago Press, Chicago, 1998, chapter 2.

60 For details, see, inter alia, IMF, *1989 Annual Report*, IMF, Washington, 1989, p.79.

61 G. Tily, "John Maynard Keynes and the development of national accounts in Britain, 1895–1941," *Review of Income and Wealth*, 55, 2009, pp.331–359, at p.355.

62 On this increasing distance of respective praxis, see U-P. Reich, *National Accounts and Economic Value: A Study in Concepts*, Palgrave Macmillan, Basingstoke, 2001. Note also that in the few national instances where national accounting has historically been dominated more by statisticians than by economists, the latter have tended to become relatively more influential in the last two decades. The UK is a good example of this transition (Geoff Tily, interview with author, 18 August 2010).

63 OEEC, *A Standardised System of National Accounts*, OEEC, Paris, 1952, p.52. The OEEC was the precursor organization to the OECD, which replaced it in 1961.

64 A. Smith, *The Wealth of Nations: IV-V*, Penguin, London, 2004, p.66.

65 The quotation is from Ward, *Quantifying*, p.93.

66 E.g. Speagle and Silverman, "The banking income dilemma," p.129: "As a first principle it may be postulated that the market place shall be the touchstone of the accounting value of goods and services produced. The price obtained in a (by some relaxed standards) free and open market shall measure the value contribution of the productive agent's hire."

67 Reich, *National Accounts*, p.3. While I have learned a great deal from Reich's important work on national accounts and theories of economic value, the problematic relationship between national accounting and neoclassical economics prompts a different impulse in his work than in mine: where his *National Accounts* seeks to blend *classical* value theory with neoclassicism, my preference is to seek to highlight tensions in the latter.

68 A. Marshall, *Principles of Economics* (9th, variorum, edition, ed. C. Guillebaud), vol. 1, Macmillan, London, 1961, pp.xv,67n1,66n1.

69 See Tily, "John Maynard Keynes," pp.334–335.

70 G. Pilling, *The Crisis of Keynesian Economics: A Marxist View*, Taylor & Francis, London, 1986, p.109.

71 J. Schumpeter, *History of Economic Analysis*, Routledge, New York, 1987, p.597.

72 See, respectively, J. Schumpeter, *Business Cycles: A Theoretical, Historical, and Statistical Analysis of the Capitalist Process, Volume 1*, McGraw-Hill, New York, 1939, pp.146–147, and *The Theory of Economic Development*, Harvard University Press, Cambridge MA, 1934, chapter 5 (the quotation is from p.201). R. Wolfson, "The economic dynamics of Joseph Schumpeter," *Economic Development and Cultural Change*, 7, 1958, pp.31–54, remains an excellent source on these areas of Schumpeter's work and the connections between them.

73 Schumpeter, *Theory*, p.175.

74 Stone, "Definition," p.40.

75 Studenski, *Income*, p.192.

76 Speagle and Silverman, "The banking income dilemma," p.130.

77 A. Tooze, *Statistics and the German State, 1900–1945: The Making of Modern Economic Knowledge*, Cambridge University Press, Cambridge, 2001, p.122. See also, on the early development of German national accounts, U-P. Reich, "German national accounts between politics and academics," in Kenessey (ed), *Accounts* (144–168), and

M. Perlman and M. Marietta, "The politics of social accounting: public goals and the evolution of the national accounts in Germany, the United Kingdom and the United States," *Review of Political Economy*, 17, 2005, pp.211–230. A key driver of this early development, Tooze argues, was the ongoing debate in the early 1920s over war reparations; since Germany's ability to pay was a central consideration in such debates, estimates of national income were seen to be essential.

78 P. Jostock, "The long-term growth of national income in Germany," in S. Kuznets (ed), *Income and Wealth, Series V* (Bowes and Bowes, London, 1955, 79–122), p.104.

79 Studenski, *Income*, p.192.

80 See especially F. Fourquet, *Les Comptes de la puissance: histoire de la comptabilité nationale et du plan*, Editions Encre, Paris, 1980; and the superb review essay on this book, Miller, "Accounting for progress."

81 Studenski, *Income*, p.192. This, note, was not the same approach – mentioned above – that Australia used in 1946 and 1947. The latter excluded only interest income, as opposed to all banking income.

82 See, for instance, W. Stolper, "National accounting in East Germany," *Review of Income and Wealth*, 9, 1961, pp.178–205.

83 L. Officer, "What Was the UK GDP Then? A data study," Unpublished paper, n.d., available at http://www.measuringworth.com/datasets/ukgdp/ukgdpstudy.pdf (retrieved January 2012), p.15.

84 UK Central Statistical Office, *National income statistics: sources and methods*, HMSO, London, 1956, p.145; emphasis added.

85 Perlman and Marietta, "Politics," pp.216, 211; emphasis added.

86 J. Keynes, *How to Pay for the War*, Macmillan, London, 1940.

87 Miller, "Accounting for progress," p.92; original emphasis.

88 Interview with author, 12 August, 2010.

89 Email to author, 19 August 2010.

90 Fourquet, *Les comptes*.

91 E.g. Tily, "John Maynard Keynes," p.335–340.

92 Enter these few words on any Internet search engine and you will find the full version of the quotation in question, which castigates bankers specifically in respect of their power to create money. There is, to the best of my knowledge, no reliable evidence that Stamp ever made this speech (reputedly at the University of Texas in the late 1920s). That said, and notwithstanding others' doubts, it does not strike me as unfeasible, particularly if one reads Stamp's published oeuvre. Consider, for example, his thoughtful commentary on the 1931 Report of the Macmillan Committee on Finance and Industry, in which, inter alia, he identified as a genuine public service contribution the Report's exposition of "the extent of the creation of credit by the joint stock banks and its effect on the level of prices" (J. Stamp, "The Report of the Macmillan Committee," *The Economic Journal*, 41, 1931, pp.424–435, at p.425). He had, as they say, 'form.'

93 J. Stamp, "The economic outlook," in his *Criticism and Other Addresses* (Ernest Benn, London, 1931, 318–336), especially at pp.324, 332.

94 Tily, "John Maynard Keynes," p.332.

95 Kendrick, "Historical development," p.305.

96 Vanoli, *History*, p.19. Cf. M. Perlman, "Political purpose and the national accounts," in W. Alonso and P. Starr (eds), *The Politics of Numbers* (Russell Sage Foundation, New York, 1987, 33–51), p.140: "thereafter many, indeed most, of those who worked on the national accounts wanted their work to reflect and to be integratable with what the Keynesian analysis offered."

97 Cf, here, T. Suzuki, "The epistemology of macroeconomic reality: The Keynesian Revolution from an accounting point of view," *Accounting, Organizations and Society*, 28, 2003, pp.471–517, who argues, along somewhat similar lines (and with a comparable focus on the UK), that developments in UK national accounting in this era constituted a key "foundation" of macroeconomics in general and the so-called "Keynesian revolution" in particular.

98 J. Keynes, *A Treatise on Money, vol. 2: The Applied Theory of Money*, Harcourt, Brace and Company, New York, 1930, p.125.

99 J. Keynes, "War and the financial system, August, 1914," *The Economic Journal*, 24, 1914, pp.460–486, at p.461.

100 J. Keynes, "The prospects of money, November, 1914," *The Economic Journal*, 24, 1914, pp.610–634, at p.633.

101 B. Dyason, "Scourging the money-changers," *Economic Record*, 7, 1931, pp. 227–238. The reference is to the narrative of Jesus and the money-changers, usually referred to as the "Cleansing of the Temple."

102 A critique which mirrored in a number of important ways the one earlier advanced by Max Weber, on which see especially L. Seabrooke, *US Power in International Finance: The Victory of Dividends*, Palgrave Macmillan, Basingstoke, 2001, at pp. 41–43.

103 D. Dillard, "Keynes and Proudhon," *The Journal of Economic History*, 2, 1942, pp.63–76.

104 R. Skidelsky, *Oswald Mosley*, Macmillan, London, 1975, p.141.

105 W. Hutton, "Will the real Keynes stand up, not this sad caricature?," *The Observer*, 2 November 2008.

106 Keynes, "National self-sufficiency," pp.760–761, 766.

107 Helleiner, *States*.

108 Reich, "German national accounts," p.163.

4

America, and Boundaries Breached

The criterion of productivity followed in our estimates, chosen in line with current social opinion, classifies as productive activities that, for a society organized differently from the United States in this century, might well be considered worthless and even harmful. It swells national income with items that represent what many citizens condemn as a misuse of energy and the inadequacies of the existing social structure.

Simon Kuznets (1941)[1]

Following the three-decade-long period of retrenchment discussed in the previous chapter, the financial world began to open up once again towards the very end of the 1950s. It did so at first hesitantly, but then with ever greater force and rapidity as the 1960s progressed. This chapter addresses key elements of this process of opening up through to the mid- to late 1970s, by which time many of the boundaries which had crystallized in the 1930s and 1940s had been removed.

The chapter highlights two main dimensions of this process. First, it emphasizes that, somewhat paradoxically, the global banking system re-internationalized – to the extent that it was feasible to do so – *before* global financial markets did. In other words, it became possible for banks to move relatively freely across international borders, or at least *some* international borders, before it became possible for money in many of its forms to do so. Indeed, as we shall see, in certain important instances it was precisely the ongoing use of cross-border capital controls that *stimulated* internationalization by financial institutions. Whereas banking had already undergone a massive wave of cross-border expansion by the early 1970s, extensive disassembly of international capital controls did not even begin until the mid-1970s and still had a considerable way to go a decade later. Second,

Banking Across Boundaries: Placing Finance in Capitalism, First Edition. Brett Christophers.
© 2013 John Wiley & Sons, Ltd. Published 2013 by John Wiley & Sons, Ltd.

I demonstrate that this process of banking internationalization had a very particular geographical centre of gravity. During the two decades considered in this chapter it comprised, almost exclusively, internationalization by *American* banks. The leading banks of other leading capitalist nations, as we will see in Part III, did not follow the US lead until later.

The primary thrust of my argument in this chapter is that as in the case of the French and especially UK-centered constellation of ideas and practices considered in Chapter 3, there was, in the US-centered context we turn to now, an *alignment* of "banking across boundaries" representations and realities in the period under review. In the European case, as we saw above, this alignment took the form of banks crossing neither conceptual boundaries nor geopolitical ones; they were envisioned as unproductive and they remained nationally-circumscribed, and in Keynes's multi-facetted intellectual and policy contributions we encountered arguably the critical infrastructure of this alignment. The US case constitutes an entirely different conjunctural assemblage. As various authors, not least the great Keynesian economist J. K. Galbraith, have argued, the US government was equally invested in the national accounts of the pre- and post-war years as its French and British counterparts – politically, ideologically, and economically.[2] Yet, crucially, the picture of banking and banking productiveness which the US national accounts conveyed to the country's politicians was wholly different to the one contained in the French and British national accounts of the post-war era. It showed banks as directly productive economic agents. The chapter's aim is to place the physical boundary crossings of US banks – crossings in which US politicians were no less invested, of course – firmly in the context of this conceptual picture. I argue, in essence, that it is no coincidence that the US was the first of the historically-significant Western banking powers to both re-internationalize its banking sector *and* render banking productive in its national accounts.

As indicated, the chapter takes us through only to the mid- to late 1970s. I draw the chapter to a close at that particular juncture because of five key developments that we can trace to it, and which account for a meaningful break between the preceding era – considered here – and the succeeding era discussed in Part III. The first two have already been highlighted: the beginnings of international expansion by other countries' banks, in addition to US banks; and the beginnings of the drawn-out process of wholesale international dismantling of cross-border capital controls.

The other three key developments all concern the form and substance of the relationship between the two types of boundary crossings in which we are interested in this book. In the age of "alignment" which is the focus of Chapters 3 and 4, the conceptual boundary negotiation proffered through national accounts came into close and material alignment, I am arguing, with the geopolitical boundary negotiation in which banks either did or did not engage. The alignment was to one side of these respective boundaries in the case of France and the UK, and to the other in the case of the US, but positive (in the sense of aligned, as opposed to non-aligned) in each case. Three critical things then happened from around the mid-1970s.

First, the relationship between the two boundary negotiations became both stronger and more explicit, since a condition of positive alignment increasingly became one of formal *effect*. In particular, having previously served to validate banks' geographical scope only in a rather abstract conceptual sense (productiveness according with internationalization, and unproductiveness, in the Keynesian schema, according with protectionism), the national accounts' envisioning of banks' economic role was now actively mobilized to provide such validation. The data, in other words, began to be *used* to lobby for a particular outcome – data showing banks as "adding value," specifically, being brought to bear upon the international politics of access to foreign banking markets. A relationship of alignment thus became more and more one of actual material constitution.

Second, and closely related to this, I will argue that the period covered in Part III differed substantively from that discussed here and in the previous chapter in terms of the degree of receptiveness of national banking markets to foreign incursion. Those markets "opened up" by multinational (and, as we know, overwhelmingly US-domiciled) banks in the 1960s and early 1970s were, in a sense, the low-hanging fruit: if not wide open, the door to foreign bank penetration was certainly ajar. Little resistance was encountered, either from political actors or from domestic competitors who might have sought to mobilize political support. From the early to mid-1970s, however, things became considerably tougher. US – and, now, European and Japanese – banks found that a much more proactive, systematic and politically-reinforced approach was required to further advance the internationalization agenda. And with trade negotiations becoming the main terrain of this renewed assault, economic ideas became critical ammunition. The shift in the relationship between those ideas and the material realities of international banking from one of alignment to one of constitution was, therefore, to some extent a *necessary* one.

Third, and representing the last of the five key developments occurring from the mid-1970s, the relationship in question increasingly became two-directional. To this point in the book, I have talked predominantly in terms of representations of banking productiveness validating geographical configurations of institutional financial capital – either conceptually, in the era of "alignment," or, as just intimated, literally and constitutively from the mid-1970s onwards. But this is to speak of a relationship in only one direction. How, in turn, might we conceive of the implications of the geography of financial capital *for representations of banks' productiveness*? Is it even meaningful to do so and, if so, can we discern the nature of any such implications? I will argue in Part III that it is, and that we can, and that we should therefore think in terms of *co*-constitution: that around the same time as national accounting data on banks' productiveness began to be marshaled in the service of opening up international banking markets, representations of banks' productiveness (in scholarly political economy as well as the national accounts) were *themselves* being transformed, and partly in consequence of precisely the geographical reconfigurations that their own mobilization enabled.

All of this, however, is to get ahead of ourselves. Our present focus is principally on the pertinent "conjunctural assemblage" which materialized in the US context between the 1930s and 1970s, and the chapter proceeds by considering each of this assemblage's core constituent elements in turn. The first section looks at the development of US national accounts in the 1930s and 1940s. It is of critical importance, I argue, if unsurprising, that it was in the US that the "banking problem" was first recognized, first articulated *as* a problem, and first seen as *requiring* a solution. After tracing the wider political-economic context of the emergence of the US national accounting system, I focus in on this banking problem and the solutions – there was more than one – advanced to resolve it.

The second section shifts focus to the intellectual milieu within which emerged not only this envisioning of "productive" banks but of course also – recalling the previous chapter – the parallel envisioning of "productive" capital flows. I note here a secondary literature which suggests that influential US economists in the late 1930s and early 1940s shared Keynes's critical reading of banks' role in the economy. My own reading, however, is different. There were, I argue, substantial differences between the views of Keynes and his US peers, especially when one comes to consider the individual economist who arguably played a comparably important role in the development of early US national accounting as Keynes did in relation to UK national accounting: namely, Simon Kuznets. Certainly, I submit, one would never have heard Kuznets or his national contemporaries talking in the terms used by Keynes about either bankers or – in association with this or not – about financial protectionism.

The third section assesses the developments in US banking internationalization which the chapter as a whole aims to situate in the context of the representations and worldviews considered in the first two sections. In the 1950s US banking remained essentially just as isolated as, for instance, UK or French banking. In contrast to the leading banks of the latter two countries, however, US banks had been preparing purposively and agitating forcefully for renewed overseas expansion opportunities since international banking had effectively closed down in the 1930s. While the positive perspective on banks' productiveness enshrined most visibly and materially in the US national accounts was a vital enabler of such opportunities when they did eventually arise, it clearly did not create them, nor serve in isolation to allow them to be exploited. Thus, in examining the extent and various forms of US bank internationalization in the 1960s and early to mid-1970s, this section also considers the more immediate drivers and catalysts of such physical boundary crossings.

The fourth and last section of the chapter looks beyond the US context to consider what was happening elsewhere during these two decades, in respect of both geographical and conceptual boundary crossings by banks. The geographical story, as already indicated, is a very short one, since nonUS banks remained largely nationally-bound entities. The national accounting story, meanwhile, is slightly longer and considerably more complicated, particularly in view of the publication in 1953 of the first UN System of National Accounts (SNA) in addition to – albeit intended to lead to the harmonization of – the various different national systems. The first of two principal observations here, nevertheless, is simply that in the French and UK national accounts banks *continued* to be envisioned as unproductive, with no changes in their treatment occurring until the mid-1970s; the production boundary had not yet been hurdled. The second observation gestures more explicitly to Part III of the book. It does so by raising the thorny matter of the *incremental* difficulties that the internationalization of banking began now to raise for statisticians *already* confounded by "that old National Accounting bugbear," to use Thomas Rymes's evocative phrase from 1985, of measuring banks' "output."[3] Banks' crossing of geographical boundaries, in short, made assessment of their crossing of conceptual economic boundaries even more problematic than before. I broach this broad issue by way of a little-known paper from the early 1980s on national accounting in Luxembourg, for what the author describes as the "nightmare" implications of globalized finance for the treatment of banking in the national accounts are ones that, as we will see in Part III, would come to have much wider and deeper pertinence over the following three decades.

Making Peace with Common Sense

As in numerous European territories, freestanding national income estimates of varying degrees of sophistication had been produced periodically in the US over a period of several decades by the time that such estimates began to cohere into more systematic accounts in the 1930s. The work of Willford King during World War I and the 1920s is often considered seminal, if limited, in laying important conceptual foundations for developments in the next decade, when the onset of the Great Depression prompted US political leaders to call for more reliable statistics to be produced on a more consistent basis. This systematic work really took off in the middle years of the 1930s, and was carried out at three separate institutions, between which some of the key individual protagonists moved. The first was the National Bureau of Economic Research (NBER); the second, another private independent research entity, was the Brookings Institution; the third, and the source of the government's official estimates from their inception in 1934, was the Department of Commerce.[4]

It was in the US, in these very early years of the development of systematic national accounts, that what I have been calling – following Bryan Haig – the "banking problem" was, to the best of my knowledge, first explicitly recognized. The recognition came in a 1932 paper in the bastion of neoclassical economics that was, and is, the *Journal of Political Economy* (a misleading name for a journal if ever there was one). The author was the economist Morris A. Copeland, and the article was titled, appropriately, "Some problems in the theory of national income." Foremost among these problems was the one of accounting for banks and their relative contribution to the national economy. Foreshadowing much of the welter of commentary on such matters over not just the following years but the next eight decades, Copeland identified what he saw as the "dilemma" of having to represent the "net-value-product" of banking as "a negative quantity" unless special procedures for treatment of the sector were introduced.[5]

If, by my argument, it was no coincidence that this issue was flagged in the national accounting context in the US before anywhere else, nor was it a coincidence, I will go on to argue, that unlike in the cases of France or the UK, the issue was immediately seen *as* a problem – and as a problem *requiring an immediate solution* – by most of those engaged at the time in constructing US national accounting frameworks. The one exception was the monetary economist Clark Warburton, who is usually identified as the first statistician or economist anywhere to have used the term "gross national product," in 1934. ("Few scholars," Galbraith later observed, "can claim to have launched so prodigious a contribution to the language."[6]) Working at the Brookings Institution, albeit in communication with those working on the same issues for the government and the NBER, Warburton produced estimates of US economic output for the odd-numbered years between 1919 and 1929 using both final-product and income methods. Financial services, however, were not included among the final (i.e. consumer) products that Warburton took to constitute the economy's total output, though other services (e.g. transportation and communication) were. A rationalization of this exclusion was not offered.[7]

Warburton's framework, however, was ultimately less significant than the others formulated during the same period, although as Carol Carson has noted his influence did extend beyond purely a terminological one, especially in terms of his "seeing the need for and arguing the merits of product estimates" at a time when income-based estimates, in the US at least, predominated.[8] The more enduring work was that which was carried out at the Commerce Department and the NBER. In the following paragraphs I will have occasion to refer to three main sets of estimates and their associated methodologies. Two of these were the official government estimates – firstly those produced up to 1946, and secondly those produced from 1947, when the treatment of financial intermediaries was changed – while the third was the NBER's. We will begin with the last of these; but all three, critically, envisioned and represented banks as productive economic agents.

The parallel work on measurement of the national economy conducted at the NBER was led, from 1933, by an individual whom we will have occasion to discuss in much greater detail below: Simon Kuznets. This work was considerably more comprehensive and elaborate than Warburton's, and results were not published in systematic form until the appearance of Kuznets's *National Income and Capital Formation, 1919–1935* in 1937. Citing data limitations, Kuznets explained that the only satisfactory way to estimate national economic output was via the income method.[9] Yet adopting this approach did not obviate the need to take a position on how to treat the net interest income generated through intermediation. The key feature of the Kuznets accounts from our perspective, therefore, is the fact that his chosen approach to measuring the financial sector's contribution to what he, too, now called "gross national product" – which was to add profits earned to wages and salaries paid – implied treating such interest not as a transfer item but as a net addition to national economic activity arising through the productive work of banks.

In discussing this methodology in a chapter of the first volume of the NBER's *Studies in Income and Wealth* series, published the same year, Copeland concluded that Kuznets had "attempted to make peace with common sense."[10] For at least two reasons, this particular expression of Copeland's is a tremendously important and instructive one. Let us consider, first, the idea simply of "making peace." Copeland had written five years earlier of the "dilemma" of showing banks as unproductive unless a special treatment of interest income were formulated. Yet he could have had no idea that this issue would constitute "a continuing source of bedevilment to economic accountants" for more than half a century (and indeed, remains so today).[11] In evoking, in 1937, this image of peace-making, Copeland tells us that the long and bloody battle with the "banking problem" had already begun.

Now consider what it was that Kuznets, in Copeland's view, had made peace specifically *with*: "common sense." We know from the previous chapter that it was in following the conventional national accounting treatment of interest income (i.e. the treatment applied to other industrial sectors) that the "leech upon the income stream" envisioning arose. Copeland thus posits such an approach and output as the very antithesis of common sense. "Common sense," rather, meant making an exception, treating banks differently, and representing them instead as what they – *obviously* and *transparently* – were: productive. This common sense, however, was of course a sense rooted in a very particular conceptual framework. It was what neoclassicism defined *as* common sense, namely *its* placement of the production boundary – not Smith's, not Malthus's, and not Marx's.

But perhaps most salutary of all is Copeland's admission that common sense was something Kuznets *needed* to make peace with. The "sensible" option was not one that came entirely naturally to national income statisticians of the day: the image of banks as productive was resisted, to one degree or another, precisely because it required making an exception. Accept it, nonetheless, Kuznets did; and in the next section we will see why this was an acceptance that came much more easily to him than to economists working on national accounts in other parts of the world, not least in the UK and France.

The second of the three most significant early sets of US national income calculations were the "official" Department of Commerce estimates first published in 1934. We need not dwell on the methodology underpinning these – though we will return shortly to the actual numbers generated – since where banking services were concerned, the Kuznets approach was used.[12] This, in retrospect, is not surprising: having joined the NBER in 1929, Kuznets was effectively seconded to the Commerce Department's Economic Research Division at the beginning of 1933 to oversee the production of the first official estimates. The NBER, moreover, was actively called upon for the checking and revision of these.[13]

The third and final framework will detain us for longer, since it entailed a fundamental revision to the official US methodology for calculating banks' contribution to national economic output. This revision came in 1947. With measurements of national output using the product method having been added to the existing income-based measurements during the war, it was now possible to estimate banks' product anew. Using the product method, however, brought the "banking problem" even more centrally into the spotlight. Did intermediation constitute a productive service and, if so, how, in the absence of explicit payment for such a service, could the value of the output of this service be estimated?

The answer, one enshrined in the treatment of banks in the US national accounts from 1947 until as recently as 2003, was spelled out conceptually in a paper by the economist Dwight Yntema. This answer was similar to the one offered in the UK and discussed in the previous chapter, in the sense that it used exactly the same method of imputation of output value. But there was a crucial difference, one originating in the fact that Yntema and the Commerce Department members who collaborated with him on the proposed treatment, unlike their UK counterparts, did *not* regard the "paradoxical" envisioning of banks as unproductive as one they could live with. Such an envisioning would be, Yntema insisted, "thoroughly unacceptable."[14]

What was this crucial methodological difference? In short, the net interest revenue derived from intermediation services, termed now the Imputed Bank Service Charge (IBSC), was to be treated as an input not (as in the UK) of the finance sector itself, but of other economic units. These units included both other business sectors and consumers, with the allocation between the two based upon respective levels of deposit ownership.[15] The upshot, in terms of the representation of sectoral value-added in the US production account versus the UK production account, was twofold. First, *other* business sectors were each shown to generate *less* value, since, aside from that component deemed consumed by the public, banks' collective net interest revenue was apportioned between those other sectors as deducted inputs. Second, and most importantly for our purposes, value added by the finance sector was commensurately greater to the tune of the entire IBSC.

Despite the wholesale change in methodology, therefore, the official US national accounts continued to show banks as making a positive net contribution to national output, just as they always had done. For Yntema, as for Kuznets, the neoclassical common sense resisted in the UK – and essentially dismissed in France – was one that peace could and should be made with. The only remaining question in this section is thus of relative degrees of productiveness: of the two official methodologies, namely the income method used to 1946 and the product method used from 1947, which showed banks as the *most* productive? Fig 4.1 displays the answer. It shows the percentage contribution to total national economic output of banks and of "finance" more broadly (the latter also including insurance and real estate), as estimated under the pre-1947 and post-1947 treatments.

Two important points need to be emphasized in relation to this chart. First, as it clearly demonstrates, the method used in the US from 1947 onwards entailed an amplification of the estimated productiveness of banking and finance. The latter were made even *more* productive than they had previously been shown to be.[16] The second observation does not arise from the chart itself but is equally pertinent to what it shows. This is that many national accounting practitioners outside the US, not only in countries where productiveness was withheld from banks (such as the UK and France) but also in countries that showed banks as productive (albeit *using different methods to the US*), saw even the *earlier* of the two US treatments as according too high a level of productiveness to the banking sector.

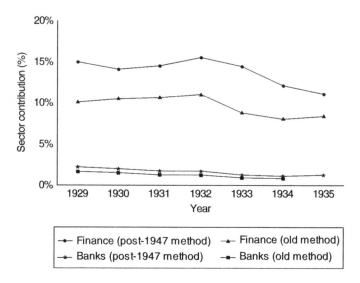

Fig 4.1   Sector contributions to US national economic output, 1929–1935.
Source: Old method, *National income in the United States, 1929–35*, pp.40, 179; post-1947 method, *National income and product statistics of the United States, 1929–46*, p.26.

Perhaps the best example of this comes from Australia, where, from 1948 to 1972, a method similar to the Kuznets treatment was used. The rationale for this was spelt out in a paper by H. P. Brown, who argued that since the function of banks, like government, was in "oiling the wheels of industry and the community generally," "the contribution of banks to the national income" should be calculated as it was in Australia at the time for government: as "equal to the wages and salaries paid by banks." Nodding to the early US treatment, Brown then raised the key question of "whether the profits of banks should also be regarded as a contribution." Kuznets and the Department of Commerce, as we know, had thought yes; Brown disagreed, averring that interest was always a transfer item (a "distribution of surplus"), and hence that "it would be inappropriate to regard the profits of banks as a contribution to national income, since these profits are merely interest passed on."[17] The significance of this perspective, of course, is that in introducing in 1947 a new treatment for banks which made them appear more productive than before, the US replaced a legacy system that, for some expert observers, already painted too positive a picture of the sector.

On the Deep Relevance of a Certain Misquotation in Financial History[18]

How are we to make sense of the fact that the primary official technical apparatus for "creating" economic productiveness made banking and finance productive in the US from the very outset, whereas it did not – and for a considerable period of time, would not – in either France or the UK? To answer this question, it is worthwhile revisiting first of all a place, time and assemblage of people, institutions and ideas that we first visited in the previous chapter: Bretton Woods in 1944. It is worth doing so because, I would argue, we can now usefully consider Harry Dexter White's powerful arguments about the danger of inhibiting "productive" international capital flows in a new, comparative light: that of the already entrenched envisioning of "productive" finance generated in and propagated by the US national accounts.

Yet immediately, and critically, the existing secondary literature on Bretton Woods and on the key US figures at the conference gives us pause for thought. Were these men, most notably White and US Treasury Secretary Henry Morgenthau, not critical of the banking system and of the role of banks in the wider economy? And, if indeed the image of "productive finance" were one with which they would not readily have concurred, would it not be misguided for us to place this national accounting-based representation alongside, and in positive alignment with, White's notion of productive capital mobility?

Certainly, there is an influential secondary literature which intimates as much. Jeffry Frieden, for instance, claims that the "New Dealers" Morgenthau and White essentially shared Keynes's distaste for private finance and financiers, and that they brought this prejudice to bear at Bretton Woods.[19] Then, strikingly, there is Morgenthau's famous statement on bankers and their "usury" at the conference itself. "As U.S. Treasury Department Secretary Henry Morgenthau told the conference," Eric Helleiner relates, "the goal of the Bretton Woods agreement was to 'drive the usurious moneylenders from the temple of international finance'." That Morgenthau believed "moneylenders," or bankers, *were* usurious, helps to explain for Helleiner and others why it was that "the Bretton Woods negotiators, under American leadership," ultimately constructed a post-war "financial order in which the use of capital controls was strongly endorsed."[20]

So much, it would therefore seem, for the idea of Morgenthau et al. endorsing the "productive finance" of US national accounting. And yet there are two significant problems with Helleiner's rendering of Morgenthau's speech, and thus of the sentiments and conceptual framework seemingly underpinning it. First, the Treasury Secretary never actually posited the banishment in question as the "goal" of Bretton Woods. His comments were made strictly in relation to *one* of the proposed Bretton Woods institutions (the International Bank for Reconstruction and Development (IBRD), which became the World Bank), and they concerned what he saw as the likely *outcome* of the IBRD providing loans when "these could not be floated through the normal channels at reasonable rates." The banishment was a foreseeable *impact* specifically of the IBRD's provision of these loans, not an a priori objective of the conference per se.[21]

Second, and just as importantly, the quotation ascribed to Morgenthau by Helleiner was not in fact what he said. What he actually said, the official conference proceedings show, was this: "The effect [of the IBRD providing such loans] would be to provide capital for those who need it at lower interest rates than in the past and to drive *only* the usurious money lenders from the temple of international finance."[22] Helleiner was not the first scholar to misquote the Treasury

Secretary (but he was a very influential one and, partly as a result of this, by no means the last), and in his case the mistake at least appears to have been an unknowing one. Unfortunately it is difficult to draw the same conclusion with regard to the scholar whom Helleiner borrowed the quotation from, the venerated Columbia Law School professor Richard Gardner. In his *Sterling-Dollar Diplomacy*, Gardner wrote – and the quotation is unalloyed, the interjecting periods inserted by Gardner, not me – of Morgenthau wanting "to drive ... the usurious moneylenders from the temple of international finance."[23] The occlusion of the small but vital word "only" was, in other words, a knowing and deliberate one; and one does wonder somewhat at the lack of curiosity in Helleiner and others in investigating what word or words Gardner had omitted, choosing instead simply to *remove* Gardner's obfuscating periods.[24]

The deep relevance of this misquotation in the present context is that through its repeated and ongoing replication, the view has come to crystallize that Morgenthau saw banking as usurious by nature and damnable accordingly. Gardner even went so far as to describe the banishment of this usurious community as Morgenthau's "lifetime ambition"![25] What the latter actually seems to have believed, if we take him at his word, is that *some* bankers were usurious, and that the IBRD would have the happy effect of exorcising from international finance only these bad apples. This, of course, is a far cry from the blanket anti-banker rhetoric and convictions with which he is often now credited; and thus Leo Panitch and Sam Gindin, while reproducing the misquotation in question, are surely correct to maintain that even in their adulterated form Morgenthau's words "should never have been taken too seriously."[26]

This is certainly a view with which I would concur. Moreover, Helleiner's own broader analysis of the Bretton Woods conjuncture makes it clear that one hardly needs to appeal to the notion of a negative attitude towards the banking sector – or, indeed, any real conviction in the likely dangers of "unproductive" capital flows – among the US negotiators to understand their immediate support for the Bretton Woods institutions or their ongoing acceptance of the use of capital controls by other states in the post-war period. Citing the undoubted importance of "American strategic goals in the cold war after 1947," Helleiner observes that "U.S. strategic thinkers were reluctant to alienate their West European and Japanese allies by pressing for unpopular liberalization moves."[27] Politics, as much as – if not more than – normative economics, is a sufficient explanation.

On my reading, therefore, we *can* legitimately align the US architects of Bretton Woods and their discourse of "productive" capital movements with the envisioning of "productive" banking and finance in the early US national accounts. Neither Morgenthau nor White would likely have opposed such an envisioning. And nor, I will suggest now, would the wider community of professional US economists within whose conceptual and institutional ambit the system of US national accounting and its treatments of financial services came into being.

Again, however, it is necessary here to disabuse ourselves of some popular misconceptions. Just as Morgenthau has come to be seen as some kind of scourge on the banks, so it is commonly perceived that US-based economists, like Keynes and

Stamp in the UK, had adopted in the early to mid-1930s a more critical stance towards the economic role of banking and bankers as the Great Depression descended on the nation. After all, was it not bank-fuelled speculative excess that led to the Stock Market Crash of 1929, which in turn precipitated US and global economic recession?

I have no intention here of entering into the protracted, messy and lingering debate about what did or did not cause the Crash or the Depression which ensued. But I do want to insist that economists were largely absent from the domestic critique of the US banking system in the 1930s, and that the envisioning of a productive banking sector in the early US national accounts is not therefore incongruous in respect of the prevailing economic episteme. I will then argue that this more favorable view of the contribution of banks was indubitably a feature of the thought of the individual economist who, in the US national accounting context, mattered most of all: Simon Kuznets.

There did emerge, of course, a strong and sustained *political* critique of Wall Street from the very beginning of the 1930s. This took its most important institutional form in the shape of the Senate Banking Committee hearings of 1932–1933, which were highly critical of the role of the banking system in the lead-up to the Great Crash. It is specifically in the context of these high-profile hearings that we can place both President Roosevelt's famous March 1933 inaugural address – in which he lambasted the failure of the "rulers of the exchange of mankind's goods" and, clearly presaging Morgenthau's speech at Bretton Woods, celebrated the fact that these "money changers have fled from their high seats in the temple of our civilization" – and the passing of the Banking Act (usually referred to as the Glass-Steagall Act, after the names of its two main political sponsors) just three months later. These political discourses and actions assuredly succeeded in persuading the public that the banks were to blame for the nation's ills. "Practices of the unscrupulous money changers," Roosevelt opined, "stand indicted in the court of public opinion."[28]

Economists, however, were never convinced. Where the original stock market collapse was concerned, blame, as Galbraith later observed in his *The Great Crash*, was more often placed at the door of a foreigner-influenced Federal Reserve for making credit too cheap. "This view that the action of the Federal Reserve authorities in 1927 was responsible for the speculation and collapse which followed has never been seriously shaken."[29] The subsequent onset and deepening of economic depression, meanwhile, was not the fault of the banks either. It was, rather, triggered in large part by yet another state-originated economic faux-pas, in this case the passing of the protectionist Smoot-Hawley Tariff Act in 1930. The then President Hoover signed this Act into being despite the vociferous opposition of the professional economics community, and hence it is not in the least surprising that economists' early readings of what caused the Depression assigned a central role to the Act.[30]

The common theme in these exercises in blame assignation, of course, was not only the absence of the private banking sector from the field of perceived culpability, but the centrality of state or quasi-state institutions.[31] The distinction with

Keynes, and his reading of what happened, is, in this respect, a vital one. At the very beginning of the 1930s, Keynes had been equally critical of government policy, blaming it for the collapse in private investment in the early months of the Depression. As Hans Jensen has shown, however, Keynes changed his mind. While government policy certainly had not helped to mitigate the consequences of Depression, the *cause* was now seen to be located "in the institutions of capitalism itself" and in particular in "the institution of rentiership," which had strangled the economy by refusing to reduce lending rates.[32]

As I argued in the previous chapter it was this later Keynes, the forthright critic of the rentier-banker, whose views came to be reflected in the treatment of the banking sector in the early UK national accounts. My argument in the present chapter, in turn, is that we can help to make sense of the very different envisioning of banks in the early US national accounts by paying heed to the contemporary perspectives on banking of US economists, and especially the fact that they did not find banks responsible for the distinctly *un*productive economic events of the late 1920s and early 1930s. One simply did not hear influential US economists of the age talking in the manner of a Keynes about either banks' economic role or, for that matter, the potential merits of national financial protectionism. The one notable American economist who might have been expected to paint a more negative picture of the role in this period of the financial sector, its long-time critic Thorstein Veblen, had died – with terrible timing – in 1929.[33]

We can cement our case further by focusing, for the remainder of this section, on the views of Simon Kuznets, for if any economist shaped the form and substance of the early US system of national accounts as closely as Keynes did the UK equivalent, then it was he. We have already seen that Kuznets played a pivotal role in formulating the treatment specifically of banking which was used in the US accounts until 1947, which only adds to the imperative of understanding his particular conceptual bearings. His wider influence on US national accounting in toto in the formative decade of the 1930s has been broadly acknowledged in the historical literature. Galbraith, mentioning the fact that, as we have seen, Kuznets worked at both the NBER and the Commerce Department, signals his "central and even decisive contribution"; Perlman and Marietta, meanwhile, label the mid-1930s simply "the Kuznets phase" in the history of US national accounting.[34]

What sort of understanding of the economy did Kuznets bring to the table in constructing the framework of a national accounting system and in identifying the "proper" place for banking therein? Two pieces of "contextual" information are extremely pertinent to this question. First, Kuznets was acutely conscious of the fact that the national accounts did not bespeak unassailable truths, but rather reflected in powerful ways the theoretical economic orthodoxy of the day. This *included*, notably, orthodoxy as to what was "productive" and what was not. "Changes in the scope of the measures and in the component parts segregated," he wrote of national accounts in 1940, "reflect the changing viewpoint of economists as to what constitutes economic and productive activities," as well as their viewpoint on other key issues. In recognizing the unavoidable imprint of "theory," Kuznets explicitly distinguished himself from many of the individuals who had produced national income estimates in previous decades and centuries. For such individuals, Kuznets claimed, the embedding of theory (*a* theory) in "measures of national income" was "often unconscious."[35]

Second, Kuznets, like Keynes, was an economist whose contributions extended far beyond simply his influence – direct and indirect – on the national accounting field. Equally, his national accounting work itself was motivated by, and thus to one extent or another internalized, a much wider set of empirical and theoretical interests than was the case for other important American national accounts practitioners of the era. As Mark Perlman has noted, Kuznets shared the concerns around the economics of class relations that spurred the national income investigations of his immediate predecessors such as King and Charles Spahr; but he was also deeply interested in the question of the causes of economic growth, and his construction of a national accounting system must be considered in this light.[36]

We can usefully highlight here a number of specific economic arguments developed by Kuznets which help illuminate and perhaps even explain the productive role accorded to banks and finance in "his" national accounts. One was his argument about the productiveness or otherwise of service activities in general. As is widely recognized, Kuznets saw services as economically productive in the same way that manufacturing or agricultural activities were.[37] He thus dismissed the views, discussed above in Chapter 1, of classical political economists such as Adam Smith, and indeed asserted that "the prevailing economic doctrine that accepted as productive only activities resulting in material goods" was *reflected in* "early 19th century" national income estimates which omitted "the value of services not embodied in commodities."[38] Seeing service activities as inherently productive, and distancing himself from measures of national income that adopted a contrary perspective, how could Kuznets *not* make financial services in their various forms productive in his own schema?

Then there was his conviction, developed over the course of his long career, that this productivity of services was significant not only in terms of the static picture of the economy we tend to associate with national accounts – a national product of such and such amount in such and such a year, made up of varying contributions from various productive industry sectors – but also for the long-run, dynamic development and growth of the economy as a whole. As indicated just above, Kuznets was fascinated by the question of what caused growth, and his answer posited a central place for services. In short, expansion of the service (tertiary) sector, and thus displacement of the so-called primary and secondary sectors, was regarded as critical to long-run economic growth. It was a classically Western conception of economic "development," whereby a large services sector comes to be seen as a mark *of* an "advanced" economy.

Within this understanding of the pivotal role of the service-based economy in wider growth dynamics, Kuznets, crucially, accorded banking a place of conspicuous privilege. He would become, over the course of several decades, a key figure in a burgeoning literature on the nature of the relationships between economic growth and the development of financial institutions and markets. He wrote the foreword to what is often considered to be the definitive study of such relationships in the

US context (Raymond Goldsmith's *Financial Intermediaries in the American Economy Since 1900*, published in 1958). He also made important contributions of his own, most notably with his 1971 book *Economic Growth of Nations*, in which his empirical analysis of different industries' shares in the economic output of different nations revealed that of all the different service sectors, "only the share of banking, insurance and real estate shows a striking rise as we shift from low to higher income countries."[39] This study may have been published some 40 years after Kuznets began his work on national accounts and made his most important contributions to this particular political-economic calculus, but he had been convinced already in the early 1930s of the positive materiality of the banking sector. Among the factors Kuznets "wanted most to stress" in his early work specifically on national accounting, Perlman observes, was the role played by banking – though not only banking – institutions "in stimulating economic growth."[40] Viewed from this vantage point, the idea of national accounts crafted directly or indirectly with his hand representing banks as anything other than productive would have seemed, to say the very least, bizarre.

The Re-internationalization of the US Banking Business

In the previous chapter we saw that internationalized finance became, at the beginning of the 1930s, a system of largely nationalized and separate financial and banking *systems*, and that things largely remained that way for three decades. In the present section I will discuss how banking, led by US financial institutions, began to re-internationalize from the late 1950s. First, however, it is important to back-track momentarily to understand a little more about some of the key, US-specific developments of the 1930s through 1950s which did not appear in the more generic, high-level overview of this period sketched out above.

A vital initial consideration in this context is that when international banking and financial markets conclusively retreated into their collective shell in the early months of the Great Depression, they had already become, by that stage, a highly *Americanized* network of institutions, activities, and flows. The whole of the 1920s was characterized in particular by massive US lending to foreign markets, and this lending – managed for the most part by US banks – continued even after the stock market crash of 1929, only dying off in the early 1930s.[41]

Equally importantly, those US banks which had been most aggressive in establishing overseas branches in the 1920s suffered less involuntary or voluntary rationalization of their international networks in the three decades of financial protectionism which followed than did their erstwhile competitors from France, Germany or the UK. Or, seen from a different angle, they made the waiting-out of a moribund international marketplace *more* of a strategic priority.[42] The best example of this was the National City bank, which had the biggest international business of any US bank throughout the period in question. It too, to be sure, endured notable episodes of constriction, closing 30 international branches in the immediate aftermath of the Great Depression and closing all of its continental

European branches at the beginning of World War II. But international profits had recovered strongly in the late 1930s, and the bank immediately began re-opening foreign offices in the late 1940s.[43]

Perhaps more importantly still, American private bankers, unlike those from the UK or continental Europe, were actively agitating for international banking and capital markets to be re-opened both before and immediately after the conclusion of World War II. The Bretton Woods documentation shows that, in Morgenthau's words, "some bankers" and – not insignificantly – "a few economists" had raised objections to the proposed IBRD in the apparent belief that it "would indeed limit the control which certain private bankers have in the past exercised over international finance."[44] Historians, interestingly, have underplayed these specific concerns, instead focusing on the same bankers' resistance to the other Bretton Woods institution, the International Monetary Fund (IMF).[45] This resistance was based in part precisely on the fear that the IMF might allow for international capital controls to remain in place, and that such controls, in Leonard Seabrooke's words, "would inhibit the spread of US banking into Europe" and thus thwart US banks' challenge to what little remained (mainly within the "sterling bloc") of the City of London's financial power.[46] As Seabrooke recounts, Wall Street lobbying led to the Congress House Banking Committee initially opposing ratification of Bretton Woods – a display of political influence worth bearing in mind in what follows.[47] Helleiner, moreover, has demonstrated that even once the Bretton Woods agreement was in place and most countries, although not the US, had implemented capital controls, US bankers spent two years (1945–1947) "applying more aggressive pressure on Western European countries to liberalize their exchange controls."[48]

All of this is important for it underlines the fact that pressures to re-internationalize banking were uniquely strong in the US in the relatively brief historical period during which banking globally became a primarily national phenomenon (and also during which, of course, national accounts came into being, with the US version offering a uniquely positive envisioning of banks' productiveness). Yet even though modest international expansion occurred in the early 1950s, with National City still in the vanguard, late in the decade international banking remained, in a historical context, firmly in the doldrums, for US as well as other countries' banks. Stefano Battilossi describes generically, for the end of the 1950s, "a world of closed and disintegrated national systems."[49] US banks like others were, for the most part, "cut off from the rest of the world."[50] Even for National City, the most internationalized US bank of all, foreign markets contributed only half (16%) as much of the company's profit in 1955 (the year it became First National City) as they had in 1930 (30%).[51]

Then, from the late 1950s through to the mid- to late-1970s, cross-border banking underwent a period of unprecedented growth, driven and dominated almost exclusively by US financial institutions. I want to focus mainly here on how we might account for these developments, but before doing so it is important to provide a summary picture of what actually happened in terms of the nature, scale, and geography of US expansionism.

The growth in US international banking activities from the end of the 1950s occurred, we can begin by observing, alongside the substantial re-emergence of cross-border private lending. Post-war reconstruction having been primarily financed, this time around, through the new multilateral agencies and the Marshall Plan, "international capital raising regained momentum only towards the end of the 1950s," and it was initially centered heavily on New York.[52] The internationalization of US banks dates from the same period, and the statistics paint a striking picture. As recently as 1955, we have just seen, First National City, the strongest US bank internationally, generated just 16 percent of its profits in overseas markets. By 1975, which turned out to be the year of peak relative profit contribution of US banks' international activities in the 1970s, international earnings contributed a weighted average share of 52 percent of total earnings for the ten largest US commercial banks. Within the mix, the figure was now as high as 71 percent for First National (now Citicorp), and above 50 percent for Citi's two most significant competitors overseas, namely Bank of America (55%) and Chase Manhattan (64%).[53]

What sorts of activities and operations, and *where*, accounted for these enormous overseas earnings? The vast majority of historical accounts point to one phenomenon above all else: the so-called "Euromarkets." This label refers to distinctive financial markets which developed from the late 1950s, and which were based largely in London. These markets processed transactions in both cash ("Eurocurrency") and debt ("Eurobonds"), with the distinguishing feature being a mismatch between the country of issue and the country of holding (in the case of cash) or of denomination (in the case of debt instruments). In other words, a Eurodollar was simply a dollar deposited outside the US, while a Eurodollar bond was simply a bond issued outside the US. The "Euro" prefix is, in this sense, misleading, for there is nothing *necessarily* European about such markets and assets – the label was used, and still is, essentially because the markets in question happened first to emerge in Europe. "Offshore" is probably a better descriptor.

The key quality of these markets, meanwhile, was the absence of regulation. The markets very much had a physical geographical grounding (in London), but, crucially, since they were not Sterling-based they were not regarded as a threat to the UK's domestic monetary conditions. Thus the UK did not regulate them – they were, Ronen Palan notes, "outside the exchange rate regulations, reserve regulations, or any other regulations of the British state" – and nor, given their location *in* the UK, did any other states, the US included. The markets were, clearly, a geo-legal and geo-political as much as a geo-economic creation, with the UK authorities playing a key role in mandating this state of financial "exception." As Palan writes, the government and the Bank of England "accepted, or even produced, an interpretation of its own laws that permitted the fiction that certain types of financial transactions did not take place within that territory."[54]

Financial historians' heavy emphasis on the Euromarkets in their analysis of international finance and banking in this period is in many respects unsurprising and justified. The emergence of the Euromarkets was a hugely significant development for all manner of different reasons, not all of which can be or need be rehearsed here. Frieden captures their overall significance nicely in observing that they came to serve to "tie the world's investors, borrowers, and banks together in a network that is at the same time part of no national financial system and part of them all."[55]

Their growth, for one thing, was startling. As defined by the Bank for International Settlements, the Eurocurrency market grew effectively from scratch in the late 1950s to over $200bn in outstanding foreign currency credits at the end of 1975.[56] This growth totally re-scripted the map of global monetary holdings and movements. More significantly, where this book is concerned, foreign banks were given free reign; there were no restrictions by nationality.[57] And amongst the banks which exploited the opportunity to set up in London (and to a lesser extent, in places like Paris and Luxembourg), American banks were immediately to the fore.[58] They soon came to enjoy "an undisputed dominant position" in the Eurocurrency market (which was largely a Euro*dollar* market) and an only marginally less dominant position in the Eurobond market; and their overall dominance of the Euromarkets, Battilossi notes, "remained uncontested until the late 1970s."[59] Thus from the end of the 1950s, for reasons we shall address below, US banks increasingly borrowed in, and lent from, Europe.

For all their undoubted importance, however, it is vital, in my view, not to overemphasize the role of the Euromarkets in the story of US bank internationalization in the 1960s and early 1970s, still less to conflate such internationalization *with* the Euromarkets. We can make this case on two linked conceptual grounds. First, if one is interested, as I am in this book, in the internationalization of finance primarily insofar as it entails banks *offering customers finance and financial services* – and thus realizing revenues and profits – in different places, then we need to be aware of a further crucial characteristic of the Euromarkets: they were, in large part, *inter-bank* markets, rather than markets where banks did business with nonbanks. The precise figure varied from year to year and between currency and debt markets, but most historians cite an inter-bank share for this period of approximately or (Frieden) "over" half.[60] Second, and related to this feature, the Euromarkets, and especially the Eurodollar market, represented in large measure a source of funding for US banks – including, as we will see below, for their *domestic* operations.[61] The significance of this is that the Euromarkets constituted a reason for banks *to* internationalize as much as a phenomenon *of* internationalization. As Palan intimates, they are perhaps better seen as enabling, rather than epitomizing, "the globalizing tendencies of the modern economy."[62]

There are also important geographical reasons for not focusing too stringently on the Euromarkets, in either their strictly European physical incarnation or indeed the more expansive spatial form associated with the generic meaning of the label. In the 1960s and 1970s, US banks increasingly operated all over the world. Some of this expansion, certainly, involved little more than a technical – as opposed to physically material – "offshore" presence, not only in Europe but also in places such as the Bahamas and Cayman Islands. (While the number of US bank "branches" in the Caribbean mushroomed from five to 166 between 1965 and 1975, most were merely shell branches, established primarily by smaller US banks for whom "the high infrastructural costs of a London base" were

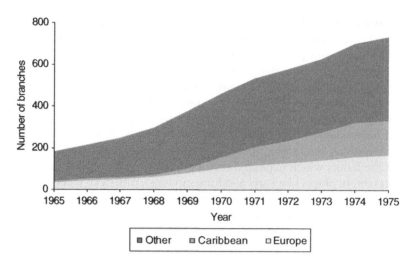

Fig 4.2 Overseas branches of US member banks (as at year start).
Source: Cho, *Multinational banks: their identities and determinants*, UMI Research Press, 1985 pp.42–43.

prohibitive and the Caribbean islands afforded a "cheaper and equally attractive regulatory environment": a Euromarket outside Europe.[63]) But US banks extended their tentacles much further afield than the historical literature's preoccupation with Euromarkets would suggest. As Fig 4.2 illustrates, in the same period that the number of Caribbean branches of US banks grew from five to 166, European branches grew from 32 to 167, but branches located in neither of these areas saw far-and-away the largest absolute increase, growing from 143 to 399.[64]

A significant component of this expansion of US banks' foreign branch networks was tied up with a boom in lending to developing countries from the mid-1960s, particularly in Latin America and Asia. In other words, a physical presence was established alongside, or in fact often in advance of, a bank's materialization as creditor. The lion's share of this funding was provided to the governments of Brazil, Mexico, Argentina, South Korea, Taiwan, and the Philippines.[65] Here, of course, was the backdrop to the famous Latin American debt crisis of the late 1970s and early 1980s. As Arthur MacEwan has noted, it was precisely the "massive expansion of international banking activity" out of the US, much of it "taking place out of the public eye," which "laid the foundation for the debt buildup."[66] A critical "moment" in these intertwined processes of US bank internationalization and developing country debt expansion was the first oil crisis of 1973–1974. Significantly higher oil prices and accompanying world recession rapidly generated large current account deficits among non-oil developing countries. American banks operating in the Euromarkets stepped in to recycle the burgeoning surpluses of the OAPEC (Organization of Arab Petroleum Exporting Countries) states into non-oil developing-country government debt, the total outstanding amount of which increased from $130bn in 1975 to $336 in 1978.[67]

By no means were the banks' international customer-facing operations all about sovereign debt provision, however. From the earliest days of US bank internationalization in the late 1950s, services were offered overseas to the US nonbank multinational corporations which were also expanding their global operations at that time. Such services typically included the full range of commercial intermediation *and* investment banking services offered to such clients in the US. As Kang Cho writes: "Most multinational banking activities of [multinational banks] are basically an extension of banking activities performed by banks on the domestic level."[68] Of course, trade financing and foreign exchange services are also important elements of the international banking mix, but these could be and were offered out of US offices as easily as through foreign branches. In addition to servicing US multinationals and nonUS governments, meanwhile, US banks' foreign branches increasingly came to encroach upon local markets for banking to foreign multinationals.

Nor did internationalization always occur through a branching model. A number of writers have developed helpful schema for classifying the different functional modes of US banks' foreign expansion. Cho, for example, distinguishes between five different models – correspondent relationships, representative offices, agencies, subsidiaries and branches – while James Houpt uses just the last two categories.[69] The two key points to note, however, are simply that there *were* different models, but that nevertheless the branch model was usually the preferred one. This, as Houpt notes, was partly because branches "are, legally, integral parts of the corporate bank and have the full authority to represent and commit the bank," and partly because "the activities of branches are typically more easily integrated into the internal reporting and control procedures of the bank."[70]

In sum, therefore, the period from the late 1950s to the mid-1970s was one of massive international growth for the US banking sector, and this expansion comprised the delivery of a wide range of services, to a diversifying spectrum of clients, using a number of alternative operating models, and within an increasing number of individual geographic markets worldwide. The Euromarkets were quite clearly an important element of this growth story but, I would re-emphasize, not its be-all and end-all; we would miss much of the wider picture if we focused only on those markets. As Ralph Bryant observes, "Eurocurrency banking is not a phenomenon sui generis, but merely one part of a general nexus of financial interrelations linking open national economies."[71]

With this observation in mind, we can turn now to the matter of explanation and understanding – the question, that is, of *accounting* for the substantial re-emergence of cross-border banking in this period, and in particular for the American dominance thereof. Inevitably, this is not a simple issue, and many different arguments have been offered in the historical literature. In what follows I will argue that six key sets of factors played an important role. In addition, I will make a case for the first and last of these to be accorded much more significance than they typically have been in the past.

The first set of important factors, then, concerns the prevailing attitudes towards banks among US policymakers, the economic representations which shaped such attitudes, and the nature of the political engagement with US banks' internationalization initiatives which those attitudes shaped in turn. I have argued at various points already that the US was home in the 1930s, 1940s, and 1950s to a significantly more positive array of economic representations of banking and finance than was the case in, most notably, the UK and France. The envisioning of productive banks in the national accounts was one such; the insistence, at and after Bretton Woods, upon the *normally* productive nature of international capital movements was another.

Earlier in this chapter, of course, I suggested that while such positive representations were perfectly understandable in terms of the worldview of key US economists such as Kuznets in the 1930s, they appeared to jar with attitudes towards Wall Street within the national political community. By the 1950s and early 1960s, however, the political negativity towards the banking sector, which had reached its zenith in the early 1930s, had substantially abated, and a more affirmative bearing was now apparent and ultimately came to bolster the banks in their foreign endeavors. As president (1945–1953), for example, Harry Truman's rhetoric lacked the anti-Wall Street content that colored it in his early days as a senator in the mid-1930s, and the man who succeeded him – Eisenhower – was generally on good terms with the banking sector. (One historian went so far as to accuse him of having "surrendered the White House to the Sacred College of Bonds and Money."[72])

We need to be careful too not to misread the substance of the "anti-Wall Street" US political discourse – and indeed, US policy instruments – of the 1930s and 1940s, or of what remained of such discourse and policy-making in the 1950s and 1960s. As Richard Sylla has demonstrated in an important essay on post-war US banking that explicitly addresses its internationalization, the heavy regulation of the domestic US banking sector in that era reflected what was more than anything else an "anti-concentration attitude" – not, I would add, an attitude of anti-banking per se, or one that condemned banks as unproductive.[73] The concern was not with "competition," so to speak, *between* banks and the rest of the economy, but with competition *within* banking; banking was not considered competitive *enough*. The watchwords of the era were therefore those of monopoly and "money trust" rather than parasitism, and it saw long and costly antitrust cases such as *United States v. Henry S. Morgan et al.* (1947–1953).[74] In this regard, the situation in banking was representative of the situation in the economy more widely, where, as Charles Maier has shown, post-war US internationalism was couched in a critique of "wasteful monopoly" alongside a celebration of "productivity" and "efficiency."[75] Returning to banking, Sylla notes that "even the largest [US banks] individually possessed no more than about 3 per cent of US bank assets" in the 1950s.[76] As such, it is no surprise that Wall Street was particularly cheered when "Harry Truman and his trust-busting administration," in the words of another historian, "were gone."[77]

It is also the case, moreover, that in the post-war era US politics featured significantly more direct banker influence and experience than it previously had done, and that this applied in terms of both the domestic and, crucially, the foreign policy arenas. As Frieden, providing a roll-call of important names, writes, "Much of the powerful cohort of wartime and postwar leaders who would rebuild the world after 1945 came from Wall Street." Battilossi makes the same point, again with a particular view to international affairs, noting that "the voice of New York bankers' [sic] became far more influential under the Truman and Eisenhower administrations."[78]

In the late 1950s and the 1960s, the cumulative upshot of these various factors was a US political environment drip-fed on an unfailing basis with evidence of banks' productiveness in its national accounts, and increasingly disposed in any event to a supportive posture towards the nation's financial sector. It is in this light that we can understand the encouragement US banks ultimately received from the US administration in their overseas expansionism, and hence can begin to understand why this expansion was so successful. It was not so much that the government was actively involved in opening up recalcitrant international markets, in the way that it would be from the late 1970s onwards (Chapter 5). It was more that it consistently chose *not* to intervene with formal regulation or other tools of intervention when it might have been expected to do so, either by skeptical domestic commentators or by foreign stakeholders in the international monetary and financial system. For the US government was, as Helleiner has shown, bent on preserving the international financial hegemony that the US had come to enjoy almost by default immediately after the war.[79] As such, when US banks began to colonize foreign markets from the late 1950s, the administration adopted a conspicuously hands-off approach which can be interpreted as one of de facto if not exactly de jure support. "International passivity," "benign neglect" and "very permissive" are just some of the phrases that have been used to capture the tenor of this approach.[80] And it is in view of this de facto support that historians of this period of US dominance in international banking point, as Seabrooke does, to the materiality of an "*interactive embeddedness* between Washington and Wall Street," Panitch and Konings similarly claiming that "the relations between financial globalization and the US state are internal and mutually constitutive."[81]

One of the most interesting things about this effective support internationally is that at least on the surface, it contrasted markedly with extensive regulation of banking domestically. Battilossi even submits that the former was some sort of "quid pro quo for over-regulating [US banks'] home-based business."[82] Perhaps, perhaps not. But what *is* clear, and what makes that domestic regulatory architecture equally interesting in the present context, is that here we encounter the second of the six sets of factors behind the boom in US international banking in the 1960s.

What particular forms of domestic regulation, then, prompted US banks increasingly to operate abroad? One we have just looked at: anti-trust reform. As Sylla notes, in the context of competition regulation which militated against profit-generative consolidation in the US banking sector, "Europe was a godsend."[83] A second, closely related to the first, were the principal provisions of the Glass-Steagall Act, which kept investment banking and commercial banking apart domestically, but which did not apply internationally and which therefore encouraged commercial banks seeking to diversify to venture overseas.[84] And a third,

worthy of slightly more extended consideration, was a series of measures that can
be viewed collectively as either a direct or indirect system of US capital controls.
Part of the reason for considering these more closely, it seems to me, is the fascinating paradox that they constituted: namely, in introducing measures to *curb*
capital mobility, the US government not only stimulated the re-internationalization of banking in advance of the wholesale liberalization of international finance
capital, but also, in the process, set in motion forces that would eventually lead to
the dissolution of its own *and others'* capital controls.

The primary provocation to these controls, which the US started introducing in
1963, was concern over the magnitude of Wall Street's lending to Europe and its
impact on America's balance of payments position. In the event, the measures put
in place not only made it more attractive for US banks to lend from abroad than
from out of the US, but also for them to accept dollar deposits there: in the former
case the key piece of regulation was the Interest Equalization Tax, which reduced
the yield on foreign bonds issued in the US, while in the latter case it was a change
in Regulation Q policy, which imposed interest rate ceilings on US commercial
banks' domestic time and savings deposits. The outcome of these and related
measures – such as the Voluntary Foreign Credit Restraint Program and the
Foreign Direct Investment Program – was to encourage US banks to conduct
more and more of their borrowing and lending business internationally, with foreign borrowing servicing not only such international lending but also domestic
loan-making.[85] Not until the mid-1970s had the US removed all such controls
(partly in the realization that the internationalization of banking stimulated by
their use materially compromised their effectiveness), and only once it had done
so did other countries also begin to dismantle theirs.

The third explanation for the surge in US bank internationalization in the
1960s and early 1970s, meanwhile, is related to this second. Simply stated, US
banks went overseas because they were making less money at home. In Helleiner's
words, they "enter[ed] the international financial arena to supplement their
declining domestic profits."[86] Certainly, Cleveland and Huertas place a heavy
emphasis on this domestic torpidity in identifying the reasons for Citicorp's
re-engagement with international banking in the early 1960s.[87] And as Seabrooke
notes, the sluggishness of the US economy more broadly at the beginning of the
1970s "only increased US banks' need to internationalize."[88] The link to the
second set of factors just discussed is, of course, that pressure on US banks'
domestic operations and profits was due in part, though by no means entirely, to
the firming of the domestic regulatory apparatus.

Fourth, and no less important, were regulatory developments in Europe.
Specifically, one of the key stimuli not only to the mass arrival of US banks in
Europe but to the connected development of the Euromarkets was the agreement
of the major Western European nations at the end of 1958 once again to make
their currencies convertible for current account transactions.[89] In some respects
the lack of ready conversion among Western currencies had been *the* key barrier
to the re-emergence of international banking in even a rudimentary form in the
post-war period. The eradication of this barrier therefore represented a seminal

moment. And as Frieden has pointedly noted, "American bankers," in particular, "had long awaited the return to currency convertibility."[90]

The fifth and penultimate category of factors which help explain the revival of international banking and the US dominance thereof is, in a sense, a noncategory, for I include within it all *other* commercial factors that I have not identified here as discernible categories in and of themselves. Here I would include (though it is clearly not a comprehensive list, nor intended to be), firstly amongst those factors driving growth in international banking generically: banks' need to follow overseas, and thus service more effectively, corporate clients whose businesses were *themselves* becoming ever more transnational; banks' increasing desire to mitigate risk through international diversification, especially in markets offering especially attractive local banking conditions; and their desire also to capture all of the value generated in such overseas markets, rather than splitting it with local representatives through such mechanisms as commission-splitting. And secondly, amongst those additional factors specifically underpinning US dominance of international banking in this period, the two most important were probably US dominance of multinational enterprise more broadly and the dominance of the American dollar in international financial markets.[91]

This therefore leaves one final, vital realm of explanation for the phenomenon we are concerned with here. I have left this until last both because I want to direct particular attention to it (in contrast to most other accounts, which tend either to ignore it or to minimize its role), and because it leads us directly into the next and concluding section of the chapter. This, then, is the substantive *lack* of competition from foreign banks – including within those banks' own domestic markets – as a further explanation for US banks' ability to dominate international banking in the 1960s and early 1970s. Not only were foreign competitors, in Frieden's words, "few and far between at the end of World War II," but even by the late 1960s they had failed to mount a serious challenge to US hegemony.[92] It was only, Houpt writes, "during the late 1970s [that] they, too, became more expansive and began to close the gap."[93]

One seeming curiosity of this history merits fleshing out here. This is that US banks established the main platform for their wider international dominance in the very place – Europe – where their principal erstwhile competitors had hailed from, and where much of their later meaningful competition would also emerge. And as Battilossi reflects, the further fact that the Euromarkets *were* mainly *Euro*markets suggests there existed, or at least should have existed, "a potential challenge brought by European to American banks." But such a challenge did not in fact materialize for the best part of two decades. Initially and ironically, "the potential threat of Europeanization of international banking in Europe led" instead, Battilossi argues, "to its heavy Americanization," with US banks' "competitive advantages as dollar-based institutions" clearly playing an important role.[94] But do *other* factors also help account for the lack of foreign bank competition? I would argue that they do. In particular, it is critical to recognize that amongst the European territories where the "potential" challenge to US bank entry failed to materialize were those – the UK and France – where, as we have seen, a much more negative view of banks' role in the economy than pertained in the US had crystallized in the 1930s and 1940s; and where, as we shall see now, such a view persisted throughout the 1950s and 1960s.

Morbid Symptoms and Nightmarish Computations

My focus in this chapter thus far has been strictly on the US and on the "alignment of worlds" that occurred and cohered there from the 1930s through to the mid-1970s: an alignment between a positive economic representation of banks and their productiveness on the one hand, and on the other a banking sector encouraged in its international aggressiveness by a government increasingly invested *in* a positive envisioning of that sector's economic role, albeit still mindful of "money trust" concerns at home. When, at the conclusion of the previous chapter, we left Western Europe, things of course looked very different: in France and the UK, where most of our attention was placed, an *obverse* alignment prevailed through the 1930s and 1940s. Banks were materially cowed – especially in terms of any renewed international ambitions – and the national accounts rendered them *conceptually* unproductive. In this final section of the present chapter, I address the question of what happened outside of the US from the start of the 1950s (which was as far as the analysis in Chapter 3 proceeded) through to the mid-1970s, which is the point at which Part III of the book picks up the narrative. In doing so, I consider developments not only in France and the UK but also, in rather less detail, further afield, with national accounting becoming in the 1950s and 1960s a more-or-less universal calculus of nation-state administration.

As we have just noted, the 1950s, 1960s, and early 1970s saw very little in the way of the internationalization of banking except for that which took place out of the US; and as I have intimated at a number of points, this was arguably only surprising in regard to countries such as the UK and France which *had* had substantively internationalist financial institutions prior to the effective closing down of transnational finance in the 1930s. This, I hasten to note, is not to argue that there were no significant nonAmerican international banks operating in the postwar years. There clearly were. But in the majority of cases, including those of France and the UK (though not, notably, Germany, which I will return to presently), such banks were not in an expansionist, offensive phase.

In fact the opposite was true. The big internationally-distributed French and British banks such as, most materially, Crédit Lyonnais and Barclays, which still possessed hundreds of foreign branches between them (most, however, in ex- or soon-to-be-ex-colonies), were timid organizations in the 1950s and 1960s. As much as anything this timidity was a function of state intervention which was arguably much more fundamental than the anti-concentration and rate-adjustment mechanisms applied in US banking since it went closer to the core of what being a deposit bank was all about. As Youssef Cassis explains, the nationalization of the Banque de France and the four major national deposit banks in 1945 gave the French state complete control of credit creation, while in the UK the "Big Five" clearing banks were rigidly, if not legally, controlled to the extent of receiving "precise instructions from the Treasury concerning not only their liquidity but also their lending priorities."[95] In such a hobbling context, limited international ambition was inevitable. Perhaps nobody expressed the degree of circumscription specifically attending UK banking in this period better than Oliver Franks, chairman of Lloyds Bank in the late 1950s. "It was like driving a powerful car at twenty miles an hour," he later told the writer Anthony Sampson. "The banks were anaesthetised – it was a kind of dream life."[96]

There was, of course, something of a paradox in this state of affairs, particularly from the beginning of the 1960s when the Euromarkets had come into being and were enjoying their rise to preeminence in international financial markets terms. As we have seen, through their decision to treat the London-based Euromarkets as somehow extra-territorial and thus beyond regulation, the UK government and Bank of England actively bolstered and championed those markets' development. In other words, a very permissive approach to a certain type of financial *market*, and indeed to the participation of banks of *any* nationality in such markets, sat cheek-by-jowl with a very conservative approach to the operations of British banks. How can we reconcile these approaches? Indeed, *can* we do so?

I think we can. The UK's financial authorities, as many historians have observed, "remained wedded to the notion that London should be an international financial center" long after the City had essentially lost such a status. Realizing that positioning London as *the* premier location for emergent offshore finance offered a potential means of re-establishing London's role "led to [British financial authorities'] support for the Eurodollar market in the 1960s."[97] But this, critically, was about the role of *London* as a place-bound hub of financial flows and economic transactions, not the role of *banks* as economic agents – still less of British banks specifically. For the UK financial authorities, there was nothing contradictory about supporting London as a financial center while closely regulating the activities of British banks. And it was partly this disjuncture that enabled US banks rapidly to attain dominance *in* London. For, while the UK's and France's banks were anaesthetized, America's banks found that "the Europeans were welcoming, particularly the British."[98]

Meanwhile, to account for the evident lack of support for aggressively commercial banking sectors in 1950s and 1960s France and Britain, *including* in an international context, it is vital to recognize the persistence in both countries of the types of concerns about banks' and bankers' role in the economy that we touched upon in the previous chapter, especially in association with Keynes. Though Keynes died in 1946, what has come to be known as the "Keynesian era" in British economic history had only just begun, and is traditionally thought to have lasted until the mid-1970s. While revisionist historians have recently questioned aspects of this neat historical narrative, even the most skeptical accept that "Keynesian economics was the dominant discourse among the British policy elite" from the mid-1940s until, at the very least, the end of the 1950s – and this discourse was, as we know, anything but positive regarding the productiveness of banks.[99] It is thus understandable that rather than being given their head to – as a more charitable economic perspective would have had it – create economic value, British banks in this period were instead *used*, as Duncan Ross asserts, largely as "a tool of policy."[100] The same was very much true in France. Although the specifically Keynesian flavoring was missing from French discourse, the prevailing perspective on banking amongst the relevant authorities was, if anything, even more cautious. The banking sector, as Gerald Epstein and colleagues have argued, was to be mobilized in the service of a "public purpose ethic that promoted," to use their salutary phrase, "'finance without financiers'."[101]

Critically, this more negative perspective on what banks *did* economically remained embodied in the pictures generated by the French and UK national accounts throughout this period – and embodied too, of course, in the assumptions underlying the production of those statistics. As we saw in the previous chapter, the earliest national accounting systems of France and the UK showed banks as being without output (no measurement was even attempted), and as generating minimal or often "negative" output, respectively. From their inception in the 1940s (the UK) and the early 1950s (France), these systems did not change the way they accounted for the banking sector until decades later, and this despite the United Nations' increasingly influential System of National Accounts (SNA) – which we shall consider shortly – offering not one but *two* alternative methodologies for treating intermediation services in particular and thus the banking sector generically, in 1953 (the first SNA) and then in 1968 (the first major SNA revision). French and British national income statisticians ignored these, at least insofar as banking was concerned, until 1973 and the first substantive change in the treatment of banking in either country's (the UK's) accounts – a change coinciding, not coincidentally, with the break between Parts II and III of this book.

So, until the early 1970s, there was no move in France or the UK to "make" finance productive, just as there was little evidence of moves to re-internationalize indigenous banking. Germany, however, which had been the third significant European power in international banking before World War I, presented a rather different configuration of things. In Chapter 3, we observed that the initial system of national accounts which was developed in Germany between the World Wars skirted the question of banks' productiveness altogether by employing the income rather than product method of presentation. We also noted, however, that when national accounts ultimately re-emerged in systematic form in West Germany after the war, the milieu in which they were authorized and produced was now entirely different.

That new milieu, as intimated at the conclusion of the previous chapter, was one of post-war political and economic reconstruction in the immediate historical and geographical shadow of the Eastern Bloc – and therefore of, more pointedly, commanding American influence exerted both directly and, through the Organization for European Economic Co-operation (OEEC, formed in 1948) in particular, indirectly. As various writers both then and more recently have documented, this influence thoroughly infiltrated the techno-political domain of official national economic statistical practice.[102] The upshot, where the representation of banking sector output in the national accounts was concerned, was that the

Yntema method of dealing with intermediation services and net interest income –
in other words, the method used in the US from 1947 – was applied, and banks
were rendered productive economic institutions accordingly.

Moreover, while the conceptual and material "worlds" being explored in this
book were not aligned as intimately in the case of West Germany as I have argued
that they were in the case of the US, German banks *were* nonetheless more energetic
than their immobilized British and French counterparts in attempting to re-colonize
international markets in the 1960s. They were enabled in this respect by a policy
environment which, in line with the more positive envisioning of banks' economic
contribution just discussed, gave them considerably more latitude to expand not
only than French and British banks, but banks in more-or-less any other European
country in the post-war era. As Panitch and Gindin write, the Bundesbank and
German Finance Ministry "espoused neoliberal monetarist policies" with consistent "determination," and this determination was clearly evident, as Battilossi shows
in a fascinating paper, in thoroughly market-oriented banking regulation which
served to induce – rather than dissuade – commercial banks to conduct international banking.[103] This they did, with the rapid expansion of the leading German
banks' international activities beginning a good decade earlier, in the 1960s, than
that of the big British and French financial institutions.[104] Even so, such activity was
still dwarfed during this period by the international activities of US banks.

More widely, it was not just Germany that came now to replicate the American
prototype of a visibly value-adding banking sector in its national accounts. The
1950s, it is important to recognize, was a period of swift international proliferation of national accounting practices. What had been the preserve before World
War II of a small number of "advanced" industrialized countries typically developing their own systems became, within 10 years of the war ending, an increasingly common governmental calculus worldwide, and one ordinarily employing
a single standardized model. That model was the first (1953) SNA published by
the United Nations (UN).[105] The twin purposes of the SNA were to enable international comparisons and to serve as a guide to countries in the development of
their own accounting systems. The latter rationale was seen to be especially pertinent for smaller, less wealthy states lacking the necessary resources, and perhaps
also the aspiration, to formulate proprietary approaches.

Most of those countries which began producing official national accounts for
the first time in the mid- and late 1950s followed the US method of handling
banks and their intermediation services, and the reason they did so was simply
that the UN's first SNA – the template for the vast majority of these newcomers –
itself recommended this method. That it did so is not, in retrospect, difficult to
understand. For while the first SNA was, as Carson and Honsa explain, "drafted
by a group of experts from various countries (including the United States)," the
core framework was the system elaborated for and by the OEEC the previous
year – and the OEEC, created to administer Marshall Plan economic aid, was a
distinctively American creation.[106] The key individual behind the OEEC national
accounting system was, somewhat ironically, Richard Stone, an Englishman who
had worked on the UK national accounts during the war, but who arguably had

a much more significant and enduring impact on practices of national accounting *outside* the UK – via his formative OEEC work – than in it.[107] In any event, it was the US system of national accounting, of all existing country-specific systems, that the 1952/53 OEEC/UN system most closely approximated to; and in the case specifically of accounting for the banking sector, this approximation was exact.

Yet while the US national accounts used the Yntema method of treating financial intermediaries until into the twenty-first century, the recommendation of this method by the UN, and thus its use *outside* America, was relatively short-lived. Despite it being America's favored approach to dealing with the "banking problem," the SNA 1953 treatment received heavy criticism from practitioners in other territories, typically on the grounds that in allocating the IBSC on the basis of levels of deposit ownership it effectively misconceived the main functions of banks.[108] When the UN's SNA underwent its first major revision in 1968, therefore, it was decided that an alternative treatment of banks' nominally "free" services – those financed through margins as opposed to explicit charges – should be recommended.[109] The newly preferred treatment, originating this time out of Norway (and the key persona of the economist Odd Aukrust) rather than the US, differed in one key respect from the Yntema/SNA-1953 methodology; and yet, critically, it too showed banks to be productive economic institutions.[110]

Before highlighting this one key amendment in the recommended UN treatment, it is apposite here, I want to suggest, to recall a dictum of Antonio Gramsci, who famously argued that a historical period during which the old is dying out but the new cannot yet be born represents an "interregnum" in which "a great variety of morbid symptoms appear."[111] I have always liked this quote, the images it helps summon, and the understanding of historical change that it articulates, but I had never happened upon what I considered to be such "morbid symptoms" in my own research – until, that is, I encountered SNA 1968 and its recommended treatment of banks. If we think of national accounts, as I suggested in Chapter 3 we might do, as a technology of representation striving to escape from the dying world of nineteenth-century political economy and its Manichean categories and to embrace instead the brave new world of neoclassicism, then arguably no more morbid symptom of the eternal interregnum inhabited by the national accounting calculus is imaginable than the treatment in question.

How so? Under SNA 1968, the *quantum* of the IBSC was to be calculated in exactly the same way as before (i.e. as the differential between banks' intermediation-derived interest earned and interest paid), but instead of being treated partly as final demand and partly as intermediate demand, this imputed output of the banking sector was now to be considered wholly intermediate consumption and, more pointedly, as the input/expense exclusively of a notional industry sector *with no output of its own.* That is correct: an *imaginary* industry supplying no products or services was theorized into being as the "buyer" of banks' intermediation. The "services" of financial intermediaries were still deemed productive outputs, therefore, yet rather than being traceable to other, tangible sectors of the national economy, they now disappeared into what was effectively the black hole of a dummy industry with a negative value-added equal (but opposite in sign) to the IBSC.

The morbidity of this treatment lay in its work of obfuscation. The treatment recognized the "banking problem" that was the unbearable burden of unproductiveness and its manifestation in the image of the "leech on the income stream." But as opposed to solving the problem (which SNA 1953 had done, however unsatisfactorily), it hid it. It removed the burden of unproductiveness from the shoulders of the banking sector and invented a fictional industry to bear this burden instead. Not surprisingly, many practitioners, not least in the US and Canada, attacked the recommendation for the fudge it was. A later user guide to the Canadian system of national accounts was exacting in its critique: in "assigning the entire [IBSC] to a dummy or fictional industry," SNA 1968 "simply has the effect of transferring the negative output from the banks to a dummy industry," and thus "does not solve the problem but makes it less visible."[112] Peter Hill, a key figure in the construction of the 1993 SNA which replaced the 1968 version (and which we shall consider closely in Chapter 5), called the treatment "expedient" and, hence, "no solution" to the banking problem. "It is debatable," he argued, in terms echoing those earlier used in the UK to justify its own way of handling this problem, "whether inventing an imaginary industry with negative value added is much better than recording negative value added for financial intermediaries. It is certainly much less transparent to users."[113]

We must pay genuinely close heed, I believe, to this SNA 1968 recommendation for the treatment of financial intermediation services, and not only in view of its ungainly and flagrant machinations. Two other factors make it, in many respects, pivotal to the wider arguments of this book. First, despite its self-evident oddity, this method of ascribing a negative income to an imaginary industry sector has probably been *the* most used for financial intermediation services in the entire history of Western national accounting. The UN, as noted, only came up with a new official recommendation in 1993, meaning that SNA 1968 was in place for 25 years. Furthermore, many of those countries which have subsequently adopted the newer UN treatment only did so very recently, and thus a large number of Western nations – Finland, France, Italy, the Netherlands, Norway, and Spain among them – were still using the dummy sector method into the new millennium.[114]

Second, there is something almost exquisitely revealing about the very *awkwardness* of this method, and the fact that it is so blatant in its concealment of the banking problem. If I had to try to capture this revelatory quality in one sentence, I would say that SNA 1968 exemplifies the perennial muddle that Western statisticians have got into in trying to show what simply has never come "naturally" in the national accounting tradition: envisioning banks as productive.

Meanwhile, as if the basic underlying problem of conceptualizing and representing banks' value contribution in the national accounts were not troubling enough, a whole additional layer of complexity began to be added to this now-longstanding problem in the 1960s and 1970s. To understand this incremental difficulty it is vital to appreciate the significance of the particular economic-geographical circumstances in which national accounting had first become systematized in the 1930s and 1940s. As we have seen, these were highly idiosyncratic decades where the historical geography of capitalism – and especially of financial capitalism – was concerned. War and then global economic recession had shrunk what Marx theorized as capital's "circuits" to accord more closely with individual nation-state spaces than at any time in living memory, and nowhere was this restriction more striking than in the case of money capital. As such, when *national* income statisticians set about measuring the notional *national* economy in this protectionist era, there was a certain spatial logic to their initiative: one *could* talk meaningfully of such a "national economy," and the types of cross-border flows that could feasibly make the representation of such an economy problematic were relatively limited, largely visible and, in general, readily manageable. In terms specifically of the activity that mattered most in measuring bank sector output, namely intermediation, there simply was not much cross-border flow: even the restless US banks were, as noted, "cut off from the rest of the world."

A key argument of this chapter, however, has been that from the late 1950s this all began to change, as banks once again began to operate substantially across national boundaries. The spatial correlation between the actual geographical economy of the world and theoretical national economy of the national accounts rapidly diminished. And while the wider importance of this relational dissolution will become clearer in the final part of the book, we can begin to foreground it here, since the "fictional industry" SNA 1968 treatment we have just been discussing brought it into especially sharp focus. It did so precisely because it assumed that *all* of the output associated with banks' intermediation services constituted "intermediate" consumption: the consumption, that is to say, of other industries *within the national economy*. (For SNA 1968 the consuming industry happened to be a fictional one, but that is not the key issue at stake here.) This, of course, had never been the case in reality, since even in a totally isolated economy in the 1930s or 1940s there would always have been a component of consumer, and thus final, demand. But even if we leave aside this particular caveat and assume, for the sake of argument, that all bank intermediation is indeed consumed by other businesses, the presumption that such businesses were always domestic – which is precisely the presumption entailed in the wholesale allocation of the IBSC to intermediate demand – became less and less true from the 1960s onwards, starting with America. The irony of SNA 1968 being published *in 1968* is, in this sense, a stark one.

If this all sounds a bit abstract, consider a notional country with a GDP estimated, under the SNA 1968 system, to be $100bn. Within the mix, it is estimated that this country's banking sector has an output of $15bn, of which $10bn is represented by the IBSC – in other words, two-thirds of the output of the bank sector represents its services of intermediation. The accounts also therefore show a dummy industry with a value-added of *negative* $10bn. But forget, for now, this particular elephant in the room, and consider how the top-line accounts would look different if the IBSC were, say, $20bn instead. The bank sector would look even more productive (with output totaling $25bn), but since all intermediation services are considered to be consumed domestically by other businesses, there would be *no change to total GDP* – the increase in banks' positive output simply being offset by a commensurate increase in the dummy industry's negative output.

Finally, consider the question of geography. Were the banks' intermediation services indeed all consumed in the way presumed by SNA 1968, then the lack of change in headline GDP in the second scenario presented here would be the correct outcome. What if, however, the reality is that all such services are actually consumed overseas? As a rule, national accounts treat all exports as final demand, and thus as wholly incremental to national output.[115] But one of the many problems with SNA 1968 is that it does not allow for any export component to financial intermediation services. As critics immediately pointed out, therefore, a treatment of such services that *did* make such an allowance could potentially generate entirely different outcomes – not so much for the represented output of the bank sector itself, but, arguably more importantly, for headline GDP. Again, take our example. In the first scenario, if the $10bn IBSC fully represents final (exported) demand, then not only do we have no fictional industry, but GDP would be $110bn rather than $100bn, or 10 percent higher; in the second scenario, it would be $120bn and thus 20 percent higher.

Perhaps not surprisingly, given what we learned earlier about the development of the Euromarkets, it was in one of the countries where such markets most fully flowered that the most vociferous objections to SNA 1968 from this specific angle emerged. That country was Luxembourg: a country, of course, that through the 1960s and 1970s saw its economy become more and more dependent on a financial sector supplying financial services of all types largely to *overseas* customers. As the banking sector grew larger and larger in the 1970s, Luxembourg's national accounts showed this sector registering a bigger and bigger share of GDP; but, because of the treatment recommended in SNA 1968 (and used in Luxembourg), with zero impact on the total level *of* that GDP. And so it was that in 1983 the national accounting practitioner Georges Als, prompted by grumbling from within government as well as the statistical community, penned an article with the felicitous title of "The nightmare of economic accounts in a small country with a large international banking sector." The "nightmare" in question, to reiterate, was, in Als's own words, that under SNA 1968 "the most prosperous branch of the economy had no effect on GDP." [116]

I raise this quandary here since it sets the scene ideally for Part III. There, prompted by the issues just highlighted, I expand the discussion in two key directions which are implicit in the analysis so far, but which I will be making much more explicit. First, there is the matter of what I referred to in the book's introduction as the *dialectical* implication of economic ideas in economic history. I will be arguing in Chapter 5 that banks' crossing of the productive/unproductive *conceptual* boundary, first and foremost in the national accounting realm – a process led, as we saw here, out of the US, with key "unproductive" holdouts such as France and the UK still to follow at the beginning of the 1970s – helped enable them to more systematically cross *geographical* boundaries from the mid-1970s onwards. In other words, ideas shaped practices. But as the Luxembourg example hints at, those reoriented practices inevitably "react back" in turn on ideas, and it is this relation I shall explore in Chapter 6: the impact of geographical boundary crossings on the *representational* boundary negotiations which, all the while, were informing those crossings. Second, I insist that we need to be thinking about this reciprocal relationship between ideas and practices much more widely than in relation solely to Luxembourg. If that relationship appears most knotty and pertinent in "a small country with a large international banking sector," for example, then at the very least we need to widen our lens to take in countries falling into the same category – countries like, I would suggest, the UK.

Notes

1   S. Kuznets, "Concept of national income," in S. Kuznets, L. Epstein and E. Jenks (eds), *National Income and Its Composition, 1919–1938, Volume I* (National Bureau of Economic Research, New York, 1941, 1–60), pp.19–20.

2   J. Galbraith, "The National Accounts: arrival and impact," in N. Cousins (ed), *Reflections of America: Commemorating the Statistical Abstract Centennial* (U.S. Government Printing Office, Washington, 1980, 75–80).

3   T. Rymes, "Inflation, nonoptimal monetary arrangements and the banking imputation in the National Accounts," *Review of Income and Wealth*, 31, 1985, pp.85–96, at p.85.

4   For more information on the development of US national accounting in this period, see the following, to which I am indebted for my summary account: P. Studenski, *Income of Nations*, New York University Press, New York, 1958, pp.149–151; C. Carson, "The history of the United States National Income and Product Accounts: the development of an analytical tool," *Review of Income and Wealth*, 21, 1975, pp.153–181; Galbraith, "National Accounts"; M. Perlman and M. Marietta, "The politics of social accounting: public goals and the evolution of the National Accounts in Germany, the United Kingdom and the United States," *Review of Political Economy*, 17, 2005, pp.211–230, at pp.217–221.

5   M. Copeland, "Some problems in the theory of National Income," *Journal of Political Economy*, 40, 1932, pp.1–51, at p.18.

6   Galbraith, "National Accounts," p.76.

7   C. Warburton, "Value of the Gross National Product and its components, 1919–1929," *Journal of the American Statistical Association*, 29, 1934, pp.383–388. The wider Brookings work on national product estimates was brought together in the volume by E. Nourse, F. Tryon, H. Drury, M. Leven, H. Moulton and C. Lewis, *America's Capacity to Produce*, Brookings, Washington, 1934.

8   Carson, "History," p.163.

9   S. Kuznets, *National Income and Capital Formation, 1919–1935*, National Bureau of Economic Research, New York, 1937, p.5.

10   M. Copeland, "Concepts of national income," in Conference on Research in Income and Wealth, *Studies in Income and Wealth, Volume 1* (National Bureau of Economic Research, New York, 1937, 3–63), p.24.

11   C. Carson and J. Honsa, "The United Nations System of National Accounts: an introduction," *Survey of Current Business*, 70(6), 1990, pp.20–30, at p.24.

12   As noted by, inter alia, R. Speagle and L. Silverman, "The banking income dilemma," *Review of Economics and Statistics*, 35, 1953, pp.128–139, at p.139.

13 Carson, "History," p.157.

14 D. Yntema, "National Income originating in financial intermediaries," in Conference on Research in Income and Wealth, *Studies in Income and Wealth, Vol. 10* (National Bureau of Economic Research, New York, 1947, 23–50); the quotation is from p.39.

15 This method of allocation was the main basis for numerous attacks on the methodology in question over the following years and decades, both within the US (e.g. Speagle and Silverman, "The banking income dilemma"; G. Jaszi, "The conceptual basis of the accounts: a re-examination," in National Bureau of Economic Research, *A Critique of the United States Income and Product Accounts* (Princeton University Press, Princeton NJ, 1958, 13–148)) and further afield (e.g. B. Haig, "The treatment of banks in the social accounts," *Economic Record*, 49, 1973, pp.624–628).

16 One data-related caveat is in order here. The exact definition of the "finance" sector for which data were presented changed slightly from one method to the other: most materially, security and commodity brokerage were included post-1947 but excluded pre-1947. Nevertheless, the estimates for "finance" generated by the later method would still be substantially higher than those generated by the earlier method, even if security and commodity brokerage were excluded.

17 H. Brown, "Some aspects of social accounting-interest and banks," *Economic Record*, 25, 1949, August Supplement, pp.73–92; the quotations are from pp.77, 83–84.

18 A paraphrasing of David Harvey's article "On the deep relevance of a certain footnote in Marx's capital," *Human Geography*, 1, 2009, pp.226–231.

19 J. Frieden, *Banking on the World: The Politics of American International Finance*, Harper & Row, New York, 1987, pp.59–61. See also, for a similar argument, E. Helleiner, "When finance was servant: International capital movements in the Bretton Woods order," in P. Cerny (ed), *Finance and World Politics: Markets, Regimes, and States in the Post-Hegemonic Era* (Edward Elgar, Aldershot, 1993, 20–48), pp.23–25.

20 E. Helleiner, *States and the Reemergence of Global Finance: From Bretton Woods to the 1990s*, Cornell University Press, Ithaca, 1994, p.4.

21 Department of State, *Proceedings and Documents of United Nations Monetary and Financial Conference. Bretton Woods, New Hampshire. July 1–22, 1944, vols I and II*, GPO, Washington, 1948, p.1119.

22 Ibid; emphasis added.

23 R. Gardner, *Sterling-dollar Diplomacy: The Origins and the Prospects of our International Economic Order*, McGraw-Hill, New York, 1969, p.76.

24 Among those to reproduce the misquotation in the form used by Helleiner in the past five years alone (citing sometimes Helleiner and sometimes Gardner himself), and usually submitting that bankers' exile was a Bretton Woods *objective*, are the historians Martin Daunton ("Britain and globalization since 1850:II. The rise of insular capitalism, 1914–1939," *Transactions of the Royal Historical Society (Sixth Series)*, 17, 2007, pp.1–33, at p.33) and Harold James ("The multiple contexts of Bretton Woods," *Past and Present*, 210, 2011, pp.290–308, at p.300), the political economist George Lambie ("Nemesis of 'market fundamentalism'? The ideology, deregulation and crisis of finance," *Contemporary Politics*, 15, pp.157–177, at p.158), and the legal scholar Michael Gadbaw ("Systemic regulation of global trade and finance: a tale of two systems," *Journal of International Economic Law*, 13, 2010, pp.551–574, at p.558).

25 Gardner, *Sterling-Dollar Diplomacy*, p.xxvi.

26   L. Panitch and S. Gindin, "Finance and American Empire," in L. Panitch and M. Konings (eds), *American Empire and the Political Economy of Global Finance* (Palgrave Macmillan, New York, 2008, 17–47), p.21.

27   Helleiner, *States*, p.5.

28   The text of Roosevelt's address is widely available online. E.g. here: http://www.guardian.co.uk/theguardian/2007/apr/25/greatspeeches.

29   Galbraith, *The Great Crash 1929*, Penguin Books, London, 1975, p.39. Galbraith himself, in his inimitable style, dismissed said explanation as "a tribute only to a recurrent preference, in economic matters, for formidable nonsense."

30   See, for instance, B. Eichengreen, "The political economy of the Smoot-Hawley Tariff," *Research in Economic History*, 12, 1989, pp.1–43.

31   A theme which actually persists in the readings of most economic historians to this day. L. Ahamed, *Lords of Finance: 1929, The Great Depression, and the Bankers Who Broke the World*, William Heinemann, London, 2009, is a recent exemplar, arguing that "the Great Depression was not some act of God or the result of some deep-rooted contradictions of capitalism," or indeed of the actions of reckless bankers; it was, rather, "the direct result of a series of misjudgments by economic policy makers, some made back in the 1920s, others after the first crisis set in" (p.501).

32   H. Jensen, "J. M. Keynes on the working class," in P. Arestis, G. Palma and M. Sawyer (eds), *Capital Controversy, Post-Keynesian Economics and the History of Economic Thought: Essays in Honour of Geoff Harcourt, Volume One* (Routledge, New York, 1997, 243–250); the quotations are from p.245.

33   On Veblen's thought, see especially J. Hobson, "The economics of Thorstein Veblen," *Political Science Quarterly*, 52, 1937, pp.139–144.

34   Galbraith, "National Accounts," p.76; Perlman and Marietta, "Politics," pp.218–219.

35   S. Kuznets, "National and regional measures of income," *Southern Economic Journal*, 6, 1940, pp.291–313, at p.292.

36   M. Perlman, "Political purpose and the National Accounts," in W. Alonso and P. Starr (eds), *The Politics of Numbers* (Russell Sage Foundation, New York, 1987, 33–51), p.136; Perlman and Marietta, "Politics," pp.218–219.

37   E.g. I. Hashimoto, "The productive nature of service labour: a criticism on the controversy concerning productive labour," *The Kyoto Economic Review*, 36, 1966, pp.56–71, at p.56.

38   Kuznets, "National and regional measures of income," p.292.

39   S. Kuznets, *Economic Growth of Nations: Total Output and Production Structure*, Harvard University Press, Cambridge MA, 1971, p.107, and see the underlying table (#12) on p.104.

40   Perlman, "Political purpose," p.138. According to Perlman, Kuznets also placed heavy emphasis on the role of government institutions.

41   Frieden, *Banking*.

42   Cf. Frieden, *Banking*, p.76.

43   H. Cleveland and T. Huertas, *Citibank 1812–1970*, Harvard University Press, Cambridge MA, 1985.

44   Department of State, *Proceedings*, p.1118.

45   Especially Frieden, *Banking*, pp.63–65.

46   L. Seabrooke, *US Power in International Finance: The Victory of Dividends*, Palgrave Macmillan, Basingstoke, 2001, p.52. See also Helleiner, *States*, to which Seabrooke's account is heavily indebted; also F. Block, *The Origins of International Economic*

Disorder: A Study of United States International Monetary Policy from World War II to the Present, University of California Press, Berkeley, 1977, pp.52–53.

47 Seabrooke, US Power, p.53.

48 Helleiner, States, p.6, and pp.51–58.

49 S. Battilossi, "Financial innovation and the golden ages of international banking: 1890–1931 and 1958–1981," Financial History Review, 7, 2000, pp.141–175, at p.169.

50 T. Huertas, "US multinational banking: history and prospects," in G. Jones (ed), Banks as Multinationals (Routledge, London, 1990, 248–267), p.260.

51 Cleveland and Huertas, Citibank, p.262.

52 S. Battilossi, "Introduction," in S. Battilossi and Y. Cassis (eds), European Banks and the American Challenge: Competition and Cooperation in International Banking Under Bretton Woods (Oxford University Press, Oxford, 2002, 1–35), p.12.

53 A. Porzecanski, "The international financial role of U.S. commercial banks: past and future," Journal of Banking and Finance, 5, 1981, pp.5–16, at p.10. On the relative importance of Citicorp, Chase and Bank of America during this period, see especially Huertas, "US multinational banking."

54 R. Palan, The Offshore World: Sovereign Markets, Virtual Places, and Nomad Millionaires, Cornell University Press, Ithaca, pp.28, 32. See also, on these matters: G. Burn, "The state, the city and the Euromarkets," Review of International Political Economy, 6, 1999, pp.225–261; and C. Schenk, "Crisis and opportunity: The policy environment of international banking in the city of London, 1958–1980," in Y. Cassis and É. Bussière (eds), London and Paris as International Financial Centres in the Twentieth Century (Oxford University Press, Oxford, 2005, 207–229), and "International financial centres, 1958–1971: competitiveness and complementarity," in Battilossi and Cassis (eds), European Banks (74–102).

55 Frieden, Banking, p.90.

56 Bank for International Settlements, 46th Annual Report: 1st April 1975–31st March 1976 (available at http://www.bis.org/publ/arpdf/archive/ar1976_en.pdf), p.75.

57 And thus the "birth and growth of the Eurocurrency market was the single most important postwar development for international banking." Y. Park and J. Zwick, International Banking in Theory and Practice, Addison-Wesley, Reading MA, 1985, p.13.

58 On Paris, see the essays by Éric Bussière and Olivier Feiertag in Cassis and Bussière (eds), London and Paris.

59 Battilossi, "Introduction," pp.2,27.

60 Frieden, Banking, p.91. The figure was sometimes much higher: see, for instance, R. Bryant, International Financial Intermediation, The Brookings Institution, Washington, 1987, p.29.

61 B. Scott-Quinn, "US investment banks as multinationals," in Jones (ed), Banks as Multinationals (268–293), pp.280–281; see also Park and Zwick, International Banking and Cleveland and Huertas, Citibank.

62 Palan, Offshore World, p.12.

63 A. Hudson, "Off-shores on-shore: new regulatory spaces and real historical places in the landscape of global money," in R. Martin (ed), Money and the Space Economy (John Wiley, Chichester, 1999, 139–154), p.143.

64 These data are taken from K. Cho, Multinational Banks: Their Identities and Determinants, UMI Research Press, Ann Arbor, 1985, pp.42–43. J. Houpt, "International activities of US banks and in US banking markets," Federal Reserve Bulletin, 85,

1999, pp.599–615, at p.614, provides different numbers, but showing comparable trends. R. Sylla, "United States Banks and Europe: strategy and attitudes," in Battilossi and Cassis (eds), *European Banks* (53–73), p.56, usefully emphasizes this fact that in the 1960s the leading internationalist US banks had "far more" foreign branches outside Europe than in it. And see Cleveland and Huertas, *Citibank*, pp.260–276, for data on the geography of international branching specifically for the ever-important Citicorp.

65 Porzecanski, "International financial role," pp.4–5; also Frieden, *Banking*, chapter 6.

66 A. MacEwan, *Debt and Disorder: International Economic Instability and U.S. Imperial Decline*, Monthly Review Press, New York, 1990, p.14.

67 Park and Zwick, *International Banking*, p.111. C.f.G. Szegö, "The role of international banking in the 'oil surplus' adjustment process," *Journal of Banking & Finance*, 7, 1983, pp.497–518.

68 Cho, *Multinational Banks*, p.16.

69 Cho, *Multinational Banks*, pp.8–16; Houpt, "International activities," pp.600–602. See also Scott-Quinn, "US investment banks," on the models used specifically by US investment banks abroad.

70 Houpt, "International activities," p.600.

71 Bryant, *International Financial Intermediation*, p.24.

72 E. Canterbury, *Wall Street Capitalism: The Theory of the Bondholding Class*, World Scientific Publishing, Singapore, 2000, p.53.

73 Sylla, "United States banks," p.54.

74 On this history, see especially V. Carosso, "The Wall Street Money Trust from Pujo through Medina," *Business History Review*, 47, 1973, pp.421–437.

75 C. Maier, "The politics of productivity: foundations of American international economic policy after World War II," *International Organization*, 31, 1977, pp.607–633.

76 Sylla, "United States banks," p.54.

77 C. Geisst, *Wall Street: A History*, Oxford University Press, Oxford, 1997, p.276.

78 Respectively: Frieden, *Banking*, p.49; Battilossi, "Introduction," p.8. For wider accounts of the relationships between banking and (especially American) foreign policy, see B. Cohen, *In Whose Interest?: International Banking and American Foreign Policy*, Yale University Press, New Haven CT, 1988 and A. Sampson, *The Money Lenders: Bankers and a World in Turmoil*, Viking Press, New York, 1981.

79 Helleiner, *States*.

80 See, respectively, Seabrooke, *US Power*; M. Konings, "American finance and empire in historical perspective," in Panitch and Konings (eds), *American Empire* (48–68); and Battilossi, "Introduction."

81 Seabrooke, *US Power*, p.45 (original emphasis); L. Panitch and M. Konings, "Demystifying imperial finance," in Panitch and Konings (eds), *American Empire* (1–13), p.2.

82 Battilossi, "Introduction," p.16.

83 Sylla, "United States banks," p.54.

84 L. Goldberg and D. Johnson, "The determinants of U.S. banking activity abroad," *Journal of International Money and Finance*, 9, 1990, pp.123–137, at p.124.

85 See, for instance, M. Moffitt, *World's Money: International Banking from Bretton Woods to the Brink of Insolvency*, Simon & Schuster, New York, 1983, pp.41–42, 45–48; Cho, *Multinational Banks*, p.41; Seabrooke, *US power*, pp.59–60; Battilossi, "Financial innovation," pp.160–166.

86 Helleiner, *States*, p.7.

87 Cleveland and Huertas, *Citibank*.

88   Seabrooke, *US Power*, p.89. As Moffitt writes in *World's Money*, p.51, "the 1970s were dismal years in domestic [US] banking."

89   Note that properly understanding the origins of the Euromarkets per se naturally requires appeal to lots of other factors, too, some of which I have alluded to here but many of which I have not – the latter including, notably, the decision of the UK government in 1957 to restrict foreign trade financing in Sterling, on which see Park and Zwick, *International Banking*, p.12.

90   Frieden, *Banking*, p.76. See also Cho, *Multinational Banks*, p.39, and Battilossi, "Financial innovation," pp.158–159 on the importance of the resumption of convertibility.

91   On these factors and more, see, inter alia, Cho, *Multinational Banks*, pp.33–41; Park and Zwick, *International Banking*, pp.26–30; Goldberg and Johnson, "Determinants"; and regarding investment banking specifically, Scott-Quinn, "US investment banks."

92   Frieden, *Banking*, p.52.

93   Houpt, "International activities," p.600. C.f. D. Fryer, "The political geography of international lending by private banks," *Transactions of the Institute of British Geographers*, 12, 1987, pp.413–432.

94   Battilossi, "Introduction," pp.11,15.

95   Y. Cassis, "Before the storm: European banks in the 1950s," in Battilossi and Cassis (eds), *European Banks* (36–52); the quotation is from p.38. On UK banking in the post-war years, M. Ackrill and L. Hannah, *Barclays: The Business of Banking, 1690–1996*, Cambridge University Press, Cambridge, 2008, pp.114–155, is very useful, as is G. Jones, *British Multinational Banking, 1830–1990*, Clarendon Press, Oxford, 1995, chapter 9.

96   Sampson, *Money Lenders*, p.108. Cf. D. Ross, "British monetary policy and the banking system in the 1950s," *Business and Economic History*, 21, 1992, pp.199–208, at p.207: "The long-term restrictions on the functions and alternative avenues of competition which were imposed on the banks encouraged apathy and blunted the sharpness of British banks' entrepreneurial and inventive thinking."

97   The quotations are from Helleiner, *States*, p.14, who draws on various other historical accounts.

98   Sylla, "United States banks," p.55.

99   The quotation is from A. Booth, "New revisionists and the Keynesian era in British economic policy," *The Economic History Review*, 54, 2001, pp.346–366, at p.346, who helpfully delineates the key contours of those recent debates as to the Keynesian influence on British post-war economic thinking and policy.

100 Ross, "British monetary policy," p.208.

101 G. Epstein, D. Plihon, A. Giannola and C. Weller, "Finance without financiers," *Papeles de Europa*, 19, 2009, pp.140–178, at p.160.

102 See especially the papers collected together as "National accounting practice in the German Federal Republic," *Review of Income and Wealth*, 10, 1964, pp.337–345.

103 Respectively: Panitch and Gindin, "Finance and American empire," p.23; Battilossi, "The regulation of international banking as an agency problem: the Deutsche Bundesbank and the Bank of Italy under Bretton Woods, 1958–71," Paper presented at the Department of Economics, Universidad Pompeu Fabra, 14 December 2001, available at http://www.econ.upf.edu/~penalva/seminar/01_3Fall/batilosi.pdf.

104 See especially U. Ramm, "German banks and the American challenge," in Battilossi and Cassis (eds), *European Banks* (177–199).

105 United Nations, *A System of National Accounts and Supporting Tables*, United Nations, New York, 1953.

106 The quotation is from Carson and Honsa, "United Nations system," p.20.

107 On Stone's work on the UK national accounts, see G. Tily, "John Maynard Keynes and the development of national accounts in Britain, 1895–1941," *Review of Income and Wealth*, 55, 2009, pp.331–359, at pp.350–352; on the importance of his OEEC work to the 1953 UN SNA, see M. Ward, *Quantifying the World: UN Ideas and Statistics*, Indiana University Press, Bloomington, 2004, pp.45,78.

108 Haig, "Treatment of banks," discusses such criticism.

109 United Nations, *A System of National Accounts*, pp.97–98.

110 On Aukrust's role, see, for instance, A. Vanoli, *A History of National Accounting*, IOS Press, Amsterdam, 2005, p.155.

111 A. Gramsci, *Selections from the Prison Notebooks*, Lawrence and Wishart, London, 1971, p.276.

112 Statistics Canada, *A User Guide to the Canadian System of National Accounts*, Minister of Supply and Services Canada, Ottawa, 1989, p.91.

113 P. Hill, "The services of financial intermediaries or FISIM revisited," Paper presented to the Joint UNECE/Eurostat/OECD Meeting on National Accounts, Geneva, 30 April-3 May 1996, available at http://www.oecd.org/dataoecd/13/62/27900661.pdf (retrieved Jul 2009), p.2.

114 OECD, "National accounts: OECD input-output database, Agenda Item 6," 1 October 2001. Document reference STD/NA(2001)22, p.8.

115 "Services rendered to non-residents represent final products, whether the customers are business enterprises or not." H. Arndt, "Measuring trade in financial services," *Banca Nazionale del Lavoro Quarterly Review*, 149, 1984, pp.197–213, at p.205.

116 G. Als, "The nightmare of economic accounts in a small country with a large international banking sector," *Review of Income and Wealth*, 34, 1988, pp.101–110; the quotation is from p.102. See also Arndt "Measuring trade," who (p.205) confirms this point that "the new [1968] SNA treatment understates GNP to the extent that financial [intermediation] services are exported."

Part III

Co-Constituted Worlds
The Age of Financialization?

Part III

Co-Simulation of Worlds

5

Layering the Logics of Free Trade in Banking

[Developing countries] are not so happy sometimes with the American Express offices, or Bank of America, or Chase in their countries. They do not know why they need these foreign banks and foreign financial experts. To us, free competition helps development. They do not always agree. We will win this battle, but it will take many, many years of discussion, scholarly writing, and all kinds of communication.

Harry Freeman (2000)[1]

Subsequent to the boom in US-led cross-border banking activity in the 1960s and early 1970s, a slowdown occurred around the middle years of the latter decade. Pertinent statistics bear this out: having risen relentlessly and rapidly to 52 percent by 1975, for instance, the proportional contribution of internationally-derived earnings to the total earnings of America's ten largest commercial banks suddenly plateaued, stagnating at 51 percent in each of the following two years before dipping *below* half in 1978 and 1979.[2] An impasse, it seems, had been reached; America's banks had managed, more-or-less unilaterally, increasingly to prise open foreign markets from the late 1950s onwards, but having reached a certain level of penetration they began to struggle to progress any further. Why was this so?

The problem was not, for the most part, competition from newly ambitious European or Japanese banks, although it was around this time that some of these did begin to explore international commercial possibilities more actively. Rather, with the low-hanging fruit of welcoming foreign markets already cheerfully plucked, the Americans, we shall see in this chapter, were now more and more often encountering resistance at the international borders they sought to breach. The nature and locations of such resistance represent key components of the argument that follows, but

Banking Across Boundaries: Placing Finance in Capitalism, First Edition. Brett Christophers.
© 2013 John Wiley & Sons, Ltd. Published 2013 by John Wiley & Sons, Ltd.

its core theme concerns the ideational struggle that underpinned the long – and very much ongoing – campaign to overcome that resistance. Further progressing the colonization of international markets, initially still largely on their own but then increasingly alongside Western European banks with similar ambition, has required American banks, I argue, to engage forcefully in what two protagonists appropriately labeled a "battle over ideas."[3] And it has done so in part because the barriers encountered at the boundaries of those obdurate international markets were themselves buttressed *by* ideas.

The central objective of this chapter, therefore, is to trace this battle over ideas – to demonstrate how the formulation and mobilization specifically of *economic* ideas, particularly (though not only) ideas concerning economic productiveness, has played a pivotal role in the largely successful dismantling of barriers to cross-border banking over the past three decades. As will soon become apparent, the world of international trade negotiations and thus of organizations such as the World Trade Organization (WTO) constitutes a – and arguably the – key socio-institutional context for the waging of this protracted battle. *Why* the world of trade politics and economics should have been such a crucial staging ground for the opening up of national economies to overseas financial institutions may not be immediately self-evident. Nor, necessarily, should it be. In fact the question of how banks' access to international markets became proactively envisioned and institutionalized *as a trade "issue"* is a central part of the ideational story narrated here.

The battle over ideas which facilitated the opening up of foreign markets to US and other Western banks from the mid-1970s onwards was fought, I argue, on two related political and geographical fronts: "internal" and "external." On the external front, governments and regulators in many countries worldwide had to be – and in some cases, still have to be – persuaded that opening their doors to foreign financial institutions was in their national interest. As we will see, economic arguments have been consistently deployed to achieve this end, most emphatically in the context of the various "rounds" of WTO negotiations relating to the General Agreement on Trade in Services (GATS) treaty. Some countries "bought" these arguments readily and rapidly; others, among them the likes of Brazil and India, have required considerably more persuasion.

Yet before this international ideational battle could even be joined, and indeed alongside its ongoing propagation, banks in America in particular were compelled to contest a comparable "internal" battle. Recognizing early on that persuading foreign governments to open up resistant markets to US financial institutions would be a significantly easier task if the active support of their own government could be enlisted, such banks focused initially on winning over domestic politicians to the cause. They argued, in other words, that there were economic reasons for the US government to invest time, effort and political capital in assisting the US financial sector in achieving its international ambitions. Some of the economic arguments invoked on this internal front were the same as, or at least closely related to, those mobilized "externally"; some, however, drew upon wholly different premises and logics.

The cumulative outcome of this bi-frontal ideational aggression was the crystallization of an enormously powerful and *novel* discourse, one perhaps best styled "free trade in banking." This discourse, the chapter shows, materialized gradually, at a range of sites and scales, through the work of a host of different epistemic communities, and came to consist of a series of putative geographical-economic logics layered upon – and mutually constitutive of – one another. It pulled together and in the process reconstituted a previously disparate assemblage of "objects": financial institutions, classical writings on trade, national accounting data, modern development theory, and others besides. (It also, meanwhile, severed links between objects that *had* been discursively connected.) As Michel Foucault reminds us is true of all such discourses, the relations between these objects did not simply "come about of themselves," but were always "the result of a construction ... the justifications of which must be scrutinized."[4] The archaeo-logical exercise I pursue here is one of just such scrutiny, and it demonstrates that the discursive construction in question invariably involved the positing of, again following Foucault, "resemblances that relate things together."[5]

With its focus firmly on the nature and effectivity of the various ideas brought to bear in the trade-centered battle to dissolve boundaries within the international banking landscape, the chapter is inevitably light on a number of indisputably important dimensions of the multi-facetted process whereby such boundaries have, over the past 30 years, been whittled away. I do not enter into detailed dis-cussion either of the GATS negotiations themselves or of the various agreements made, though I do summarize the key events and milestones specifically where trade in financial services has been concerned; a large literature exists already on the empirical minutiae of what has been haggled over, where and when.[6] Nor do I assess the various *other* material ways in which the opening up of international markets to US and other Western financial institutions has been effected – the overt exercises, some linked to trade negotiations but many not, in latter-day "dollar diplomacy," and the only slightly less overt pressure to liberalize applied through such disciplinary instruments as the loan conditions of multilateral institutions like the International Monetary Fund.[7] I do not for one moment mean to downplay the importance of these parallel developments. I focus on economic ideas, rather, because their own materiality *has* been underplayed. A clear rationale for exploring these ideas is afforded, moreover, by the fact that the trade negotiations they have colored *have* demonstrably led to the wholesale removal of barriers to cross-border banking, and that such removal in turn – and as we shall see in the following chapter – *has* facilitated massive growth in the activity those barriers previously served to prohibit.

The chapter contains four sections: one in which I describe and analyze the most pertinent aspects of the political-economic context within which the cam-paign to open up foreign banking markets has been conducted, and then three in which the emphasis is squarely on the ideas mobilized during this campaign.

In the first, contextual section, I pause to reflect briefly on US and – from the early 1980s, at any rate – European banks' seemingly unquenchable thirst for geographic expansion, showing that a consistent feature of the past three decades has been bankers' recurring insistence that for all the territorial gains already made, more expansion is *always* still required. I also observe in this section that at the beginning of the period we are concerned with here, namely in the mid-1970s, the capital controls we encountered in Chapter 3 in relation to the Bretton Woods agreements remained one key form of obstacle to such cross-border banking activity. Relying on what is, once again, a large secondary literature, I provide a brief overview of how, when and where these controls gradually came to be loosened. As elsewhere in the book, however, it is banking, not financial capital that primarily interests me. Certainly the loosening of capital controls helped banks grow international operations, and certainly this loosening was itself enabled in part by shifts in discursive formations – just as the use of those controls in the immediate post-war era had been justified in part by the legitimation of the idea of "unproductive" capital flows. Yet when capital controls were removed, substantial barriers to cross-border banking very often remained. And in the drive to dismantle these other barriers – barriers to banks, not to the capital they manipulated – the work of economic ideas was, I argue, even more material.

Those ideas and the work they have "performed" are therefore the focus of the rest of the chapter. The second section argues that before Western bankers could begin actively lobbying their own governments for support, let alone begin the job of trying to persuade foreign governments to open their doors, some preparatory ideational groundwork was required. This came, and to a certain extent still comes, in the shape of two interlinked economic arguments. One, not to be underestimated, is the argument that services in general represent tradable economic phenomena. In the 1970s this was by no means a standard tenet of conventional economic wisdom. But if it had not subsequently been *made* so, services, including financial services, could never have made it onto the WTO liberalization agenda, and the barriers to international banking which the pursuit of that agenda helped dismantle would potentially still be in place today. The second argument, meanwhile, was more specifically about banking and finance. This argument, equally critical, is that banking, or "finance," is *itself* an economic service; that there is such a thing as "financial services." Today, of course, this is essentially taken as read; but in the 1970s it was not. It is of no small significance, I will argue, that much of the work of yoking "finance" and "services" to one another was effected *specifically* in the context of the attempt to internationalize American banking. Nor is it insignificant that at the same time, the world of national accounting, long stymied by the conceptual quandary precisely of what banks' intermediation "service" truly consisted in (Chapter 3), was finally closing in on a consensus answer to this element of the "banking problem."

In the third section, I focus on arguments that US bankers, in particular, have invoked in seeking to secure domestic government support initially for hoisting financial services onto the official international negotiating platform that was and is the WTO, and subsequently for doggedly pursuing multilateral liberalization initiatives in this realm. It is here, I show, that we first encounter arguments explicitly about economic productiveness, and moreover arguments underpinned by national accounting data testifying to the productiveness specifically of the financial sector.

In the US context, of course, where these arguments were first mobilized, locating and using such data was unproblematic, since as we saw in the previous chapter the US national accounts always *had* envisioned banks as productive economic actors. In Europe, however, where these arguments would increasingly also come to be posited in the 1980s, the national accounts were not necessarily always so obliging. The UK, I argue, is a striking and important example of a country whose financial institutions leveraged economic arguments that would have been much more tenuous – if not entirely untenable – were it not for contemporary moves, which I also document, to "make" banking productive within the national accounting calculus.

The fourth and final section of the chapter follows the banks as, now joined at the hip with converted domestic governments and trade representatives, their arguments were transplanted to the all-important "external" front: the WTO negotiating forum, and the resistant worldview shared by governments of territories where substantive barriers to foreign bank entry remained. Such governments have been subjected over time to a veritable barrage of economic arguments as to why they should open their borders to US and other major international banks. Here, too, ideas relating to "productive finance" have been consistently material; and here, too, the "proof" contained in national accounting's envisionings has been vital. From the very first appearance of financial and other services on the WTO agenda for the Uruguay Round of negotiations beginning in 1986, all the way through to the current conjuncture of ongoing-but-stalled Doha Round negotiations nearly three decades later, the resistance of protectionist nations and, with it, their remaining barriers to incursion by foreign financial institutions, have gradually but ineluctably been worn down. I examine the ideas that have helped make this possible.

Restless Capital and the Eternally Elusive Spatial Fix

The 1960s and early 1970s represented, I argued in the previous chapter, the first important period of renewed international expansion by America's largest commercial banks in the post-war era. This expansionist phenomenon was extraordinary in at least a couple of senses. First, it was achieved, as Ingo Walter later remarked, "all without formal negotiations or the pro-active involvement of the GATT, the OECD, the EEC, or any other official body."[8] Second, and all the more remarkable given this first feature, it occurred on a gigantic scale, whether measured by branch numbers or by revenue and profit achievements.[9] One might be forgiven for thinking, therefore, that American financial institutions would have been satisfied with their overseas successes to this point, and perhaps even relatively sanguine about the plateauing of foreign profit generation in the second half of the 1970s. Yet not a bit of it: "In 1979," Harry Freeman – whose words form the epigraph to this chapter – would later recall, "I was in New York with the American Express Company and was in charge of strategic planning and acquisitions. We were having problems, which we now call *market access problems* (we did not have this kind of terminology at that time), in thirty or forty countries."[10] These problems had become a matter of urgent consideration.

For American Express and other major US financial institutions, it was very much a case of the glass being half-empty rather than half-full. Yet if one reads the now longstanding literature on the structural dynamics of capitalism's geographical political-economy, and especially the seminal work of David Harvey from the late 1970s and early 1980s (the timing being far from coincidental here), there appears nothing surprising in this. Arguably Harvey's unique contribution to Marxian theory has been rigorously to incorporate spatiality into its primarily temporal architecture, and he has done so in part through his argument that capitalism seeks spatial as well as temporal "fixes" to its recurrent episodes of systemic crisis.[11] One such "spatial fix," he has claimed, is a restless and unceasing search for new geographical spaces of accumulation. Thus capitalism, Harvey summarized recently, can be said to be "addicted to geographical expansion much as it is addicted to technological change and endless expansion through economic growth. Globalization is the contemporary version of capitalism's long-standing and never-ending search for a spatial fix to its crisis tendencies."[12]

Freeman, American Express and other leading finance companies were displaying symptoms of just such an addiction as the 1970s drew to a close. Large parts of the world had already been colonized; but attention rapidly came to be focused instead on the "30 or 40" countries *resisting* colonization. Many of these did come to be colonized to varying degrees in the 1980s and beyond; but still this was not enough. (Harvey's argument, of course, is that it never is, further geographical expansion being a structural necessity under capitalism.) Thus, a decade after Freeman registered his grievance, the further gains made were still not considered sufficient, with Walter lamenting (in 1988) that in much of the world "the ability of foreign based players to supply financial services remains severely restricted."[13] Nor were they sufficient in 1995, when a director of the Ford Financial Services Group gave testimony in US Senate hearings that many countries continued to "restrict the ability of US-based financial services companies from gaining market access," or in 1999, when the British banker Andrew Buxton lamented in turn that "hardly any progress" had been made in countries such as India and that therefore "more pressure" was needed. [14] And nor, it appears, are they sufficient today, with industry lobbyists in both the US and Europe continuing to push over the past decade for "the expansion of market access for financial services firms."[15] Such firms have proven over the past half-century to be territorially voracious and, as such, quintessentially capitalist.

In the next three sections, I discuss some of the key ideational dimensions of American and European banks' drawn-out struggle to break down barriers to banking across borders. But before doing so, it is important to recognize that some of the most material obstacles standing in the way of expanded international banking in the early 1970s were of course barriers not so much to the banks themselves but to the financial capital they worked with: they were, in short, *capital* controls. It is important also to recognize that while it is easy to conflate barriers to the mobility of financial capital and of financial institutions – how, one might ask, can banks operate overseas if capital flows are substantially impeded? – it is only minimally accurate. Capital *can* flow without banks necessarily "following" them across borders; equally, banks *can* internationalize in the absence of capital freedom, and indeed did so, as we saw in the previous chapter with US banks, in the 1960s. Hence, in a speech given in 2002, Stanley Fischer, chairman of Citigroup, made the following helpful observation: "[C]apital account liberalization and opening of the domestic financial sector to foreign entry, while related, are not identical issues. A country may permit foreign firms to compete in the domestic financial sector even while restricting capital flows... It is also possible that a country may permit a wide range of capital flows but seek to protect the domestic financial sector by excluding foreign firms."[16]

Nevertheless, while capital controls are not as thoroughly disabling as is sometimes assumed, they do clearly present formidable barriers to particular activities – cross-border lending being an obvious one – and thus certainly preclude a full flowering of international banking. And in the early 1970s such controls, having been introduced widely in the turbulent period between the World Wars and then given a seal of approval at Bretton Woods, remained extensive and substantive. As long as they did so, international banking would continue to butt up against a relatively low ceiling of opportunity. It was therefore a development of enormous significance for the global banking sector, and specifically for its cross-border possibilities, when the existing system of international capital controls rapidly began to unravel from the mid-1970s onwards.

The vast literature on the history of this capital account liberalization points to a number of crucial explanatory factors.[17] Certainly, various "background" market and technological developments provided a powerful impetus to the loosening of controls, these including increasing demand for international financial services with the rapid growth in international commodity trade and multinational corporations, restoration of confidence in the safety of international financial transactions, the possibilities opened up by innovations in derivatives, and the adoption of floating exchange rates in the early 1970s. But it has become increasingly clear that state and multilateral institutions played a pivotal and necessary role. Eric Helleiner points to the actions in particular of the US, UK, and French governments; Rawi Abdelal, meanwhile, focuses on the activities of German and especially French policymakers within the institutional contexts of the EC/EU, the OECD, and the IMF.[18]

The upshot of the various decisions taken and initiatives pursued by these agents was the dismantling of capital controls more-or-less globally over a 20-year period. The US, which had never employed such controls vigorously or comprehensively, began the trend in 1974, with the UK following suit in 1979. Once these two had taken the decision to liberalize unilaterally, it became increasingly difficult for others to maintain restrictions. But while some countries proceeded to abolish their controls "voluntarily," others waited to be forced, most notably by a 1988 EC directive requiring members to remove all restrictions on capital movements, and by a 1989 amendment of the OECD's Code of Liberalization of Capital Movements. By 2005, Abdelal reports, these EU/OECD rules on liberalization "governed some 70 to 80 percent of the world's capital flows."[19] There has, interestingly, been something of a renewal of interest in – and, within the key global multilateral institutions such as the IMF and World Bank, of acceptance of – the use of capital controls in the past few years as first the Asian financial crisis of the late 1990s and then the global financial crisis a decade later put the issue of destabilizing capital flows squarely in the political spotlight. And in the afterword to the book I will return to this development: which is *especially* pertinent, I argue, in view of a conspicuous *lack* of any similar trend towards advocacy of national protectionism in financial services in general, or banking in particular.

Here, I want merely to make one final set of observations, beyond noting that such progressive capital account liberalization represented a substantial boon to cross-border banking operations from the mid-1970s through to as recently as 2007. (The impact was not only in one direction, either: as Kevin Gallagher has importantly shown, the liberalization of cross-border financial services provision through trade treaties, which we turn to later in the chapter, has very often mandated *also* "the unbridled opening of the capital account without safeguards."[20]) These final observations pertain to the fact that for all the importance of state and multilateral institutional power and of background market and technological drivers, *ideas* were important here, too – that is to say, in enabling the opening up of international capital flows as well as of (as we shall see below) international banking markets. This, obviously, should not surprise us: the idea that capital flows could be somehow "unproductive" was, as we saw in Chapter 3, crucial to the materialization of a consensus view at Bretton Woods that capital controls should be permissible, notwithstanding Harry White's insistence that such flows were *normally*, or by their nature, productive; one would therefore imagine that a shift in such ideas might have facilitated – or perhaps even have been necessary for – restrictions on capital controls being removed.

And so indeed, to a certain extent, it proved. Through the 1970s and 1980s, it became increasingly accepted wisdom among Western policymakers not only that capital should be able to flow to where it could be put to most "productive" use, but that state intervention was not required to ensure that it *would* flow thus – markets, functioning efficiently, would take care of that.[21] As Helleiner has observed, the growing hegemony of such a view was part-and-parcel of the wider rise of a neoliberal consensus during the period in question.[22] And one could add, of course, that this argument's increasing purchase was encouraged also by the simultaneous strangling of the political-economic orthodoxy that neoliberalism ultimately supplanted: namely, the Keynesian welfare-statism whose policy autonomy had been seen to *require* the judicious use of capital controls.

Thus the concern that cross-border capital flows could be unproductive, or even destructive, effectively dissipated as neoliberal policymaking colonized Western institutions of national and multinational governance from the mid- to late-1970s onwards. In its place emerged a pervasive discourse on the desirability and "rightness" of capital freedoms that took both overt and more subtle forms. The overt form amounted to, as Jagdish Bhagwati styles it, a "hijacking" of "the idea and the ideology of free trade and its benefits."[23] As I showed in Chapter 2, the classical theories of free trade offered by Adam Smith and David Ricardo were theories about trade in goods, not (also) in capital. Moreover, even as late as the 1940s, those like White who argued in favor of capital mobility did so without invoking the theory of free trade as conceptual support – Smith's and Ricardo's arguments were simply not seen as relevant.[24] When, therefore, the US "Wall Street-Treasury complex" identified by Bhagwati began in the 1980s to posit international capital mobility *as a free trade issue*, it represented a novel historical development. Bhagwati's critique of this populist hijacking of Smith and Ricardo is nothing short of withering. With Wall Street and its lobbyists seen to have gained influence not only over the US Treasury but also the IMF and World Bank, a deep-seated and broadly-based adulteration of classical free trade theory served from the 1980s "to bamboozle us into celebrating the new world of trillions of dollars moving about daily in a borderless world."[25]

Meanwhile, the "idea" of free capital mobility also gained momentum in other, less conspicuous, but arguably no less significant ways. A more subtle ideational shift occurred, for example (and perhaps most pointedly), in the realm of mainstream academic neoclassical economics, which all the while was becoming a, if not *the* principal scholarly buttress – to the degree that one was needed – for the ascendant neoliberal political project.[26] But the relationship between academic concepts of capital mobility, and the propagation of policies geared towards capital mobility in the "real world," was by no means straightforward. This much is clear from the account provided by Matthew Watson. Where capital mobility entered into the models constructed by economists, Watson shows, it tended to be more as an assumption than as a recommended policy approach. This does not mean that such models of capital mobility had no effective materiality, but rather that their "effects" were of a more indirect nature. As Watson notes, "acting upon the prescriptions" of models that assumed perfect capital mobility manifestly "encouraged governments to cede their capital controls."[27] It did so, presumably, precisely because those models' constitutive assumptions ruled out, by definition, such controls.

Setting the Discursive Scene

Where and when capital controls were removed, however, formidable barriers to cross-border banking often still remained. What types of barriers are we dealing with here? Essentially, these barriers were, and in some cases still are, of two inter-connected forms. The first are *entry* restrictions.[28] Such restrictions can either be total, or can allow some types of foreign banking presence (a representative office, for instance) while excluding others (e.g. acquisition of a majority interest in an indigenous bank). The second form of barrier, meanwhile, pertains to restrictions on *operating activities* where entry is permitted. Again, such restrictions can be extremely varied, ranging from highly targeted interventions such as denying or curbing foreign bank access to certain funding sources, to a more wholesale disqualification from engaging in particular intermediation, advisory or investment practices.

In the mid-1970s, very few countries around the world had liberalized to the extent of allowing effective freedoms in terms of both the entry *and* operation of foreign banks. It was when US banks began to be materially constrained overseas by the barriers of this kind which remained that the contribution of foreign markets to their total earnings began, as we have noted, to level off. My argument in the rest of this chapter will be that the battle to break down such barriers depended to a very significant degree – and much *more* so than was the case with capital controls – upon banks waging and winning a battle at the level specifically of economic ideas.

In the current section, I explore what we can think of as the ideational preparation of the wider battlefield: the forceful establishment of *where*, institutionally and thematically, efforts to open up international markets should be focused, and why such a focus was conceptually appropriate. As I indicated at the outset of the chapter, it was upon the world of international trade negotiations that this focus came to alight. As such, the preparatory conceptual groundwork I discuss here amounted in large part to the positing of the internationalization of financial services as an issue *of* trade. This work began early, in the mid-1970s, but it continued long after the battle proper had begun: as obstacles to the further liberalization of international banking were encountered over the following decades, it was repeatedly necessary to remind naysayers of why cross-border banking activities had entered the trade domain in the first place.

The original and primary impetus to conceiving and negotiating access to overseas banking markets in terms of trade came, perhaps not surprisingly, from within the US finance sector. Increasingly frustrated internationally by the types of entry and operating restrictions alluded to above, companies such as American Express, Citigroup and American International Group (AIG) collectively made a crucial observation: whereas they were attempting to overcome such obstacles more-or-less independently, their counterparts in goods production and distribution not only received extensive support from the US government, but did so explicitly in the realm of negotiations such as the GATT aimed at the reduction of foreign trade barriers. Might a similar form and direction of support, they began to wonder, be useful in their own sector?[29] In the belief that it *could* be, the three aforementioned companies spearheaded the organization in 1974 of "a full-fledged campaign to extend many of the provisions of the [US Trade Act of 1974] to services."[30]

It would ultimately take more than a decade, however, before services formally joined goods on the WTO negotiating agenda. (Indeed as late as 1986 US banking chiefs were still telling the US government that foreign markets remained impenetrable, "we basically need help in this situation ... [and] need to use the GATT. It is the best thing we have got."[31]) A large part of the reason for this delay, I want to argue, was that the US financial sector firms and executives who first mooted the conjoining of trade and financial services were entering, in the mid-1970s, decidedly inauspicious conceptual territory. Quite simply, "trade" and "services" were rarely, if ever, spoken of in the same breath. Geza Feketekuty, a senior figure at the Office of the U.S. Trade Representative in the 1970s and 1980s and a key individual in what follows, noted in this vein that "before 1973 there had been no public discussion of trade in services."[32] Similarly, Vinod Aggarwal, writing specifically about the heterogeneous trade "community" which existed in the early 1970s, had this to say: "Almost everyone in the United States government, business, academics, press, and policy elites – as well as their international counterparts – felt that services were uninteresting and unimportant."[33] Confronted with this inopportune conceptual environment, it was clear to the AIGs of the world that for financial institutions and other service providers to secure domestic government support for advancing their interests in the trade arena – not to mention winning over overseas trade negotiators – existing mindsets had to be thoroughly recast.

This recasting entailed, I submit, making two fundamental, interlinked economic arguments. I will analyze these in turn, but in advance of doing so it is important to register a critical feature that they share. In both cases, the argument put forth effected a discursive rapprochement. By this, I mean that the protagonists of each argument put into conversation, and in the process bound together, economic terms that historically had circulated largely independently of one another. In one case the terms in question were, as previously foregrounded, "services" and "trade"; in the other they were "services" and "finance."

Taking trade and services first, the core problem for those minded to make services a trade issue was not so much that people inside and outside the trade community appeared uninterested in services trade, but a deeper concern which, in many respects, explains this very lack of interest: the belief that services were simply not tradable phenomena. This belief, it turns out, characterized the bulk of mainstream economic theory until as recently as 40 years ago. Ronald Shelp, an AIG executive in the 1970s and another key figure in my narrative, has noted that there were two main reasons for this. "First, as the classical economists observed, [services] cannot be stored. How, after all, can a loan or an accounting service be warehoused? And if services cannot be stored, how can they be shipped to another country? Second, services do not physically cross borders the way goods and commodities do."[34] The upshot was that economists traditionally tended to believe services must be produced where they are consumed; and that, as Eugene Beaulieu has noted, services were therefore "treated in economic analysis as the proverbial non-tradable."[35] Clearly, it would remain inconceivable for services to become a trade negotiations issue until such time as this prevailing conceptualization had been supplanted.

Far and away the fullest and most penetrating account of how it came to be argued that services *were* actually tradable, and thus *could* be legitimately presented for discussion at the WTO, has been provided by William Drake and Kalypso Nicolaïdis.[36] As they observe, economic actors in one territory had been providing services to economic actors in other territories for several centuries, but since such service provision had never been considered "trade," services were not included in any of the first five, pre-1970s rounds of the GATT. The earliest intimation that this might change came in 1972 when, Drake and Nicolaïdis claim, the term "trade in services" was first used, in a report into the long-term outlook for trade commissioned by the OECD and authored mainly by economists. They further show that the "services trade" discourse thus initiated came to be rapidly embraced firstly in the US and the UK, and then from the early 1980s – and stimulated by the evangelizing work of organizations such as the Coalition of Service Industries (CSI) in the US and the Liberalization of Trade in Services Committee in UK, both launched in 1982 – further afield.[37] This new epistemic consensus regarding tradable services was circulated and recirculated within an ever-growing community of believers, "with analysts from academia, research institutes, corporations, consulting firms, business associations, and governments joining in from an increasing number of countries." Drake and Nicolaïdis offer an unambiguous assessment of the long-term significance of this discursive transformation. "The shift to a trade discourse," they conclude, "was a revolution in social ontology: it redefined how governments thought about the nature of services, their movement across borders, their roles in society, and the objectives and principles according to which they should be governed."[38]

Drake and Nicolaïdis's account is important for at least one further reason. On the face of it, the argument that services were in fact tradable phenomena did not necessarily carry with it any prescriptive judgment about what sort of international trade regime was preferable. It was, merely, an assertion that services could be traded – not that they should be, nor that they should be in a particular manner. But when services were co-opted into the discourse of trade, they clearly did not enter a judgment-free realm. On the contrary: they became immersed in a political and theoretical world long soaked in powerful convictions regarding how trade *should* be conducted and administered. More specifically, with five GATT rounds already complete, "free trade" was well established in the West as the default stance on trade policy. As such, it would be naïve to imagine that making services a trade issue in the 1970s could ever have been a neutral conceptual coupling. Indeed, only assertions explicitly to the contrary could realistically have prevented the new services-trade discourse from immediately assuming free trade characteristics; and none, unsurprisingly, was forthcoming. "The very act of defining services transactions as 'trade'," Drake and Nicolaïdis thus observe, "established normative presumptions that 'free' trade was the yardstick for good policy."[39] The importance of this associational effect will become clear in the following sections of the chapter.

From our perspective here there is, however, one crucial limitation to the analysis provided by Drake and Nicolaïdis: they largely overlook the fact that while the insertion of services into the trade domain was increasingly effected and supported by a broadly-based epistemic community as the 1970s seeped into the 1980s, the most forceful proponents of this new discourse in its formative stages in the former decade hailed almost exclusively from the world of finance. It was financial institutions that *made* services tradable in a generic, conceptual sense. And doing so entailed intense engagement in a range of writing, lobbying, and networking activities that together *constituted* the discourse in question. AIG executives were to the fore here: Shelp, and also chief executive Hank Greenberg, who was appointed to the Presidential Advisory Committee for Trade Negotiations.

But they were not alone. Feketekuty describes how they and other financiers brought the discourse to life:

> In addition to Shelp, Harry Freeman and Joan Spero from the American Express Company assumed leading roles in organizing conferences, developing press material, lobbying in congress, and building support in the business community at home and abroad. Freeman and Spero used their participation in bilateral business meetings with business leaders from other countries to develop statements of business support for negotiations on trade in services. Together with other business leaders, they helped to support conferences on trade in services in the United States and abroad. They also used their membership in a variety of business organizations and public policy research institutes to persuade these organizations to launch research studies on trade in services. When the time came to establish a senior advisory committee to the U.S. trade representative on services trade policy, Freeman persuaded James D. Robinson, the chairman and CEO of the American Express Company, to become its chairman.[40]

The key point to emphasize here is that through their efforts to make access specifically to overseas financial markets a trade issue, US financial institutions actually succeeded in lodging services *in general* within the ambit of trade discourse and policy. This was a major development, as David Hartridge, formerly director of the WTO's Trade in Services Division, has since acknowledged: "Without the enormous pressure generated by the American financial services sector, particularly companies like American Express and CitiCorp, there would have been no services agreement and therefore perhaps, no Uruguay Round and no WTO."[41]

There was nonetheless a distinct irony about the fact that of all service providers, it was financial institutions that led the initiative to reconceptualize services as tradable phenomena. The irony was that if one had asked US or UK economic policymakers of the era to list the main components of the tertiary (or services) sector of the economy, many, if not most, would likely have left finance off the list. This was not because finance was seen as unimportant to the functioning of the economy, but rather because what banks and other financial companies "did" was traditionally not regarded as "service provision." Banks were banks: they acted first and foremost as intermediaries between those with financial surpluses and deficits, and outside of the world of national accounting – a notable exception, of course, and one I turn to presently – such intermediation had long been considered less a service than a "position" or role. Banks made money not so much through what they provided as by virtue of where, in a wider network of economic actors, they stood.

If US financial institutions were ever going to be able to force their international market access problems onto the radar of trade negotiators *as a services issue*, therefore, a second argument needed to be made: not only that services were tradable, but that "finance" was *itself* a service. In short, "finance" had to become "financial services." It is of no small significance to the wider narrative of this book that much of the discursive work of effecting this coupling indeed occurred precisely in the context of the attempt to internationalize American banking. And our best guide here is the man we encountered earlier in the context of his grumbles regarding resistant overseas markets: American Express executive Freeman.

> Another thing that we had to deal with very, very early on is the meaning of financial services. The first thing we did in 1979 was to coin the phrase. You will not see the term "financial services" before 1979. We did that by asking everybody in the company to talk about financial services particularly with the media, and in about two years the term financial services was part of the lexicon. ... We were quite successful in the Uruguay round in defining financial services as "any service of a financial nature." This allowed us to have more and more allies, and you have to take care of your allies.[42]

Rarely does one come across such stark testimony to the power of language or to, more broadly, the materiality of discourse.

Freeman is absolutely correct that the concept of "financial services" only took meaningful root and began to flower within public and policy discourse from the beginning of the 1980s (even if his claim that "you will not see the term" before 1979 is not strictly accurate). Yet as we saw in Chapter 3, there did exist one "expert" community within which the intermediary function of banks *had* been conceived as a service of sorts for several decades: the community of national accountants. Indeed the "banking problem" as I articulated it in that chapter was, in part, a conceptual one: the question not so much of whether financial intermediaries performed a service, but of what this service actually comprised. To the extent that they had been theorizing finance in service-oriented terms since the 1940s national accountants were, it is clear, some way ahead of the wider conceptual curve.

As late as 1990, I noted in Chapter 3, two well-known authorities on national accounting were still in a position to observe that practitioners remained split on what the core intermediation service was.[43] And here, it is true, the most recent UN System of National Accounts (1968) had not been of much help: it merely recommended that national authorities impute a charge equivalent to banks' "excess of the property income they receive over the property income they pay out" (ideally excluding the value of any property income receivable from the investment of their own funds) and label this a "service charge," without ever saying what the service in question specifically consisted of.[44] But, crucially, while Freeman and his collaborators had been busy through the 1980s telling the world that finance was in fact a service, national accountants *had* been steadily converging in the background upon a consensus answer regarding the nature thereof – at least insofar as banks, as intermediaries, were concerned. This consensus view was spelt out unequivocally, if somewhat tortuously, in SNA 1993. The service provided by financial intermediaries, which represents their unique contribution to national economic output, and which therefore justifies the net interest revenues they thereby accrue, was *the assumption of risk*:

> [Financial intermediaries] obtain funds by incurring liabilities on their own account, not only by taking deposits but also by issuing bills, bonds or other securities. They use these funds to acquire financial assets, principally by making advances or loans to others but also by purchasing bills, bonds or other securities. *A financial intermediary*

does not simply act as an agent for other institutional units but places itself at risk by incurring liabilities on its own account.[45]

This newly-acquired certainty with regards to the service *of* finance was manifest not only in the definition of financial intermediation services in SNA 1993, but also in the new label given to the measurement of their value: FISIM, which, as noted in the introduction, stands for "financial intermediation services indirectly measured." Later in this chapter I will turn to FISIM in more detail, for its recommended method of derivation, which differed substantially from the methods advocated in previous versions of the SNA, was integral to the redoubled endeavor in SNA 1993 to envision banks as definitively productive. At this juncture I am interested more in the terminology. For the previously-employed term "imputed bank service charge" was now regarded as altogether too tentative: it *intimated* that banks performed valuable services, but it did not specify what those services were, and in requiring a value to be "externally" attributed to those services it communicated the fact that this value could not simply be measured. "FISIM" was subtly, but substantively, different. Not only were the services in question now labeled, but a rather abstract and cautious exercise in "imputation" had now become a putatively robust and transparent process of measurement – albeit, still, an indirect one.

At a point in time, therefore, when the cumulative preparatory discursive work of making "services" a trade issue and making "finance" a service had been underway for nearly two decades, SNA 1993 emerged to rubber-stamp the latter rapprochement by giving financial (intermediation) services official, "expert," and precise authentication. It did so, assuredly, in the background; Shelp, Freeman et al. were doubtless quite oblivious to this development. Yet, if this conceptual work remained hidden in the shadows, the quantitative picturing of financial sector productiveness that it enabled and rationalized did not. The likes of Shelp and Freeman were nothing if not cognizant of the power of the GDP and GVA data generated by national accountants. And as we shall see now, they showed no hesitation in putting these data tangibly to work, domestically and overseas, in the service of arguments explicitly for the opening up of international markets to Western financial institutions.

Comparative Advantage and Just Desserts

The arguments investigated in the previous section were key to establishing – and continuing over time repeatedly to *re*-establish – the basic rules of engagement of the broader internationalization project explored in this chapter. If it were to prove possible to use the domain of trade negotiations to lever open resistant overseas markets to US and other Western financial institutions, it was, bluntly, *necessary* to envision finance as a service and services as tradable. Yet such envisionings were never likely to be *sufficient*: either in winning over protectionist foreign governments and regulators, or in gaining meaningful and actionable support from domestic authorities. In the final section of the chapter I will turn to the ideational battle waged on the former, "external" front. Here, meanwhile, my focus is on the latter, "internal" struggle. Through what *additional* economic arguments did financial firms and their champions, in the US and then increasingly in Western Europe, set about persuading their governments to go into battle in the trade arena on their behalf?

My claim is that a further two arguments served this purpose. But, more than that, and picking up again the central thread of the book, it is that both arguments depended squarely on conviction in and quantitative substantiation of the economic productiveness of the financial sector. Such conviction and substantiation could, I argue, be found most readily and advantageously – in the sense of the authenticity and neutrality it theoretically possessed – in national accounts. This was all well and good in the all-important American context where, as we know from the previous chapter, the national accounts had never shown banks as anything other than unambiguously productive. In Europe, however, and in particular the UK and France, things were less straightforward, since the 1970s dawned with the accounts of both those nations still providing altogether more equivocal perspectives on financial sector productiveness. As such, I examine in this section not only how national accounting data was used to buttress the two arguments deployed to garner government support for taking services to the WTO, but also simultaneous shifts in French and British national accounting treatments which *allowed* a positive picture of productiveness to be uniformly painted.

The first important topic to consider, though, is the domestic political contexts within which the financial institutions agitating for state support were operating. What type of challenge did they face? Given the leading role of Citigroup, American Express and AIG, the American context in the late 1970s and early 1980s is the critical one. As we noted above, perhaps the best way of summarizing the initial political standpoint on the services industries, insofar as their early articulations of enlarged international ambitions were concerned, was disinterest. Writes Aggarwal: "No immediate crisis faced the service industry, and thus government officials saw little reason to respond."[46] This, as Murray Gibbs noted, changed somewhat with the coming to power in 1981 of the Reagan Administration, which had a "stated commitment to free trade" and proved immediately more receptive.[47] Even then, however, skepticism and even opposition remained, especially in the form of an "increasingly protectionist Congress."[48]

The tactics adopted by US financial services companies to sway those not convinced by the cause were, as Sharon Beder has shown, extremely aggressive. Coordinated from 1982 onwards by the CSI, which was chaired by Freeman, these companies targeted three constituencies: "public opinion, the US Congress, and the US Executive." They did so, moreover, by strategically aligning themselves with other "service" companies under the CSI umbrella, recruiting these various "'allies', including non-financial service companies, to better influence Congress. Until this point," Beder continues, quoting US diplomat James P. Zumwalt, "corporate executives in fields as diverse as entertainment, engineering, transportation and finance did not identify as 'part of a coherent "services" sector with common interests'."[49]

In this assault on domestic public and political opinion, as indicated, two further economic arguments were layered on top of those already discussed. We can start by identifying what those arguments were, before moving on to consider who mobilized them, when and where, and with what effects.

The first argument was that the US government – and later, various Western European governments – should support their domestic financial institutions in making services a formal trade negotiations issue because it was here, in the services sector, that their national "comparative" or "competitive" advantage now resided. This argument appealed directly to the trade theory of David Ricardo and to, more recently, Eli Heckscher and Bertil Ohlin's extensions to the Ricardian framework. We do not need to get into the details of such theory here, but we do need to recognize those elements of the theory that were put to work domestically. (Others, we shall see below, were then put to work "externally" in negotiations with foreign governments.) Specifically, Ricardo had suggested that each country should allocate resources towards, and thus concentrate export trade in, activities in which it enjoyed not so much *absolute* competitive advantage – which some countries might not enjoy in any sector – as *relative* competitive advantage. The argument now put forth by Citigroup and its peers, therefore, was that whatever America's relative strengths had been in the past, financial services was where it was most productive and competitive today, and the government should play to these strengths by helping US firms compete without hindrance abroad.

The second argument was perhaps less theoretically pure, but it was equally forceful and equally reliant on notions of productiveness. We can think of this argument as quite simply one of "just desserts." Look, its proponents said, at the scale of the contribution that the financial services sector makes to national economy and society: the jobs created, the tax dollars delivered, the balance of payments benefits *already* being realized, and, not least, the economic output generated. Given these highly quantifiable and substantive contributions, surely the very *least* the sector deserved was a modicum of support for expanding its business overseas and, in the process, reinforcing its value to the nation?

The leading financial companies in the US and Western Europe have petitioned their governments time and again with these arguments over the years, from the mid-1970s until right up to the present. In fact with current levels of internationalization, as discussed earlier, still deemed insufficient, and with Western governments *still* not seen to be doing enough to unlock closed markets through new trade treaties, the arguments in question are no less visible today than they were three decades ago.

They were first marshaled, however, in the mid-1970s, and certainly for the rest of that decade and into the early 1980s the "comparative advantage" argument was the more prominent of the two. Among the first to make the case were, as Geoffrey Underhill has noted, a number of Washington-based think-tanks.[50] But it was not long before bankers and other financiers themselves latched onto the argument and made it their own. In Senate hearings into the service industries in 1981, for example, Richard Wheeler, an executive of Citibank, spoke forcefully and explicitly of those industries as "a great strength and a potentially important competitive advantage and comparative advantage in terms of future trading patterns."[51] Around this time, furthermore, a number of trade economists published books and papers containing the same argument, thus lending it a scholarly imprimatur.[52] Deepak Nayyar, writing in 1988, summed up the prevailing mood that had resulted by the middle of the decade: "There is a perception in the United States that the increase in the share of the services sector in output and employment reflects a shift in its comparative advantage out of manufacturing activities and into the services sector."[53] And nor, we should note, was this solely an argument coming out of the US. On most measures the countries of Western Europe enjoyed collectively in the early 1980s a significantly higher share of worldwide services exports than the US, and thus it was hardly surprising that similar assertions as to the comparative advantages – and thus trade policy priorities – of European nations began appearing at this time.[54]

Already by the early 1980s, especially in the US, the notion that financial services companies should be given political assistance in the international domain as a "reward" or quid pro quo for their multi-facetted "contribution" at home was circulating in lockstep with the comparative advantage argument. Here, again, the CSI was immediately an active and powerful player.[55] If anything, however, this particular argument has become *more* entrenched and insistent over time, while the more "conceptual" case for comparative advantage has quieted somewhat. Witness, for instance, Congressional hearings in 1994 on the results of the Uruguay Round of GATT negotiations, where finance sector lobbyists seeking to stake their claim focused explicitly on "the importance of financial services and services generally *to the U.S. economy*."[56] Thirteen years later, as the latest (Doha) round of WTO talks stumbled from one collapse to another, the chief executives of the 20 member companies of the US Financial Services Forum made the "just desserts" argument in strikingly clear terms in a letter to President Bush. "We understand," they wrote, "that the administration and Congress must take into account the interests and objectives of all sectors of the U.S. economy in a way that is most beneficial to the nation as a whole. We are concerned, however, that the financial services sector is not receiving the attention it deserves based on its contribution to the national economy."[57] The Liberalization of Trade in Services Committee of International Financial Services London (IFSL) – which hails, like so many comparable entities, from the early 1980s – has continued in recent years to make more-or-less the same argument vis-à-vis the UK economy and the implied "obligations" of the UK government in multilateral trade negotiations.[58]

The various companies and industry lobby groups responsible for formulating and articulating these two economic arguments over the past three decades have always placed great weight on using data to cement their case. Comparative advantage and "just desserts" could, in other words, be "proven" quantitatively. Both were and are, of course, fundamentally *relative* rather than absolute arguments: they attest to the level of contribution made by the (financial) services sector *in comparison to* contributions made elsewhere, more than they are about the quantum of such a contribution per se. What is particularly important to note here, however, is exactly what, where and whom the comparison is being made to. In the case of comparative advantage, the comparison is with the (financial) services sector contribution in other countries, a higher relative contribution representing evidence of such sector-specific "national advantage." In the case of the argument for just desserts, by contrast, the comparison is with the contribution of other industry sectors in the same country, a higher contribution justifying a relatively stronger claim on the support of the domestic state.

Unsurprisingly, the two main economic metrics mobilized in both cases have consistently been employment and GDP data (although contribution to the national balance of payments position has often also been added to complete a fuller picture). Yet the emphasis placed on these two metrics has never been quite equal; of the two, GDP data have been invoked more frequently, more widely, and more forcefully. How might we account for this bias? There are, in my view, two explanations. I alluded to one of these in the introduction to the book, where I argued that where the question specifically of economic *productiveness* is concerned, GDP or GVA data offer something that employment or, say, taxation metrics do not. That special "something" is an impression of augmentation – of *adding* something to the economy that might not otherwise exist. (Health services, government, and education, by way of counter-example, employ large numbers of people in most countries, but those people are typically not regarded as economic producers in the sense of adding directly to the size of the economic pie.) Clearly, in the context of soliciting government support for advocacy in trade negotiations, being able to argue that the sector for which support is being sought is a productive one has never been an idle consideration.

The second explanation for why GDP or other output data have been privileged somewhat over employment data is a more straightforward one. It is, quite simply, that in relation to *financial* services in particular, the former data have tended to be more flattering and, hence, more suasive. As we shall see below when we consider specific examples of data that have been used, the reported percentage share of national economic output generated by the financial services sector has – in countries such as the US and UK, in recent decades – typically been higher, and sometimes considerably higher, than the share of national employment accounted for by that sector. On reaching for numbers to demonstrate how important the financial sector is, therefore, *particularly* in relation to the contribution of other industry sectors within the same country, GDP data have inevitably been the preferred ammunition for most proponents of the arguments in question.

The penchant for mobilizing such data became apparent, as noted, almost as soon as those two arguments began, in the late 1970s and early 1980s, to cohere. Indeed, it would perhaps not be stretching the case to suggest that the data were always an integral part *of* those arguments; that the arguments could not have crystallized without them and the substance they conferred. Citibank's Wheeler, for example, furnished his 1981 Senate testimony with "The fact that more than 50 percent of our GNP is represented by the services sector."[59] At around the same time, the CSI began feverishly, Beder relates, to "put together and [publicize] data and statistics to prove what a large proportion of exports, gross domestic product and jobs could be attributed to service industries."[60] "The US interest," confirms Underhill, summarizing the broad message, "was clear: America possessed the

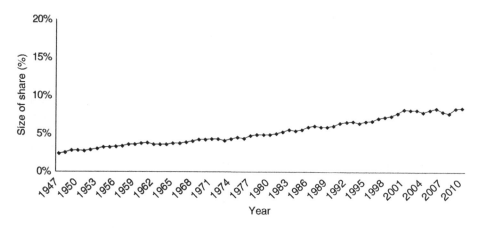

Fig 5.1   Finance and insurance share of US value-added, 1947–2010.

Source: Bureau of Economic Analysis Gross-Domestic-Product-(GDP)-by-Industry Data (here http://
www.bea.gov/industry/xls/GDPbyInd_VA_NAICS_1947-1997.xls and http://www.bea.gov/industry/
xls/GDPbyInd_VA_NAICS_1998-2010.xls).

largest service economy, with over 75 per cent of the workforce and 69 per cent
of gross national product dependent on service industries."[61]

The above examples, of course, all relate to the services industries in general,
and while such data certainly supported the financial sector's case for governmental assistance, data pertaining more narrowly to financial services were and are,
nonetheless, critical. Examples abound of these being invoked, also. Two follow. I
have selected these because one (the first) illustrates data being co-opted explicitly
in the service of the comparative advantage argument, while the other is oriented
categorically towards the theory of "just desserts." "Within services," claimed
IFSL's Liberalization of Trade in Services Committee in giving evidence in 2008 to
the EU Committee of the UK's House of Lords, "financial services in particular
are an area of especial interest for the UK. The sector represents 10.1% of the UK
economy, a far larger proportion than that of any of the UK's EU counterparts."[62]
On the other side of the Atlantic, meanwhile, America's financial companies could
be seen differentiating themselves from domestic rather than foreign peers:
financial services, President Bush was informed, account "for more than five per
cent of all American jobs and more than $1 trillion, or eight percent, of U.S.
economic output – two-thirds of the combined value of all types of manufacturing
and eight times greater than total U.S. agricultural output."[63]

Had American banks or other financial institutions wanted to similarly invoke
positive output data in the 1950s, 1960s or 1970s as opposed – as above – to the
1980s and later, it would have been straightforward for them to do so. To be sure,
the picture has become steadily *more* positive over time (Fig 5.1): having hovered
between 2.5 and 4 percent in the 1950s, the combined reported "finance and
insurance" share of US value added averaged just under 4 percent in the 1960s,
4.5 percent in the 1970s, 5.5 percent in the 1980s, 6.7 percent in the 1990s, and

8.0 percent between 2000 and 2009. Nevertheless, the fact remains that the figures *have always been positive.*

Yet in various other countries, as we know from Chapters 3 and 4, that has not always been the case. Having been deemed unproductive by the great pre-twentieth-century political economists, banking and finance *remained* such in the estimation of the post-war national accounts of, most notably, the UK and France. There were, as we have learned, different reasons for this, and different respective envisionings *of* financial "unproductiveness": the French accounts simply excluded all financial institutions from the list of economic actors considered productive, whereas the UK accorded banks a productive value but rendered it null or negative by effectively stripping out any value associated with the perennial hot potato of intermediation services. Such differences notwithstanding, banks – our chief concern here – were yet to be "made" productive in both the UK and French accounts as late as the beginning of the 1970s, which was precisely when US banks began agitating for financial services to be made an international trade liberalization "issue."

Had no changes to the accounting calculus occurred in those two countries, therefore, it would have been impossible for French or British banks to lobby their respective governments for support in the trade negotiations domain in the way their US counterparts did – which is to say, by, inter alia, actively mobilizing supportive GDP data. Coincident precisely with this critical period in the history of financial border politics, however, changes to the UK and French conventions for accounting for banks' productiveness *were* occurring; with the result that it *did* become possible for organizations such as IFSL, as we saw just above, not just to press domestic politicians for assistance, but to do so armed with positively legitimating economic output data.

In the following chapter, I will argue that there was nothing coincident*al* about the timing of these changes. I suggest, rather, that to understand why French and British national accounting practitioners "made" finance productive in the 1970s, we need to recognize that it was in this same decade that French and British banks awoke from their post-war slumber and began once again to expand overseas – confronting, in so doing, the selfsame barriers already frustrating America's internationalist banks; and then pressuring their own governments, from the early 1980s, to support the American push for adding services to the GATT.

At the present juncture, I want merely to date the pertinent changes in national accounting treatments. In doing so, we can identify when exactly positive output data could begin to be leveraged in the UK and France in support of domestic financial institutions' comparative advantage and "just desserts" arguments. In the UK, the change occurred in 1973, when it adopted the SNA 1968 "dummy industry" method that we reviewed in the previous chapter. And the same method was selected in France when it made its own leap into the brave new statistical world of productive banking two years later. As we noted above, it was then directly from the beginning of the following decade that EU governments, not least the government of the UK, began to come under pressure from their finance sectors to make finance an international trade issue – on the grounds of "rewarding" a domestic contribution that afforded, in turn, national competitive differentiation in the international marketplace.

What, therefore, were the practical effects of this upsurge in the lobbying of US and EU governments on services – and especially *financial* services – trade matters from the early 1980s? It would be wrong to suggest that there were no dissenting views. Plenty of economists, for instance, suspected that trade in services was *not* in fact like trade in goods, and that concepts such as comparative advantage might not be applicable.[64] Some, looking at the issue from more narrowly partisan perspectives, worried that making services a formal issue of trade negotiations failed the most basic cost-benefit analysis: that the effort and costs associated with likely painstaking negotiations and exhaustion of political capital were simply not justified by the gains potentially available.[65] And there was, perhaps more pointedly, explicit *political* resistance in the shape of the US Treasury. For a number of reasons, as Aggarwal has argued, the Treasury was highly reluctant to sanction the type of approach – "a financial services accord as part of a broader multilateral [trade] agreement" – favored by "the bulk of the [US] financial services industry."[66]

Yet despite these various conceptual quibbles and political wrinkles, the US administration was rapidly on board. It eagerly supported hoisting services onto the GATT (and later WTO) agenda, with a multilateral agreement encompassing financial services indeed the explicit objective; and, once established there, it has consistently promoted the aggressive use of that platform to break down barriers to international banking. (Persuaded by the finance lobby's "positive" arguments for such aggression, certainly,[67] but no doubt over time increasingly influenced *also* by its more "negative," indeed overtly threatening ones: James Robinson, chief executive of American Express, warning in 1990 that were no agreement reached on services in the Uruguay Round, "The US service industry would either be neutral or vocal in its opposition (to such a result)."[68])

Already by 1978, then, the US government had, through the Department of Commerce and the US Trade Representative, conducted a significant amount of proprietary research into trade in services; had succeeded in inserting references to services in three nontariff agreements in the Tokyo Round of the GATT negotiations; and had obtained an *informal* commitment from other industrial countries to undertake a full study of trade in services in the Trade Committee of the OECD. This showed that the other major Western nations – and especially the UK, West Germany, France, and Japan – were by now well disposed, at the very least, to the US agenda. The OECD work carried out in 1980 and 1981 subsequently snuffed out any meaningful, lingering misgivings.[69] The leading financial services companies had, in other words, successfully persuaded the US and other major Western governments that making services a formal and substantive international trade negotiations issue *was* a cause worth fighting for. In concluding, we can leave it to Geza Feketekuty – described by Drake and Nicolaïdis as the US government's "house intellectual" on services, and more widely as no less than the "father of trade in services" – to summarize.[70] "As a result of the work undertaken in the OECD Trade Committee," Feketekuty wrote in 1988, "most developed countries had come to the conclusion by 1981 that they had an economic interest in trade in services, and that the issue should be examined in the GATT as a possible topic for future multilateral negotiations."[71]

The Battle Over Ideas

Reporting on the state of "global competition in financial services" in 1988, Ingo Walter attempted to articulate what it was that the US and its financial-trade liberalization allies had been pushing for since the beginning of the decade. The best summary description he could come up with was "equality of competitive opportunity." Yet no sooner had he encapsulated their demands thus than he was forced to admit the problematic nature of his phrasing. Such "equality" was, he acknowledged, "an extraordinarily difficult concept to define, much less deliver."[72]

What, in practice, was sought, therefore, if not this hazy panacea of even competitive opportunity in global markets? The answer, fortunately, is relatively straightforward. Ever since the governments of the US and other major industrialized economies were first persuaded to pursue international liberalization of commercial financial services, two demands on counterpart governments have been paramount. These were first spelled out in the national study on trade in services which the US prepared in 1983 for submission to the GATT. In sum, this study concluded, "the U.S. would like to see ... all countries offer national treatment, including liberal right of establishment, to foreign banking institutions."[73] "National treatment" meant that foreign financial institutions should be accorded precisely the same treatment as (i.e. not be disadvantaged in relation to) "national," or indigenous institutions; "right of establishment" meant that foreign institutions should be able not only to provide services across borders, but to wholly control the delivery of those services locally through the ownership and operation of a permanent local branch or subsidiary. A parallel report into trade in banking services by the OECD Committee on Financial Markets – published in 1984 – made much the same recommendations as the US study, in its case placing especial emphasis on the latter of the two demands on the alleged grounds that "the most serious [existing] impediments relate to limitations to the granting of right of establishment to foreign-owned banks."[74] These two aforementioned objectives of liberalization remained equally as pivotal in the 2000s as the 1980s. And this is true not only in relation to multilateral trade initiatives.[75] In the case of recent US- or EU-led bilateral trade agreements, also, it has been national treatment and the right of establishment that financial services negotiators have invariably targeted.[76]

The first lobbying of international – as opposed to domestic – governments by financial institutions and the lobbying assemblages they formed took place, as Feketekuty has related, from the very beginning of the 1980s. Whilst the Trade Committee of the OECD was carrying out its generic study into trade in services,

Feketekuty, "in cooperation with a loose international coalition of about a dozen key business executives and government officials," developed a strategy designed, inter alia, to "engage trade officials in other governments on issues dealing with trade in services."[77] But the response from governments outside the small core of supportive industrialized economies ranged from lukewarm at best to, at worst, outright hostility. Indeed, had the reaction *not* been so negative, it would not have taken until 1986 for the US and its allies to achieve the relatively small (and in practice, exceedingly painful) first step of persuading the GATT membership to formally launch negotiations – let alone make agreements – on trade in services. Here, again, is Feketekuty, recalling the tone of the initial response: "Developing countries, however, strongly resisted the discussion of trade in services in the GATT, and this set the stage for a confrontation at the [trade ministers' meeting in November 1982]."[78]

Neither that ministerial meeting, nor the explorations of services trade issues by those skeptical "developing" countries over the next two years, did anything to assuage such countries' concerns. In fact, as Ronald Shelp later observed, "Third World opposition, led by Brazil and India, had hardened" by the end of 1984. Shelp points here to the importance of a document produced by the secretariat of the UN Conference on Trade and Development (UNCTAD), *Services and the Development Process*, which, he says, "strongly suggested that subjecting services to the GATT rules was not in the Third World's interest."[79] Such resistance to liberalization of financial services across large parts of the Global South reflected varying combinations of multiple arguments in favor of financial protectionism: the desire for national control over monetary policy; the desire to protect domestic firms from powerful foreign competition; the desire to maintain full control of the local regulatory environment; and the desire to prevent destabilizing inflows and outflows of capital.[80]

What was immediately apparent, therefore, was that the preparatory ideational work discussed in the section before last – positing finance as a "service" and services as tradable phenomena – had either not been sufficiently compelling to such international ears, or had simply not been fully absorbed and understood. (Shelp appears to have suspected the latter, making the fantastically patronizing statement in 1988 that "Developing countries must first familiarize themselves with this novel subject."[81]) Either way, it was rapidly perceived that further arguments were needed to move the debate forwards and to precipitate action. These arguments, and their formulation and dissemination from the early- to mid-1980s to the present day, are my concern in the rest of the chapter. I aim to demonstrate that just as was the case "internally," such "external" arguments were multiple; were layered upon one another discursively; were grounded, however tenuously, in economic "theory," or in Chakravarthi Raghavan's words "propelled by economic theories on the 'role of services';" were reliant upon a conceptual envisioning, and quantitative substantiation, of banks as productive economic actors; and were widely propagated in the form of books, articles, briefing papers, and other written and spoken texts authored by Western policymakers, economists, and financiers themselves.[82]

The central and most crucial argument consisted of an extension and realignment of the comparative advantage thesis that was mobilized internally within the US and the EU territories. In its "internal" form, as we have seen, this argument was that such countries had a relative competitive advantage in services in general, and financial services in particular, and should focus their resources and export enterprises accordingly. The critical extension, which *also* drew upon classical trade theory in its Ricardian form, was that "free" trade conducted on the basis of the international distribution of comparative advantages in different industry sectors benefitted *everyone* – not just those who happened to enjoy competitiveness in financial services.

Once more, the benchmark US study of 1983 set the tone for the broader discourse which subsequently crystallized. Liberalizing services trade would, it asserted forcefully, assist "developing countries" too, not least since some "have important service industries which figure in the international marketplace" and since "the availability of the best services at competitive prices will be crucial for countries that seek to improve their competitiveness in goods production."[83] Key "intellectual" voices in the US pro-trade camp then set to work reiterating and puffing out this core theme. Feketekuty, for instance, wrote that "The unique characteristics of trade in services do not invalidate the application of existing international trade theory," in particular the core comparative advantage dictum that "every country can gain from trade if it concentrates its energies in the industries that make best use of its resources and skills."[84] Walter concurred. "There is no greater justification for protection (appropriately defined) in financial services than there is for steel, automobiles, or telecommunications equipment." Indeed for him, freeing up services trade was thus not so much an ideal as an obligation – one ordained by the righteousness of free trade theory: "countries that have a competitive advantage in this sector have the *right* to seek access to foreign markets as a matter of general reciprocity, in return for access to their own domestic markets for goods or services in which they have a competitive disadvantage."[85]

If this discourse originated in the US, it had, by the turn of the decade, been fully absorbed by the other industrialized nations pushing for services trade liberalization, and also, critically, by the WTO's internal group of "expert" economists and lawyers – the Secretariat – whose role it was and is to supply technical support and advice to WTO members, and whose personnel were and are drawn disproportionately from those same countries. A group of such Secretariat "experts," for example, penned a highly influential study on *Opening markets in financial services and the role of GATS* in 1997, which was a highly-charged moment in the longer negotiations process. "From an economic perspective," they asserted in their report, "trade in financial services is no different from trade in other goods or services" and hence liberalization "can have strong positive effects on income and growth, driven by the same factors as in other sectors – specialization on the basis of comparative advantage, dissemination of know-how and new technologies, and realization of economies of scale and scope."[86] Wagner, meanwhile, surveying the broader "persuasive-discursive" milieu of the 1990s, observes that "negotiators from the United States and other developed countries emphasized to developing countries the virtues in economic terms of free trade in financial services and the gains to producers and exporters in such countries of importing cheaper and more efficient banking and insurance services."[87] And underlying this discourse, vitally, there always existed a conviction – sometimes spelled out, though often not, and one we will turn to in more detail presently – about not only the nature of trade dynamics but the nature of the economic dynamics of financial "services" per se. This conviction concerned economic productiveness; it was, as we shall see, specifically and only the productiveness *of* finance that rendered free trade theory applicable. "As in any other productive sector," wrote Richard Webb of the Brookings Institution in 1994, and making this coupling explicit, "the output of financial services is cheapened, improved, and increased by specialization and by trade across borders."[88]

Yet over the past three decades, countries outside the Global North have raised at least three key sets of suspicions in relation to the argument that the iron laws of comparative advantage would deliver benefits to all from liberalizing international banking markets. The first of these suspicions was, we saw above, also raised internally – if less vociferously – within the US and various Western European countries. This was that trade in services was materially *different* from trade in goods, and that the concept of comparative advantage was thus potentially redundant. Those Western economists hinting at this heretical view were essentially drowned out by a cacophony of free-trade voices in the US and Europe, but when policymakers and their advisers in the Global South articulated this same suspicion in the combustible context of live trade politics, an *answer* of some sort was required; and it could never consist solely of a simple negation. In the event, the response from the ideologues of financial services trade was actually still relatively limp. Provide us *evidence*, they said, that, in Shelp's words, "something about services *invalidates* the principle that countries should trade what each can most efficiently produce."[89] This was the infuriating logic of Occam's razor. "[N]one of the potential difficulties of applying the normative theory of comparative costs to trade and investment in service industries," argued Brian Hindley and Alasdair Smith in a contorted double negative in 1984, "appears to yield any a priori reason to suppose that the theory does *not* apply."[90] Or as Shelp, more succinctly, expressed it: "The burden of proof lies with those who disagree."[91]

The second suspicion takes us back to an issue with which we began this chapter: the issue of capital movements and of capital controls. Since the beginning of the process of widespread removal of capital controls and especially since that process gathered pace in the context of the Global South in the late 1980s and early 1990s, exposure to unsettling flows of capital has been a recurrent political and policy concern for many of the countries which, simultaneously, have resisted – to varying degrees, and with varying intensity at different junctures – financial *services* liberalization. Perhaps unsurprisingly, therefore, often-longstanding concerns about the former have periodically bled into beliefs and policies regarding the latter; almost anything which smacks of greater mobility for "finance," even if the "finance" in question actually pertains to financial *institutions*, has raised the specter of free capital movements in some quarters. The US and its allies in the trade domain have long recognized this locus of suspicion, and their words and actions have been crafted accordingly. On the discursive front, while explicitly coupling concepts with little or no historical inter-relation ("services" and "trade," for example), proponents of free trade in services have striven to *un*-couple discussion of freedoms for financial capital on the one hand and for financial companies on the other – freedoms which historically were, rightly or wrongly, accorded close conceptual proximity. Meanwhile a parallel severance was consciously effected on the policy front. As Raghavan, among others, has noted, "the rules of GATS were designed to decouple liberalization of trade in financial services from that of capital account transactions."[92]

The third and final suspicion takes us back not to the first part of this chapter, but all the way back to the first chapter of the book. In invoking not only David Ricardo but also Adam Smith to propound the merits of free trade, the champions of liberalized financial services markets were venturing onto decidedly thin ice. The laws of comparative advantage, the countries of the Global South were told, mean that everyone gains from trading in the outputs of productive economic activities, whether the latter consist of producing goods or providing services. But hold on, those countries were entitled to (and did) say: did not Adam Smith, your free trade priest, claim that services, and the labor invested in them, were wholly *un*productive? Indeed, as we saw in Chapter 1, he – and Ricardo – did. As such, perhaps the greatest single conceptual hurdle confronted by the Western financial services trade lobby over the past 30 years has been this particular Smithian legacy. Nobody, on my reading, grasped this as clearly as Ronald Shelp, who repeatedly lamented "the 200-year-old picture of services as at best a necessary evil, leeching the productive areas of the economy" and the way in which this picture obstructed efforts to liberalize services trade. "A trade negotiation on services," he wrote in 1988, which was still early in the first GATT round formally to feature services discussions (the Uruguay Round, 1986–1994), "will be plagued by theoretical questions derived from the classical economic view that services are fundamentally different from other kinds of economic activity."[93]

And so it proved. For the first time in history, and thus representing a conjuncture of seminal importance to the overall narrative arc of this book, enabling banks to cross geopolitical boundaries *required* demonstrating that they had also crossed a conceptual boundary – the boundary separating the productive from the unproductive. This, therefore, was the task assumed by Shelp, Feketekuty, and the other leading theorists of free and open services trade. In many respects it was a curious thing to behold: acolytes of one part of Smith's conceptual scaffold busily dismantling another. But they set about the task with a characteristic intensity. Shelp did so from as early as the late 1970s, publishing in 1982 the book *Beyond Industrialization* in which he meditated – in an early chapter – on "The meaning and significance of services" and began the task of rebutting the Smithian inheritance.[94] His later work continued this effort.[95]

But, of the two, Feketekuty was probably the more prominent and respected "thinker" (Shelp, with his AIG background, was much more transparently partisan), and it is telling that in his hugely influential text on *International Trade in Services* (1988) he devoted an entire chapter (number 4) *specifically* to confronting the classical unproductive envisioning.[96] Smith, he claimed, had got it wrong. To the notion that services were unproductive Feketekuty leveled two ripostes. One was "ample" – though actually entirely unspecified – "evidence to the contrary." The other, somewhat more persuasive, was that it had been "natural" for Smith "to conclude that workers producing services rather than industrial goods were not productive" since he was, of course, a creature of his time, "when English factories began to produce the goods that energized British trade" and "the factories turning out industrial goods were the key source of economic power and national wealth." Smith's perspective was, in short, an anachronism. "As more consumers are able to satisfy their needs for the basic goods associated with the average life-style," Feketekuty insisted, jumping to the present-day economy, "consumer demand has shifted toward buying more services such as health, education, tourism, and entertainment. There should be no reason why anyone should feel that producing these services is less productive than growing food or producing manufactured goods."

Whatever the merits of such arguments – and again, the tendency for double negatives and occamian logic is noteworthy – they rapidly gained traction and rapidly infiltrated the wider discourse of free trade in finance with which the hold-outs of the Global South were bombarded. It was a simple but powerful claim: services, including financial services, produced value and wealth. It featured explicitly and implicitly in trade negotiations from the late 1980s onwards. And it spread to become dogma within the other Western-led multilateral institutions of global political economy. In a forthright paper supporting the role of foreign banks in developing countries, for example, the influential American economist Ross Levine – at the time (1996) a principal economist at The World Bank – elaborated this "basic theme" about financial services: namely, that they "constitute real value added; financial institutions are not simple balance sheets, and financial markets are not simple veils for the functioning of the real sector."[97]

To understand how and why it was possible for the assertion of financial sector productiveness to be made relatively unproblematically, however, we need to recognize that it enjoyed a crucial and effectively uncontested source of both conceptual and empirical validation. A clue to the location of that source lies in Levine's choice of words: "value added." As I argued in Chapter 3, the middle decades of the twentieth century had seen the emergence of a new and ultimately dominant forum for the adjudication of what constituted productive economic activities, what activities were unproductive, and where the boundary between them lay; and that forum, which was of course the techno-political calculus of national accounting, quantified each industry's productive output specifically in terms of (gross) value-added.

Why, then, did Feketekuty himself not draw upon national accounting statistics to buttress his argument against Adam Smith? This is where Feketekuty's account is actually at its most revealing, for he clearly *wants* to use output or value-added data, but he senses that they do not quite tell the story he would like to relate: "it is very difficult," he grumbled, "to develop an objective measure of output in services, and this tends to result in a consistent understatement of gains in the real value of services produced in the economy."[98] Shelp, interestingly, had been even more up-front about such "problems" with the representation of services – and in his narrative, specifically *financial* services – output in national accounts, singling out the traditional French system in which all financial activities were regarded as effecting a redistribution of existing income rather than a generation of output.[99]

Yet as we have already seen, the statistical world lamented by Shelp and Feketekuty was rapidly becoming a thing of the past; the various constituent parts of national accountants' "banking problem" either had been, or were close to being, resolved, in theory at least. Both France and the UK, during the 1970s, had switched to the SNA 1968 treatment, which, if clunky and widely criticized, nonetheless rendered banks productive in statistical terms. And when Feketekuty published his text in 1988, SNA 1993, with its formalized identification of the nature of the underlying "service" provided by financial intermediaries, was only five years away.

Where SNA 1993 would *really* come to the assistance of those who waged the "battle over ideas" around financial services trade from the mid-1990s onwards, however, was not so much in its isolation of financial intermediaries' "service" as in its decisive categorization of such service *as explicitly productive* and its recommended method for measuring this productive value. The 1953 and 1968 SNAs, while making net interest revenue an output but not an input of the banking sector and hence according that sector a positive output value, had both been somewhat equivocal; the issue of accounting for intermediation clearly remained a highly and explicitly troublesome one. Neither SNA reads as if the authors had come to a consensus that intermediation services *were* productive – certainly they are never described in those terms – and that the methods for showing this were self-evident. Rather, the two documents give the cumulative impression of intermediation being nudged tentatively, if not quite covertly, towards the productive domain; *not* lodged there by right. Writing in 1986, Bryan Haig perfectly captured this sense of intermediation services having been "made" productive not so much because they were genuinely and unanimously believed to be so, but because their representation as *un*productive would be so discomfiting. The arguments hitherto advanced for treating interest as anything other than a transfer item, he argued, "amount often to little more than the assertion that a change in treatment of interest is necessary in order to solve the banking problem."[100]

SNA 1993 broke free of this history of equivocation, discursively and methodologically. Paragraph 4.78 cuts immediately to the chase, leaving the reader in no doubt as to how the service of intermediation is now to be conceptualized: "*Financial intermediation may be defined as a productive activity* in which an institutional unit incurs liabilities on its own account for the purpose of acquiring financial assets by engaging in financial transactions on the market."[101] And methodologically, while the recommended treatment of financial intermediation services was in one respect a throwback to the past – by advising that the imputed charge for these services, now labeled FISIM, be allocated to both consumers *and* other business sectors (as in SNA 1953) rather than just the latter (SNA 1968) – there was also a significant step in a new direction.[102] This concerned not the allocation but the derivation of the imputed value of banks' output. With both

SNA 1953 and 1968 having based this value on the difference between interest earned from borrowers and that paid to lenders, SNA 1993 now recommended a new derivation.

Instead of assessing banks' borrowing and lending activities together, and intimating that the combination constituted a portfolio of services whose collective value could be imputed by deducting interest paid on the former from interest generated by the latter, SNA 1993 separates the two functions and defines each – *independently* – as a productive activity whose output can be measured. It does this by introducing the pivotal idea of a "reference" rate of interest, which is defined as "the pure cost of borrowing funds," and for which, it is suggested, either the inter-bank lending rate or the central bank repo rate could serve as a meaningful proxy. The productive output of financial intermediaries' borrowing activities (which consist not only of taking deposits, of course, but also "issuing bills, bonds or other securities") is then defined as "the difference between the interest [creditors] would receive if a reference rate were used and the interest they actually receive"; and the output of the banks' lending activities becomes "the difference between the interest actually charged on loans, etc. and the amount that would be paid if a reference rate were used."[103]

This mobilization of a "reference rate," enabling the output of borrowing and lending activities to be measured independently of one another, is absolutely fundamental to the attempt, in SNA 1993, to show intermediation services as explicitly productive. For the very notion of "production" *requires* a base of some kind against which the extent of productive activity can be assessed. In the world of material goods production, this base is the raw commodities whose transformation into final goods constitutes the productive process. SNA 1993 claims that financial intermediation represents something similar: the quantum of "production" effected by banks is represented by the differential between the reference rate and the actual rate of interest, because the former is the rate that would be payable/receivable were no "productive service" performed. That service, we now know, is seen to be the taking of risk, with the reference rate of interest thus representing that "from which the risk premium has been eliminated to the greatest extent possible and which does not include any intermediation services."[104] Financial intermediaries contribute to economic output, in other words, by assuming financial risk; and we are able to measure the amount of such output because the gap between actual and "base" interest rates signals the level of risk and hence "the extent of intermediation supplied."[105]

And so, when the Global North's trade negotiators insisted to the countries of the Global South that banking and other financial services, contra Smith and Ricardo, *were* productive, they drew liberally – from the mid-1990s onwards in particular – on national accounting data, just as lobbyists within the US and various EU countries did in order to get their domestic governments to the negotiating table in the first place. The WTO Secretariat's 1997 *Opening Markets* study, which I referred to above, is just one example among many of texts peppered with this "evidence-based" discourse. The "important role of the financial services sector" was manifested in the fact that such services "constitute a large and growing sector in virtually all economies." "Value-added" metrics were the main proof of this: "All industrialized countries for which data are available reported a value-added share of about 2–4 per cent of GDP for this sector in 1970. By the mid-1990s, the United States and Switzerland reported value-added shares of 7.3 and 13.3 per cent respectively, the highest among industrialized countries. Other industrial countries reported value-added shares of 2.5 per cent to 6 per cent of GDP in the same period."[106] Given these impressive numbers, how could finance *not* be considered productive and, as such, subject to free trade laws?

This insistence on productiveness, we should be clear, was not equivalent to the "weaker" Smithian argument that banking played a vital facilitating role in the economy more broadly. Smith, as we saw in Chapter 1, mobilized the metaphor of a "waggon-way through the air" to envision banking as a practice that, judiciously operated, allowed the nation's *productive* workforce "to increase, very considerably, the annual produce of its land and labour." Banking was not productive itself; it merely allowed other sectors to be *more* productive. Hence Feketekuty made it clear that his beef with Smith was specifically with the notion that financial services "have no *independent* value," not that they have no value tout court. They were, he countered, "*themselves* productive."[107] Others made the same distinction, thus clarifying that their argument was a categorically stronger one than Smith's. To be sure, financial services were, as Pierre Sauvé and James Gillespie – "leading advocates" of the GATS initiative – put it, "key inputs in the production of all that a nation produces."[108] But they were more besides. *As well as* being "the backbone of modern economies" the financial sector contributes a substantial "direct share" of output; as well as providing "an essential infrastructure for the functioning of the entire economy" it "contributes directly to output and employment."[109]

This, therefore, was how the Western advocates of liberalizing trade in financial services sought to alleviate the third suspicion raised by holdouts in relation to the "trade benefits all" argument – by taking the source of that suspicion (Adam Smith) to task, conceptually and empirically. But if, as I have suggested, such extension and realignment of the comparative advantage thesis has been the central and most crucial argument mobilized to break down resistance to internationalized banking in the Global South, it has not been the only one. Weaved into this discourse are other economic arguments, often not explicitly *about* trade, but nonetheless trumpeted by those championing the trade cause. Two such arguments have been especially prominent and important.

The first of these we have already touched upon tangentially, and I will not belabor it here. This is an argument about the merits of increased competition, as generated through market liberalization, per se – whether such liberalization and the competition resulting from it arise through trade initiatives or not. Surely you should want and encourage trade liberalization and thus more competition, the likes of Brazil and India were told, because more competition means a more efficient marketplace and a better deal for users of financial services. At a meeting of the WTO working group on financial services in 1990, the EC representative pressed this case. "Liberalization of financial services had its *own* merits and would especially benefit those countries that suffered from a closed market. Foreign competition introduced into the market the innovation and expertise that was important both for developing and developed countries."[110] A decade later, Citigroup chairman Stanley Fischer could be heard emphasizing the same point in a speech on "Liberalization of global financial services": "George Stigler used to argue that you need only one good reason to do something. There is one good reason for a country to allow foreign firms to participate in the home financial market – competition. ... [M]ore competition holds the promise of more efficiency and more innovation – and a better deal for both producers and consumers in captive domestic markets."[111] All the while, supportive economists were busy in the background making the same case in more academic terms.[112]

The second, somewhat comparable argument is about the relationship between liberalization and not competition but "development," or "advancement." Do you not want to be a more developed, more *modern* country, as well as a more efficient one? Liberalizing the domestic financial sector, it has consistently been claimed, is an indispensable means of attaining such advancement. The basis for this assertion is that in the world's "developed" countries the services sector in general, and the financial services sector in particular, accounts for a larger share of employment and GDP than in "developing" countries; ergo an enlarged financial sector *equals* development, and development can only be achieved through means designed to secure such enlargement. "Financial services have a crucial role to play in accelerating the development of emerging economies," begins IFSL's July 2006 briefing document on *Benefits to Emerging Economies of Liberalising Financial Services & Promoting Access to Finance.*[113] Similarly, according to the WTO Secretariat economists, "countries with open financial sectors have typically grown faster than those with closed ones."[114]

This latter argument, of course, bears very strong echoes of the theories of Simon Kuznets and others, which we encountered in the previous chapter, on the relationship between service sector expansion and economic growth and development. Kuznets had claimed that the transition to a tertiary-sector-led economy was part-and-parcel of the modernization process. And for the proponents of late twentieth-century financial trade liberalization, countries such as Australia and Singapore represented proof positive that such a relationship did indeed exist. They were therefore invoked widely. Singapore's "far-sighted policies and regulations to promote Singapore as an international financial centre" since the late 1960s were eulogized by those same WTO economists as "a key element in Singapore's impressive economic success."[115] Meanwhile, Australia's WTO delegates enthusiastically explained to the unconverted, in 2002, how by signing up in 1998 to the 1994 GATS Understanding on Commitments in Financial Services (which will be discussed below), Australia had achieved "a sustained period of strong growth in economic activity."[116]

Alongside these various arguments about the benefits of financial market liberalization in both generic and trade-specific senses, one other extremely important "message" was impressed from the start upon those countries not initially willing to entertain the free trade principle. This was, once more, posited as a theoretically-derived – or, at the very least, historically-substantiated – economic principle. The argument was that national treatment was a necessary but not sufficient condition of meaningful financial market opening; only where the right of establishment was *also* proffered to foreign financial institutions could a market be regarded as genuinely liberalized, since, as the OECD Committee on Financial Markets stipulated as early as 1984, "access to the local market through authorisation to have a physical, operative presence is a prerequisite to the pursuit of banking business proper."[117] This was very much the US stance from the outset, with negotiators insisting, as Raghavan later observed, that "the only effective way" for financial services "to be provided on the spot" to foreign consumers "was through establishment or investment."[118] In other words, this was never a question of "mere" trade imperialism; it was to be an exercise, from the beginning, in institutional *colonization* of foreign markets. Among those to attempt to justify this principle were Ingo Walter and Peter Gray. "The history of the great banking houses, dating back to the Italian banks of the fifteenth and sixteenth centuries," they claimed, "illustrates the importance of a direct presence through FDI in the foreign markets to be served."[119]

This last argument, Heinz W. Arndt reflected around the same time, was an extremely "dubious" one. It was by no means clear, he submitted, that free and open trade in banking and insurance services "requires the 'right of establishment'."[120] And Arndt's misgivings were, no doubt, justified. Yet to question the validity of this and the other arguments mobilized to lever open resistant international financial markets from the mid-1980s is not my concern here. Assuredly, all manner of contradictions and ironies did characterize those arguments: the need for skeptics to "prove" that comparative advantage did *not* apply to services trade, when of course nothing like "proof" had ever been furnished for its application to trade in goods; the imperative for financial market opening internationally, but not for full liberalization of a still highly-regulated market in the US itself; the fact that banking was to be considered "just the same" as other businesses in terms of trade dynamics, but not when it came to the treatment of interest in national accounts; and, last but not least, the blinding circularity inherent in arguing, as the WTO's economists did, that "development" requires financial sector deepening on the grounds that "countries with the smallest banking sectors and banking assets of less than US$ 1 billion are also among the least well-off in the world."[121] My concern, rather, has been to examine how and where these various ideas, *whatever* their warts, have been put to work.

And they have been put to work, the historical record shows, with clear, direct, and traceable effects. This of course is not to suggest that all those governments that initially resisted the idea of dismantling barriers to foreign financial institutions were immediately persuaded by the logic of beneficence emanating from the Global North. The negotiations around financial services trade which began in the mid-1980s originally progressed at little more than snail's pace, and obstinate mindsets were a big part of the "problem." "Such negotiations often reached an impasse," Wagner confirms, specifically "because these economic arguments were not compelling to trade negotiators used to talking in terms of gains and losses."[122] The alluring idea that *everyone* would gain was a foreign one. Many governments were ultimately won over or, at any rate, ground down, but there have always been – and there remain today – some that steadfastly refute the "reason" of financial free trade. It was, after all, as recently as 2000 that the call for a vigorous rejoining of the necessary "battle over ideas" was put out (by the aforementioned advocates Sauvé and Gillespie); and, in the same year, that Harry Freeman appealed for "many, many years of discussion, scholarly writing, and all kinds of communication" to win that battle.

Nor is it to suggest that the process of liberalization of financial services trade – and of, therefore, removal of entry and operating restrictions on foreign financial companies – is now complete around the world. Far from it: the disassembly of remaining financial services trade barriers has been a central priority for the countries of the Global North during the Doha Round of WTO negotiations, which began as long ago now as 2001; and repeated failure to reach agreement on precisely these services has been one of the main reasons for the wider failure of the round to reach a conclusion.[123] This stalling in the past decade, moreover, has occurred despite not only predictable, ongoing lobbying by the usual suspects (the CSI and IFSL in particular), but also the explicit backing of the WTO Secretariat and of, most notably of all, the WTO Director-General Pascal Lamy.[124] Alongside President Obama's US Trade Representative Ronald Kirk, Lamy, for instance, delivered one of the keynote speeches at the 2009 Global Services Summit – held in Washington D.C. and organized by the Global Services Coalition, which counts the CSI and IFSL among its members. In the midst of the global *financial* crisis, Lamy insisted that further trade services liberalization would be key to economic recovery, and emphasized the proselytizing work still needed: "continued policy and regulatory reform in favour of services trade will be vital to supporting economic recovery. This may be clear to all of you attending this Summit, but you are the 'converted.' The challenge is to take this message beyond these walls. ... [O]ne very obvious step that can be taken in this direction is the timely conclusion of the Doha Development Round."[125]

Yet, slowly but surely, the economic ideas and arguments discussed in this final section *have* over time come to permeate substantial blocks of thinking on trade and finance well beyond the restricted geographical and institutional spaces where they were originally formulated. Conceptual and political heresy became, in the process, conceptual and political orthodoxy. Striking evidence of this transformation was apparent, for instance, when the Committee of Ministers of Trade and Industry from the 14 members of the Southern Africa Development Community (SADC) approved a regional Protocol on Services Trade Liberalization in 2007. What was especially illuminating was not so much the decision itself but the palpable familiarity of the imported language used to justify it. "By opting for a Protocol on Services," the UNCTAD press release noted, "SADC Member States recognize the increasing importance of services for development. For most SADC countries, the services sector has become the driving force for structural change in their economies and is now a major contributor to employment. Services have become the most productive sector, contributing about 57% to the region's GDP." (Only marginally less striking, meanwhile – and testifying to the continued application of the forces enumerated above – was the acknowledgment that the decision in question "benefited from the technical support of the UNCTAD Secretariat. This support was financed by the European Communities.")[126]

And, just as victories on various fronts increasingly punctuated the global battle over ideas, so, in turn, the barriers those ideas were designed to destabilize *have* fallen. In some cases the barriers have been taken down through the signing of *bi*lateral agreements. The EU, for example, has since 2000 negotiated bilateral free trade agreements with Chile, Korea, Mexico, and South Africa, all of which include financial services liberalization provisions.[127] Significantly, the EU also expects to finalize a major bilateral agreement with India soon.[128] Banking services have been a major point of focus within the negotiations towards this agreement since they began in 2007, with the UK and Germany in particular pushing the case for wholesale liberalization in the form of national treatment and right of establishment.[129]

The most material elimination of barriers, however, has undoubtedly occurred in the domain of WTO-centered *multi*lateral negotiations and agreements. I offer here only a synoptic overview of the key developments in this history.[130] As I have previously indicated at a number of points, the ideological battle waged to pre-cipitate such developments, rather than those developments themselves, has been my main concern. The first breakthrough came in 1986 when, at the outset of the Uruguay Round, the member countries of the GATT agreed to launch negotia-tions on trade in services. By the time of the conclusion of the Uruguay Round in 1993, however, negotiations specifically on *financial* services remained incom-plete, mainly because the commitments offered by other governments did not satisfy the US. It took another four years for a deal on financial services to be hammered out, ultimately taking the form of the December 1997 Agreement on Financial Services (FSA) – the most significant multilateral agreement on cross-border financial services provision in history.

The FSA was not in point of fact a single agreement; what is referred to as the FSA actually comprises six interlocking parts, *including* the 1994 Understanding on Commitments in Financial Services referred to above.[131] Together, these six components formed a framework of "principles" according to which the signa-tory nations would regulate financial services trade, some of which were general principles while others were subject to individual member commitments. A number of countries, importantly, made only partial market access concessions, the US having failed in its attempt to make market access and national treatment *general* obligations. These countries included Chile, India, South Korea, and Thailand; were it not for such resistance, of course, *further* liberalization would not have become a core plank of the Global North's Doha Round demands.[132] Nevertheless, as many as 70 countries did sign up to the FSA, and the WTO esti-mated at the time that the agreement covered more than 95 percent of interna-tional trade in banking, insurance, securities, and financial information.[133] What is more, the varying commitments made by a large number of major countries across the Global South were in many cases substantive, deep, and historically-transformative.[134]

The upshot of all this is that since 2000 the world has been characterized by much lower and much less widespread barriers to cross-border banking than obtained in the world of the late 1970s, the 1980s, and even the early 1990s. And, as surely as day follows night, the removal of restrictions to entering and operating in previously-closed markets has been swiftly followed by a new wave of internationalization by the major financial institutions of the Global North. In the next, final chapter of the book, I will attempt to paint a high-level picture of the degree to which such latter-day internationalization has occurred. But I will also connect back to the central subject matter of this chapter, specifically by arguing that the intensification of banking across boundaries has had a reciprocal impact upon the types of ideas *about* the economic nature of banking and finance discussed here.

Notes

1 H. Freeman, "Comments by Harry Freeman," in R. Litan and A. Santomero (eds), *Brookings-Wharton Papers on Financial Services: 2000* (Brookings Institution, Washington, 2000, 455–461), p.458.

2 A. Porzecanski, "The international financial role of U.S. commercial banks: Past and future," *Journal of Banking and Finance*, 5, 1981, pp. 5–16 , at p.10.

3 P. Sauvé and J. Gillespie, "Financial Services and the GATS 2000 Round," in R. Litan and A. Santomero (eds), *Brookings-Wharton Papers on Financial Services: 2000* (Brookings Institution, Washington, 2000, 423–452), p.446.

4 M. Foucault, *The Archaeology of Knowledge*, Tavistock, London, 1974, p.25.

5 M. Foucault, *The Order of Things*, Tavistock, London, 1970, p.143.

6 See especially the overviews provided by C. Wagner, "The new WTO agreement on financial services and Chapter 14 of NAFTA: has free trade in banking finally arrived?," *NAFTA: Law and Business Review of the Americas*, 5, Winter 1999, pp. 5–90; and C. Raghavan, *Financial Services, the WTO and Initiatives for Global Financial Reform*, G-24 Research Paper, 2009 (available at http://www.g24.org/Publications/ResearchPaps/cr0909.pdf).

7 See, for instance, J. Stremlau, "Clinton's dollar diplomacy," *Foreign Policy*, 97 (Winter 1994–1995), pp.18–35, and S. Beder, *Suiting Themselves: How Corporations Drive the Global Agenda*, Earthscan, London, 2006, p.135, respectively.

8 I. Walter, *Global Competition in Financial Services: Market, Structure, Protection and Trade Liberalization*, Ballinger, Cambridge MA, 1988, p.181.

9 See Chapter 4.

10 Freeman, "Comments," p.456: emphasis added.

11 See especially D. Harvey, *The Limits to Capital*, University of Chicago Press, Chicago, 1982, chapter 13.

12 D. Harvey, "Globalization and the 'spatial fix'," *Geographische Revue*, 2, 2001, pp.23–30, at pp.24–25.

13 Walter, *Global Competition*, p.181.

14 Respectively: James F. Gwaltney, cited in Wagner, "New WTO agreement," p.10; A. Buxton, "Keynote speech to the Preparatory Conference for the World Services Congress, Washington," June 1999 (available at http://www.esf.be/new/wp-content/uploads/2009/07/spab0699.pdf), p.4.

15 This particular quote is from a 2007 letter signed by chief executives of the 20 member companies of the US Financial Services Forum and addressed to then President George W Bush. See D. Palmer, "Financial services firms chide Bush," *Reuters*, 16 April 2007, available at http://www.reuters.com/article/2007/04/16/us-usa-trade-financialservices-idUSN1633526620070416.

16 S. Fischer, "Liberalization of global financial services," Speech at the Institute for International Economics, Washington, June 2002, available at http://www.iie.com/fischer/pdf/fischer060502.pdf.

17 I am guided here primarily by the influential accounts provided by E. Helleiner, *States and the Reemergence of Global Finance: From Bretton Woods to the 1990s*, Cornell University Press, Ithaca, 1994, and R. Abdelal, *Capital Rules: The Construction of Global Finance*, Harvard University Press, Cambridge MA, 2007.

18 Helleiner, *States*, esp. chapters 6 and 7; Abdelal, *Capital Rules*, esp. chapters 4–6.

19 Abdelal, *Capital Rules*, p.12.

20 See especially K. Gallagher, *Policy Space to Prevent and Mitigate Financial Crises in Trade and Investment Agreements*, G-24 Discussion Paper, 2010 (available at http://www.ase.tufts.edu/gdae/Pubs/rp/KGCapControlsG-24.pdf). The quotation is from K. Gallagher, "US trade agreements threaten emerging markets' financial stability," *Financial Times*, 11 May 2010.

21 E.g. D. Harvey, *A Brief History of Neoliberalism*, Oxford University Press, Oxford, 2007, ch. 4.

22 Helleiner, *States*, esp. pp.15–16.

23 J. Bhagwati, "The capital myth: the difference between trade in widgets and dollars," *Foreign Affairs*, 77(3), 1998, pp.7–12.

24 See E. Helleiner, "When finance was servant: International capital movements in the Bretton Woods order," in P. Cerny (ed), *Finance and World Politics: Markets, Regimes, and States in the Post-Hegemonic Era* (Edward Elgar, Aldershot, 1993, 20–48).

25 Bhagwati, "The capital myth," p.11.

26 See esp. R. Van Horn and P. Mirowski, "The rise of the Chicago School of Economics and the birth of neoliberalism," in P. Mirowski and D. Plehwe (eds), *The Road from Mont Pélerin: The Making of the Neoliberal Thought Collective* (Harvard University Press, Cambridge MA, 2009, 139–180).

27 M. Watson, *The Political Economy of International Capital Mobility*, Palgrave Macmillan, Basingstoke, 2007. The quotation is from p.79.

28 I am guided here primarily by I. Walter and H. Gray, "Protectionism, and international banking: Sectorial efficiency, competitive structure and national policy," *Journal of Banking and Finance*, 7, 1983, pp.597–609, at pp.601–604; C. Neu, "International trade in banking services," in R. Baldwin, C. Hamilton and A. Sapir (eds), *Issues in US-EC Trade Relations* (University of Chicago Press and National Bureau for Economic Research, 245–269) at pp.248–251; and Wagner, "New WTO agreement," at pp.23–25.

29 G. Feketekuty, *International Trade in Services: An Overview and Blueprint for Negotiations*, Ballinger, Cambridge, 1988, pp. 295–300.

30 Ibid, p.300.

31 George Clark, Executive VP, Citibank, cited in Underhill, "Negotiating financial openness: the Uruguay Round and trade in financial services," in Cerny (ed), *Finance and World Politics* (114–151), p.126.

32 Feketekuty, *International Trade in Services*, p.295.

33 V. Aggarwal, "The political economy of service sector negotiations in the Uruguay Round," *The Fletcher Forum of World Affairs*, 16, 1992, pp.35–54, at p.38.

34 R. Shelp, "Trade in services," *Foreign Policy*, 65, 1986–87, pp.64–83, at p.66.

35 E. Beaulieu, "Trade in services," in W. Kerr and J. Gaisford (eds), *Handbook on International Trade Policy* (Edward Elgar, Aldershot, 2008, 150–162), p.150. Cf D. Nayyar, "The political economy of international trade in services," *Cambridge Journal of Economics*, 12, 1988, pp.279–298, at p.280: "economists have paid scant attention to services in the context of international trade."

36 W. Drake and K. Nicolaidis, "Ideas, interests and institutionalization: 'Trade in Services' and the Uruguay Round," *International Organization*, 46, 1992, pp.37–100. See also M. Gibbs, "Continuing the international debate on services," *Journal of World Trade Law*, 19, 1985, pp.199–218.

37 See also J. Kelsey, *Serving Whose Interests?: The Political Economy of Trade in Services Agreements*, Routledge, New York, 2008, pp.78–80, on this evangelizing work. That the UK should have been the most receptive country to this US-originated discourse is, in retrospect, not the least surprising, since along with their US counterparts UK companies dominated what international services trade existed at that time (i.e. before such trade was recognized, as it were, *as* trade) – they had, therefore, the most to gain, in the short term at least, from further liberalization. The combined US/UK share of global services exports in 1970 was estimated to be 35 percent by UNCTAD. See Nayyar, "Political economy," p.288.

38 Drake and Nicolaïdis, "Ideas, interests, and institutionalization." The quotations are from pp.59, 38. I would reiterate here, however, the observation I made earlier that such preparatory discursive groundwork was never – and perhaps never is – quite complete. It required continual restating in the face of the periodic surfacing of resistant worldviews. Indeed as late as 2000 Freeman, previously of American Express, argued that "ignorance" remained widespread and that the message thus needed ongoing propagation. "I will not belabor the point about understanding trade in services, but it is probably our biggest problem. Most people do not understand what we are talking about." Freeman, "Comments," p.458.

39 Drake and Nicolaïdis, "Ideas, interests, and institutionalization," p.40.

40 Feketekuty, *International Trade in Services*, p.308.

41 Cited in Raghavan, *Financial Services*, p.5. Cf. Underhill, "Negotiating financial openness," p.126: "private groups and firms ... were perfectly clear about their interest in bringing the service sectors under the umbrella of the GATT, and no group was so unequivocal as the major US banks."

42 Freeman, "Comments," p.457.

43 C. Carson and J. Honsa, "The United Nations system of National Accounts: an introduction," *Survey of Current Business*, 70(6), 1990, pp.20–30, at p.23.

44 United Nations, *A System of National Accounts*, United Nations, New York, 1968, p.97.

45 United Nations, A *System of National Accounts 1993*, United Nations, New York, 1993, p.117; emphasis added.

46 Aggarwal, "Political economy," p.38.

47 Gibbs, "Continuing the international debate," p.200.

48 Underhill, "Negotiating financial openness," p.126.

49 Beder, *Suiting*, p.128.

50 Underhill, "Negotiating financial openness," p.125.

51 *Hearings before the Subcommittee on Business, Trade, and Tourism ..., United States Senate, 97th Congress, First Session, October 20 and 21, 1981*. S. 1233. US Government Printing Office, Washington, 1982. Statement of Richard W. Wheeler, p.100.

52   See especially A. Deardorff, "Comparative advantage and international trade and investment in services," in R. Stern (ed), *Trade and Investment in Services: Canada/U.S. Perspectives*, Ontario Economic Council, Toronto, 1985, pp.39–71; B. Hindley and A. Smith, "Comparative advantage and trade in services," *The World Economy*, 7, 1984, pp.369–390.

53   Nayyar, "Political economy," p.291.

54   E.g. N. Oulton, *International Trade in Services Industries: Comparative Advantage of European Community Countries*, EC Commission, Brussels, 1982.

55   Beder, *Suiting*, p.130.

56   Wagner, "New WTO agreement," p.9n5; emphasis added.

57   Palmer, "Financial services firms chide Bush."

58   E.g. IFSL, "Written evidence from the International Financial Services London," in House of Lords European Union Committee, *Developments in EU Trade Policy: Report with Evidence* (HMSO, London, 2008, 100–106).

59   Statement of Richard W. Wheeler, *Hearings Before the Subcommittee...*

60   Beder, *Suiting*, p.130.

61   Underhill, "Negotiating financial openness," p.125.

62   IFSL, "Written evidence," p.101.

63   Palmer, "Financial services firms chide Bush."

64   E.g. B. Herman and B. van Holst, *International Trade in Services: Some Theoretical and Practical Problems*, Netherlands Economic Institute, Rotterdam, 1986; J. Nusbaumer, *Les services: nouvelle donné de l'économie*, Economica, Paris, 1984.

65   See especially Neu, "International trade in banking services."

66   Aggarwal, "Political economy," at p.42.

67   "[The US government] accepted the economic logic in favour of liberalizing financial services trade." Underhill, "Negotiating financial openness," p.126.

68   Cited in Aggarwal, "Political economy," p.41.

69   See P. Carroll and A. Kellow, *The OECD: A Study of Organisational Adaptation*, Edward Elgar, Cheltenham, 2011, pp.90–92; Drake and Nicolaïdis, "Ideas, interests, and institutionalization," pp.50–51; Gibbs, "Continuing the international debate," p.200.

70   Drake and Nicolaïdis, "Ideas, interests, and institutionalization," p.50n21.

71   Feketekuty, *International Trade in Services*, p.319.

72   Walter, *Global Competition*, p.164.

73   US Trade Representative, *U.S. National Study on Trade in Services*, US Government Printing Office, Washington, 1984, p.139.

74   OECD, *International Trade in Services: Banking*, OECD, Paris, 1984, pp.23–24.

75   Where Fischer, "Liberalization," represents a particularly striking example of the standard substance of the wishes of Western financial institutions.

76   See, for instance, Kavaljit Singh's illuminating recent discussion of the UK and Germany's aggressive championing of financial services liberalization under the proposed India-EU free trade agreement, which has been in negotiation since 2007. "The EU-India free trade agreement, banking sector liberalization," 24 March 2011, available at http://www.themarketoracle.biz/Article27152.html (retrieved April 2011).

77   Feketekuty, *International Trade in Services*, pp.306–307.

78   Ibid, p.319.

79   Shelp, "Trade in services," pp.73–74.

80   I draw here on Wagner, "New WTO Agreement," p.16.

81   Shelp, "Trade in services," p.82.

82   Raghavan, *Financial Services*, p.30.

83   US Trade Representative, *US National Study*, p.11.
84   Feketekuty, *International Trade in Services*, p.92.
85   Walter, *Global Competition*, pp.190–191; original emphasis. Writing in 1988, Walter was confident that forward-looking countries in the Global South would ultimately see the light and therefore "will eventually come to see the inconsistency and economic 'drag' that is the product of the combination of a highly competitive industrial sector, export-led economic growth, and a 'retarded' financial service industry" (p.219).
86   M. Kono, P. Low, M. Luanga, A. Mattoo, M. Oshikawa and L. Schuknecht, *Opening Markets in Financial Services and the Role of GATS*, WTO Secretariat Special Study, 1997, available at http://www.wto.org/english/news_e/pres97_e/finance.pdf, p.17.
87   Wagner, "New WTO agreement," p.17.
88   R. Webb, "Comments by Richard Webb," in R. Herring and R. Litan (eds), *Financial Regulation in the Global Economy* (Brookings Institution, Washington, 1995, 163–166) p.163.
89   Shelp, "Trade in services," pp.68–69; emphasis added.
90   B. Hindley and A. Smith, "Comparative advantage and trade in services," *The World Economy*, 7, 1984, pp.369–390, at p.386; emphasis added.
91   Shelp, "Trade in services," p.69.
92   C. Raghavan, "Financial services talks as contentious as overall Doha talks," *Third World Network*, 14 October 2004, available at http://www.twnside.org.sg/title2/5667a.htm (retrieved January 2010).
93   Shelp, "Trade in services," p.65.
94   R. Shelp, *Beyond Industrialization: Ascendancy of the Global Service Economy*, Praeger Publishers, New York, 1982.
95   See especially Shelp, "Trade in services."
96   Feketekuty, *International Trade in Services*. The chapter in question can actually be read online at http://www.commercialdiplomacy.org/articles_news/trade_inservices4.htm.
97   R. Levine, "Foreign banks, financial development, and economic growth," in C. Barfield (ed), *International Financial Markets: Harmonization Versus Competition* (American Enterprise Institute, Washington, 224–254), p.229.
98   Feketekuty, *International Trade in Services*, p.63.
99   Shelp, *Beyond Industrialization*, p.61.
100 B. Haig, "The treatment of interest and financial intermediaries in the National Accounts of Australia," *Review of Income and Wealth*, 32, 1986, pp.409–424, at p.415.
101 United Nations, *System of National Accounts 1993*, p.117; emphasis added.
102 Where SNA 1993's recommendation for allocation differed from the 1953 method was primarily in the fact that the split of the imputed charge between consumers and business – and, within the business category, between industries – was now to factor in respective levels of borrowing from, as well as lending to, financial intermediaries.
103 United Nations, *System of National Accounts 1993*, p.172.
104 Ibid.
105 I. Begg, J. Bournay, M. Weale and S. Wright, "Financial intermediation services indirectly measured: estimates for France and the U.K. based on the approach adopted in the 1993 SNA," *Review of Income and Wealth*, 42, 1996, pp.453–472, at p.455.
106 Kono et al., *Opening Markets in Financial Services*, p.7.

107 Feketekuty, *International Trade in Services*, p.60; emphasis added.

108 Sauvé and Gillespie, "Financial services," p.424. The label "leading advocates" is taken from Kelsey, *Serving Whose Interests?*, p.43.

109 These pairs of quotations are from, respectively, Kono et al., *Opening Markets in Financial Services*, p.7; Export.gov, "U.S.- CAFTA-DR Free Trade Agreement: Financial services," available at http://www.export.gov/FTA/cafta-dr/eg_main_017557. asp (retrieved Nov 2009).

110 WTO, MTN.GNS/FIN/1, "Note on the meeting of 11–13 June 1990, Working Group on Financial Services including Insurance," ¶ 123 (5 July 1990); emphasis added.

111 Fischer, "Liberalization."

112 See especially Levine, "Foreign banks."

113 IFSL, "Benefits to emerging economies of liberalising financial services & promoting access to finance," July 2006 (available at http://www.thecityuk.com/assets/Uploads/ Liberalistion-in-Emerging-Markets-2006.pdf), p.1.

114 Kono et al., *Opening Markets in Financial Services*, p.17.

115 Ibid, p.20.

116 WTO, S/FIN/W/23, "Communication from Australia; Australian Experience with Financial Market Reform, Committee on Trade in Financial Services" (24 October 2002).

117 OECD, *International Trade in Services: Banking*, p.24.

118 Raghavan, *Financial Services*, p.13.

119 Walter and Gray, "Protectionism and international banking," p.598.

120 H. Arndt, "GATT and the developing world: agenda for a new trade round," *Weltwirtschaftliches Archiv*, 123, 1987, pp.705–718, at p.714.

121 Kono et al, *Opening Markets in Financial Services*, p.10. Cf. IFSL, "Benefits to emerging economies," p.1: "The problems caused by the inadequacies of financial services are most severe in the poorest economies."

122 Wagner, "New WTO Agreement," p.17.

123 See, for example, F. Williams and A. Beattie, "WTO talks on services markets face 'crisis'," *Financial Times*, 1 March 2005; J. Hilary, "Time to kill off Doha," *The Guardian*, 25 November 2009.

124 Perhaps the Secretariat's most explicit advocacy is contained in WTO, S/C/W/312, S/FIN/W/73, "Financial Services: Background note by the Secretariat; Council for Trade in Services, Committee on Trade in Financial Services" (3 February 2010).

125 WTO NEWS, "Speeches — DG PASCAL LAMY," 14 October 2009, available at http://www.wto.org/english/news_e/sppl_e/sppl138_e.htm (retrieved January 2011).

126 UNCTAD/PRESS/IN/2007/037, "Ministers of Southern African Development Community approve protocol on services trade liberalization" (10 July 2007).

127 http://ec.europa.eu/enterprise/policies/international/facilitating-trade/free-trade/ index_en.htm#h2–1 (retrieved Nov. 2011).

128 "EU hopeful FTA negotiations will be completed by February," *The Hindu Business Line*, 14 November 2011 (available at http://www.thehindubusinessline.com/indus-try-and-economy/article2626995.ece).

129 "The EU-India free trade agreement, banking sector liberalization."

130 Guided primarily by Wagner, "New WTO agreement" and Raghavan, *Financial Services*.

131 See Wagner, "New WTO agreement," p.68.

132   On which see especially S. Key, *The Doha Round and Financial Services Negotiations*, American Enterprise Institute, Washington, 2003.

133   WTO PRESS/86, "Successful conclusion of the WTO's financial services negotiations" (15 December 1997).

134   See especially A. Mattoo, "Financial services and the WTO: Liberalisation Commitments of the Developing and Transition Economies," *The World Economy*, 23, 2000, pp.351–386.

6

Anaemic Geographies of Productive Finance

Accounting is an inherently territorializing activity. Put differently, the forming of calculative assemblages is itself a type of territorializing, for there is no assemblage without territory. The calculative instruments of accountancy transform not only the possibilities for personhood, they also construct the calculable spaces that individuals inhabit within firms and other organizations.

Andrea Mennicken and Peter Miller (2012)[1]

The last few years of the twentieth century and the early years of the twenty-first saw moves to make banking and finance productive not only in national accounting but also within the representative domain responsible for the original forging of a conceptual distinction *between* the economically productive and unproductive: the domain of Western political economy. Such moves have not been ubiquitous. In certain isolated pockets, most notably orthodox Marxian political economy, finance has remained categorically unproductive, to the extent that the question of its "location" is ever posed as such. Elsewhere, however, and within cognate academic fields, a number of high-profile scholars have converged on the view that the classical political economists, Marx included, were wrong. The operations and labors of finance do not merely redistribute value already created (thus constituting, in Marx's terms, a tax on surplus generation) – they contribute, rather, to the creation of value. Banking is productive, and financial labor is productive labor.

In this final chapter of the book, I argue that key to understanding this particular conceptual shift is *precisely* the recent deepening of the internationalization of banking that, as we have seen, changes in the envisioning of financial productiveness – specifically within national accounting – themselves helped to precipitate.

Banking Across Boundaries: Placing Finance in Capitalism, First Edition. Brett Christophers.
© 2013 John Wiley & Sons, Ltd. Published 2013 by John Wiley & Sons, Ltd.

The argument, in other words, is that effects have manifested in *both* directions: ideas have influenced economic regulations and practices, but so in turn those practices have impacted back on the ideational realm.

To make this case, I focus – critically – on the widely-mobilized concept of "financialization," or at least on one particularly influential variant thereof. This is the thesis that recent decades have seen a fundamental mutation in capitalist accumulation dynamics, whereby the structural balance of the economy under advanced capitalism has shifted towards the financial sector and away from the nonfinancial sector. The economy, or capitalism, has *financialized*. The reason for my focusing here is that those scholars who argue now for banks' productiveness typically cite financialization as their grounds for doing so. How else, they submit, if not by appeal to the inherent productiveness of finance, can one account for such a deep-seated rebalancing of the economy, and for the "surface" phenomena taken to signify such a rebalancing: namely, growth in recent decades in the contribution of financial activities and financial sources of income to corporate profitability in mature capitalist economies such as the US and the UK?

There are at least a couple of different possible responses to this submission. One would be to point out that the assumption of productiveness by no means follows automatically from the concept of financialization. Or, to put it another way: it is entirely credible that a particular sector of the economy could account for a substantial share of overall profit realization without contributing to the underlying generation of value. This, more or less, is the view of Marxists such as David Harvey, who agrees that there has been a financialization of late capitalism, but who stridently refutes the assignation of productiveness to the financial sector. For Harvey, interest and rent, for all their contemporary quantitative importance, remain qualitatively derivative, their extraction still representing – as for Marx – a "costly drag upon productive forms of capitalist activity."[2] In this reading, financialization is about not productiveness but *power*: the power of parasitical institutions to extract value from the seams of its creation.

Such, however, is not the case I wish to present here. My argument, contra Harvey as well as the concept's more recognized proponents (such as Greta Krippner and Gerald Epstein), is that the idea of financialization is *itself* problematic. What if, I ask, the increasing profit share captured by financial activities and income sources in the US and UK since the early 1980s has resulted not from structural shifts within capitalism, but from geographical shifts – and in particular from rapid growth outwards from the US and UK in the international provision of finance and of financial services? If that were indeed the case (and I will suggest that it might well be, though 'proving' this is next to impossible), then this process of internationalization could be seen to lie back of the move to render finance productive in political economy by virtue of scholars' *mis*-reading – as evidence simply of "financialization" – of the surface profitability trends it has generated. In short, through the analytical neglect of its shifting geographical constitution, capitalism has been conceptualized as if situated on the head of a pin: "finance" has grown, meaning capitalism has financialized, meaning finance *must* after all be productive. Introducing geography into the picture unsettles this chain of spatially-anaemic logic.

I make this argument over the course of the chapter's four sections. The first section considers the two aforementioned conceptual claims: first, the claim that advanced capitalism, as manifested in its US and UK incarnations in particular, is a financialized form of capitalism; and second, the claim, building directly on the financialization argument, that classical political economy's relegation of finance to the unproductive sphere needs to be reversed. In each case I examine the details of the claims made, the identity of the scholars who have formulated them, and – especially in the former case – the nature of the quantitative evidence marshaled to support such claims.

In the second section I begin by formulating an explicitly spatially-oriented critique of the financialization narrative. As an example of what is often referred to as the "varieties of capitalism" school of comparative political economy, the thesis that capitalism has financialized tends to fetishize the national scale and, in doing so, offer a geographically anaemic reading of the aforementioned historical changes in profit shares between the "financial" and "nonfinancial" parts of the economy. To properly understand what has been driving those changes, I argue, it is necessary to consider cross-border flows of financial assets and of services provided by the financial sector.

I also emphasize in this section, however, that this geographical anaemia is to some extent unavoidable; that it is, in profoundly material respects, inherent to the particular data sources that the student of historical economy has available to her. It is no coincidence that national accounts materialized as a technology of political calculation and intervention in the period in modern human history that witnessed both the strictest protectionism *of* national economies and – through the work of Keynes in particular – the most concentrated efforts to identify and model the dynamics specifically thereof. National accounts were the accounts *of nations*, delimited precisely as such; and national accounts, directly or indirectly, constitute the historian of the macro-economy's main holistic data hunting-ground. Granted, the accounts do factor export and import flows into GDP measures, and balance of payments data can help with loosening somewhat the rigid scalar circumscription of the economic picture the national accounts provide. But trying to paint a geographically-accurate picture of phenomena such as profit generation and realization at the international scale is, as we will see, very hard – *particularly* where "financial" profits, variously defined, are concerned. As noted in Chapter 4, for instance, SNA 1968, by assuming all consumption of financial intermediation services to be intermediate demand, allowed for no export component thereof. No wonder, then, that as I will also discuss, champions of financial services trade liberalization like Harry Freeman and Geza Feketekuty repeatedly bemoaned the lack of data to better demonstrate the materiality of such trade; and that, later on, the enduring scalar fixedness of the national accounts calculus should lead to financial outcomes "in" particular countries being interpreted as evidence of structural transformation *of* those "national economies" per se.

The chapter's third section attempts to unpack – by situating geographically – the US and UK profitability trends invoked by proponents of financialization. It does so by exploring the renewed wave of banking internationalization that the lowering of trade barriers precipitated. I ask how much internationalization has since occurred, what forms it has taken, and, critically, what principal geographies it has assumed: where have banks internationalized *from*, and where to. I argue that it is certainly significant, if not surprising, that the two countries which led the charge to crack open resistant international financial markets – the US and the UK – are the two whose resident financial institutions have benefitted most from the removal of entry and operating restrictions. But I suggest that it may be even *more* significant that it is these same two countries that are most often posited as exemplifying a financialized form of capitalism. To understand why "financial profits" have become so much more material in the US and UK, I suggest, we may not *need* to conclude that the way advanced capitalism "works", or is structured, has changed; rather, the fact that UK and US-based financial capitalists have so successfully colonized new international markets, repatriating profits accordingly, may itself be a sufficient explanation. Anglo-American capitalism's financial profit "excess" of recent decades, by this reading, is of geographical rather than structural derivation.

The conceptual implications of this argument are the focus of the last section. I argue firstly that it destabilizes – though does not necessarily disprove – the claim by some contemporary political economists that the financial sector is a site of value creation, since the latter claim is based squarely on financialization having occurred. Yet more significantly it implies, I submit, that political economy's rendering of finance as productive has at least in part been *enabled by* our "other" boundary crossing, namely banks' crossing of international borders. It implies this because such internationalization *generated*, to one extent or another, the profitability shifts (mis)read as financialization and as, in turn, evidence of productiveness. And I speculate, finally, that a comparable instance of geographical materiality shaping economic ideas has occurred in the realm of national accounting itself, in terms of its own reconceptualization and re-envisioning of finance as productive. That is to say, I will argue that the "productivization" of finance in national accounting, as in political economy, was promoted, in part, by financial internationalization. Constrained by the peculiar geo-scalar epistemological world they inhabited (and its manifestation in treatments such as SNA 1968), national accounting practitioners have, I suggest, been equally susceptible to overlooking the materiality of major geographical shifts in capital accumulation dynamics.

Rethinking the Place of Finance

Financialized capitalism

What is meant by "financialization," and more particularly by the financialization *of capitalism*? In a short period of time the term financialization has come to be used relatively promiscuously, so it is vital to be clear about the meaning intended here. The specific understanding of financialization I will be considering is concerned, as indicated above, with the *structural dynamics* of the capitalist economy.

It distinguishes most importantly between activities and income sources that are deemed financial in nature, and those that are not. While definitions vary, financial activities comprise those pursued designedly, if not uniquely, by financial institutions (financial intermediation, financial advisory, financial investment, and so on); financial income sources include such things as interest and dividends, although once again classifications differ. The claim that capitalism has financialized is essentially a claim that the balance of the capitalist economy has changed, becoming more weighted to financial as opposed to nonfinancial activities and income sources.

Two other understandings of financialization, among the many now in evidence, are also especially prominent and hence important to identify and distinguish here.[3] One invokes the term to depict an ascendance in the role of financial concepts, languages and evaluative practices in everyday political and cultural life. Finance, it is asserted, has increasingly and relentlessly colonized all kinds of ostensibly extra-economic life worlds, generating financialized cultures and even financialized identities.[4] The other extremely important stream of research in the financialization literature has been that which draws attention to the growing importance of models such as "shareholder value" to practices of corporate governance in the contemporary business world in general.[5] The hegemony of such models, it is claimed, speaks to the heightened influence not only of financial concepts themselves but of the financial markets and institutions which propagate them. Although I do not explicitly consider in this book these (and other) alternative understandings of financialization, I do recognize their salience.[6]

Arguably the first study formally to theorize the idea of financialization as a reorientation of late capitalism towards finance was Giovanni Arrighi's *The Long Twentieth Century*. Published in 1994, it was certainly this book that introduced the notion of capitalism's financialization to mainstream scholarly debate, and which triggered much of the subsequent research in this area. Here, Arrighi argued that "the 'financialization' of capital," particularly in the US context, had been a key feature of global economic crisis in the 1970s and "the absolutely predominant feature" of such crisis in the 1980s.[7] He did so by drawing upon, but departing substantially from, the theory of "finance capital" put forward by Rudolf Hilferding in the early twentieth century. "Finance capital," in Hilferding's rendering, was an *organizational* concept, alluding to a perceived merging of industrial-, merchant- and financial-capitalist interests; Arrighi's "financialisation," by contrast, was about the underlying *processes* of capital accumulation.[8] Financialization refers to where "accumulation proceeds through financial deals."[9]

Yet Arrighi offered no analytical, data-based corroboration of capitalist financialization, and so it was left to others to take up this challenge. To the best of my knowledge, however, only three studies, to date, have done so in substantive empirical depth and with an emphasis squarely on structural dynamics: those by Gerald Epstein and Arjun Jayadev, by Greta Krippner, and by Özgür Orhangazi.[10]

Krippner's and Orhangazi's studies are very similar to one another, so we can deal with them together. Each focuses solely on the US; and each attempts to measure financialization in two distinct but related keys. First, they look at overall levels of US corporate profits, and then track the trend in the share of such profits accruing to financial institutions. Second, they look at the levels of profits accruing specifically to US corporations categorized as "nonfinancial" (those, in other words, where the core business activity is deemed to be something other than a financial service), and then track the trend in the share of such profits derived from what are categorized as "financial" – and thus considered noncore – sources: interest payments, dividends, and (in Krippner's case only) capital gains on investments. Both report data going all the way back to the 1950s, with Orhangazi's more recently-published research bringing the story further forward (up to 2006) than Krippner's (up to 2001).

Epstein and Jayadev's analysis, meanwhile, differs from the two aforementioned studies in four significant respects. First, and most obviously, it offers much broader geographical coverage, investigating trends not just in the US but also in the UK and 13 other OECD countries (attempting to do so for the period 1960–2000, but with data limitations restricting the analysis to much shorter periods in certain cases). Second, it consolidates the two "indicators" of financialization that Orhangazi and Krippner treat separately – (1) finance sector profits, and (2) financial sources of nonfinancial sector income (the nonfinancial sector extended here beyond just nonfinancial corporations to "the rest of the private economy," and thus including households and not-for-profit bodies; but with financial income limited solely to interest payments) – into a single proxy for what the authors label "rentier income," tracking the ratio of this income to total gross national product. Third, it offers a narrower definition of the finance sector, focussing specifically on "firms engaged primarily in financial intermediation," whereas Krippner includes insurance companies within the "financial" designation, and Orhangazi switches between various different categorizations. Finally, it explicitly recognizes that the rate of inflation needs to be factored into the analysis of financial versus nonfinancial sources of profit to account for its impact on the real value of financial assets.

All three of these studies conclude that financialization has occurred; and while it is not necessary to reproduce their respective findings in full, three particular conclusions are especially relevant here. First, all three analyses indicate that the 1980s saw the most intense period of financialization. Second, financialization is not just a US phenomenon: in the analysis presented by Epstein and Jayadev, all but two of the 13 OECD countries for which data were available for more than a decade (the exceptions being Italy and Denmark) saw increases in rentier share. Third, and most importantly, all three authors emphasize that the changes observable in the national economies that they studied represent changes *in capitalism*, as this mode of socio-economic organization happens to be manifested in those territories. Thus Krippner asserts that the "underlying shift" she documents is one in "the nature of contemporary capitalism"; Orhangazi speaks explicitly of "financialized capitalism"; and Epstein, in the introduction to the book on *Financialization and the World Economy* in which his co-authored essay appears, similarly claims that this and other essays in the volume signal "structural shifts of dramatic proportions."[11]

Meanwhile, alongside these detailed attempts empirically to confirm the financialization of contemporary Western capitalism, we find a large and ever-increasing number of other studies that effectively take this structural financialization as read. Some, to be sure, cite isolated statistics to back up this affirmation; and interestingly, it is almost invariably the same metric that is invoked – the rise in the "share of corporate profits generated in the financial sector" in the US "from 10% in the early 1980s to 40% in 2006." (This quotation is taken from James Crotty; other influential scholars to point to the same numbers include Ronald Dore, Peter Gowan, and David Harvey.[12]) But most studies appealing to financialization do not provide empirical evidence, merely nodding non-specifically to, for instance, the "larger share of overall profits that recently went to finance" or finance having become "the principal means of generating profit."[13] It is assumed simply to be established fact that capitalism, particularly of an Anglo-American guise, *has* financialized. Nowhere, perhaps, is this assumption more egregious than in the cases of John Bellamy Foster and Costas Lapvitsas's disquisitions on, respectively, "the financialization of capitalism" and "financialised capitalism."[14]

Productive finance?

Twentieth and twenty-first-century Marxian political economy is the only scholarly domain in which the old debate about productive and unproductive labors has lived on in more-or-less its original Smithian form – which is to say, positing hard-and-fast distinctions between productive and unproductive labor, and concerned not only to identify the precise conceptual location of the all-important production boundary, but to categorize different contemporary labors and economic sectors accordingly. This Marxian school, however, is not my focus in this chapter, for the simple reason that within it the placement of banking has not changed. Banking continues to be viewed as categorically unproductive. Indeed, so axiomatic is this particular placement that when Sungur Savran and Ahmet Tonak, two important figures in this debate, argue for including various consumer services within the productive sphere, they parenthesize that such an inclusion should occur "with the exception *naturally* of financial services."[15]

Our interest, by contrast, is in contemporary scholarship that does question the envisioning of finance in general, and banking in particular, as economically unproductive. Some writers to have trodden this path are certainly influenced by Marx, to one degree or another. But none positions their argument as an intervention strictly into Marxian debates, and few draw explicitly on the classical (and heavily loaded) distinction between productive and unproductive labors per se. The terms "productive" and "unproductive" survive; but the "labor" component of the couplet typically does not.

The writings I examine in this section aver, individually and collectively, that the traditional placement of finance in the unproductive sphere must have been wrong – or, at the very least, that that traditional placement no longer holds in the particular context of contemporary Anglo-American-style capitalism. As such these writings, by influential figures in and around the critical political economy field, effect a form of border crossing. The result of this crossing, I show, has been a substantive if sometimes partial, cagey and ambiguous reconceptualization of the productiveness of finance, with the latter no longer seen to be definitively segregated from productive sectors of the economy. This is not to say that banking and finance are necessarily now cast in a less "critical" light, any more than the classical Smithian delineation of unproductive labors was a pejorative one. (It was not, even though it often came to be seen as such; as John Stuart Mill emphasized: "the term unproductive does not necessarily imply any stigma; nor was ever intended to do so."[16]) It is to say, rather, that the potential for financial activities directly to create economic value has begun to be retheorized.

In examining the ways in which and extent to which finance has been shifted towards the productive sphere in such scholarship, I will focus on three contributions in particular, although certainly comparable conceptual manoeuvres exist elsewhere and could be similarly considered.[17] The first contribution is in the work of Leo Panitch and Sam Gindin; the second, that of Edward LiPuma and Benjamin Lee; and the third, that of Christian Marazzi.[18] As I will demonstrate, important differences assuredly distinguish their respective arguments from one another. Yet they share, nonetheless, two vital qualities: they refute the classification of the financial sector as unproductive, and they regard the putative financialization of capitalism as the reason for doing so. How could it be that the financial sector dominates contemporary capitalist economies and the realization of profits within them *unless* it is in some measure productive of wealth?

Panitch and Gindin are prominent figures within the critical political-economic literature on contemporary capitalism, with questions of finance representing a major theme in their work. Their reconceptualization of the "place" of finance can be broken down into two components. The first involves a brief historical overview of important developments in the actual practices of Western finance and banking, the authors claiming that from the 1960s onwards "major change occurred in the very nature of what financial institutions do." While they do not offer a detailed description of what those changes actually were, they do refer to banks' "expansion of services beyond the acquisition of savings and the provision of credit" and there is every indication that the changes they have in mind comprise the evolution and enormous growth of derivatives markets and, in particular, of practices of securitization. As they write: "Forms of money themselves became commodities that could be packaged and sold to an unprecedented degree."[19]

It is, however, the second component of Panitch and Gindin's conceptualization that is of most relevance here: namely, their thoughts on what such historical developments might mean in terms of "larger questions about the contributions of finance." As they point out, such questions have long been "controversial." And, harking back to the traditional political-economic perspectives on the productiveness of finance which I surveyed in Chapter 1, they acknowledge that in the late twentieth century "credit creation in itself did not necessarily imply an increase in productive activity." Yet they are convinced, nonetheless, that something fundamental *has* changed – persuaded, in this respect, by the "financialisation" of capitalism that is avowedly manifested in the "larger share of profits that recently went to finance."[20]

Some of this increased share could, admit Panitch and Gindin, be traced to "speculative and rentier gains" (which is the Harvey explanation). *But not all*: "it also represented in part a return for finance's contribution to keeping general profits higher than they would otherwise have been." In other words, far from representing, as in the Smithian or Marxian scheme of things, a mere transfer mechanism or background facilitator of value creation, finance was now seen to be "placed directly at the heart of the accumulation process." What, therefore, did this mean in terms of its inherent productiveness? Directly invoking the productive/unproductive dichotomy discussed above, Panitch and Gindin assert that finance can no longer be deemed unproductive; but that, equally, it is not categorically productive either. It has moved some, but not all of the way across this divide. In a rather ungainly formulation, then, they write of finance in terms of "a new sector that straddled credit and production."[21]

If Panitch and Gindin's reconceptualization shifts finance only some of the way towards the productive sphere, that offered by LiPuma and Lee is bolder still, positing that finance has fully bridged the divide between unproductive and productive capitals (if, indeed, it ever properly belonged among the former). They make this case in their influential book on financial derivatives. What is especially fascinating and striking about their account is the fact that it is so implicitly indebted to – while simultaneously departing decisively from – Marx. For, on the one hand, they draw heavily upon the prototypically Marxian distinction between production and circulation that we encountered in Chapter 1, and continue to classify finance as part of the latter. But on the other hand, they break from the Marxian thesis that the activities of circulation do not contribute to value creation. Let us look now at both of these elements in their work.[22]

The central plank of their thesis is to argue that circulation in general, and finance in particular, *can* produce surplus. Not only that, but circulation has now, they insist, surpassed "production" in terms of its contribution to capitalist value creation: "wealth generation seems to have seismically shifted from productive labour … to cultures of circulation." In the process, they further submit, the very relationship between production and circulation has also been reconfigured. For Marx, circulation was dependent upon production not merely for its ongoing sustenance (surplus value) but for its very existence; circulation, as realization, could not be envisaged in the absence of the process of production. LiPuma and Lee, by contrast, argue for a severing of this essential connection.[23] Thus the financial "cultures of circulation" that they regard as value-generative now constitute "a relatively autonomous realm." Part of the reason why derivatives assume center stage in their account is that "the power of financial derivatives" is seen to be emblematic of precisely this decoupling.

Only in a footnote to the book – where LiPuma and Lee write of how circulation has become "a quasi-independent sphere of the capitalist economy" – is there
any hint of the type of equivocality and imprecision that characterizes Panitch
and Gindin's incomplete migration of finance towards the productive economic
realm. Elsewhere, their analysis of the re-placement of finance is stark and decisive. They even speak of contemporary finance-led circulation "redefining the
production and possibilities of value itself." They depict, in fact, nothing less than
a deep-seated structural shift in the capitalist regime of accumulation – the emergence of a new capitalist genus, as it were. And it is circulation in general, and
finance in particular, that represents "the cutting edge of [this] capitalism."

The third selected study that renders finance productive in conceptual
terms is Christian Marazzi's *The Violence of Financial Capitalism*. In many
respects Marazzi's account is similar to LiPuma and Lee's (albeit even more
forthright in its claims). He is keen throughout to emphasize, in contradistinction to classical Marxian theory, the "*non*-parasitic role of finance"; and
like LiPuma and Lee he does so by rebutting the orthodox association of
"production" with productiveness and "circulation" with unproductiveness,
identifying instead an "externalization of value production … into the sphere
of circulation."[24]

Marazzi's account is of particular interest, however, in view of its explicit
mobilization of "financialization" as the historical development that *justifies*
this re-conceptualization. The other two accounts also point for legitimation to
the profitability trends underpinning the financialization thesis – Panitch and
Gindin emphasizing the "larger share of profits that recently went to finance,"
LiPuma and Lee privileging finance/circulation in view of it having seemingly
become "the principal means of generating profit" – but Marazzi is much more
overt about the link to financialization. That a "financialization of economy"
has occurred is not, in his view, debatable (and he quotes Greta Krippner's work,
via Giovanni Arrighi, as evidence of this). And it is this structural shift that
proves, for Marazzi, the existence of a new sphere of value creation.
Financialization, he thus insists, is "*not an unproductive/parasitic deviation of
growing quotas of surplus-value and collective saving, but rather the form of
capital accumulation symmetrical with new processes of value production.*" Or,
to summarize: "The increase in profits [to finance] over the last 30 years is thus
due to a production of surplus-value by accumulation … external to classical
productive processes."[25]

What is explicit in Marazzi is, however, only marginally less so in the two other
accounts considered here. The professed empirical stimulus is consistent. All three
accounts, in short, extract from the putative financialization trend a series of
wider conclusions about the place of banking and finance within basic classificatory
schema of "productive" and "unproductive" capitals. With financial institutions
seen to be recording strongly increasing shares of profits in mature capitalist
economies, they conclude, it is simply inconceivable that such institutions can
continue to be considered – as they were by Smith, Malthus, and Marx –
unproductive of wealth.

Spaces of Economy and of Economic Calculus

Anaemic geographies

My objective in this section, and in the chapter more widely, is not to dispute the data presented by the three empirical studies of financialization discussed above. It is, rather, to question the logic of the conclusions drawn from such data. What the data show, first and foremost, is "finance" in many mature Western capitalist countries taking a rising share of profits recognized – which is to say, profits accounted for – in those individual countries. What has been concluded from the data is something subtly but crucially different. It is that this profit share has changed because the type of capitalism exhibited by the countries in question has changed. Capitalism has (been) financialized. The profitability trends documented in such studies are thus seen to represent something *structural*: namely, that the balance between the financial and nonfinancial parts of the economy, as evidenced in their respective profit shares, has fundamentally, if not permanently, shifted.

My argument is that this conclusion, and the analytical logic underlying it, is a geographically anaemic one. While I borrow the term "anaemic geography" from Matthew Sparke, the theoretical impetus for my argument is wider.[26] Particularly important in this regard is a critique of what is known as the "varieties of capitalism" school of political economy. Closely associated with scholars such as Peter Hall and David Soskice, the "varieties" school essentially submits that capitalism varies from place to place, materializing in different incarnations in different environments.[27] But as Jamie Peck and Nik Theodore, among others, have argued, such a positing of different national capitalisms is not unproblematic. A key issue highlighted by Peck and Theodore is that this approach tends to fetishize the national scale, meaning that it treats the nation-state as an inherently meaningful scale at which to analyze and theorize capitalism.[28] The reason why such a treatment is problematic, of course, is that capitalist "systems" rarely, if ever, exist as self-contained national silos – they typically spill across those silos, variously connecting nation-states to one another, and thus rendering characterizations of "national capitalisms" moot. As Paul Krugman observes, "there is no particular reason to think that national boundaries define a relevant region" for economic analysis of any variety.[29] David McNally, meanwhile, objects to nationally-constituted conceptualizations even more force-fully. "Much discussion of the neoliberal period has focused on a number of capital-istically developed nations – most frequently the US, Germany and Japan – and treated the world-economy as largely an aggregate of these parts. This," he main-tains, "is both methodologically flawed and empirically misleading."[30]

Concurring fully on this point, I argue here that we can apply McNally's and Peck and Theodore's generic critiques of the "varieties" school *specifically* to the concept of "financialised capitalism." For, although it might not be articulated literally as such by its proponents, this concept displays all the hallmarks of the "varieties" model in terms of its empirical substantiation and territorial applica-tion. All three of the empirical studies of financialization discussed in the previous section are based on analysis framed exclusively at the national scale, examining trends in national income streams; and, as such, "financialised capitalism" is posited as existing in specific countries (most notably the US and UK), both in these individual studies and in the broader literature on the financialization of capitalism.[31] The US and UK are held to be "financialised economies" – prototypes *of* "financialised capitalism."

There are two linked senses in which this prevailing national conceptualization of financialization is geographically anaemic, and we can briefly consider each in turn. One, already pointed up, concerns the fact that capital simply does not "exist," or circulate, solely at the national scale; and that this is particularly true of contemporary *financial* capital. Saying this, note, is categorically not to deny the importance of the national scale altogether: as the locus of financial regulation and compliance, and thus of competition between regulatory regimes, the nation-state clearly remains a materially vital scalar configuration. The problem, rather, lies with framing the analysis of *economic outcomes* purely, and in isolation, at this scale. McNally helpfully distinguishes these two issues. "Nation-states and 'national economies' cannot be the fundamental units of analysis," he argues, "however much we need to attend to their importance as points of concentration within the system."[32] The second, linked form of anaemia concerns levels of reflexivity. As I will show, there has been an inadequate theorizing of the *implications* of the national scale upon which the thesis of financialization is both analytically and conceptually predicated: its implications for what nationally-constituted analysis can, and cannot, reveal.

Both forms of anaemia, then, are present in the three empirical "substantiations" of financialization discussed earlier. Each study claims to substantiate financialized capitalism without addressing the international, cross-border nature of contemporary capitalist finance; and none satisfactorily addresses how this absence might have shaped – unconsciously – their conclusions. In fact two of the studies do not reflect on their national circumscription at all, be it with regard to financial capital or, for that matter, nonfinancial capital. The only study to do so is Krippner's, which I will discuss in more detail now. I should emphasize that my critical focus on Krippner's work is perhaps in one sense unfair, given that hers is comfortably the most reflexive of the three studies where issues of geographical scale are concerned. But this, and the fact that hers has also proven the most influential study (witness, for instance, Marazzi), is precisely what makes it worth close attention: for even here, the critical consideration of scale is limited and, in respect particularly of financial capital, materially lacking.

The limitations are both conceptual and analytical. Conceptually, Krippner wonders whether the observed growth in the shares of US profits accounted for by the finance sector and by financial income sources might actually result not from financialization of "American capitalism" but from "spatial restructuring of economic activity where production increasingly occurs offshore but financial functions continue to be located in the domestic economy" – from, in other words, the US non-financial sector shrinking (by virtue of being exported) more than from US "finance" growing.[33] But the parallel possibility – not the expatriation, and thus relative domestic decline, of the nonfinancial economy, but rather the controlled overseas expansion, and thus domestically-repatriated growth, of the financial economy – is not mentioned. This conceptual limitation then feeds through into Krippner's empirical analysis, where internationalization is only quantified at a very high and relatively abstract level, and in such a way that a consideration of the extent of contribution of international markets to financial profits realized in the US is precluded.

More broadly, Krippner's seeming relative indifference to questions of scale is evident in the dismissal of such matters with which she ends her analysis. Intimating that her brief empirical foray into international statistics is sufficient to allay concerns about spatial patternings of profit derivation and thus about her envisioning of *American* financialized capitalism, she further states, as if to cement her case, that "US profits earned abroad are relatively insignificant when compared to profits earned in the domestic economy."[34] But let us actually examine the data on this ratio from the source (the US Bureau of Economic Analysis) on which Krippner herself relies. These show (Fig 6.1) that earnings from the rest of the world have accounted for over 15 percent of US corporate profits in each of the last 20 years, with the ratio peaking at 47 percent – or fully *69 percent* if, as Krippner suggests, we compare overseas earnings not to total profits but to "profits earned in the domestic economy" – in 2008.[35] To be fair to Krippner, the highest levels of overseas contribution came in the 2000s, after the end, in 2001, of the period she studied; nevertheless, the two ratios in question had reached 25 percent and 30 percent respectively by 2000. Plenty of adjectives could be legitimately invoked to capture this level of contribution, but "insignificant" is not one of them.

If these data demonstrate one thing above all else, of course, it is that contemporary capitalism, as experienced and shaped from the US corporate perspective, is a comprehensively internationalised political-economic system. It is surely the case, therefore, that any identification of fundamental structural shifts in capitalism, such as its "financialization," must be framed at the international scale – or, at the very least, must critically interrogate the full array of international capital flows in which individual "national economies" such as the US are embedded. It is in recognition of this that Peck and Theodore argue for the analysis not of national varieties of capitalism but of a transnational, "variegated" capitalism; and that, where more specifically financial matters are concerned, Shaun French and colleagues press the case for "a network approach" in place of the restrictive "scalar geographical imaginary" that dominates the financialization literature.[36] In a similar vein, McNally insists that since "capitalism is a world-system whose imperative is the unbounded drive to accumulate, not to develop 'national economies'," and since it is "at the level of world-economy that the laws of capitalism are most fully and concretely enacted," it follows that "explanatory priority must be placed on the operation of capitalism as a *global* system."[37]

I endeavor to provide just such a transnational perspective later, when I turn to examine in detail the "US" and "UK" profitability trends invoked by proponents of financialization. Here, the final important point is to reiterate the implications

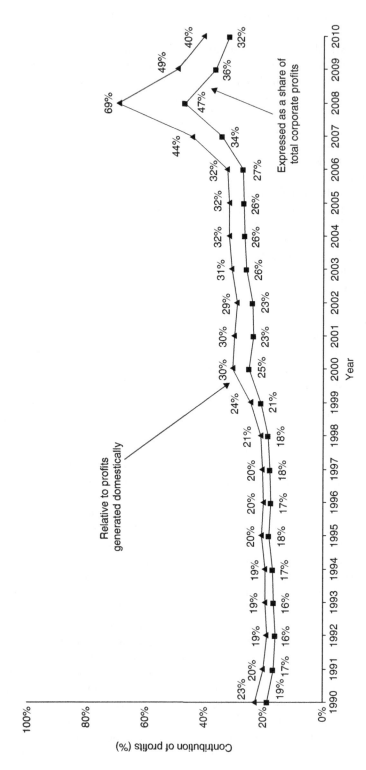

Fig 6.1 Contribution to US national corporate profits of earnings from the rest of the world, 1990–2010 (based on profits shown with inventory valuation and capital consumption adjustments).

Source: US Bureau of Economic Analysis.

of *not* adopting such an analytical approach – of, that is, attempting to diagnose capitalism's structural forms and mutations by examining the surpluses generated by different capitals as if those surpluses somehow attached to individual nation-states. For to do so is, I argue, to fall into what John Agnew memorably labelled the "territorial trap": it is to treat the *idea* of a "national economy" as an economic *reality* by searching for explanations of "national" economic outcomes exclusively in "national" economic dynamics.[38] The perils of such a methodology are profound. Put simply, examining one country in isolation is akin to extracting one piece from a larger jigsaw puzzle: we may think that we know what this piece shows, but it inevitably looks different when viewed as part of the wider, interconnected whole to which it belongs. Looking only at such pieces in isolation, all three of the above studies of "financialization" necessarily exclude the possibility that rising financial profits in the US and other OECD countries have been driven by changing relationships with international markets as well as – or perhaps even instead of – structural adjustments within those economies themselves.

National accounts and "national economies"

Yet it is difficult not to empathize with those who have sought to analyze the historical macro-development of capitalism as a constellation of interlocking commercial activities and monetary flows and ended up being lured into the trap of a rigid territorial framing. There is, I want to argue now, nothing coincidental about this particular geo-scalar approach to the analysis of the economic past. Quantitatively-oriented historians of capitalism tend to fetishize the national scale, I suggest, in part because the principal data sources they have available to them – the national accounts of different countries – themselves fetishize the national scale.

The history of how and why this fetishization came about is of no small significance to this book. As we saw in Chapter 3, the original systematization of national accounting in the Western world occurred primarily in the 1930s and 1940s. But these, as we have *also* seen, were no typical decades where the historical geography of capitalism was concerned. Recall the metaphor of an accordion that I used in Chapter 2: having been stretched out relatively freely across national borders in the late nineteenth and early twentieth centuries, global capitalism (including the world of finance) retreated into highly protected national enclaves for much of the 1920s through 1950s before then expanding out once more. It was this idiosyncratic world of – more than at any time in history – *national economies* that Keynes, in particular, set about modelling; and *national* accounts became at once the principal tool of envisioning such economies and the main proving ground for Keynes's equations. As Timothy Mitchell observes: "The statistical figures with whose help the economy was gradually constructed – national income (later called the gross national product), investment, savings, and money supply – were all measures of the movement of money from hand to hand *within the nation*."[39]

Following Mitchell's promptings, one could actually push this argument a step further. Not only, Mitchell argues, has the primary quantitative apparatus of macro-economic visualization always been nationally enframed; but so too, more fundamentally, has our underlying understanding of "the economy" per se. To make this case one could, perhaps, go back to Adam Smith and his tract on the wealth *of nations*. But Mitchell maintains that the idea of "the economy" as it coheres today – a self-contained system, separate from the spheres of politics, law, and culture, and one "whose internal parts are imagined to move in a dynamic and regular interaction" – did not exist in Smith's day. "The economy" as idea was made, rather, in the twentieth century, and specifically in the era of Keynes. And it was made, says Mitchell, "by definition and default" as a national space: "The nation, and the national economy in particular, provided the format of what could appear as a postimperial political topography."[40] On this interpretation, the scalar epistemology that "fixes" the nation as the space of economy runs much deeper than the technology of national account-ing – making the fetishization of the national scale in the historical analysis of capitalism's economics all the more explicable.

Since Keynes's day, of course, repeated waves of globalization of both financial and nonfinancial capital have decisively put paid to the national economy as a material reality. But even if, as a result, the national economy can legitimately now be considered, as Hugo Radice put it, a "Keynesian myth," we all know that myths persist and exercise power.[41] Nowhere, perhaps, is this truer than in the case of national accounts, which, almost by definition, still live and breathe the Keynesian myth and have, in consequence, long struggled to keep up with eco-nomic-geographical realities.

My own analysis of cross-border banking in the next section is itself unavoid-ably compromised by this struggle. It is true that the national offices of economic statistics that produce the national accounts have always attempted to factor cross-border transactions into their analysis through international investment and export and import line items, which are usually most fully documented in balance of payments publications. (The UK, as an example, has a Pink Book – the balance of payments – and a Blue Book – the national product, income, and expenditure.) But these cross-border computations, so critical of course to the differentiation between "domestic product" and "national product," have always been fraught with difficulty and have often appeared to be a step or two behind the pace of real-world developments.

Consider the US Bureau of Economic Analysis's (BEA) figures on internation-alization by US banks. If we are primarily concerned, as in this book, with banks' crossing of geographical borders *as physical, operating organizations*, two forms of internationalization are especially salient to our analysis: first, exports of finan-cial services (i.e. services supplied by banks in one territory to customers in another); and second, the establishment of owned operations in other territories. (These two, of course, corresponding approximately to the respective "national treatment" and "right of establishment" demands which, as we saw in the previ-ous chapter, dominated the US and Western European trade-in-services agenda from the mid-1970s). But how well equipped are the BEA's records to allow us to analyze the history of outwards US banking internationalization in these two particular dimensions? For financial services exports, the answer is "quite well"; global totals for financial services exports are available back to 1997, while totals for unaffiliated exports (only) are available back to 1986. In terms of foreign direct investment (FDI) by US financial corporations, however, while the BEA does publish estimates for the value of services provided to international markets through corporate affiliates that are located in the markets that they serve, banks were not included in these statistics prior to 2004, making any sort of comprehensive longitudinal analysis impossible.[42]

Nor, we should note, is the problem of sourcing a spatially-sensitive empirical picture of banking's history of internationalization confined solely to the realm of the national accounts and their own peculiarly "nationalist" geographical imagination. Consider also the data that the practitioners of national accounting *themselves* rely upon in seeking to develop a spatially-faithful representation. These, based on returns submitted by financial institutions either directly or indirectly (for example, via central banks), are hardly unproblematic. Only businesses required to – or wanting to be seen to – conform to International Financial Reporting Standards need segment their revenues and profits by geographic area in their official filings. And even this segmentation is, in practice, highly discretionary and opens considerable scope for "questionable" allocations in the sense of revenue/profit being recognized wholly in one place (say, in the US) when the practical reality is that the service is either being exported or is being consumed *and* provided in large part elsewhere. As is widely recognized, the question of where banks book profits is often as much about internal transfer pricing and tax "efficiency" mechanisms as it is about actual activity locations.[43]

To illuminate the problematic let us take two examples: first, Goldman Sachs, and the geographic data provided in its annual report for the financial year ending November 2008.[44] The report states that the "methodology for allocating the firm's profitability to geographic regions is dependent on the judgment of management," and it is this methodology, which varies by business division, that is of interest. A geographical "mismatch" of the kind hypothesized above seems possible in at least three areas of its business. First, "Trading", where geographical allocation of profits from market-making and from executing and clearing client transactions is based on the "location of the trading desk" but where clearly a service *is* often being exported (from the London desk to a client in Africa, for instance) and yet will not be recorded as such; second, "Asset Management", where the determining factor is the home "location of the sales team" but where, once more, cross-border activity is extremely common; and third, "Securities Services", where allocation depends upon "location of the primary market for the underlying security" but where a not-uncommon business scenario might be Goldman's New York office lending the shares of a company operating in Asia but listed in London to a hedge fund based in Germany. In this last case, Goldman's profits would appear in its accounts, and thus *also* in the national accounts, as UK profits; it would, however, be awfully tenuous to read those profits as in some way representative of developments in the UK "national economy."

Geographical allocation and reporting of finance sector profits is, in other words, relatively arbitrary. A second short example will illustrate, moreover, that such allocation is often not even consistent in its arbitrariness. The example this time comes from the UK, and specifically Barclays Plc, a quintessential example of the modern diversified, globalized financial services company. To make the point about lack of consistency, we need to compare the company's accounts for the years 2001 and 2002 respectively.

The former report allocates total 2001 gross income of £19.1bn to five main geographic regions. Three are straightforward: other EU (£1.3bn), the US (also £1.3bn), and rest of the world (£1.1bn). It is the two final categories that are of interest. The largest by some margin, at £14.1bn, is called simply "UK." The last, at £1.3bn, is labelled "foreign UK-based," which comprises firstly "activities in the UK with overseas customers, including sovereign lendings," and secondly "the main foreign exchange trading business arising in the UK."[45] Yet by the time the 2002 annual report was published a year later, something strange had happened to the geographical allocation of this £19.1bn of 2001 gross income. The allocations to other EU, the US and the rest of the world were still the same, but the remaining £15.4bn was now *all* allocated to the UK. And while the notes to the accounts identify various other restatements vis-à-vis the previous year's report, nothing at all is said about this rewriting of the geographies of income origination. In fact the category of "foreign UK-based" disappears from the accounts altogether.[46] The £1.3bn of relevant income, meanwhile, has not so much disappeared as been "domesticated." What had been inscribed in Barclay's earlier accounts as, at least in part, globalized finance, would be visible henceforth – both for 2001's £1.3bn and indeed for all income, of unknown quanta, deriving in subsequent years from the same activities – as a wholly domestic manifestation of demand for, and supply of, financial services.

All of which is to say that if national accounts fetishize the national scale and struggle in so doing to capture the "true" texture of financial internationalization, they are clearly not helped by the underlying architecture of data provisioning constituted by financial institutions' own geographical income-allocation procedures. And we should be aware that it is not only analysts of financial and economic history who have been hamstrung – consciously or unconsciously – as a result. It is, in my view, highly significant that many of the key personalities we encountered in the previous chapter repeatedly lamented the paucity of usable data on the international dimensions of financial services delivery. As we know, national accounting metrics were vital ammunition in the battles over ideas waged both internally and externally by the Western champions of open international banking markets, and the likes of Geza Feketekuty and Harry Freeman insisted that the picture of international activities contained in these and other official statistical envisionings simply was not good enough.

"People have such a hard time believing that trade in services is important", Feketekuty, for instance, argued, "because they cannot see it and it is very difficult to measure."[47] This was an essentially unanimous conviction in the 1980s and 1990s among those individuals and organizations seeking to progress services trade liberalization. Indeed the introduction internationally of systems capable of satisfactorily recording services trade volumes, and especially volumes of *financial* services trade, was one of the primary initiatives of the Western nations throughout the multilateral trade negotiations that took place during those decades.[48] Freeman captured the mood of frustration perfectly when he wrote in 1990 (and in terms directly echoing our Goldman and Barclays examples): "How do you compute the export of services? At American Express, three teams spent one day each examining the annual report and computing the company's exports. One came back with something like $1 billion, one came back with $2 billion, and one came back with $4 billion. Pick one!"[49] Quite. Chakravarthi Raghavan argues that even after two decades of work on such issues by the UN Statistical Commission and various affiliated task forces, the resulting 2001 manual on Statistics of International Trade in Services intended for use by national statistical offices was so ineffectual that it would "not serve trade negotiators at all."[50]

Perhaps most pointedly of all, it is evident that the treatment of international economic activities specifically in national accounts has long been *particularly* problematic in respect of financial services. That is to say, some of the problems associated with envisioning the international dimensions of financial services in the accounts have been its – financial services – alone. Heinz Arndt alluded to these in an important article from 1984, in which he observed that the difficulties involved in measuring trade in financial services "are closely related to the difficulties that have been encountered in the treatment of financial enterprises in social accounts for national economies" – namely to, he further specified, *precisely* the "banking problem" introduced in Chapter 3 and further explored in Chapters 4 and 5.[51]

Thus we can usefully conclude the present section by focusing on this particular statistical-analytical conjuncture. Consider the situation facing someone searching, in the early 1980s, for evidence of the magnitude of financial *intermediation* services exports from the two countries that were leading the push around that time for the lowering of global services trade barriers: the US and the UK. Crucially, it would have been impossible to find any such evidence. The US BEA did not at that time include "implicitly" charged-for financial services – such as loan-making and deposit-taking – within its services exports estimates (and did not begin to do so until 1985).[52] The UK did not either.

And the latter, UK example is especially interesting, important and revealing. The "problem," if we can posit it as such, related to the treatment of such "free" services recommended by the UN's 1968 SNA and specifically to the allocation (rather than derivation) of the imputed charge associated with such services. Because it was assumed to represent intermediate demand in its entirety, there actually *could be*, as we saw in Chapter 4, no export component to intermediation-based output. Hence Luxembourg's gripe that growth in its international-facing financial industry generated little growth in reported national GDP under SNA 1968 since all such output was assumed to be consumed domestically by other businesses.

The UK, as we saw in the previous chapter, had adopted the SNA 1968 treatment in 1973. But the historical incongruity in this timing was that it was just around this time that the UK's finance sector *did* begin to re-internationalize after the relative slumber characterizing the immediate post-war era. With this incongruity in mind, the final section of the chapter will consider the long-term implications of the disjuncture epitomized by the UK (but not only the UK) from 1973 – between an internationalizing finance sector and a national accounting framework that structurally underestimated such internationalization – for representations of the productiveness of banking in the world of national accounting. First, though, we need to examine the actual shape of post-1970s financial services internationalization more widely, and to reframe the thesis of financialization – which essentially ignores such internationalization – in this light.

From Financialized Capitalism to Globalized Finance

Banking across boundaries

In absolute terms, the period since the early- to mid-1970s – which was the point at which, in Chapter 4, we left off the story of post-war banking internationalization – has seen far-and-away the most substantial and widely-dispersed process of geopolitical boundary-crossing by financial institutions in history. Such boundary crossing has occurred in all of the three main registers in which banks can and do internationalize: in the provision of financial services from one place to another (exports); in the establishment of proprietary banking operations overseas (foreign direct investment); and, with the simultaneous dismantling of capital controls occurring more-or-less worldwide, in the cross-border provision of financial capital (international portfolio investment).

In the following pages I provide a high-level overview of this process. While I do touch on the last of the three aforementioned forms of boundary crossing, my focus, as in the rest of the book, is on the first two: in other words, on *bank* rather than capital mobility. I will begin by considering the major patterns of where banks of the Global North have tended to internationalize *to* – for it *has* been almost exclusively such banks, as we shall then see below, that have substantially internationalized.

The strongest current of bank internationalization over the past three to four decades has been into countries in Central and Eastern Europe, Latin America, and sub-Saharan Africa – countries often referred to as either "emerging" or "developing" markets, or both. While this process has of course been highly uneven across both time and space, we can helpfully highlight two of its key features. First, a large component of this internationalization has entailed FDI as well as, or instead of, export: the organic establishment or, more commonly, acquisition of a permanent foothold in the territory in question. Often this has occurred through the privatization of troubled state-owned banks (as in much of Eastern Europe) or directly following financial crises (as in Mexico in 1995).[53] And second, the heaviest period of such internationalization occurred in the 1990s and 2000s once capital controls and then barriers to trade in financial services – including restrictions on the right of establishment – had begun to be widely removed.

The most striking outcomes of this internationalization can be readily illustrated. On average across all "developing" countries, Robert Cull and Maria Peria estimate that the share of bank assets held by foreign banks increased from 22 percent in 1996 to 39 percent in 2005, reaching or exceeding 50 percent in each of sub-Saharan Africa and Eastern Europe.[54] UNCTAD, meanwhile, reported that in 2001 there were 29 countries in which foreign banks accounted for more than 70 percent of total banking assets, with the figure exceeding 90 percent – and in some cases reaching 100 percent – in the likes of Estonia, the Czech Republic, Botswana, Lesotho, Gambia, Belize, and Aruba. Cross-border banking mergers and acquisitions, described by UNCTAD as "the principal mode of foreign entry into developing countries and [Central and Eastern Europe] during the 1990s," amounted to nearly US $80bn for the period 1995–2003 compared with just $2bn for 1987–1994.[55]

Of course, internationalization has also taken place *into* the territories of the Global North which, as we shall see below, have been home to the world's most aggressive internationalist banks. American banks have continued to set up shop en masse in London, just as they did in the 1960s; they have been joined there by German and other continental European banks; and major American and continental European financial centers have been similarly colonized by foreign banks from the other leading banking nations. But three caveats regarding the importance of such higher-income market "interpenetration" – specifically in the context of this book and this chapter – are in order. First, despite such cross-colonization, foreign shares of domestic banking markets remain much lower in the countries of the Global North than in the world regions discussed in the previous paragraph. Second, and related, setting up banking operations in overseas international financial centers is often as much about establishing new footholds from which to better serve (other) far-flung markets, and new nodes for co-ordinating highly mobile international capital flows, as it is about serving customers *in* those markets per se. Third, and most important here, internationalization into countries such as the US, the UK and in Western Europe, *unlike* internationalization into the "developing" and "emerging" world, did not require the waging and winning of the battles over ideas and trade restrictions that we examined in the previous chapter.

Connected to this point, it is also particularly important to note that the major aforementioned pattern of FDI-driven banking internationalization into "developing" countries has largely not been mirrored, in the past two decades, in the third register of internationalization indicated above: cross-border financial investment more generally. As we observed in Chapter 2, levels of international capital mobility in the late twentieth century began once again to approach the levels last witnessed in the "first" era of financial globalization before World War I. Yet recent research has shown that this latter era of international financial integration displays a markedly different geography to the former one. Whereas investment in developing countries was central to late nineteenth-century financial globalization, today's financial globalization, especially in the aftermath of the Latin American debt crisis of the 1980s, is characterized primarily by capital flows between higher-income economies and their respective financial centers. "By historical standards," writes Moritz Schularick, "poor countries are marginalized in the contemporary global financial market."[56]

Amongst the major regions of the Global South, the only one where the picture in the 1990s and 2000s was *not* for the most part one of widespread foreign bank incursion was Asia. At the same time as the number of foreign banks relative to the total number of banks was increasing – by 2005 – to more than 50 percent in each of sub-Saharan Africa and Eastern Europe and to 42 percent in Latin America, the same ratio, while rising, was doing so much more slowly and at much lower absolute levels across Asia: reaching 19 percent in East Asia and just 8 percent in South Asia.[57] A primary reason for these relatively low figures concerns the historical situations specifically in the key territories of China and India. In both cases, while foreign banks have been making determined efforts to establish themselves for many years now, and while domestic regulators – especially in India – are increasingly relaxing the pertinent entry and operating restrictions, such banks' presence remains limited. In China, for instance, PricewaterhouseCoopers recently estimated that foreign banks' market share remains below 2 percent.[58] In India, it is estimated that 32 foreign banks collectively run just 310 branches, representing less than 0.5 percent of the 72,000-strong branch network across the nation; and that their share is below 10 percent in terms of each of banking assets, profits, and deposits.[59]

If we know, then, that it is primarily Eastern Europe, Latin America, and sub-Saharan Africa that have been colonized, who have been banking's latter-day colonizers? They have certainly included, we can begin by noting, American banks, buoyed from the mid-1990s by the services trade liberalization developments that they themselves, in large part, engendered. Such banks have essentially carried on the process of international expansion that we tracked through to the mid-1970s in Chapter 4, although the period since has seen a relative withdrawal from particular *components* of international banking, the most notable – Citicorp apart – being retail banking.[60] Between 1975 and 1998, the number of foreign branches of US-insured commercial banks swelled from 762 to 935, while the total assets held by these branches rose from US$163bn to over $700bn. Comfortably the largest growth in branch numbers and assets came in Latin America (from 133 to 354 branches) and Asia (112 to 220).[61] But expansion has by no means been limited to commercial banks, with investment banks also aggressively extending their international presence.[62] Among the large number of US banks operating internationally – in 1960, over two-thirds of the largest 25 US banks had been wholly domestic operators, whereas by 1978 none was – the major players in the past three decades have been Citcorp, JP Morgan, and Chase Manhattan.[63]

A critical difference between US bank internationalization before the early 1970s and in the period since, however, is that such banks have not been left effectively unchallenged in the latter era. Throughout the 1980s, a major competitive challenge came, in particular, from Japanese banks. Such banks "increased international activities sharply from the early 1980s fuelled by strong domestic economic growth, a fast pace of domestic regulation, and large flows of foreign direct investment by Japanese industrial firms."[64] Japanese banks' overseas offices, branches and subsidiaries increased in number from 299 to 913 between 1980 and 1988; by 1985, in tandem with this *institutional* internationalization, Japan had become the world's largest creditor; and by 1986 12 of the world's largest 20 banks (ranked by assets), including all of the top five, were Japanese.[65] Yet this extraordinary burst of internationalization, which was primarily focused on other industrialized markets, was relatively short-lived. By the turn of the century most Japanese banks had retreated from the international arena, "in large part due to the restructuring and consolidation of the Japanese banking industry in response to widespread banking distress during the economic recession of the 1990s."[66]

The more enduring competitive challenge to international US banks has come from Europe and, in those above-discussed regions of the world where foreign banks have come to assume such a formidable presence in the wake of capital account and banking market liberalization, from two European countries in particular: the UK and France. Despite the relative lethargy in the immediate post-war era we observed in Chapter 4, UK banks had never *lost* their longstanding overseas presence. They remained extremely powerful in many former settler colonies, for example; as at 1970, two UK banks between them held fully 73 percent of commercial bank deposits in South Africa.[67] But it was not until the early 1970s that UK banks began in earnest to *re*-internationalize, and to do so not only in countries where they had long been active but also in entirely new regions.[68]

In this process of re-internationalization, which continues very much to this day and which has increasingly incorporated international investment banking as well as commercial banking, three UK-headquartered banks have been especially prominent: Barclays, HSBC, and Standard Chartered.[69] The last of these now employs approximately 85,000 people in over 1,500 branches across 71 different countries, 15 of which deliver more than US$100 million individually in annual profits. The group is especially strong in Asia, the Middle East, and Africa, operating branches in 14 different sub-Saharan African territories and 26 in Nigeria alone.[70] Barclays is a similarly dispersed – though even more operationally diversified – beast. It employs over 145,000 people in over 50 countries, with a broadly similar geographic footprint to Standard Chartered: Asia, Africa, and the Middle East being its main sources of income outside of Europe and North America (although it is also active in Brazil, Argentina, and Mexico).[71] HSBC, meanwhile, is the largest and most internationalized of the three. A truly global operation, it has around 7,500 offices in 87 countries, with those countries in which it has more than 50 offices including, inter alia, Brazil (1,358), Mexico (1,162), Turkey (336), Indonesia (202), China (176), Argentina (150), India (122), Saudi Arabia (104), Egypt (87), El Salvador (84), Honduras (75), Panama (71), and Malaysia (58) – a list which indicates just how geographically dispersed the company is.[72]

Alongside UK banks, the other most geographically-ambitious European banks over the past 30 years have been those hailing from France.[73] Jean-Marie Fournier and Denis Marionnet report that at the end of 2007, France's eight largest banks had bases in 87 different countries. And, as is the case with the UK, it is three banks that account for the lion's share of this international activity: BNP Paribas, Société Générale, and Crédit Agricole, which employ more than half of their personnel outside France and which, between them, are estimated to have accounted in 2007 for 83 percent of all international operations carried out by French banks.[74] BNP Paribas alone has operations in more than 80 countries. All three of these banks, like their UK counterparts, began to substantially ramp up their international operations from the early 1970s onwards.[75] Indeed, research for the Commission Bancaire into the foreign branches of 24 leading French banks found that the net profits generated by those branches delivered 54 percent of the banks' global profits by as early as 1981.[76]

This emphasis on US, UK, and French banks is not intended to suggest, of course, that no other banks have engaged in large-scale international diversification. The argument, rather, is that it has been *mainly* US, UK, and French banks that have benefitted from the widespread removal of previously-forbidding entry and operating restrictions around the world. Others have also moved to exploit those greater freedoms, of course. Switzerland has two major international players in UBS and Credit Suisse; the Netherlands has ING Bank; Germany has Deutsche Bank; and Spain has Banco Santander. But several of these – especially the Swiss pair and Germany's Deutsche – are heavily focussed on OECD territories where, for the most part, gaining access did not require active political petitioning through trade negotiations or otherwise.[77] And only in the case of the UK, the US, and France can we legitimately speak, it seems to me, of a multiply-constituted financial *sector* with global – or very nearly global – commercial ambition.

Yet when we consider all of the ways in which banks operate internationally, French banks ultimately lie a considerable distance behind their American and UK counterparts. My focus in the immediately preceding paragraphs has been primarily on internationalization in the guise of physical, branch-based colonization of foreign markets. But as we know, the internationalization of banking is not only about such FDI. We must also explicitly factor in export volumes since a large component of contemporary international banking is executed through cross-border service flows. With this in mind, Fig 6.2 charts the annual value of financial services exports from 1995 to 2010 for France and for each of the six countries for whom this value exceeded US $10bn in 2010.[78]

Before considering the data pertaining to France and their relation to the US and UK data, it is important to address briefly an apparent anomaly thrown up by this chart: Luxembourg. In the above discussion of major internationalized banks, Luxembourg did not feature at all; and yet Fig 6.2 shows it as the world's third largest exporter of financial services. What is going on here? The answer, of course, is that Luxembourg is a very "special" place in international finance. It is, in short, an offshore financial center and tax haven. More pointedly, it is a financial center populated overwhelmingly by *foreign* banks, from which

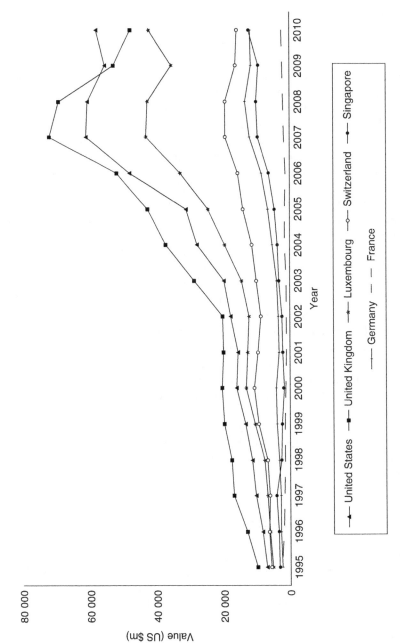

Fig 6.2 Value of national financial services exports, 1995–2010 (excludes insurance services).
Source: UNCTADstat.

those foreign banks themselves export financial (and largely wealth management) services overseas, and very often "back" to the territories where those banks are domiciled – to Germany, to France, to Switzerland, to the US, and so on.[79] It would, as such, be stretching things conceptually to posit Luxembourg as a home to internationally-expansionist banks in the same way that the US and the UK clearly are.

Meanwhile, the data charted in Fig 6.2 demonstrate unambiguously that French banks are simply not in the same bracket as US and UK banks when it comes to financial services export activities. To the degree that they have internationalized, they have evidently done so almost exclusively through FDI – a model that US and UK banks have used too, of course, but not in isolation. By 1995 – one year after the signing of the WTO's Understanding on Commitments in Financial Services, and two years before the signing of the wider Agreement on Financial Services – the US and UK were already established as the world's largest financial services export-ers; over the next 15 years, as they expanded their branch networks overseas, they simultaneously surged far ahead of their erstwhile competitors in cross-border financial services trade.[80]

It is, then, no surprise that when we scan the various tables and rankings that attempt to identify the world's largest banks, US and UK banks tend today to dominate. Take, as a typical example, *The Banker's* rankings for 2010. Fully seven of the top 10 banks ranked by Tier 1 capital, and *all* of the top six, were US or UK banks; China (with ICBC), Spain (Santander) and France (BNP Paribas) accounted for one each.[81] For all its extensive branch footprint, French banking, with an extremely limited export business, has not exploited the new, liberalized land-scape of open global banking markets to anywhere near the same diversified extent as American and British banking. But *neither*, critically, is France ordinarily invoked alongside the US and the UK as an exemplar of contemporary "financial-ized" capitalism. Is there a connection between the two? I want to argue that there is. Thus, how we can think about Anglo-American bank dominance – and spe-cifically its fundamentally internationally-distributed foundations – in relation to arguments about the financialization *of* the UK and US economies is the question I turn to now.

Geographies of "financialization"

In what follows, I extend the above findings on prevailing recent patterns in inter-national banking markets to reflect specifically upon some of the key profitability trends mobilized by theorists of "financialization" as evidence thereof. As previ-ously intimated, such trends tend to pertain to the two territories from which, as we have just seen, banking has most fully and forcefully internationalized in recent decades: the US and the UK. These two are widely "considered to be exemplar financialized economies" or, in the words of another study, as the two economies "which arguably have moved furthest in the direction of being truly 'financialized'."[82] Krippner and Orhangazi , as we have seen, both look exclusively at the US in seeking to substantiate financialization; Willem Buiter, meanwhile, is one of many to comment on the UK's own "excessive financialization."[83]

Before attempting to cast historic trends in "US" and "UK" profit realization in a more geographically nuanced light, we must first remind ourselves of what exactly those trends are – in other words, what specific empirical patterns have been read as indications of "financialization." There are, in broad terms, two: first, the increasing share of corporate profits accruing to the finance sector; and second, the increasing share of nonfinancial companies' profits taking the form of financial (versus nonfinancial) categories of income. (Epstein and Jayadev's analysis of "rentier share" consolidates these two trends into one measure and, incidentally, validates the US/UK focus of the financialization critique: finding that while the inflation-adjusted rentier share of national income typically increased by between 5 and 10 percent for those OECD countries for which there are data available from the 1960s through the 1990s, it did so by 11.5 percent for the UK and by fully 18.1 percent for the US.[84])

My argument will essentially be that in the cases of both the US and the UK, the *first* of these trends is in fact substantially explicable in terms of the internationalization of financial services provision. The conceptualization of a structural mutation in advanced capitalism is in this sense, I argue, unnecessary – or, to put it another way: is necessitated only by the *neglect* of capitalism's geographical mutations. What we *know* is that the geography of capitalism has changed (and has, in the process, lifted finance sector profits in the US and UK); the structural dynamics of capitalism, meanwhile, may not have.

But what of the second "financialization" trend: the increasing quantum of profits realized as financial rather than nonfinancial income for companies not themselves categorized as financial institutions? I have elected not to examine this development – not because I consider it uninteresting or unimportant, but because, for two reasons, I regard it as a particularly unreliable indicator of structural change towards finance-based accumulation. These reasons relate to what those studies invoking this trend typically treat as the two main components of "financial income": dividends and interest. A brief comment on each is merited.

A dividend is simply a portion of profits paid out to shareholders rather than retained and reinvested in a business. For scholars such as Krippner, dividends represent "financial" income for recipients since they do *not* represent operating or "nonfinancial" income; they are, as Epsetin and Jayadev would have it, rents rather than "productive" revenues. My unease with this distinction, however, is that it seems much too sharply drawn. After all, growth in a company's dividend income could equally well reflect corporate restructuring – a partial spinning-off of a business division, for instance, with a share of the latter's profits subsequently being accounted for as dividends rather than as wholly-owned operating income – as it could a process of financialized rent-seeking. The same possibility applies at the scale of the economy as a whole. The broader point here is that the matter of determining what is a "financial" source of income and what is not is, in my view, fraught with ambiguity and difficulty and is, as such, wholly unreliable as a basis for structural economic analysis.

Interest income is, I think, no less problematic. Again, the premise is quite straightforward: "nonfinancial" companies generating profits increasingly through interest as opposed to through normal, core business activities bespeaks a structural change in the economy towards "finance." Yet why should such a trend imply structural change (and remember that Krippner et al. *do* insist on viewing financialization in terms of "structural shifts" in "the nature of contemporary capitalism")? Could it not represent something entirely cyclical or even ephemeral, and nothing to do with structural adjustment? It is widely recognized, for example, that nonfinancial corporations in the US and the UK have been building up record cash surpluses for many years now, with most commentators treating this behavior as evidence of managers' prevailing belief that surpluses cannot be (more) profitably invested in those corporations' core activities.[85] Is this – and the greater interest income flows it has generated – evidence of a structural "financialization" of the economy or simply of, as Marxian economists would have it, the type of crisis of overaccumulation to which capitalism is endemically prone? There is, it seems to me, no easy answer to this question; and hence no more sound a basis for relying on interest income growth as evidence of "financialization" than there is dividend income growth.

As such, I focus here instead on the "other" signifier of financialization, namely the finance sector's growing share of overall corporate profits – which, as it happens, is very much regarded as *the* "proof" of financialization in the wider literature on the phenomenon. Krippner's and Orhangazi's studies, drawing on BEA sources, both present plenty of data attesting to this trend for the US. For the UK, however, demonstrating the trend in question is slightly less straightforward, primarily because there is no directly comparable line in the UK national accounts to the BEA's "corporate profits." Nevertheless, proxies are available, and certainly point to similar trends. Financial corporations' share of the total *gross operating surplus* generated by all UK corporations, for instance, increased from under 5 percent in the first half of the 1980s to 22 percent by 2009.[86]

But where, geographically, are these growing UK and US financial sector profits being extracted? It is, unfortunately, extremely hard to say for sure, since neither the BEA nor the UK's Office of National Statistics (ONS) provides estimates of the geographical breakdown of profits for particular industries. One can, nonetheless, build an instructive – if not comprehensive – picture from those data that are available. In attempting to do this now, I focus throughout on what the national accounts treat as *operating* income, which is the same profit delimitation used by the above-mentioned studies of finance's rising profit share.[87] Capital gains and dividends are therefore excluded.[88]

Let us take the UK first. The ONS does not provide estimates of profits derived from cross-border services, but it does provide exported *output* figures. Thus, Fig 6.3 charts for the years 1986–2008 the value of all exports by UK-resident financial corporations (here including insurance companies). It shows that the value of this exported output grew from just £5bn in 1986 to £60bn in 2008: a compound annual growth rate (CAGR) of 11.7 percent. The chart also expresses each year's export value as a proportion of the total domestic output (exported *or*

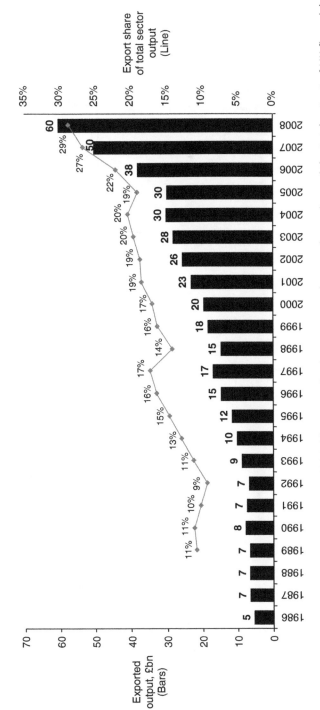

Fig 6.3 UK financial services exports, 1986–2008 (shown as absolute output values, and as a share of the total output of UK financial corporations).

Source: UK Office of National Statistics.

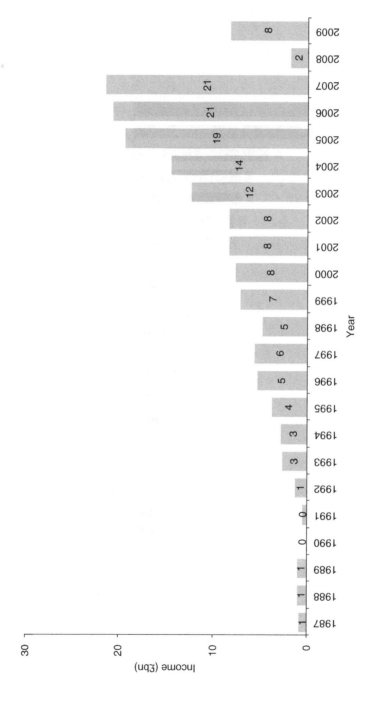

Fig 6.4 UK financial corporations' foreign direct investment income, 1987–2009.
Source: UK Office of National Statistics.

domestically-consumed) of financial corporations for that year. Due to data limitations it is only possible to track this proportion for the years 1989–2008, but the trend
illuminated is in any event a striking one. We can see that exports' share of total
finance sector domestic output rose from 11 percent in 1989 to 29 percent in 2008.
Indeed, perhaps most strikingly of all, the domestically-consumed component, which
can be isolated by deducting the value of exports from total output value, can be seen
to have grown at a CAGR of only 5.5 percent during this period – exactly the same
as the equivalent-period rate of growth in UK GDP as a whole. To be sure, the chart
tracks overseas' markets increasing contribution to finance sector output, *not profits*.
But with no a priori reason to believe that profit margins are materially different on
output consumed overseas as opposed to domestically, we can only assume that profit
growth has similarly been based disproportionately on the former geographical realm.

Exports, however, are of course not the only available route to growing over-
seas-derived profits. The other possibility, as we have noted, is through FDI. To
what extent have UK-based financial corporations profited from this approach?
Again, the figures (see Fig 6.4) are striking. Having begun to exhibit meaningful
growth from very low levels in the middle of the 1990s (coincident, unsurprisingly, with the beginning of the widespread removal of international restrictions
on banks' hotly-disputed right of establishment), repatriated earnings – and this
is a profit figure – from UK financial corporations' FDI had risen to around £20bn
per annum by the middle of the last decade.

What, then, if anything, can we conclude about the *total* overseas contribution
to UK finance sector profits – the contribution of exports and FDI earnings combined – and thus about the spatial underpinnings of finance's own growing contribution to UK corporate profitability? Given that it requires making a number
of assumptions, any such conclusion can only be tentative and must be heavily
caveated, but it certainly seems clear that since the late 1980s (before which point
the necessary data are unavailable), overseas markets have contributed the bulk
of the growth in UK finance sector profits. My calculations indicate that the total
overseas contribution to those profits climbed from below 20 percent two decades ago to in the region of 50 percent in recent years.[89]

The picture for the US is not quite as clear, partly because the same quality
and consistency of data are not available. Starting, as for the UK, with exports,
we already know from the UNCTAD figures charted above that since the mid-
1990s the value of US financial services exports has in most years been broadly
comparable to that of UK exports. (Fig 6.5 charts the BEA's own data back
to 1986, the first year for which figures are available; I have included insurance
services exports since the pertinent profitability data also incorporate the insurance sector.[90]) This in itself is highly significant because, by contrast, US finance
sector domestic profits – profits generated through domestic activity, whether
the output is consumed domestically or exported – have typically been larger
than UK finance sector profits by several orders of magnitude. To illustrate this
latter gap, Fig 6.6 charts the gross operating surplus of UK financial corporations alongside those domestic US financial sector corporate profits for each
year since 1980.

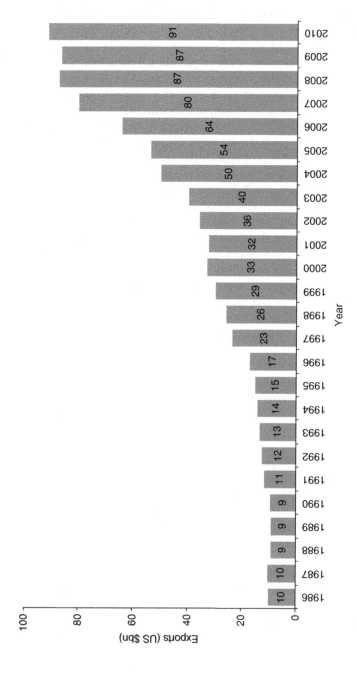

Fig 6.5 US financial services exports, 1986–2010 (includes insurance services, and imputed value of services furnished without payment).

Source: US Bureau of Economic Analysis. Note: Up to 1996, only unaffiliated financial services exports are included; thereafter, figures are for affiliated and unaffiliated exports.

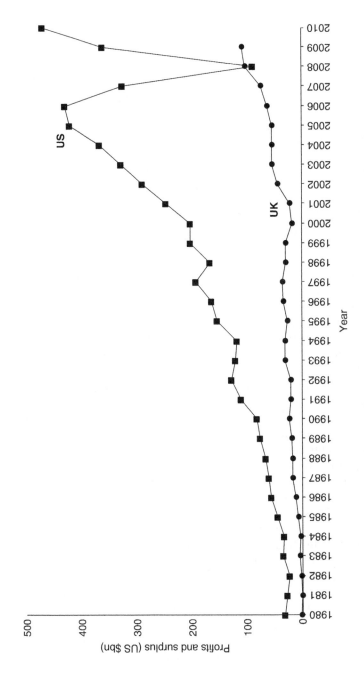

Fig 6.6 US finance sector corporate profits and UK financial corporations' gross operating surplus, 1980–2010.

Source: UK Office of National Statistics; US Bureau of Economic Analysis. Note: UK figures assume a fixed exchange rate of £1:$1.60.

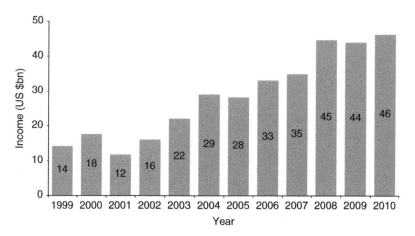

Fig 6.7 US finance sector income from foreign direct investment, 1999–2010.
Source: Bureau of Economic Analysis.

US financial services exports have assuredly shown rapid growth in recent decades, rising at a CAGR of 5.6 percent from 1986–1996 (unaffiliated exports only) and then 11.1 percent from 1997–2010 (total exports). But such growth was no stronger than the parallel growth in US financial sector corporate profits to which it contributed. Those profits (Fig 6.6) grew at a CAGR of 9.3 percent between 1986 and 2010. The implication of this is that over the two-and-a-half decades in question, export growth was not contributing *disproportionately* to growth in US finance sector profits, and nor therefore to the finance sector's rising share of US corporate profits as a whole.

Yet as we saw with the UK, exports do not represent the entire overseas story. We must also consider earnings from FDI, and although data for such earnings are only available as far back as 1999 they do allow us to assemble an altogether more nuanced picture for at least the period since. As discussed in Chapter 4, US financial institutions had already made significant inroads into foreign markets long before drawn-out trade negotiations began to pay further dividends in the mid- to late 1990s. Thus, while UK banks' FDI earnings were modest until quite recently, the US finance sector was already repatriating $14.2bn in FDI earnings per annum in 1999. This figure has since grown apace, at a CAGR of 11.3 percent, to reach nearly $50bn by 2010 (Fig 6.7).

As such, it is clearly the case that overseas markets have delivered more of an impetus to the growth in US finance sector profits than an exclusive focus on exports would suggest. The pity is that we are incapable of assessing the extent of the relative overall overseas contribution any further back than 1999, before which point we have only the export data (and even that we have only back to 1997 for total exports). What we are able to say is that *since* 1999 overseas markets *have* made a disproportionate contribution to US finance sector profit growth, which is to say that the rate of such growth – and hence the degree of "rebalancing" between the financial and nonfinancial sectors, viz. "financialization" – would have been lower without the contribution from overseas markets. By my calculations – again, incorporating important assumptions and caveated as such – total US finance sector profits, based on BEA measures and including both profits on export and repatriated FDI earnings, grew at a CAGR of 8.2 percent between 1999 and 2010; within the mix, the two-part overseas component thereof grew at 11.8 percent.[91]

Even this, however, likely presents a distorted picture not only of the overseas contribution to growth in US finance sector profits, but of this latter growth trend itself. Why? Recall, firstly, the discussion above regarding the complexity of financial institutions' geographical income-allocation procedures, and management's broad discretion in making such allocations. It has become increasingly clear in the last few years that for reasons related largely to tax policy, a significant quantum of profits earned overseas by US corporations is overlooked by the BEA despite appearing in those corporations' accounts as foreign profits. The reason for this is that only profit repatriated to the US is captured in the US national accounts and – more materially – *taxed* in the US. The relatively high tax rate on such repatriated earnings has, it is argued, motivated many large US corporations to book and *retain* substantial profits overseas.[92] One such company is Citigroup: sitting in early 2011 on $32bn in untaxed foreign profits, according to the accounting commentator Jack Ciesielski.[93] (Ironically, the OECD has claimed that while retaining foreign profits overseas, many multinational corporations, and *especially* financial services companies, happily repatriate foreign *losses* for the domestic tax benefits they can confer.[94]) The upshot of such practices is that the BEA's figures almost certainly understate the level of profits generated overseas by US financial corporations; a systematic analysis of those companies' own financial accounts would indicate a substantively higher foreign share.

Perhaps a bigger problem with the type of analysis conducted by theorists of US financialization, however, and one that an attempt to minimize the anaemic geographies of such analysis can not in itself overcome, is with the BEA's very categories "financial" and "nonfinancial." The "finance sector" which the BEA's figures – and, in turn, Krippner and Orhangazi – show taking a larger share of US corporate profits in recent decades includes not just bank holding companies but, critically, *all* holding companies, whatever the nature of their constituent holdings.[95] Hence it includes, perhaps most conspicuously and materially, Warren Buffett's famous Berkshire Hathaway investment vehicle. This, to be sure, numbers *some* financial services companies (in particular insurance companies) amongst its holdings; but it also has sizeable investments in sectors ranging from energy to apparel and from building products to retail. It is, moreover, ranked as one of the 20 largest companies in the world.[96] And then, even more incongruously, there are US holding companies with *no* financial services holdings at all – the likes of, for instance, United Continental Holdings, a publicly-traded holding company whose sole purpose is to own and operate United Airlines, which by employee numbers is presently the largest airline in the world. Thus, in a bizarre crystallization of classificatory quirks that goes unacknowledged by Krippner and Orhangazi, purported growth in US "finance sector" profits actually incorporates growth in the profits of companies only partly engaged in "finance", or indeed not engaged in finance at all.

I make these observations merely to underscore the following central point: the BEA data on sector profitability, and on the geographies of such profitability, are highly problematic for all manner of reasons. As such, my preference here is to focus not on what we do not know – how much finance sector profits in the US have grown, and how far their contribution to total US corporate profits has risen – but on what we do know. We *know* that US exports of financial services have been growing at least as fast as finance sector profits; that repatriated FDI earnings in the finance sector have been growing faster still; and that the latter trend has occurred *despite* US multinational corporations resisting the repatriation of a substantial component of total foreign-sourced profits.

Where, then, does all of this leave the financialization argument? The answer remains unclear. It is surely no coincidence, however, that today's two most nominally financialized economies are quite clearly those from which financial institutions have most forcefully internationalized, drawing more and more countries into their profit-extracting ambit. In view of the scale of this internationalization, it is at best misleading to read off from trends in spatially-circumscribed profitability metrics – notably the rise in UK and US financial versus nonfinancial profits – a fundamental mutation in contemporary or "advanced" capitalism. For, as we have seen, growth in financial sector profits has been driven in substantial part by increased demand from overseas. Domestic demand has grown less strongly; and *much* less strongly in the case of the UK, where the value of financial services supplied domestically has only just kept pace with the expansion of the UK economy as a whole over the past 20 years. This is hardly emblematic of a structural adjustment in the overall economy towards finance.

One possible objection to this critique might be to argue that the location of ultimate purchase of financial services which we have examined here is immaterial: that if financial activities are generating an increasing share of corporate profits realized *in* the UK and US, then financialization *of* the UK and US is, by definition, occurring. Yet whether one prefers to think in terms of "capitalism" or "the economy," supply and demand are clearly *both* crucial constituents, so we cannot focus only on the geography of the former to the neglect of the geography of the latter. And it is, of course, precisely changes in "the economy" and "capitalism" that financialization's protagonists posit.

As will hopefully become more apparent in the next section, this is about much more than mere semantics. On the basis of the analysis provided here, the furthest that the notion of financialization can be safely extended is to the supply-side of the UK and US economies. To stretch the notion of financialization to "the economy" or "capitalism" at large is a conceptual as opposed to merely terminological slippage, since to demonstrate the evolution of financialized capitalism we would need to substantiate the financialization of economic supply *and* demand. At smaller geographical scales, we usually recognize this; no scholar, after all, would propose Luxembourg, with its intensive national agglomeration of internationally-oriented financial service suppliers, as an example of "financialized capitalism." But making such a claim of the UK or US is arguably different only in degree, not kind. Luxembourg, and the financial corporations clustered there, is thoroughly embedded in a global capitalist economy, and represents an extreme case of specialization in finance within a wider system of different-but-largely-complementary national supply-side specialisms, the so-called "new international division of labor." So too, arguably, do the US and the UK.

A World of Productive Finance

This book started out in Chapter 1 with a consideration of the question of the productiveness of finance – how and when did it first become possible for such a question to be posed, and what initial answers to the question were posited? – and that is where it returns now in concluding. In Western political economy from its birth through to the late nineteenth century, finance and banking were uniformly conceived as economically unproductive. Only once the question of economic productiveness formally resurfaced in twentieth-century national accounting did banking manage to hurdle the pivotal production boundary: first in the US accounts then later, by turns, elsewhere. And as we saw earlier in this chapter, this more positive conceptualization of the productiveness of finance has most recently breached the very domain where the "idea" of economic productiveness first materialized – various contemporary political economists, in defiance of their forebears, *making* finance productive.

The political-economic argument that financial activities create rather than merely redistribute value has been predicated, I demonstrated, on the powerful notion of "financialization" – the notion that the very structure of the capitalist economy has, in particular locations, changed, with the financial sector progressively eclipsing the nonfinancial sector in scale. But that notion is a problematic one. Once we reinsert the wider geographies of capitalist accumulation into the spatially-anaemic conceptual framework that the notion of financialization inhabits, the need for a theory of structural change ebbs away; geography can explain much, if perhaps not all of the finance sector's apparent ascendancy. And if we doubt the financialization of capitalism, of course, we must *also* question the conclusions that have been drawn from it – not least the conclusion that a larger financial sector must perforce be a productive one.

Such a skepticism, however, is only one aspect of the questioning that a more critical perspective on financialization seems to warrant. As I have sought to emphasize throughout this book, its interest is less in the "rightness" or "wrongness" of economic representations than in their effects and their etiologies. Where, in the latter regard, do changes in ideas come from; what forces catalyze such changes? The large-scale internationalization of US and UK financial capital in recent decades, I have argued, *generated*, to one degree or another, the re-weighting of US and UK corporate profitability towards the financial part of the economy. But if it did so, then it *also* contributed towards the conceptual shifts that this re-weighting has itself elicited: the theory of financialization and of, in turn, productive finance. One form of "boundary crossing" has, in other words, stimulated another; without the internationalization of banking, it is questionable whether finance "in" the UK and

US would have expanded sufficiently to prompt the scholarly envisioning of financialization and of a financial sector traversing the production boundary. Yet a cardinal feature of this effectivity – the precise mirror image of the effectivity analyzed in Chapter 5, where conceptual boundary-crossing enabled material migrations – has been, it seems to me, its unknowingness. Had the internationalization of US and UK banking, and its implications for headline profitability trends, been recognized for what it is, demand for a theory of structural economic transformation would clearly have been commensurately lower.

Nor, I have argued, is it only in the realm of political economy that we encounter anaemic analytical geographies. Indeed: this anaemia *reflects*, I suggested, an underlying geo-scalar rigidity in the epistemology of the national statistical apparatuses upon which the study of political-economic trends so heavily relies. If this is true, might it be the case that, in a comparable "unknowing" way, national accounting's *own* relocation of finance across the production boundary has also been shaped by financial internationalization?

I want to suggest in conclusion that this is certainly conceivable. I will develop this suggestion by considering two "events" in the history of national accounting's long struggle with the eternal "banking problem" and the central paradox – that of a prosperous industry potentially being envisioned as unproductive or destructive of value – it entailed. The first is the broadly contemporaneous decision of both the UK (in 1973) and France (in 1975) to switch to the treatment of financial intermediation services recommended in SNA 1968; the second is the development, and subsequent staggered adoption, of the later recommended treatment of financial intermediation services in SNA 1993.

I argued in the previous chapter that France's and the UK's decision to switch to SNA 1968 was critical for what it *allowed*: inter alia, the mobilization of positive value-added data on the banking sector in fora such as international trade negotiations. But *why* did the UK and France shift; and why *then*? Ultimately the answer to this question is unclear; in my research for this book, despite looking, I have not been able to find for either country either documentation explaining the rationale for the change or individuals able directly to recollect such a rationale. What I did encounter, however, was a widespread conviction among today's practitioners and students of national accounting that the change to the SNA 1968 method in 1970s France and Britain represented a reconciliation with "reality." What the UK and French statistical offices had done, it was felt, was exactly what Morris Copeland, back in 1937, argued Simon Kuznets had done, too, in finding his own way of showing banks as productive: "made peace with common sense." In early-1970s France and the UK, the banking sector was growing rapidly, and becoming more and more profitable; as it did so, it would have become more and more anomalous to the "sense" of neoclassically-trained economists to envision banks as *un*productive. "Banking was becoming a bigger and bigger part of modern economies," Iain Begg observes, "and the national accounts needed to recognize this."[97] Or as Hugh Skipper writes, again in relation to the UK specifically: "at least part of the reason would have been that the SNA 68 approach would be seen to give a truer reflection of the contribution to GDP."[98]

The critical issue to consider here, however, is *why it was* that in the UK and France the banking sector was getting "bigger and bigger" at this particular time. And the answer, in part at least, is that as we saw above, it was at this particular historical juncture that French and UK banks began once more to pursue aggressive internationalization. They did so through both exports and, predominantly, FDI. During the decade 1974 to 1984, for instance, FDI by French banks grew *sevenfold*, from an amount outstanding of 2.8 to 20.8bn francs.[99] Simultaneously, the proportion of the profits of the UK's "Big 4" banks – Barclays, Lloyds, Midland, and NatWest – earned internationally was relentlessly rising: from just 15 percent at the beginning of the 1970s to 33 percent by 1978.[100] As earnings from overseas markets flowed back to the UK and France, those countries' banks became – and were *seen* to become – bigger and bigger. And as they did so, national accountants' disquieting banking problem, as yet unresolved in either country, became, by its very nature, increasingly acute. Seen from this historical-geographical perspective, it is not surprising that it was now that the conceptual tension became too much – the UK becoming the first to "snap" in 1973, followed by France in 1975. One boundary crossing – banks' crossing of the national accounts' production boundary – was, in this view of things, inextricably bound up with another.

Twenty years later, the UN's statistical office replaced SNA 1968 with SNA 1993, and one treatment of financial intermediation services with another. Both treatments have been discussed in detail in previous chapters. It took some time for the new accounting system (in its entirety) to be adopted in many places and this was especially true of its banking services recommendations, with FISIM at their core. Most countries had no problems with the *derivation* of FISIM, which, as discussed in Chapter 5, suggested the use of reference rates to enable the estimation of output on borrowing and lending activities separately. But the *allocation* of FISIM was a different matter; and because the new recommendations for allocation were regarded, especially in Europe, as so difficult to implement, a compromise position was reached whereby (until more than a decade later) countries could choose to allocate newly-derived FISIM to the "old" dummy industry sector. This was what happened in the UK, among other places: it switched to SNA 1993, and began calculating FISIM (in place of the Imputed Bank Service Charge), in 1998; but it did not switch to the new method for *allocation* of FISIM until 2008.[101] Even so, and allowing for ongoing international variations specifically in FISIM allocation, SNA 1993 has now been implemented more-or-less universally, including in Russia, China, and other former users of the Material Product accounting system.[102] As the ONS baldly states in the preface to the latest version of its Blue Book: "The SNA 1993 has been adopted world wide."[103]

In earlier discussion of FISIM (Chapter 5), I focussed largely on its effects, particularly insofar as it encompassed a categorical clarification of the nature of the financial intermediary's service *and* defined this service as explicitly productive. What I did not discuss were the reasons for its development, other than to situate it within the vital context of the extended struggle to "resolve" the aforementioned banking problem. But among the chief catalysts was criticism of SNA 1968 in regard especially to the question of allocation of the Imputed Bank Service Charge (IBSC). Part of this critique concerned the patent unsatisfactoriness of a dummy industry approach. In addition, however, critics noted that because all consumption of financial intermediation services was assumed under SNA 1968 to be intermediate (that is, consumed by other domestic industry), total GDP was entirely insensitive to the quantum of such services. If the IBSC increased, so too did banking sector value-added and dummy industry *negative* value-added; but GDP was unaffected. This, it was argued, made no sense. The problem, then, was that the SNA 1968 allocation did not allow for any demand for intermediation services that would add to overall GDP – specifically, as Begg and colleagues observe, "neither the substantial final demand from households for financial services, nor," of course, "for net exports."[104]

This latter exclusion is the critical one in the present context. For SNA 1968 rigidly enframed the financial sector at the national scale. It embedded financial sector domesticity in the national accounting framework and in the process, through the 1980s, showed the rapidly internationalizing banking sectors of several notable countries – France and the UK, certainly, but also Luxembourg, the Netherlands, and Spain, all of which also used SNA 1968 – becoming ever larger components *in and of national economies*. The profound *geographical* shifts taking place in global finance in that era could not be interpreted, within the prevailing, spatially-anaemic national accounting calculus, as anything *but* a structural shift instead. This was the shift, theoretically completed in SNA 1993 after decades of conceptual wrestling, to enlarged and thus productive finance.

Banks effectively function, national accounting historian Paul Studenski had pithily summarized in 1958, by "withholding all or a large part of the interest earned on the loans and investments made with their depositors' funds": a scholarly envisioning of banking's modus operandi captured more bluntly by the populist "3-6-3 rule" of banking of the 1960s and 1970s (borrow at 3 percent, lend at 6 percent, and be on the golf course by 3 p.m.).[105]

By 1993, in the wake of progressive waves of financial internationalization inadequately captured by national accounting or, for that matter, by methodologically-nationalist political economy, "withholding" had become "producing."

Notes

1   A. Mennicken and P. Miller, "Accounting, territorialization and power," *Foucault Studies*, 13, 2012, pp.4–24, at p.20.
2   D. Harvey, *The Enigma of Capital and the Crises of Capitalism*, Profile Books, London, 2010, p.182.
3   On the proliferation of meanings of the term, see R. Guttmann, "A primer on finance-led capitalism and its crisis," *Revue de la Régulation*, no. 3/4, 2008, and R. Lee, G. Clark, J. Pollard and A. Leyshon, "The remit of financial geography— before and after the crisis," *Journal of Economic Geography*, 9, 2009, pp.723–747.
4   E.g. R. Martin, *Financialization of Daily Life*, Temple University Press, Philadelphia, 2002; P. Langley, "'The uncertain subjects of Anglo-American financialisation," *Cultural Critique*, 65, 2007, pp.66–91, and "Financialization and the consumer credit boom," *Competition & Change*, 12, 2008, pp.133–147.

5   E.g. W. Lazonick and M. O'Sullivan, "Maximizing shareholder value: a new ideology for corporate governance," *Economy and Society*, 29, 2000, pp.13–35; J. Froud, C. Haslam, S. Johal and K. Williams, "Financialisation and shareholder value: consultancy moves, management promises," *Economy and Society*, 29, 2000, pp.80–120; J. Peters, "The rise of finance and the decline of organised labour in the advanced capitalist countries," *New Political Economy*, 16, 2011, pp.73–99.

6   Equally, in focusing on just one theoretical formulation of financialization, I am neither reducing the wider literature to this single conceptualisation, nor privileging it above all others.

7   G. Arrighi, *The Long Twentieth Century: Money, Power, and the Origins of Our Times*, Verso, London, 2010, p.xi.

8   D. Harvey, *The Limits to Capital*, University of Chicago Press, Chicago, 1982, ch. 10, is particularly helpful on this distinction.

9   Arrighi, *Long Twentieth Century*, p.6.

10 G. Epstein and A. Jayadev, "The rise of rentier incomes in OECD countries: financialization, central bank policy and labor solidarity," in G. Epstein (ed), *Financialization and the World Economy* (Edward Elgar, Northampton MA, 2005, 46–74); G. Krippner, "The financialization of the American economy," *Socio-Economic Review*, 3, 2005, pp.173–208; Ö. Orhangazi, *Financialization and the US Economy*, Edward Elgar, Northampton MA, 2008. There are certainly other studies that attempt to trace "financialization" empirically, but these focus on metrics not specifically related to the financial/nonfinancial weighting of economic processes and income sources. See, for instance: D. Duménil and D. Lévy, "The real and financial components of profitability (United States, 1952–2000)," *Review of Radical Political Economics*, 36, 2004, pp.82–110, and *Capital Resurgent: Roots of the Neoliberal Revolution*, Harvard University Press, Cambridge MA, 2004; E. Engelen and M. Konings, "Financial capitalism resurgent: comparative institutionalism and the challenges of financialization," in G. Morgan, J. Campbell, C. Crouch, O. Pedersen and R. Whitley (eds), *The Oxford Handbook of Comparative Institutional Analysis* (Oxford University Press, Oxford, 2010, 601–624); and E. Engelen, M. Konings, and R. Fernandez, "Geographies of financialization in disarray: the Dutch case in comparative perspective," *Economic Geography*, 86, 2010, pp.53–73. For different territories, these studies examine, inter alia: asset type splits, the size of financial markets, degrees of asset securitization, forms of wealth holdings, and levels of savings.

11 Krippner, "Financialization," p.174; Orhangazi, *Financialization*, p.132; G. Epstein, "Introduction: Financialization and the world economy," in Epstein (ed), *Financialization* (3–16), p.4.

12 J. Crotty, "Structural causes of the global financial crisis: a critical assessment of the 'new financial architecture'," *Cambridge Journal of Economics*, 33, 2009, pp.563–580, at pp.575–576; R. Dore, "Financialization of the global economy," *Industrial and Corporate Change*, 17, 2008, pp.1097–1112, at p.1098; P. Gowan, "Crisis in the heartland: consequences of the New Wall Street system," *New Left Review*, 55, 2009, pp.5–29, at p.7; Harvey, *Enigma*, p.51.

13 The quotations are from, respectively, L. Panitch and S. Gindin, "Finance and American Empire," in L. Panitch and M. Konings (eds), *American Empire and the Political Economy of Global Finance* (Palgrave Macmillan, New York, 2008, 17–47), p.38; and E. LiPuma and B. Lee, *Financial Derivatives and the Globalization of Risk*, Duke University Press, Durham NC, 2004, p.9.

14   J. Foster, "The financialization of capitalism," *Monthly Review*, 58, 2007 (April), pp.1–12; C. Lapavitsas, "Financialised capitalism: crisis and financial expropriation," *Historical Materialism*, 17, 2009, pp.114–148.

15   S. Savran and A. Tonak, "Productive and unproductive labour: an attempt clarification and classification," *Capital & Class*, 68, 1999 (Summer), pp.113–152, at p.137; emphasis added.

16   J. Mill, *Principles of Political Economy*, Prometheus Books, New York, 2004, p.70.

17   One example is in the work of – ironically, given my broader argument about geographical anaemia – the geographers Andrew Leyshon and Nigel Thrift. In their influential *Money/Space: Geographies of Monetary Transformation* (Routledge, London), p.55, Leyshon and Thrift argue that continuing to view finance and financial workers as constituting "a drain on the economy of producers of things … is clearly an unsustainable position."

18   Panitch and Gindin, "Finance and American empire"; LiPuma and Lee, *Financial Derivatives*; C. Marazzi, *The Violence of Financial Capitalism*, Semiotext(e), Los Angeles CA, 2011.

19   Panitch and Gindin, "Finance and American empire," p.38.

20   Ibid, p.38.

21   Ibid, pp.38–39.

22   The quotations in the following two paragraphs are taken from LiPuma and Lee, *Financial Derivatives*, pp.8–9, 11, 15, 19, 22–23, and 195n1.

23   As do Leyshon and Thrift, *Money/Space*, pp.55–56, in their own critique of the conventional classification of finance as unproductive.

24   Marazzi, *Violence*, pp.44, 51, original emphasis.

25   Ibid, pp.67, 49, 63; original emphasis.

26   M. Sparke, "White mythologies and anemic geographies: A review," *Environment and Planning D: Society and Space*, 12, 1994, pp.105–123, and *In the Space of Theory: Postfoundational Geographies of the Nation-State*, University of Minnesota Press, Minneapolis, 2005.

27   P. Hall and D. Soskice (eds), *Varieties of Capitalism: The Institutional Foundations of Comparative Advantage*, Oxford University Press, New York, 2001.

28   J. Peck and N. Theodore, "Variegated capitalism," *Progress in Human Geography*, 31, 2007, pp.731–772.

29   P. Krugman, *Geography and Trade*, MIT Press, Cambridge, 1991, p.71.

30   D. McNally, "From financial crisis to world-slump: accumulation, financialisation, and the global slowdown," *Historical Materialism*, 17, 2009, pp.35–83, at p.43.

31   Ironically, the one meaningful exception to this rule is the study that precipitated the wider literature: Arrighi's *Long Twentieth Century*, which conceptualizes eras of "financialization" as "long periods of fundamental transformation of the agency and structure of *world-scale processes* of capital accumulation" (p.87; emphasis added).

32   McNally, "From financial crisis to world-slump," p.44. Interestingly, and not insignificantly I think, the paper in which McNally criticizes the "varieties of capitalism"-type analysis of political economy sees him *also* mobilize (yet) another conceptualization of "financialization." Lamenting the "bad theorizing often associated with the [financialization] concept" (p.56), McNally invokes the term to refer to something at once more specific, but also more (geographically) generalized, than a structural shift towards finance within certain "national capitalisms": namely, the increasing penetration of relations between capitals, and of relations between capital and

wage-labour, by interest-bearing capital (cf. B. Fine, "Locating financialisation," *Historical Materialism*, 18, 2010, pp.97–116).

33 Krippner, "Financialization," p.193. Cf. W. Milberg, "Shifting sources and uses of profits: sustaining US financialization with global value chains," *Economy and Society*, 37, 2008, pp.420–451.

34 Krippner, "Financialization," p.198.

35 These percentages are different from those I cited in the equivalent analysis in B. Christophers, "Anaemic geographies of financialisation," *New Political Economy*, 17, 2012, pp.271–291. This is because the BEA has since revised its corporate profits figures for 2007 through 2009.

36 Peck and Theodore, "Variegated capitalism"; S. French, A. Leyshon and T. Wainwright, "Financializing space, spacing financialization," *Progress in Human Geography*, 35, 2011, pp.798–819, at p.809.

37 McNally, "From financial crisis to world-slump," p.44; original emphasis.

38 J. Agnew, "The territorial trap: the geographical assumptions of international relations theory," *Review of International Political Economy*, 1, 1994, pp.53–80.

39 T. Mitchell, *Rule of Experts: Egypt, Techno-Politics, Modernity*, University of California Press, Berkeley, 2002, p.99; emphasis added.

40 Ibid., pp.82–83.

41 H. Radice, "The national economy: a Keynesian myth?," *Capital & Class*, 22, 1984, pp.111–140.

42 Jennifer Koncz-Bruner (Economist, Balance of Payments Division, U.S. Bureau of Economic Analysis), communication to author, 21 June 2010.

43 E.g. R. Palan, *The Offshore World: Sovereign Markets, Virtual Places, and Nomad Millionaires*, Cornell University Press, Ithaca, p.30.

44 *2008 Goldman Sachs annual report*, p.135. Available at http://www2.goldmansachs. com/our-firm/investors/financials/archived/annual-reports/2008-entire-annual-report.pdf (retrieved Jan 2010).

45 *Barclays Plc Annual Report 2001*, pp.163,111. Available at http://www.investor. barclays.co.uk/results/2001results/annual_report/website/pdf-new/full_ra.pdf (retrieved April 2010).

46 *Barclays Plc Annual Report 2002*, p.191. Available at http://www.investor.barclays. co.uk/results/2002results/annual_report/website/pdf/full.pdf (retrieved April 2010).

47 G. Feketekuty, *International Trade in Services: An Overview and Blueprint for Negotiations*, Ballinger, Cambridge, 1988, p.27.

48 See, for example, A. Cornford, *Statistics for International Trade in Banking Services: Requirements, Availability and Prospects*, UNCTAD Discussion Paper No. 194, June 2009.

49 H. Freeman, "Comments by Harry Freeman," in R. Litan and A. Santomero (eds), *Brookings-Wharton Papers on Financial Services: 2000* (Brookings Institution, Washington, 2000, 455–461), p.457.

50 C. Raghavan, *Financial Services, the WTO and Initiatives for Global Financial Reform*, G-24 Research Paper, 2009 (available at http://www.g24.org/Publications/ResearchPaps/cr0909.pdf), p.32. pp.29–35 provide an excellent overview of the wider, longstanding problem of data on services trade in the context of the WTO.

51 H. Arndt, "Measuring trade in financial services," *Banca Nazionale del Lavoro Quarterly Review*, 149, 1984, pp.197–213, at p.197.

52 K. Howell and R. Yuskavage, "Modernizing and enhancing BEA's international economic accounts," *Survey of Current Business*, 90(5), 2010, pp.6–20, at p.12. In my

article "Anaemic geographies," published in 2012, I stated that the BEA *still* does not provide estimates for such services. This, I have subsequently learned, was incorrect, and based on this author's misunderstanding: the actual situation was (and is) that the BEA does not provide such estimates *in its international transaction accounts*, but it *does* do so in the national income and product accounts.

53 A. Berger, "Obstacles to a global banking system: 'Old Europe' versus 'New Europe'," *Journal of Banking and Finance*, 31, 2007, pp.1955–1973, at p.1967.

54 R. Cull and M. Peria, *Foreign Bank Participation in Developing Countries: What Do We Know About the Drivers and Consequences of this Phenomenon?*, World Bank Policy Research Working Paper No. 5398, 2010, pp.2–4.

55 UNCTAD, *World Investment Report 2004: The Shift Towards Services*, United Nations, New York and Geneva, 2004, pp.102–104, 136. See also D. Domanski, "Foreign banks in emerging market economies: changing players, changing issues," *BIS Quarterly Review*, December 2005; G. Clarke, R. Cull, M. Peria and S. Sanchez, "Foreign bank entry: experience, implications for developing economies, and agenda for further research," *The World Bank Research Observer*, 18, 2003, pp.25–59.

56 M. Schularick, "A tale of two 'globalizations': capital flows from rich to poor in two eras of global finance," *International Journal of Finance and Economics*, 11, 2006, pp.339–354, at p.343.

57 Cull and Peria, "Foreign bank participation," p.4.

58 PricewaterhouseCoopers, *Foreign banks in China*, June 2011 (available at http://pwccn.com/webmedia/doc/634442705425169010_fs_foreign_banks_china_jun2011.pdf), p.4.

59 T. Bandyopadhyay, "Foreign banks set to play bigger role," *Mint*, 5 October 2010.

60 T. Huertas, "US multinational banking: history and prospects," in G. Jones (ed), *Banks as Multinationals* (Routledge, London, 1990, 248–267), p.256.

61 J. Houpt, "International activities of US banks and in US banking markets," *Federal Reserve Bulletin*, 85, 1999, pp.599–615, at pp.603, 614. See also S. Miller and A. Parkhe, "Patterns in the expansion of US banks' foreign operations," *Journal of International Business Studies*, 29, 1998, pp.359–390.

62 B. Scott-Quinn, "US investment banks as multinationals," in Jones (ed), *Banks as Multinationals* (268–293).

63 The statistic is provided by Huertas, "US multinational banking," p.257. A. Slager, *Banking Across Borders: Internationalization of the World's Largest Banks between 1980 and 2000*, Unpublished PhD thesis, Erasmus University Rotterdam, 2004, pp.258–268, provides detailed case studies of individual US banks' internationalization strategies.

64 Slager, *Banking Across Borders*, p.8.

65 E. Helleiner, "The challenge from the east: Japan's financial rise and the changing global order," in P. Cerny (ed), *Finance and World Politics: Markets, Regimes and States in the Post-hegemonic Era* (Edward Elgar, Aldershot, 207–227), at pp.212, 209; UNCTAD, *World Investment Report*, p.109.

66 UNCTAD, *World Investment Report*, p.109. See also Slager, *Banking Across Borders*, p.385.

67 G. Jones, *British Multinational Banking, 1830–1990*, Clarendon Press, Oxford, 1995, p.185.

68 See especially Jones, *British Multinational Banking*, chapter 10.

69 Slager, *Banking Across Borders*, pp.286–300.

70   *Standard Chartered Annual Report 2010*, pp.1, 9, 110. Available at http://annualreport. standardchartered.com/downloads/5840_SCB_Annual_Rpt_2010.pdf.

71   *Barclays Plc Annual Report 2010*. Available at http://www.barclaysannualreports. com/ar2010/.

72   "International network," http://www.hsbc.com/1/2/about/network (retrieved Dec 2011).

73   C. Michalet (ed), *Internationalisation des banques et des groupes financiers*, CNRS, Paris, 1981; J. Métais, "International Strategies of French banks," in C. de Boissieu (ed), *Banking in France* (Routledge, London, 1990, 136–187).

74   J. Fournier and D. Marionnet, "Measuring banking activity in France," *Quarterly selection of articles – Bulletin de la Banque de France*, 16, 2009, pp.5–32, at p.16.

75   Slager, *Banking Across Borders*, pp.341–355; Métais, "International strategies."

76   Cited in Métais, "International strategies," p.149.

77   On German banks' circumscribed internationalization, see especially C. Buch and A. Lipponer, *FDI Versus Cross-Border Financial Services: The Globalisation of German Banks*, Deutsche Bundesbank Economic Research Centre Discussion Paper No. 05/2004.

78   The data for US exports should be read with the caveat identified earlier – that prior to 1997 figures are unavailable for affiliated exports – in mind. And even after 1997, UNCTAD's figures for the US do not exactly match up to the figures provided by the BEA (nor, indeed, in the case of the UK, to those provided by the UK's Office of National Statistics). I use the UNCTAD figures here only since I am also using the UNCTAD figures for the other countries.

79   On the nationality of Luxembourg-based banks, see PricewaterhouseCoopers, *Banking in Luxembourg*, December 2011 (available at www.pwc.lu/en/banking/docs/pwc-banking-luxembourg.pdf), p.18.

80   A. Webster and P. Hardwick, "International trade in financial services," *The Service Industries Journal*, 25, 2005, pp.721–746, provide an insightful and much broader quantitative analysis of relative national strengths in financial services trade.

81   http://www.relbanks.com/rankings/top-1000-world-banks (retrieved Dec 2011).

82   Respectively: French et al., "Financializing space," p.805; E. Engelen, "The case for financialization," *Competition and Change*, 12, 2008, pp.111–119, at p.114.

83   W. Buiter, "Why the United Kingdom should join the Eurozone," *International Finance*, 11, 2008, pp.269–282, at p.281.

84   Epstein and Jayadev, "Rise of rentier incomes."

85   Elsewhere (B. Christophers, "Revisiting the urbanization of capital," *Annals of the Association of American Geographers*, 101, 2011, 1347–1364, at pp.1360–1361), I have charted this build-up of surplus money capital for UK nonfinancial corporations, showing that it began in earnest around 2002–2003.

86   Christophers, "Anaemic geographies," p.281.

87   A. Hodge, "Comparing NIPA profits with S&P 500 Profits," *Survey of Current Business*, 91(3), 2011, pp.22–27, is an excellent overview specifically of why US corporate profits as reported by the BEA differ from those reported collectively by companies – on a financial accounting basis – themselves.

88   In the following analysis I draw upon, but also rework and extend, my previous analysis in "Anaemic geographies."

89   Calculations available from author. Total UK finance sector profits are assumed to be the sum of gross operating surplus and FDI earnings; the total overseas component thereof is assumed to be the sum of FDI earnings and an imputed export earnings figure, where the latter is calculated as a proportion of gross operating surplus equivalent to the exported output share of total sector output.

90 The inclusion of insurance services is not the only reason for the discrepancy between the BEA and UNCTAD figures: the latter, to the best of my knowledge, exclude (the imputed value of) services furnished without payment, whereas I have included these in the BEA data.

91 Calculations available from author. Total US finance sector profits are assumed to be the sum of domestically-generated profits and repatriated FDI earnings; the total overseas component thereof is assumed to be the sum of repatriated FDI earnings and an imputed export earnings figure, where the latter is calculated as a proportion of domestically-generated profits equivalent to the exported output share of total sector output.

92 E.g. J. Chambers and S. Catz, "The overseas profits elephant in the room," *The Wall Street Journal*, 20 October 2010.

93 J. Ciesielski, "10 companies with the most untaxed foreign income," *CNN Money*, 14 April 2011.

94 OECD, *Corporate Loss Utilisation through Aggressive Tax Planning*, OECD Publishing, Paris, 2011.

95 R. Kozlow, *Investment companies: what are they, and where should they be classified in the international economic accounts?*, IMF BOPCOM-03/22, Sixteenth Meeting of the IMF Committee on Balance of Payments Statistics, Washington DC, December 1–5, 2003.

96 "Fortune Global 500 2011," available at http://money.cnn.com/magazines/fortune/global500/2011/full_list/index.html.

97 Interview with author, 6 August 2010. Begg is an academic who has written widely on financial intermediation, including in relation to national accounting.

98 Email to author, 23 Nov 2011. Skipper works for the ONS, and is an expert on the treatment of financial intermediation services.

99 Métais, "International strategies," p.140.

100 P. Cottrell, "The financial system of the United Kingdom in the Twentieth Century," in L. De Rosa (ed), *International Banking and Financial Systems: Evolution and Stability* (Ashgate, Aldershot, 2003, 43–72), at p.58.

101 Note that in the UK the term Financial Services Adjustment was used for the Imputed Bank Service Charge.

102 On the adoption of the SNA in the former communist countries, see Y. Herrera, *Mirrors of the Economy: National Accounts and International Norms in Russia and Beyond*, Cornell University Press, Ithaca, 2010. Meanwhile, note that although there is an SNA 2008, this is an *update* of SNA 1993 rather than a new system in its own right.

103 ONS, *United Kingdom National Accounts – The Blue Book, 2011 edition*, Office for National Statistics, Newport, 2011, p.6.

104 I. Begg, J. Bournay, M. Weale and S. Wright, "Financial intermediation services indirectly measured: estimates for France and the U.K. based on the approach adopted in the 1993 SNA," *Review of Income and Wealth*, 42, 1996, pp.453–472, at p.456. Cf. K. Lal, *Measurement of output, value added, GDP in Canada and the United States: Similarities and Differences*, Research paper 13F0031MIE-No.010, Statistics Canada, Ottawa, 2003, p.40.

105 P. Studenski, *Income of Nations*, New York University Press, New York, 1958, p.192.

Afterword

The ideas of economists and political philosophers, both when they are right and when they are wrong, are more powerful than is commonly understood. Indeed the world is ruled by little else. Practical men, who believe themselves to be quite exempt from any intellectual influences, are usually the slaves of some defunct economist. Madmen in authority, who hear voices in the air, are distilling their frenzy from some academic scribbler of a few years back. I am sure that the power of vested interests is vastly exaggerated compared with the gradual encroachment of ideas.

John Maynard Keynes (1936)[1]

Among the most interesting effects of the financial crisis that has rocked the world over the past five years has been something of a reconsideration by policymakers of the potential merits of capital controls. Having been resoundingly dismissed throughout the 1990s and, despite the Asian financial crisis of 1997–1998, for most of the 2000s, capital controls have begun to be seen in a new light. The International Monetary Fund (IMF), long one of the primary opponents of the use of such controls, has epitomized this tentative shift, arguing in its April 2010 Global Financial Stability Report that capital controls could "usefully complement the policy toolkit" available to national monetary authorities.[2] Various other mainstream multilateral institutions and central banks have gone even further, intimating that controls are not only viable but necessary. "These statements," as Kevin Gallagher observes, "would have been unthinkable a decade ago."[3]

Equally interesting, however, is the fact that there has been no comparable change of heart vis-à-vis international banking and controls on the entry and operations of foreign banks. Indeed one could argue that, if anything, attitudes

Banking Across Boundaries: Placing Finance in Capitalism, First Edition. Brett Christophers.
© 2013 John Wiley & Sons, Ltd. Published 2013 by John Wiley & Sons, Ltd.

have hardened. To ad hoc suggestions that the internationalization of financial services in recent decades may have contributed to economic instability, the WTO delivered a stinging rebuke in early 2010, insisting on the contrary that "none of the root causes of the financial crisis can be attributed to services trade liberalization as provided for in the GATS, namely granting market access and national treatment."[4] Nor have any of the other leading global multilateral institutions pointed the metaphorical finger at open banking markets.

This seems curious for a number of reasons, but one in particular bears comment. A great deal has been said and written since 2007 about the self-evident perils of allowing financial institutions to become "too big to fail"; permit banks to assume such a scale that letting them fail risks precipitating systemic crisis, and the socialization of losses via state subvention becomes inevitable in the event of insolvency. But much less has been said about the processes whereby Western financial institutions have been able to *become* too big to fail (or at least, to be perceived as such). The dismantling of capital controls clearly played an important role, enabling banks to accumulate international financial assets and liabilities on a scale previously unimaginable. Yet so too, surely, did the *banking* internationalization that has seemingly eluded recent critical scrutiny.[5] Those banks routinely identified today as being "too big to fail" are, to an institution, internationally-diversified operating groups.[6]

And it is not like politicians and policymakers were not warned. The RAND Corporation economist C. Richard Neu wrote an extremely prescient article on international trade in financial services in 1988 in which he reflected that "if we are trying to design the global banking system for tomorrow, we ought to be seeking ways to produce banking institutions that are … not so large that they cannot fail from time to time." Part of Neu's unease about the liberalization of services trade – a process which, of course, was in its infancy when he was writing – related precisely to its likely implications for institutional scale. Hence his observation that "freer trade may result in bigger banks whose failure is likely to be less thinkable."[7] This, as we know, is *exactly* what has since happened: Lehman Brothers was allowed to fail, but AIG and Citigroup – not just quintessential contemporary global financial services companies, but two of those who of course led the initiative to tear down international barriers in the first place – were not.

How, then, might we seek to account for the lack of critical attention to the geography of banks' operations in the political and regulatory response to the crisis? Part of the explanation may have to do with the credibility of those representations of productiveness I have been examining in this book. Why, after all, would governments and regulators want to stamp down on a productive, value-adding industry sector – and one evidenced as such not only in historic national accounts, but also, as we shall presently see, in accounts produced in the very midst of the financial crisis? The more material understanding of banks' productiveness, however, has almost certainly been not this generic envisioning embedded in the calculus of national accounting, but a much more spatially-circumscribed and geographically-selective one, and one associated directly with financial internationalization. In short, the key consideration has probably been not "are banks productive," but "are *our* (international) banks productive *for us*"?

In the bulk of the industrialized countries that continue to play a leading role in shaping global monetary and financial regimes – not least the G7 of Canada, France, Germany, Italy, Japan, the UK, and the US – the answer to this latter question has been "yes," in significant part because those countries tend to be the world's leading exporters of banking services. Not only do their banking sectors provide a highly valued source of tax revenues: they make a vital contribution to a balance of payments position that would otherwise be less healthy or, in the case of the UK and US in particular, even more dismal. In the current political conjuncture, the question of whether financial services are productive in a generic, conceptual sense is, in a sense, a secondary consideration; what matters, for the US and UK administrations most notably of all, is that they are productive *for* the countries in question by virtue of bringing more revenue into the country than they take out. Hence, in part at least, British Prime Minister David Cameron's high-profile decision in late 2011 to veto changes to the EU's Lisbon treaty aimed at addressing the euro crisis on the grounds that he did not secure sufficient safeguards on financial regulation.

The irony in this decidedly more partial notion of productiveness is that it harks directly back to a conceptualization that, as we saw in Chapter 1, long predated even Adam Smith, not to mention the twentieth-century-born tradition of national accounting. For the idea that a trade surplus *represents* productive wealth creation was the classic mercantilist thesis – maximize exports and minimize imports – which Smith sought to scotch.

In any event, it is to be expected that preventing their banks from venturing as freely as possible overseas would be the very last thing that the US, UK or other Western European governments would be likely to recommend in response to the recent crisis. And Neu, interestingly, displayed uncanny prescience on this front too. "Imagine what might happen," he wrote 25 years ago, "if trade in banking services became a major item in some countries' balance of payments." Conjuring such a scenario, Neu envisaged "international competition among national bank regulators, each trying to make banks in his own country more competitive," perhaps through "lax regulation, low reserve requirements, and relaxed attitudes towards capital adequacy."[8] Imagine, indeed.

If, perversely, the financial crisis has not cast a spotlight on banks' crossing of geographical boundaries, the other boundary-crossing examined in this book – banks' crossing of the production boundary, specifically within the realm of national accounting – has, perhaps surprisingly, become a point of discussion. The reason for this was foregrounded in the introduction: the fact that the national accounts of a number of countries implausibly showed banks generating record value-added growth during the period when threats to their very existence prompted state bail-outs. The US was one such country.[9] Another was the UK. "According to the National Accounts, the nominal gross value-added of the financial sector in the UK grew at the fastest pace on record in 2008Q4," observed the

Bank of England's pugnacious Andrew Haldane. "At a time when people believed banks were contributing the least to the economy since the 1930s, the National Accounts indicated the financial sector was contributing the most since the mid-1980s. How do we begin to square this circle?"[10]

The answer, as Haldane explained, lay in FISIM, and in its method of derivation. While there are a number of different dimensions to this issue, perhaps the key one concerns the gap between actual rates of interest charged by banks on loans, and the "reference" rate of interest with which those actual rates are compared in the national accounts in order to compute the level of banks' intermediation-based output. During the crisis, as central banks rapidly lowered base rates, the reference rate – the "pure" cost of borrowing, or the rate from which the "risk premium" assumed by commercial banks has theoretically been removed – went down. But *actual* loan rates went up in response to increases both in the expected level of defaults and in perceived liquidity risk. The result? A large increase in lending FISIM, and thus in the reported level of bank output.

Plainly, this statistical outcome is not far short of absurd. If the national accounts are showing banks as more productive than ever at a time when their destructive capacities are writ largest, then there is something unequivocally awry with their methodology for calculating and envisioning such productiveness; the "banking problem" clearly has *not* been solved, after all. And equally incongruous, in this particular context, is national accounting's understanding of the underlying nature of the productive service performed by financial intermediaries. As discussed in Chapter 5, SNA 1993 identified this service as the assumption of risk. Yet with national governments standing ready to bail out failing institutions, the question of how "at risk" such institutions really were and are is obviously a moot one. For small, systemically-unimportant banks, perhaps risk is indeed an appropriate means of conceptualizing the intermediation service; but for banks deemed "too big to fail" and thus for the banking sector at large, we have seen that the real risk often lies elsewhere.

How, then, have national accountants responded to this apparent failure of the FISIM approach to measuring the output of banks? Predictably, there has been a renewed drive to make the national accounts' treatment of banks *better*; to improve the methods used. The objectives and philosophy of this approach are encapsulated in Australian statistician Michael Davies's reference to "FISIM misbehavin'" in his paper on "The measurement of financial services in the national accounts and the financial crisis."[11] For the inference is, of course, that FISIM *can* behave; that a better, more accurate, even "correct" method of measuring banks' output *is* attainable.

Reflecting on this conviction, it is salutary to recall in the first place the words of the US statistician George Jaszi – also quoted in the book's introduction – who surmised of the "banking problem" already in 1958 that "it seems to me unlikely that a really satisfactory solution will ever be found."[12] But it might also be salutary to consider what Karl Marx, almost a century earlier, had to say about the classical political economists' *own* wrestling with a production boundary – in their case the boundary between generically productive and unproductive labor.

To be sure, Marx, like Smith and Thomas Malthus before him, sought to identify where the boundary lay and which labors belonged on either side. But he actually devoted little attention to this exercise; he was arguably *more* interested, on my reading at least, in understanding why the question had become such a central one for political economy in the first place. (The answer: as a means of determining who did, and did not, contribute to the economic growth of nations.) And perhaps his most original contribution to the debate was to ascertain why making such distinctions is so difficult. What he realized was that there is nothing incidental about our perennial confusion over what is and is not productive. Such confusion, he claimed, actually "arises from" the capitalist mode of production "and is typical of it."[13] Furthermore, he said, this confusion spreads and intensifies as capitalism develops and as more and more services become embraced by the market economy.

As such, one imagines Marx would not have been in the least surprised by the course of development of national accounting in the twentieth century – by the extraordinary mushrooming and complexification of the UN's periodically-rewritten System of National Accounts (from fewer than 50 pages in 1953 to just under 250 in 1968 and over 800 in 1993); and, within it, the increasing intricacy and impenetrability of its recommendations specifically for measuring the output of banks. Marx recognized that in view of its growth imperative, capital was prone to self-analyze its own internal fault-lines – what generates surplus value and thus growth for capital, and what does not – to the point of compulsion. The history of national accounting has proven an exercise in *exactly* such compulsive adjudication.

As a measure of economic productiveness FISIM has of course been shown to be highly problematic. But perhaps the lesson we should draw from Marx is a deeper one: that the real problem lies not so much with particular measures of productiveness but with our underlying social fixation with identifying the economically productive and distinguishing it from the unproductive. Either way, the suspicion must be that only once we have moved beyond this obsessive questioning – and perhaps also the growth obsession that gave rise to it, and which still fuels it – will we be on the way to a healthier global political economy.

Of course the objective of this book has not been to try to envision the possible contours and form of the latter. Rather, it has been to encourage and begin to undertake the type of conceptual work required to begin that journey. For, while the last half-decade has generated a colossal amount of thinking, writing, and talking about banking, there has been relatively little by way of thinking about *thinking-about-banking* – about the entrenched discourses which embody and reproduce it (even in nominal opposition), where they derive from, and what purposes they serve. Until we fully recognize and understand the power of discourses such as those associated with national accounting's eternal "banking problem" – and after all "[n]ational accounting is," as André Vanoli observes, "a language" – it is hard to envisage any solution to society's much more obvious banking problems: those associated with risk, stability, inequality, and ultimately exploitation.[14]

Radical (geographical) political economy must, in short, be constantly, critically attuned to the dominant economic ideas and theories that format our social totality, and to how those ideas and theories are themselves shaped, in turn, by the social processes to which they give rise. As such, the questioning or challenging of evaluative, dualistic categorizations such as productive/unproductive should always be effected with care and *especially* with due heed to the very conditions of possibility of such conceptual distinctions. Marx was the theorist par excellence of such conditions, and his appreciation thereof underwrote his wariness of exercises in Manichean economic classification.

In closing, therefore, we can speculate that if Marx would have raised a wry smile at the contortions undertaken by twentieth-century national accountants in their negotiations of the economy's production boundary, he would also have smiled at the conclusion reached by another, later philosophical skeptic – Michel Serres – regarding dualistic economic logic more widely. "Thus you cannot discourse on money by using a bivalent kind of mathematics," submits Serres in *The Parasite* (*not*, I should emphasize, a book about banking!). "Thus all your models of mathematical economy are disqualified. Marx was wrong, Freud was wrong, Zola was wrong, I am wrong, economists are wrong. The only kind of mathematics applicable to economics is the theory of fuzzy subsets."[15] Recalling my comments on directions in critical geographies of money and finance in the introduction, this does not, it seems to me, mean throwing away Marxism, or indeed any other "totalizing" conceptual architecture of political economy. It means, ultimately, judging them, including any "bivalent" logic they contain, on the basis not of narrow empirical accuracy – the theory says banking is productive, the numbers indicate it is not – but of their holistic ability satisfactorily to account for the dynamics and disposition of the world as it is.

Notes

1 J. Keynes, *The General Theory of Employment, Interest and Money*, Macmillan, London, 1936, p.383.
2 IMF, *Global Financial Stability Report*, April 2010, p.131.
3 K. Gallagher, "US trade agreements threaten emerging markets' financial stability," *Financial Times*, 11 May 2010.
4 WTO, S/C/W/312, S/FIN/W/73, *Financial Services: Background note by the Secretariat; Council for Trade in Services, Committee on Trade in Financial Services* (3 February 2010), p.96.
5 Other contributing factors are usefully discussed by A. Haldane, "The doom loop," *London Review of Books*, 34(4), 2012, pp.21–22. See also B. Christophers, "Banking and competition in exceptional times," *Seattle University Law Review* (forthcoming).
6 See, for example, Forbes' list of "The 29 global banks that are too big to fail," available at http://www.forbes.com/sites/afontevecchia/2011/11/04/the-worlds-29-most-systemically-important-banks/.
7 C. Neu, "International trade in banking services," in R. Baldwin, C. Hamilton and A. Sapir (eds), *Issues in US-EC Trade Relations* (University of Chicago Press and National Bureau for Economic Research, 1988, 245–269), pp.265–266.

8   Ibid, p.264.

9   See J. Kay, "The beauty is in the data," *Financial Times*, 5 April 2011.

10   A. Haldane, *The contribution of the financial sector: miracle or mirage?*, Speech at the Future of Finance Conference, London, 14 July 2010, available at www.bankofeng land.co.uk/publications/speeches/2010/speech442.pdf.

11   M. Davies, "The measurement of financial services in the national accounts and the financial crisis," *IFC Bulletin No 33*, available at http://www.bis.org/ifc/publ/ifcb 33aj.pdf.

12   G. Jaszi, "The conceptual basis of the accounts: a re-examination," in National Bureau of Economic Research, *A Critique of the United States Income and Product Accounts* (Princeton University Press, Princeton NJ, 1958, 13–148), p.63.

13   K. Marx, *Capital, Volume I*, Harmondsworth, Penguin, 1976, p.1042.

14   A. Vanoli, *A History of National Accounting*, IOS Press, Amsterdam, 2005, p.xvii.

15   M. Serres, *The Parasite*, trans. L. Schehr, University of Minnesota Press, Minneapolis, 2007, p.150.

Index

Note: Page numbers in *italic* refer to figures.

Banking Across Boundaries: Placing Finance in Capitalism, First Edition. Brett Christophers.
© 2013 John Wiley & Sons, Ltd. Published 2013 by John Wiley & Sons, Ltd.

Printed and bound by CPI Group (UK) Ltd, Croydon, CR0 4YY

13/04/2025

14656463-0004